SECOND EDITION

HEALTH POLICY ANALYSIS

AN INTERDISCIPLINARY APPROACH

CURTIS P. MCLAUGHLIN, DBA

PROFESSOR EMERITUS
KENAN-FLAGLER BUSINESS SCHOOL AND SCHOOL OF PUBLIC HEALTH
UNIVERSITY OF NORTH CAROLINA AT CHAPEL HILL
CHAPEL HILL, NORTH CAROLINA

CRAIG D. MCLAUGHLIN, MJ

HEALTH POLICY SPEAKER AND CONSULTANT
BERKELEY, CALIFORNIA

JONES & BARTLETT
LEARNING

World Headquarters
Jones & Bartlett Learning
5 Wall Street
Burlington, MA 01803
978-443-5000
info@jblearning.com
www.jblearning.com

Jones & Bartlett Learning books and products are available through most bookstores and online booksellers. To contact Jones & Bartlett Learning directly, call 800-832-0034, fax 978-443-8000, or visit our website, www.jblearning.com.

Production Credits

Executive Publisher: William Brottmiller
Publisher: Michael Brown
Associate Editor: Chloe Falivene
Editorial Assistant: Nicholas Alakel
Production Manager: Tracey McCrea
Associate Production Editor: Kristen Rogers
Director of Marketing: Alisha Weisman
Senior Marketing Manager: Sophie Fleck Teague
Production Services Manager: Colleen Lamy
Senior Production Editor, Digital Products:
   Tiffany Sliter
Art Development Editor: Joanna Lundeen
Art Development Assistant: Shannon Brady
Manufacturing and Inventory Control Supervisor:
   Amy Bacus
Composition: Cenveo Publisher Services
Cover Design: Kristin E. Parker
Rights and Photo Research Coordinator:
   Ashley Dos Santos
Cover Image: (Top) © Orhan Cam/ShutterStock, Inc.,
   (Bottom) © unopix/Shutterstock, Inc.
Printing and Binding: Edwards Brothers Malloy
Cover Printing: Edwards Brothers Malloy

To order this product, use ISBN: 978-1-284-03777-7

Library of Congress Cataloging-in-Publication Data
McLaughlin, Curtis P., author.
   Health policy analysis : an interdisciplinary approach / Curtis P. McLaughlin, Craig D. McLaughlin. -- Second edition.
      p. ; cm.
   Includes bibliographical references and index.
   ISBN 978-1-284-05818-5 (pbk. : alk. paper)
   I. McLaughlin, Craig, author. II. Title.
   [DNLM: 1. Health Policy—United States.   2. Health Planning—United States.   WA 540 AA1]
   RA395.A3 23
   362.1—dc23
                           2014015113
6048

Printed in the United States of America
18 17 16 15 14   10 9 8 7 6 5 4 3 2

Dedication

To our talented wives, Barbara Nettles-Carlson and Karen Janowitz, and to the three generations of health professionals in our extended family who patiently share so much with us.

Contents

Preface

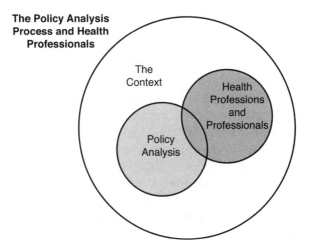

The Policy Analysis Process and Health Professionals

The Context

Health Professions and Professionals

Policy Analysis

This text is about the process of developing health policy relevant to the United States. We have included the perspectives of a number of disciplines and professions. Because our country has many actors but no coherent, integrated, systematic health policy at the federal level, even after the passage of the Patient Protection and Affordable Care Act (ACA), we have drawn heavily on our personal experiences and backgrounds, which include economics, political science, management, communications, and public health. We have also drawn on the experiences of other countries. Although the federal government has taken on a greater role with the passage of the ACA, states and even smaller jurisdictions will continue to play a major role in health planning. Values, economics, and health risks may vary among them, which suggests a need for independence in planning and execution. Canada's experience with a broad policy and specific health systems for each province has seemed to work as well, or better than, a centralized bureaucracy might have. Even the health services of a number of European countries have tended toward more decentralization as time has passed.

This text is organized into three parts: "The Context," "The Policy Analysis Process," and "The Professional as a Participant." We have anticipated that this text will be used to review health system issues and policy planning for health in a variety of graduate professional programs. We have not assumed zero knowledge of the U.S. health system, but we have not anticipated that the reader will have a great deal of background about how and why the U.S. health system developed as it did, nor about the efforts that took place in the past to reform it. Therefore, Part I, "The Context," explores current issues with the system (Chapters 1 and 2) and the history of how that system has evolved (Chapter 3). Chapter 4 challenges readers to ask about where we want to be, and Chapters 5 and 6 review policy alternatives that seem to have strong support for getting from where we are to where we might want to be. Some of these are reflected in the ACA, while others are not. These chapters do not purport to be "value free," but this text is different from most books on health policy because it does not attempt to push a single solution set. Studying the present is important for research and understanding, but the educational purpose of this book, and presumably of any course in which it is assigned, is to prepare students to meet whatever new, and perhaps unforeseen, challenges that develop in the future.

Part II, "The Policy Analysis Process," develops a set of tools for use in the future. Chapter 7 deals with identification and definition of the issues to be studied. Chapter 8 introduces some of the concepts of technology assessment applicable to health care. Chapter 9 adds more concepts of technology assessment related to evidence-based clinical innovation and management. Chapter 10 reviews the political processes that influence planning in various settings, especially the public-sector health arena. Chapter 11 presents the accepted methods of economic and financial analysis that determine the economic viability of health care plans. Chapter 12 addresses the ethical and other value considerations that must enter into the health policy process. In our deeply divided country, value issues are important. They crop up in just about every context and influence the outcome of most analyses. We have put this chapter after the other three process chapters to try to offset the tendency of many less sophisticated students to start with the qualitative and never get to the rewarding, but demanding, work of including the quantitative. Part II ends with Chapter 13, which focuses on implementation. Policies and plans must take into account the capacities of organizations and societies to implement them. At the same time, how the policy-making process proceeds becomes a part of the context within which the implementation will take place. Yes, there is a problem of circularity here, but that is real life.

Part III, "The Professional as a Participant," deals with the roles, skills, and leadership that health professionals can bring to the policy-making process in their local and national communities. It also acknowledges that one has to act out of a personal set of values and point of view, while at the same time preserving one's flexibility to make incremental progress if that is all that can be achieved. Chapter 14 reviews the overall planning processes in our society and suggests some things that professionals might strive for in the short and long run. The emphasis in that chapter is on what is likely to work, rather than the ideal. Chapter 15 suggests that there are important roles for health care professionals in the change process. It also discusses the skills that health professionals need to acquire if they are going to be accepted into the process and work effectively on its tasks, either from the inside or the outside. Chapter 16 provides summary and concluding material for the text.

Acknowledgments

Curtis McLaughlin would like to recognize a number of individuals who helped steer him in the direction of health policy and administration and supported him to continue in it for more than 40 years. They include Roy Penchansky and the late John Dunlop while at Harvard, and Sagar Jain, Arnold Kaluzny, and the late Maurice Lee at UNC-Chapel Hill.

Craig McLaughlin would like to extend his appreciation to the members and staff of the Washington State Board of Health during his tenure there, as well as the many other talented leaders in state and local public health in Washington State, for their tutelage. In particular, he would like to recognize his former supervisors for their patient mentoring—chairs Linda Lake, Dr. Thomas Locke, Dr. Kim Marie Thorburn, and Treuman Katz, and former executive director Don Sloma.

About the Authors

Curtis P. McLaughlin, DBA, is professor emeritus at the Kenan-Flagler Business School of the University of North Carolina at Chapel Hill and Senior Research Fellow Emeritus at the Cecil B. Sheps Center for Health Services Research. He was also Professor of Health Policy and Administration in the School of Public Health. Prior to coming to North Carolina, he was Assistant Professor at the Harvard Business School and also taught in the Harvard School of Public Health. He is the author or coauthor of several hundred publications, including the first three editions of *Continuous Quality Improvement in Health Care* with A. D. Kaluzny and *Implementing Continuous Quality Improvement in Health Care: A Global Casebook* with J.K. Johnson and W.A. Sollecito for Jones & Bartlett Learning.

He received his BA with honors in chemistry from Wesleyan University and his MBA with distinction and his DBA from Harvard Business School. While there, he studied and then taught in the Harvard interdisciplinary program in health care economics and management. At the Business School in Chapel Hill, he developed management programs for health professionals and directed the Operations Management Area and the Doctoral Program. He has served as a consultant to the World Health Organization and a number of businesses and organizations.

Craig D. McLaughlin, MJ, is a public health policy consultant as well as a freelance journalist and motivational speaker. He was executive director of the Washington State Board of Health when he coauthored the first edition of this text. He joined the board as senior health policy manager in 2001 and served as executive director from 2004 to 2011. Immediately prior, he served as director of college relations and adjunct faculty for The Evergreen State College. As a newspaper editor and freelance journalist for more than a decade, Mr. McLaughlin wrote and edited articles on a broad range of health issues. He has served as a communications consultant to foundations and as a management consultant to media organizations. Mr. McLaughlin earned his BA in biology from Wesleyan University and his masters in journalism from the University of California at Berkeley. He also completed all coursework toward an MPA with a concentration in health administration at the University of New Mexico.

Chapter 1

Introduction

If everyone is in charge, then no one is in charge. Health policy is problematic throughout the world, but it is particularly challenging in the United States, where there is no consensus about which government agency or social institution, if any, has an accepted, legitimate role of developing or implementing national health policy. The U.S. Constitution is silent on the subject of health and health care. Although its preamble promises "to promote the general Welfare," the Tenth Amendment states, "The powers not delegated to the United States by the Constitution, nor prohibited by it to the States, are reserved to the States respectively, or to the people." Neither education nor health care powers are specifically allotted to the federal government in the Constitution. The omission of health, however, cannot be attributed solely to the framers' intent, despite the presence of three physicians at the Constitutional Convention. They lived in a world of "evil humours" where one visited "barbers and churgeons."

Constitutional issues almost derailed the Patient Protection and Affordable Care Act (ACA) of 2010 before the Supreme Court. In 2012, the Court, by a 5–4 vote, upheld the constitutionality of the "individual mandate" provisions that require most individuals to carry basic health insurance or pay a penalty on their income tax return. At the same time, it overturned a provision requiring states to expand Medicaid access, ruling that it was unconstitutional because it did not provide states enough latitude.

President after president has pushed for an overhaul to our health care system and remedies to the access problems it creates. Only Lyndon Johnson and Barack Obama have succeeded. Attempts by Truman, Eisenhower, Nixon, and Clinton were less successful. In the more recent past, the rapid growth of health care costs has expanded the policy debate, as has growing recognition of medical errors and other quality problems. In the meantime, policy analysts struggle to make progress with a highly fragmented system and a divided body politic.

THE MANY ACTORS

Policy decisions are made at multiple levels of U.S. society:

- National government
- State and local governments
- Health care institutions
- Provider professionals
- Payer organizations (employers and insurers)
- Employers (meeting the mandate)
- Individuals (consumers)

Tables 1-2 through **1-7**, which are distributed throughout this chapter, provide samples of major health policy questions faced in each of these domains. Like most tables and lists in this text, they are meant to be illustrative, not exhaustive.

In such a decentralized environment, government may take a hands-on approach, treating health care as a public good, as it does transportation and education, or a hands-off approach, favoring market-driven outcomes. Therefore, government's stance and specific policies may swing dramatically as political power shifts. For example, during the 2012 presidential campaign, one side vowed to repeal the ACA if it gained complete control of the political process, undoing a major accomplishment of the Obama administration. Sharp changes in public attitudes are not unknown. The 1988 Medicare Catastrophic Coverage Act had a favorable rating with the public when passed, but was repealed in November 1989 as the public, especially the wealthier elderly, learned more about it.

This chapter describes what health care policy is, how the policy analysis process works, and the different roles health professionals can play in setting and implementing health policy over time. The role of a policy analyst is described quite completely in the excerpt from the U.S. Office of Personnel Management Operating Manual displayed in **Table 1-1**. As you

Table 1-1 Excerpts from the Office of Personnel Management Qualification Standards for General Schedule Positions—Policy Analysis Positions

· Knowledge of a pertinent professional subject-matter field(s). Typically there is a direct, even critical, relationship between the possession of subject-matter expertise and successful performance of analytical assignments.

· Knowledge of economic theories including micro-economics and the effect of proposed policies on production costs and prices, wages, resource allocations, or consumer behavior; and/or macro-economics and the effect of proposed policies on income and employment, investment, interest rates, and price level.

· Knowledge of public policy issues related to a subject-matter field.

· Knowledge of the executive/legislative decision making process.

· Knowledge of pertinent research and analytical methodology and ability to apply such techniques to policy issues, such as:

· Qualitative techniques, such as performing extensive inquiry into a wide variety of significant issues, problems, or proposals; determining data sources and relevance of findings and synthesizing information; evaluating tentative study findings and drawing logical conclusions; and identifying omissions, questionable assumptions, or inadequate data in the analytical work of others.

· Quantitative methods, such as cost benefit analysis, design of computer simulation models and statistical analysis including survey methods and regression analysis.

· Knowledge of the programs or organizations and activities to assess the political and institutional environment in which decisions are made and implemented.

· Skill in dealing with decision makers and their immediate staffs. Skill in interacting with other specialists and experts in the same or related fields.

· Ability to exercise judgment in all phases of analysis, ranging from sorting out the most important problems when dealing with voluminous amounts of information to ensure that the many facets of a policy issue are explored, to sifting evidence and developing feasible options or alternative proposals and anticipating policy consequences.

· Skill in effectively communicating highly complex technical material or highly complex issues that may have controversial findings, or both, using language appropriate to specialists and/or nonspecialists, facilitating the formulation of a decision.

· Skill in written communication to organize ideas and present findings in a logical manner with supporting, as well as adverse, criteria for specific issues, and to prepare material complicated by short deadlines and limited information.

· Skill in effective oral communication techniques to explain, justify, or discuss a variety of public issues requiring a logical presentation of appropriate facts and information or analysis.

· Ability to work effectively under the pressure of tight time frames and rigid deadlines.

Source: Reproduced from: http://www.opm.gov/qualifications/standards/Specialty-Stds/gs-policy.asp; accessed 12/01/12. For more detail see Section IV-A (pp33-34) of the Operational Manual for Qualification Standards for General Schedule Positions.

Table 1-2 Illustrative Health Policy Issues at the U.S. Federal Level

- How should otherwise healthy people be motivated to participate in health insurance programs, thus lowering the average premium?
- What population groups should receive subsidized coverage from tax revenues?
- Because the Constitution does not include the topic of health care as a federal responsibility, how should the federal government participate in supporting health care for all?
- How should the federal government support quality improvement efforts if state boards are not effectively addressing medical error rates?
- The cost of malpractice insurance in some states threatens the supply of providers in some specialties and appears to raise the cost of care, so what is the role of the federal government in avoiding the negative effects of malpractice lawsuits?
- Progress in information technology implementation in health care has lagged behind most other information-intensive service sectors. Are the provisions of the Health Information Technology for Economic and Clinical Health (HITECH) Act sufficient to overcome this problem?
- What services should be covered under Medicare? Medicaid?
- How many health professionals in a subspecialty are sufficient? Armed with the right answer, what should we being doing about any shortages? About any surpluses?

proceed through the text, you will likely note many parallels between that role description and the organization of this text, even though this text is meant to outline health policy analysis for health care professionals rather than cover the full training needs for a career in policy analysis. We then provide an overview of some of the major policy issues facing health care in this country. Finally, we address how certain potentially confusing terms are employed throughout this text and suggest ways to integrate the material that you will be learning with your knowledge from other disciplines.

HEALTH CARE: WHAT IS IT?

The terms *health* and *health care* are used loosely in U.S. policy debates. Often what people mean by health is an absence of notable ailments. The World Health Organization (2005), however, defines health as "a state of complete physical, mental and social well-being and not merely the absence of disease or infirmity."

Similarly, when people utter the phrase *the health care system*, they often are talking about the system for financing and delivering personal medical services—what some refer to as illness care and we will refer to primarily as the medical care system. The entire system that promotes health and wellness is actually much more complex. Other health systems include public health, mental health, and oral health. Moreover, much of our health is the result of *social determinants*, such as housing, education, social capital, our natural environment, and the way we construct the *built environment* around us. These are shaped by policy decisions made outside the health care system.

Thinking about health in terms of population outcomes can dramatically shift the way problems are defined and addressed. One example is identifying the leading causes of death. Using a disease model, the leading killers are ailments such as heart disease, cancer, stroke, injury, and lung disease, but McGinnis and Foege (1993), using a population-based, prevention-oriented perspective, identified the "real causes of death" as behaviors such as tobacco use, improper diet, lack of physical activity, and alcohol misuse. They argued that 88% of what we spend on health nationally pays for access to medical care, but in terms of influence on health status, medical care accounts for a mere 10%. This view attributes 50% of our health status to our behaviors, 20% to genetics, and 20% to environmental factors. Yet only 4% of health spending has been going to promote healthy behaviors and 8% to all other nonmedical health-related activities (Robert Wood Johnson Foundation, 2000). Since the mid-1960s, public health spending as a percentage of overall spending on health care has fluctuated between 1% and 1.5% (Frist, 2002), and yet 25 years of the 30-year increase in life expectancy between 1900 and 1995 can be attributed to public health interventions.

Some examples used to illustrate points throughout this text draw on material from outside the realm of medical care finance and delivery. One case study discusses folic acid fortification of foods, an example of a population-based public health intervention. This text, however, focuses mostly on access, cost, and quality issues related to personal medical services. That is because the primary intended audience is health care professionals (people who operate primarily from within the medical care system) and also the simple fact that the United States is currently wrestling with many critical issues related to health care access cost and quality. Readers are urged, however, to keep that intentional bias in mind and to think about how a big-picture view of health might change the way problems and solutions are identified. For instance, one reform proposal currently in vogue, and discussed in several places in this text, is pay for performance, also known as pay for quality. Pay-for-performance programs provide financial incentives for providers to meet certain process and outcome measures. Kindig (2006, p. 2611) has proposed a "pay-for-population health performance system" that "would go beyond medical care to include financial incentives for the equally essential nonmedical care determinants of population health."

Table 1-3 Illustrative Health Policy Issues at State and Local Levels

- What services should be provided and to whom under Medicaid options and waivers?
- How should the professional licensure be conducted so as to encourage quality of care, adequate access, and appropriate competition?
- How should the public university system decide how many professionals to train to ensure adequate access to all sections of the state? To all target groups?
- How aggressive should our state be in implementing and supporting health insurance exchanges?
- What should be the roles of the state insurance regulations and oversight boards in ensuring access to care for the general public and for special populations?
- Should the curative health care system, the mental health system, and public health clinics be merged as health care access becomes universal?
- What are intended and unintended consequences of sex education policies on health and health services?
- How do we undertake health care emergency planning for responses to floods, earthquakes, pandemics, and terrorism? What is the relationship between the state systems (public health and military) and local first responders?

HEALTH POLICY: WHAT IS IT?

Beyond the scope issues just described, most of us are clear on what health policy is about in general terms. Simply stated, health policy addresses questions such as:

- Where are we with our health care?
- How did we get here?
- Where do we want to be?
- What other alternatives are available here and throughout the world?
- What is likely to work in the future given our political process?
- What roles should health professionals and ordinary citizens play in this process?
- How can we become better prepared for such roles?

We cannot expect any representative cross section of participants to agree on the answers to all of these questions because their interests often conflict. A goal of this text is to encourage development of an objective, managerial approach to decision making—one that uses precise definitions of terms and relationships and carefully considers the key issues (and walks in the shoes of key actors) before reaching individual conclusions. Readers should come away with a set of tools for interpreting and analyzing events,

Table 1-4 Illustrative Health Policy Issues for Health Care Institutions

· How much charitable (uncompensated) care should we provide beyond that which is mandated?

· What should be our health information technology strategy?

· Should we undertake joint planning for future services with our local health department?

· How should we go about increasing the proportion of the local population who volunteer as local organ donors?

· Can we rationalize the services provided by local providers, reducing duplication and waste, and still avoid charges of anticompetitive practices?

· What should we be doing to become an effective learning organization?

situations, and alternatives—tools that can add to the skills already developed through professional training and experience. No one need abandon what has worked, but we hope to empower analysts to do a better job using a broader array of methods that fit a greater variety of situations.

THE POLICY ANALYSIS PROCESS

The policy analysis process usually involves the following activities:

· **Problem identification.** Why do we think we need to evaluate and possibly change the way we do things? What kinds of actions are people asking for? What are the drivers that require that scarce resources be devoted to this policy area? What is the intended output? What is the expected result?

· **Process definition.** What is the current situation? What concerns are people citing? Why are current results unsatisfactory to some? What is being done about it? Who are the current actors, and what are their roles? Are people framing the issue effectively? What are reasonable expectations for results over a relevant time horizon?

· **Process analysis.** What is happening in practice? How are outputs and outcomes measured, and why? What are interested parties recommending? What are the resource inputs? Are they appropriate? Are the outputs distributed fairly? Policy analysis can be approached rationally using a consistent set of steps:

  · Map out the existing processes that yield the outputs and outcomes of concern in as much detail as necessary to be operational.

  · Generate a list of solution strategies and narrow it to viable alternatives.

- Map out the best processes for the more promising alternatives.
- Ask where, how, and when new technologies might change each process within the relevant time horizon.
- Determine the resource requirements of the most promising alternatives and then cost them.
- Calculate other process parameters, such as lives saved, hospital days avoided, or persons served.
- **Qualitative analysis.** Identify and assess the nonquantitative issues related to valuation of benefits, quality, equity, and perceived fairness and distribution of outcomes.
- **Evaluation and choice.** Take steps to evaluate the options and make a choice:
  - Weigh the evidence, quantitative and qualitative, and review the conclusions to evaluate for:
    - Technical feasibility (medical evidence and operational effectiveness)
    - Political feasibility
    - Economic viability
  - Choose a preferred policy.
  - Prepare to report your findings and conclusions.
- **Implementation strategy.** How do we gain public, professional, and consumer support for change and backing for the most

Table 1-5 Illustrative Health Policy Issues for Provider Professionals

- Should I accept Medicaid patients?
- What services should I provide in addition to those normally provided by my specialty?
- Should I accept an invitation to join the local consortium for accountable care organizations (ACO)?
- What should I do to help the local populace understand the risks of potential pandemics without arousing unnecessary concerns?
- What positions should I encourage my local, state, and national professional organizations to take on current health policy issues?
- Should I volunteer to serve on local or state committees assessing and advocating on health policy issues? Should I seek or accept a leadership role? How do I prepare for that possibility?
- Should I make my information systems meet current "meaningful use" standards and take the subsidy or forget about it until I'm forced to convert?
- Should I enter (or stay in) private practice, or should I join a large group with ties to a dominant delivery network (hospital, health maintenance organization [HMO], ACO, pharmacy chain, etc.)?

appropriate alternative(s)? How do we ensure early implementer and consumer buy-in and mediate conflicting interests?

- **Implementation planning.** What steps do we need to take to ensure the successful implementation of the alternative chosen? How will we evaluate the level of improvement?
- **Feedback on policy processes.** Have we been making the right choices? If not, why not? What might we do to enable better policy choices in the future?

PROFESSIONALS AND THE POLICY PROCESS

An unusual aspect of health care in the United States is the low level of influence that health professionals have on policy formulation. All too often health professionals refer to what policy makers are doing to them, not on what they are doing to contribute to the policy processes. Professionally prepared leadership is extremely important if policies are going to be accepted and effectively implemented. Later in the text we will point to how and where professionals can exert leadership in enhancing the delivery of services that is their work and their calling.

One reason U.S. health care professionals have been involved so little in policy making has been the very high opportunity cost of any time devoted to policy matters. Most countries have a Ministry of Health that oversees the national health system. Where government pay for health professionals is low, professionals compete for higher administrative posts that offer better salaries, and especially better locations. Most key positions below the political level in the ministry are held by health professionals, and the directors of most divisions, departments, and institutions are physicians. At one time, U.S. health department directors were all expected to be MDs, and so were many hospital administrators. During and after World War II, when physicians were in short supply, other administrators were called on to run those institutions and new cadres of administrators were trained in the nation's schools of public health, public administration, and business administration. Rapidly rising physician income, especially after the introduction of Medicare and Medicaid in 1965, increased the demand for physician services, but not the supply. Providing care paid so much better than administration that few health professionals sought training in health administration. Educational institutions and health agencies again expanded their training programs for health administrators without professional credentials. Only as managed care has begun to constrain provider income and consolidation has begun to increase administrator

Table 1-6 Illustrative Health Policy Issues for Payer Organizations (Employers and Insurers)

- What kinds of options should I offer as health benefits? Given that employees need choices, should I offer high-deductible insurance policies to go with medical savings accounts?
- How much money and effort should we allocate to prevention? What about the argument that people change plans so often that our investment in prevention won't pay off?
- We have a lot of data on health care utilization. Should I mine that data and suggest choices of procedures? Providers? Lifestyle changes?
- Ethically, how much should we know about our employees' (the insureds') lifestyles that may affect future health care costs, and how should we use that knowledge?
- Now that health care benefits are mandated for most employers, how do we balance competing for the right labor force, avoiding or not avoiding the tax penalties for those employees not covered, and keeping premium costs under control?
- Should we participate in the new insurance exchanges? If so, what should be offered?

incomes have professionals taken a stronger interest in managerial training programs. This interest has been reinforced by provider dissatisfaction with the changes in professional autonomy and working conditions under managed care. At the same time, the incomes and productivity demands on nonphysician professionals have also been rising, dampening their interest in participating in policy processes. Professionals are waking up to the need to participate, but often feel constrained by their lack of skills and confidence to participate effectively in the policy process.

NATIONAL SYSTEMS DIFFER BUT PARALLELS EXIST

Every country's health care system is unique, as a result of culture, history, and happenstance. Yet the issues policy makers face can parallel each other. Many developed countries are struggling with the burden of their social programs, including health care. Even in countries that have long had national health services, there have been many efforts to decentralize them, to make them more responsive to local needs, and to tap into tax revenues available at the regional and local levels. Medical care systems in the United Kingdom and Scandinavia provide examples of this. No other developed countries, however, spend as much per capita or as a percentage of the national income (gross domestic product) as the United States, and many of them have better health outcomes across the population. The results achieved in the United States should be better, given our relatively high expenditures.

Table 1-7 Illustrative Health Policy Issues for Individuals

- Should I purchase health insurance if my employer does not pay for it, or should I pay the tax penalty?
- What should I do about my increasing weight and high blood pressure?
- When I retire, how much should I plan to rely on Medicare to cover my health care costs as I continue to age?
- Certain medical specialties are not available in my area. My county government wants to issue tax-exempt bonds to finance a new doctors' office wing on the county hospital site. Should I support the referendum on the bonds?
- My daughter is 24 years old and waiting tables at the Pizza Palace. The company's health benefits are minimal. Should I keep her on my health insurance policy until she turns 26?

Although this text does not emphasize comparative international health policy, it is important to understand that both developed and less developed countries have taken rather different routes to more or less successful health care systems, leading, in turn, to differences in costs and outcomes. These results have been achieved over decades of adaptation to the cultures and institutions of those countries and may or may not be models for the United States.

All countries are aiming at targets that shift as their populations age, as new technologies become available, and as new diseases and environmental threats emerge. Many, if not most, are experimenting with one or more aspects of a market system for health care delivery, while still maintaining that health care is a basic human right. Although health care is not officially a right in the United States, all levels of government and the body politic have been concerned about the proportion of the population forced either to forgo care or to seek some form of public assistance. Even relatively conservative commentators have argued for universal participation in national or state-level health insurance schemes, partly to disengage health care financing from employment relationships and partly to avoid adverse selection by employees and underwriting discrimination by insurers. The provisions of the ACA, if fully implemented, could go a long way toward meeting those goals. Its impact on costs remains to be seen.

KEY POLICY CATEGORIES

The major policy categories in the first column of **Table 1-8** will be used to structure later discussions. They relate to quality of care, availability of resources, payment and funding, motivation of patients and providers,

Table 1-8 Matrix of Major Policy Categories Versus Major Skills Disciplines

Major Policy Categories	Major Skills Disciplines			
	Medical	Economic/ Financial	Political	Operational/ Managerial
Quality				
Access		X	X	X
Technical management	X	X		X
Interpersonal relationships	X			X
Continuity of care	X		X	
Measurement and reporting	X			X
Resource availability				
Personnel	X	X	X	
Technology				
Evidence-based medicine	X	X		X
Process rationalization	X	X		X
Information systems	X	X		X
Payment				
Insurance/allocation of risk		X	X	
Motivating patients and payers				
Consumer-oriented care		X	X	X
Mandated payments		X	X	
Price transparency			X	X
Motivating providers				
Volume				
Fee-for-service		X	X	X
Capitation/vouchers		X	X	
Bundling	X	X	X	X
Budgets/salaries				
Pay-for-performance	X	X	X	X
Price Competition				
Antitrust		X	X	
Labor substitution	X	X	X	X
Increased buyer power		X	X	
Cost-efficiency and effectiveness				
Malpractice			X	X
Fraud and abuse			X	X
Cost-reduction measures	X	X	X	X
Organizational learning	X			X

volume and price of services, competition, and cost drivers. They are based on a classification of policy interventions developed in McLaughlin (2014). The four other columns represent the major skills disciplines that are needed by the policy analysis team. Each will be the subject of one or more subsequent chapters. Any significant policy analysis is likely to need data and other contributions from experts in medicine, economics (including finance), political science, and services management (including behavioral and operational skills). The Xs identify which of those disciplines seem to have a major role in the analysis of that particular policy category. One could argue that all the boxes need to be checked for all categories. Although expertise and analytical skills across all four domains are relevant for each category, we have chosen to put Xs in a limited number of boxes to highlight the variability in major skill set requirements.

OVERARCHING MEDICO-SOCIAL ISSUES

In addition to these specific policy categories, a number of overarching social issues need to be kept in mind. They include:

- Ongoing relationships between health insurance and employment
- Employment status, compensation, and autonomy of health care professionals
- Equity in access to services
- Fairness in intergenerational transfers
- Allocation of responsibilities among federal, state, and local governments
- Professional versus institutional responsibilities for process development and improvement

Relationships Between Health Care Financing and Employment

Increasing international competition for jobs has highlighted the high costs of U.S. health care and the impact of concentrating those costs onto large employers who purchase health care or health insurance for employees and retirees. These costs have been one factor that has led international auto manufacturers to select sites in Canada over otherwise lower cost locations in the southern United States, resulting in job losses. The proportion of workers receiving health insurance coverage at their place of employment has been falling in recent years. Employers had sought to control costs through the use of managed care organizations. Because this effort seems to have reaped the bulk of its potential savings, employers now are shifting more of the burden to workers by requiring higher individual premiums, reducing subsidies for dependents' coverage, relying more on independent contractors, or eliminating benefits. This has forced the nation to wrestle with the question of whether health care insurance coverage should be dependent on employer decisions. The response in the ACA was that the employer had to contribute but the employee was to make the decision about what to purchase—how much coverage of what type—with the combination of employer and personal funds.

It remains to be seen whether this will work as planned. Small employers, the ones most likely to drop their health benefits, are initially exempt from the requirements of the ACA. There is also concern about whether the penalties are sufficient to change employer behaviors significantly (Wilensky, 2012) and whether the government subsidies to low-income employees can be offset by other revenue.

Employment Status, Compensation, and Autonomy of Health Professionals

For many years, nearly all physicians and pharmacists were independent businesspeople. Hospitals employed some specialists (e.g., radiologists, pathologists, anesthesiologists), often under profit-sharing agreements, but medical practice acts in many states prohibited the use of employed physicians. Movement toward managed care and the consolidation and industrialization of the health care industry, however, prompted more and more organizations to buy practices and to serve customers that had previously turned to private practices and independent pharmacies. The ability of large organizations to buy and sell goods and services at deep discounts forced more and more small provider groups to sell out. Increasingly, health care professionals are employed by large organizations and are experiencing conflicts around their professional independence and autonomy. This has led to patient concerns about providers' disinterestedness, a concern that tends to weaken the status of the health professions.

Equity in Access to Services

The Centers for Disease Control and Prevention (CDC) has issued a set of targets for *Healthy People 2020*, a federal strategic plan for improving health status and reducing health disparities. Reducing health disparities involves easing the disproportionate burden of disease, disability, and death among a population or group. Disparities can result from cultural factors, behaviors, social determinants (such as low socioeconomic status), lack of access to care, not seeking or being provided with care when it is available, and not receiving quality or culturally and linguistically appropriate care when it is accessed. The problem of health disparities is not unique to the United States. The equivalent term used in much of the rest of the world, and increasingly in the United States, is *health equity*. **Table 1-9** shows some of the baselines and the targets displayed in the CDC's *Healthy People 2020 Objectives* (2010). More data about the disparities in health status of minorities are presented in Chapter 2.

Fairness in Intergenerational Transfers

Recent debates about the national debt have focused on entitlement reform. Recommended reforms include raising the starting age for full

Table 1-9 Selected Objectives for *Healthy People 2020*

- Increase the proportion of population of all ages with a specific source of ongoing care from 86.4% in 2008 to 95.0%.
- Reduce U.S.-acquired measles cases from 115 in 2008 to 30.
- Reduce age-adjusted deaths from HIV infections in those over 13 from 3.7 per 100,000 population in 2007 to 3.3.
- Reduce age-adjusted smoking rates by persons over 18 from 20.6 in 2008 to 12.0.
- Reduce the rate of infant deaths in the first year of life from 6.7 per 1,000 live births in 2008 to 6.0.
- Increase the age-adjusted rate of adults 18 and older whose hypertension is under control from 43.7 in 2005–2008 to 61.2%.
- Reduce age-adjusted coronary artery disease deaths from 126 per 100,000 populations in 2007 to 100.8.
- Increase the proportion of adults who engage in aerobic physical activity of at least moderate intensity at least 150 minutes/week or 75 minutes of vigorous intensity or an equivalent combination in 2008 from 43.5% to 47.9%.
- Decrease the proportion of adults 18 and over who experienced a major depressive episode in 2008 from 6.8% to 6.1%.
- Decrease age-adjusted death rate due to fatal injuries from 59.2 per 100.000 in 2008 to 53.3.
- Increase the age-adjusted rate of adults receiving colorectal cancer screening according to most recent guidelines from 52.1% in 2008 to 70.1%.
- Increase the proportion of cancer survivors living 5 years of more after diagnosis from 66.2% in 2007 to 72.8%.

Source: Reproduced from: Healthy People 2020, Topics and Objectives - Objectives A-Z. Accessed Dec. 7, 2013 at http://www.healthypeople.gov/2020/topicsobjectives2020/

Medicare benefits to 67. However, some have objected to the use of the word *entitlement* to refer to Medicare. They prefer the term *earned benefit*. For someone who has been paying into Medicare and Social Security for 20 years but is still relatively young, this represents a loss of expected return on the investment and an intergenerational transfer to the elderly who are already on Medicare. How might we deal with this fairness issue?

Allocation of Responsibilities Among Federal, State, and Local Governments

In the United States, Medicare is a federal program, Medicaid is a joint federal and state program, mental health services are joint state and local programs, and public health services are usually a local program or some blend of local and state. As we try to rationalize our system with a new focus on universal coverage, how will we allocate these responsibilities to achieve integrated and coordinated delivery? Our most expensive and neediest patients tend to have multiple diagnoses and present a special problem. Right now many are dual eligibles under Medicare and Medicaid and have treatment needs in more than one delivery system. All too often their problems are kicked back and forth from one system to the other with less than acceptable results. Who is responsible for the whole patient in such cases?

Professional Versus Institutional Responsibilities for Process Development and Improvement

A key issue in health policy is how to evaluate and rationally adopt new health care technologies. In manufacturing terms, how and when do we deploy the products of our research and development? Much of the recent increase in health care costs has been attributed to the introduction of health care technology, much of which leads to positive improvements in our ability to deal with disease but also costs more to provide.

In the past, when change information was generated more slowly and there was little concern about cost, we relied on the individual professionals to stay abreast of the new developments and decide when and where to adopt them. Many of the recommendations of management experts call for reliance on improved learning by provider organizations on top of professional competency. Because the health care marketplace is highly fragmented, most provider organizations cannot undertake research and development unless it results in a product that can be patented, as is the case with new drugs. Local providers can only amortize research and development costs over their own client base, and it would take too long to recoup their investment. Alternatives are to turn to the federal government or to vendors that have access to multiple providers. However, vendors are not disinterested parties. A number of provisions of the ACA attempt to deal with this by setting up new institutes and boards, but these provisions seem to lack the support of a broad consensus and may prove difficult to maintain and fund in the face of determined lobbying efforts.

The following new agencies and boards are included under the ACA:

- Independent Payment Advisory Board
- Center for Medicare & Medicaid Innovation
- National Prevention, Health Promotion, and Public Health Council
- National Health Care Workforce Commission
- Interagency Working Group on Health Care Quality

The role of the Medicaid and CHIP Payment and Access Commission (MACPAC) was also expanded to parallel the functions of the Independent Payment Advisory Board concerning Medicare.

Areas of research and development where government already plays some role in the United States include:

- **Basic science.** Our society has decided to fund basic research in health care through the National Institutes of Health and other government agencies. Much of this research takes place in universities that receive grants to conduct research efforts.
- **Clinical applications.** Some federal funding is available for clinical research, but much of it takes place with the support of vendors or individual or institutional providers. In some areas, a great deal of individual experimentation goes on and innovation spreads rapidly; one example is the field of surgery, which often is not subject to Food and Drug Administration (FDA) approval. In the new drug field, the FDA tightly controls experimentation. This helps to ensure consumer safety but it slows the pace of innovation considerably.
- **Testing for efficacy and safety.** Here responsibilities are shared among the vendor, the provider, and government regulators. Who does what depends on the nature of the innovation. If the technology does not offer a "blockbuster" or high-volume good or service, there is limited support for this type of research. The Agency for Healthcare Research and Quality (AHRQ) has the function of studying how to apply "evidence-based medicine" to existing treatments and practices, but its funding is not sufficient to finance many needed studies.

IMPACT OF SOCIETAL VALUES ON POLICY DECISIONS

Health care policy making does not occur in a vacuum. Health policy is profoundly influenced by value-driven issues that cut across the entire U.S. policy landscape. These include, especially, debates over the role of free versus managed market mechanisms and pro-life and right-to-die ideologies. The battle over embryonic stem cell research is a case in point. The idea of using cells from fertilized eggs that were going to be thrown out anyway might not have attracted attention if it were not for the continuing debate about abortion, much of which turns on the definition of when life begins. If "life" begins at birth, then opposition to early abortion—and the objection to using embryonic stem cells—is greatly weakened. If "life" begins with the union of the egg and sperm, then there is a logic to protecting embryos. Strong clashes among value frameworks affect other health care issues such as physician-assisted suicide or executions, contraception for minors, morning-after pills, concerns of institutional review boards, and direct-to-consumer pharmaceutical marketing.

These issues are largely beyond the scope of this text. However, we are confident that they will be introduced in your classroom discussions as you look at specific policy decisions. Although these values may or may not be subject to study using policy analysis techniques, they exist and must be taken into account.

THE CONTEXT

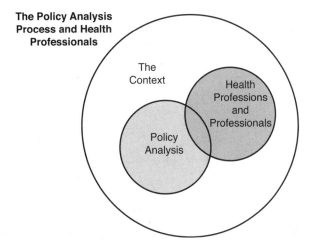

Although this book is designed to be valuable to anyone engaged in health policy development, its primary purpose is to enable current and future health professionals to understand and then participate in the health policy process. The figure above shows policy analysis and the work of the health professions taking place within the context of the health care system. The first section of this book develops that context through a discussion of the current status of the U.S. health care system (Chapter 2) and a review of factors that influenced its development as the decentralized system we have today (Chapter 3). The case accompanying Chapter 3 provides a chance to look at the experiences of other countries and develop some hypotheses about how these countries achieved their current status. Chapter 4 reviews the many and varied objectives for the U.S. health care system being expressed by various policy participants. Chapter 5 presents some of the recommendations for government action being suggested. One educational outcome you should try to achieve is to understand these positions, their underlying assumptions, and their strengths and weaknesses. This is followed in Chapter 6 by a discussion of the responses that service delivery organizations, providers, payers and employers, and initiatives they have undertaken.

These chapters provide both the context and vocabulary for moving on to the second part of this book, which outlines available tools for rational policy analysis—one of the circles within a circle in the diagram. The third part of this book looks at the role of the health professions and professionals and, in particular, how they can and should participate in policy analysis.

Chapter 2

Where Are We?

American health care is in a state of flux as new scientific knowledge and clinical experience continue to change our definitions of illness and wellness. As a society, we respond by changing the ways health care is delivered. Health services increasingly impact our society—from health status to employment to budgetary economics to recreation to professional concerns to our perceptions of our own well-being.

American health care is also in flux because now that it has grown to more than one-sixth of our economy it threatens to squeeze out public goods such as education and infrastructure maintenance. People have wanted to do something about cost and access to care problems for a long time. The 2010 Affordable Care Act (ACA) is doing much to address access issues, but opposition to certain provisions is strong. Employers are steadily shifting more risk to employees and their families, and there is a real tension between Washington and the state capitols over Medicaid expansion. Medicare trust funds are forecast to disappear over the next decade or so. Washington is unlikely to tolerate another major health reform battle, although major changes may come as a side effect of a "grand" government overhaul of spending and tax policies. The future is highly uncertain, and still we must plan and act as we go along.

This chapter reviews the current status of the U.S. health care system from several points of view:

- Current outcomes and costs
- Quality
- Leadership
- Complexity
- Industrializing structures for delivery
- Medicalization of our society
- Redistribution of wealth

CURRENT OUTCOMES AND COSTS

Health care expenditures were projected to rise to close to 20% of the U.S. gross domestic product (GDP) by 2015 (Borger et al., 2006), but more recent estimates from the Centers for Medicare & Medicaid Services (CMS) project it to be 18.2% for 2015 and 19.5% by 2021 (CMS, 2012). Average annual family health insurance premiums were estimated for 2012 at $15,745, with $11,429 paid by employers. The 4% growth rate for 2012 was slow by historical standards but still more than twice the growth rate of wage income. The comparable total insurance cost for a single individual was $5,615. Large employers (98%) offered health care benefits to workers but were cutting back on retiree health benefits. Only 50% of firms with 3 to 9 workers and 73% with 10 to 24 workers offered health benefits. Many small companies do not provide health benefits. At the same time, control of health care by health professionals is being threatened by outsiders calling for more reliance on government programs, more consumer-centered care, or both.

High Comparative Costs and Low Comparative Outcomes

The United States spends far more on health care per capita and as a percentage of GDP than other developed countries, yet does not seem to be much better off for it. **Table 2-1** illustrates this by comparing 11 countries on these two resource-input dimensions and on two outcome dimensions: overall life expectancy at birth and infant mortality rates. Similar rankings result when a number of other outcome variables are examined. The health care systems of these other countries offer virtually universal coverage, but the mechanisms they use range from mostly private insurance to a national health service. The incongruous combination of high U.S. costs and low

Table 2-1 Selected International Comparisons of Health Inputs and Outcomes, 2011

	Health Expenditures (US$) per Capita	Health Expenditures as % of Gross Domestic Product	Population Life Expectancy at Birth (Years)	Infant Deaths per 1,000
United States	$8,508	17.7	78.7	6.1
Switzerland	$5,643	11.0	82.8	3.8
The Netherlands	$5,099	11.3	81.3	3.6
Canada	$4,522	11.2	81.0**	4.9**
Germany	$4,495	11.3	80.8	3.6
France	$4,118	11.6	82.2	3.5
Belgium	$4,061	10.5	80.5	3.3
Sweden	$3,925	9.5	81.9	2.1
Australia	$3,800*	8.9*	82.0	3.8
United Kingdom	$3,406	9.4	81.1	4.3
Japan	$3,213*	9.6*	82.7	2.3

* 2010 data, ** 2009 data

Source: Data from: OECD Health Data 2013. Copyright OECD 2013. http://www.oecd.org/els /health-systems/oecdhealthdata2013-frequentlyrequesteddata.htm

U.S. outcomes does not seem to be associated with any one specific organizational or financing approach, yet that is about all on which experts seem to agree.

Anderson et al. (2003, p. 103) noted that "U.S. policy makers need to reflect on what Americans are getting for their greater health care spending," concluding that "It's the prices, stupid." Administrative costs for our system, estimated to account for as much as 30% of overall health care costs, are also high when compared with the rest of the world (Woolhandler, Campbell, & Himmelstein, 2003). Much of these overhead costs can be attributed to intermediaries who try to make up for or take advantage of imperfections in the marketplace. Examples include pharmacy benefits managers and third-party administrators.

Cannon and Tanner (2005) would explain away comparative international differences because

- Data definitions and collection methods are not comparable.
- Health care is partly a consumption good that normally rises with income.

- The U.S. infant mortality rate is increased by our efforts to save low-birth-weight infants that would be stillborn elsewhere.
- There is little proven relationship between longevity and health care expenditures.
- Our cost figures include the costs of medical research and innovation that are not incurred elsewhere.

They argue that disease-specific data are a better measure. On the mortality-to-incidence ratios for AIDS, colon cancer, and breast cancer, for example, the U.S. system looks very good.

Overinsurance and Overutilization Arguments

If the United States spends more on health care than any other nation without top-notch results across the board, does that mean we are spending too much? Overspending can be about price (paying more than we need to for a service) or quantity (buying more services than we need or not getting what we paid for). In health care, it is probably a bit of both. The number of physician visits and hospital beds per capita was lower in the United States than the Organisation for Economic Co-operation and Development median (quantity), while health care worker wages, hospital supplies, and drugs were much costlier in the United States (price) (OECD, 2013). U.S. health care wages are the highest in the world.

Quantity factors are typically discussed under the rubric of overutilization. Some argue that overutilization is due to our fee-for-service (volume-based) payment system. Others argue that it is due to patient demand; patients are insulated from risk by our tax-subsidized health insurance system. Research also shows that an increased supply of health professionals leads to more utilization, yet attempts to restrict the supply of specialists using licensing systems have led to charges of illegal restraint of trade. Like health care, professional education is a confusing mixture of a public good and a personal investment. Many alternative methods—certificate of need regulations, for example—can be used to try to control overuse or underuse by influencing the supply or demand for health care services.

Cutler, Rosen, and Vijan (2006) concluded that if 50% of the increase in longevity between 1960 and 2000 is attributable to our increased medical care expenditures, we have gotten an acceptable return on our money. They suggest that the cost of a life-year gained was reasonable, especially for those younger than 65 years. They caution, however, that the returns from added expenditures, especially for older people, have diminished over time.

Continued High Cost-Inflation Rates

The CMS Office of the Actuary is responsible for providing estimates used to assess the financial viability of Medicare and Medicaid, which are two huge government programs. Its report, *National Health Care Projections 2011–2021,* concludes that health care spending is likely to outstrip economic growth (GDP growth) throughout the next decade. Although there will be ups and downs because of specific interventions, such as Medicare Part D drug coverage and the ACA, there will be little effect on aggregate health care spending, which will grow at a rate 2% higher than the overall economy. The government share of health spending will gradually increase, leaving health expenditures financed about equally between government and private sources. Fuchs (2013) suggests that the spread between the two growth rates has been narrowing for almost a decade, but is still a serious problem. **Table 2-2** summarizes historical and forecast data on health expenditures in dollars per capita and as a percentage of GDP. **Figure 2-1** illustrates that, except for the period from 1995 to 1998, the inflation rate for health care costs and health insurance premiums has been well above the inflation rate of the consumer price index and growth of workers' earnings for most of the last 25 years. No wonder workers and employers feel squeezed by the rising costs of health care.

Disappearing Health Benefits

Employee health benefits (73% paid by employers, including government employers, in 2012) are threatening to disappear. Between 2000 and 2004, the percentage of insured people younger than age 65 in employment-based

Table 2-2 U.S. National Health Expenditure (NHE) and Percentage of GDP, Selected Years 2006–2022

	2006	2011	2014*	2017*	2022*
NHE ($ billion)	2,163	2,701	3,093	3,660	5,009
NHE per capita	7,255	8,680	9,697	11,711	14,164
NHE as % GDP	16.2	17.9	18.3	18.4	19.0

* Estimated projections include effects of the Affordable Care Act and an alternative to the sustainable growth rate.

Source: Reproduced from: Centers for Medicare & Medicaid Services, Office of the Actuary. Accessed at http://www.cms.gov/Research-Statistics-Data-and-Systems/Statistics-Trends-and-Reports/NationalHealthExpendData/downloads/proj2012.pdf

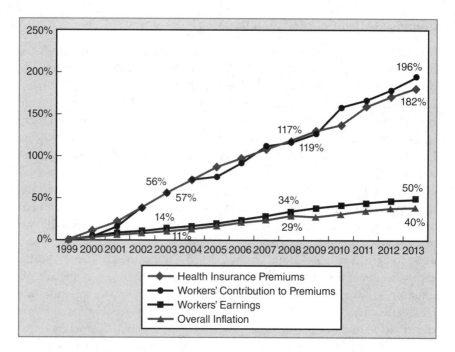

Figure 2-1 Cumulative changes in health insurance premiums, overall inflation, and workers' earnings from 2000–2013.

Source: Reproduced from: "Employer Health Benefits 2013 Annual Survey–Chartpack," (8465), The Henry J. Kaiser Family Foundation and Health Research & Educational Trust

health programs dropped 5%, to 61%. Since then the coverage rate has stayed relatively constant. However, the proportion of employers offering employee health benefits has declined.

Official federal policy has been to encourage employees to participate in health savings accounts (HSAs). The theory is that workers will choose health insurance coverage with high deductibles and coinsurance and will put savings from the reduced premiums into tax-exempt (income and interest) savings accounts that can be used in case of high medical expenses, for future retirement income, or for other uses. These plans got off the ground slowly because employers were concerned about the problem of *adverse selection*, namely that younger, healthier employees would choose the HSA option, leaving higher risk employees to draw from a different and smaller risk pool. Early returns from postal employees showed that the employees signing up for HSAs were much younger than those who chose or kept traditional coverage. By 2012, however, HSAs accounted for 19% of health plan enrollment.

Some employers are also concerned about the "portability" feature of HSAs. If the worker leaves, the premium dollar saved goes with the worker rather than staying to help cover the remaining employees' health insurance claims. Many employers see health benefits as a cost that is necessary to attract good employees and reduce employee turnover. Portability can run counter to that objective (Freudenheim, 2006).

QUALITY: A SYSTEMATIC EVALUATION

In 1980, Donabedian suggested the use of the following framework when evaluating quality of care:

- Access
- Technical management
- Management of interpersonal relationships
- Continuity of care

One could easily add additional categories, but these are a useful starting point (McLaughlin, 1998). All of these factors involve trade-offs with the cost of care, with one another, and with issues of equity and system complexity.

In this section we employ this categorization system with a modification. Donabedian developed this structure before most of our current concerns about costs and at a time when the health community shared a more homogeneous value system; therefore, we must consider the additional factors relating to costs and values, especially notions of equity in health care delivery. We have added costs to the list of categories. We will discuss value in a future chapter.

Within these now five categories, we will discuss three subcategories: structure, process, and outcome. Structure refers to available resource inputs, whereas process refers to conformance to best practices. We have already demonstrated what is meant by outcomes.

Access and Availability

If you were in a serious auto accident, you would want the ambulance to arrive as quickly as possible to stabilize you and transport you to a trauma center. You would want that ambulance to be *available*. If we are in danger, we supposedly are guaranteed *access*. If the situation is life threatening and the hospital participates in Medicare or Medicaid, it must take the patient regardless of ability to pay. For less serious situations, for emergent medical conditions, and for prevention, there are no such guarantees. Unfortunately, a significant proportion of our population lacks access, availability, or both. Estimates of the number of U.S. residents lacking health insurance coverage in 2011 began at 48 million and went up from there. Federal safety net spending, including Medicare, had decreased the lower-end number by more than a million from the preceding year. Implementation of the ACA should ameliorate many financial barriers to health care. The groundbreaking Massachusetts program reduced the proportion of nonelderly uninsured to single digits.

Numerous other perceived access problems exist. Although coverage for children has improved and the older population receives considerable benefits from Medicare and Medicaid, the working population has become worse off. Even before employer coverage decreased, the biggest access problems were among the *working poor*—those who earn too much to qualify for Medicaid but have little or no access to employer-subsidized health insurance or are unable to pay their share of the costs even when employment-based insurance is available. Even under subsidized programs, such as those offered in Maine and Massachusetts, enrollment by the working poor has been slow (Belluck, 2007).

Many improvements in coverage for children followed the creation of the State Children's Health Insurance Program (SCHIP) in 1997 and have occurred despite reduced private insurance coverage for children. Racial disparities in insurance coverage remain, with the highest rate of uninsurance occurring among Hispanic children (16% in 2011) and African American children (11%). Children uninsured for all or part of the year were more than twice as likely to receive no medical care that year (SHADAC, 2006).

Racial and Ethnic Health Disparities

In the United States, black infants are twice as likely to die as non-Hispanic white infants. A child between 1 and 14 years old in Alaska or Arkansas was about twice as likely to die in 2009 as a child in New Hampshire, Massachusetts, or Connecticut. Even worse, children in Arkansas, Alabama, Oklahoma, New Mexico, and Mississippi were more than three times as likely to die compared to their counterparts in those New England states. In 2010, the heart disease age-adjusted death rate in Mississippi was twice what it was in Minnesota and some 30% above the national average (State Health Facts, 2013).

One hopeful sign is the report from the Centers for Disease Control and Prevention (CDC) that there was no statistically significant difference in the vaccination rate of children 19 to 35 months in 2005, whether black, white, Hispanic, or Asian (CDC, 2006). There has been a continual narrowing of the gap with programs such as SCHIP and state attempts to recruit children into state programs, but the disparities are still striking.

Providers may also choose to direct their efforts toward consumers who have the greatest ability to pay. They gravitate toward more profitable specialties and may emphasize services that are most likely to generate income. In the United States, some gravitate to areas where malpractice insurance premiums are low. All of these factors can contribute to geographic and income disparities in care availability and access.

Many government and private programs bring services to special populations such as underserved rural areas, the posthospitalized mentally ill, American Indian and Alaskan Native communities, and people with AIDS. In these cases, the nation has modified its focus on a market-driven system to overcome market failures. Phelps (1997) pointed out that government involvement is one of the four features of the economics of health care delivery that differ from the delivery of most professional services. Three other economic differences that Phelps noted are uncertainty, information asymmetry, and externalities.

Structure

The United States stacks up pretty well in the developed world in terms of the total supply of services available, but services are distributed very unevenly. This is, however, a problem almost everywhere in the world. Urban centers attract trained personnel with job opportunities and educational and cultural opportunities for their families. Rural areas everywhere tend to lack personnel and facilities. That is one reason why in 2004 a third of U.S. patients could see a primary care physician the same day, but a sixth had to wait six or more days, and 16% reported going to the emergency room for a condition that could have been treated elsewhere if a regular doctor or source of care had been available (Schoen et al., 2004). Over time, this rural problem has lessened as the supply has increased and primary care physicians and even some specialists have moved to smaller communities in response to market forces (Rosenthal, Zaslavsky, & Newhouse, 2005).

Process

When asked in 2001 about prescriptions not filled; doctor visits needed but not made; and treatments, tests, or follow-ups missed, all because of costs and problems paying medical bills, 35% to 40% of U.S. respondents with below-average incomes reported experiencing such problems. This was almost double the rates in Australia, Canada, and New Zealand and six to nine times as large a proportion as in the United Kingdom. For the U.S. uninsured, the rate exceeded 50%. More than half of U.S. respondents with below-average income and a quarter of those with above-average income were delaying dental work because of the cost; however, these rates were also high in all of the five countries except the United Kingdom (Blendon et al., 2002). People everywhere seem to use every reason possible to avoid going to the dentist.

Outcomes

Outcomes reflect the fact that the greatest access barriers are economic ones. Morbidity in the nonelderly population is concentrated in the lower socioeconomic strata. Certainly, high morbidity contributes to loss of income, but that effect is small compared with the effects of social status on access to care.

Technical Management

Many efforts to improve U.S. care have focused on the processes of care delivery. For many years, medical error was an unmentionable among professionals. Finally, in the 1990s, the advent of evidence-based medicine and the resulting protocols led to the recognition that the best processes were often not used and that medical errors were all too common.

Structure

In the United States, most health professionals are well trained. Their credentials are carefully checked by the institutions where they work, and their licensing boards and certifying bodies require continuing professional education. Entry by foreign physicians is relatively tightly controlled, with requirements for additional postgraduate training and testing before practicing; however, the results of this process still show providers and institutions to be poorly distributed. Poor states, rural areas, inner cities, and areas with high minority concentrations and low incomes have very different health care utilization rates from the more privileged areas of the country.

Process

To ensure quality of care, most systems focus on the process of care delivery. They concentrate on the variability in treatment approaches among practices, among various areas of the country, and on failure to implement evidence-based practices. This focus on specific care processes, supported by measurement and reporting systems such as the National Committee for Quality Assurance's Health Plan Employer Data and Information Set (HEDIS) system, has improved the rate of conformance in the areas measured, but there is still a long way to go.

One indicator of poor resource allocation and questionable quality is variability in medical care delivery from one area to another. Wennberg, Fisher, and Skinner (2002) showed, for example, that Medicare spent twice as much per enrollee in Miami than in Minneapolis, without any apparent improvement in results. The Miami patients might have been sicker to start with, but case-mix differences were unlikely to justify a doubling of average costs in a fee-for-service program. These authors suggested that there is relatively little variability where the medical evidence for best practices is strong and much more where the evidence is less so, such as with hospital-based care during the last six months of life.

Estimates of waste in the U.S. health care system run as high as 30% to 40%. Not only are tests duplicated and medical records often unavailable, but there is little attempt to optimize processes and coordinate activities to maximize the use of personnel. Each specialty and department tends to operate to meet its own preferences and maximize revenue, rather than to improve system efficiency. Staff departments assigned to improve processes have fallen by the wayside during cost-cutting drives (Sahney, 1993). Experience at the Mayo Clinic shows the potential that can be realized by rebuilding in-house industrial engineering staff and empowering mid-level scheduling personnel (Berry & Saltman, 2007).

Outcomes

Much attention has been paid to medical error rates in recent years. The 2000 Institute of Medicine (IOM) report *To Err Is Human* and the follow-up report, *Crossing the Quality Chasm,* focused the attention of the government and a reluctant medical profession on this problem (IOM, 2000, 2001). The Leapfrog Group, an employer-oriented organization, has suggested several measures that are in the process of being implemented, including computerized physician order entry and widespread use of intensive-care hospitalists. The 100K Lives program and the Cystic Fibrosis Society databases have illustrated the magnitude of the improvements that could be achieved.

The ACA called for the formation of a Patient-Centered Outcomes Research Institute, thus institutionalizing the support of evidence-based medicine that was part of the American Recovery and Reinvestment Act stimulus package. Its effectiveness remains to be seen due to the restrictions in the legislation; for example:

> (e) The Patient-Centered Outcomes Research Institute established under section 1181(b)(1) shall not develop or employ a dollars-per-quality adjusted life year (or similar measure that discounts the value of a life because of an individual's disability) as a threshold to establish what type of health care is cost effective or recommended. The Secretary shall not utilize such an adjusted life year (or such a similar measure) as a threshold to determine coverage, reimbursement, or incentive programs under title XVIII. (PPACA [Consolidated], Sec. 6301/9511 IRC)

Management of Interpersonal Relationships

Most Americans believe it is important to have a relationship with a personal physician. Most do not want to be told which doctors they may or may not see. Many will even pay extra to have the relationships that they think will suit their needs.

Structure

Americans rebelled in the past when it was found that health maintenance organizations (HMO) could interfere with their existing relationships with their personal physicians. The public clearly values the patient–physician relationship where it exists; however, a substantial number of Americans report financial and spatial access problems and use less personal services, such as emergency rooms or urgent care centers. Many are concerned that as the ACA is implemented and financial access is improved, there will not be enough primary care providers to fulfill the demands for care.

Process

Much of the expressed dissatisfaction with interpersonal relationships in U.S. health care has to do with the brevity of encounters. Patients feel rushed by their primary care providers, who are under pressure to see more patients as preferred provider contracts and government discount pricing have eroded income per visit. This weakens patients' confidence that their providers have their welfare at heart. Clinically, it means that many emotionally fraught issues—issues that used to be addressed when the provider listened carefully for the "by the way" comment toward the apparent end of the visit, or what some counselors call the "doorknob moment"—are no longer addressed. Increased reliance on electronic medical records may or may not improve efficiency after the slowdown that typically occurs during the break-in learning period.

Outcomes

Increasingly, payers evaluate providers on the basis of questionnaires that measure consumers' satisfaction with the interpersonal aspects of their encounters. For example, the Hospital Consumer Assessment of Health-care Providers and Systems (HCAHPS) 32-Item Survey Instrument asks questions such as the following:

- During this hospital stay, how often did nurses treat you with courtesy and respect? This question is repeated to ask about interactions with doctors.
- During this hospital stay, how often did nurses listen carefully to you? This question is repeated to ask about interactions with doctors.
- During this hospital stay, did doctors, nurses, or other hospital staff talk to you about whether you would have the help you needed when you left the hospital?

The results of a hospital's HCAHPS surveys are posted for the public to see on the Hospital Compare website, http://www.medicare.gov/hospital compare/search.html.

Costs

Although a discussion of cost occurred earlier in this chapter, it is worth considering cost issues again in the context of quality using the same framework applied to the categories above.

Structure

As noted, the unit costs of health care inputs are high in the United States, especially for professional salaries, drugs, medical supplies, and devices. Health care provider salaries, are the highest in the world. Costs could go even higher as unmet needs are addressed. There are huge untapped needs in the fields of child psychiatry and community psychiatry. People report being constrained on their consumption of psychotherapy because of limitations on insurance reimbursement. We also know that the poor do not see physicians and other providers as much as those with adequate insurance, although that can beg the question of whether the problem is overutilization by those with health insurance, underutilization by the poor, or both. Given that a significant proportion of the poor are poor because of their health status, one would expect higher utilization on their part if they had sufficient insurance.

Process

Variability in processes is evident through differences in costs across areas and institutions. A substantial amount of gaming goes on between providers and the payment system. When the system will not pay for a diagnosis and an office procedure on the same visit, a dermatologist may schedule two visits. If the patient needs multiple minor procedures but the payer will not pay for each one separately, there again may be as many visits as procedures, wasting patient time and payer money. Kleinke (2005) reported that the three large independent clinical laboratory firms had failed to adopt a common reporting system that is available to them because they do not want to support electronic data interchange that might avoid tens of billions of dollars in duplicate laboratory tests. According to Kleinke,

> In an industry rife with dirty little secrets, this is health care's dirtiest: Bad quality is good for business . . . the surest road to bad quality is bad or no information. The various IT systems out there are expensive to buy, implement, and train staff to use, but this expense pales in comparison to all the pricey and billable complications those systems would prevent. (2005, p. 1250)

The second dirtiest little secret, Kleinke says, is that "[o]ne organization's unnecessary medical product or service is another's revenue source" (p. 1252).

Outcomes

Earlier sections of this chapter provided information on health costs and outcomes for the United States compared with other developed nations. They also noted that perceived cost and inability to pay were major impediments to obtaining needed health care. The magnitude of those costs is also motivating major corporations to dismantle their employment-based insurance plans for employees, families, and retirees and keeping many smaller employers from offering health care plans to their staff.

COMPLEXITY

One barrier to access may be the complexity of publicly financed programs. Some programs have been available only to those who at are below the federal poverty level (FPL), whereas other specific state programs can enroll families up to 300% of FPL. It should be noted that a family needs to make 200% to 300% of FPL before it has money left after purchasing food, shelter, and other essentials to pay for discretionary items, which have traditionally included health insurance and nonurgent health care services. Programs also have requirements for cost-sharing with premiums, copayments, and deductibles.

Health coverage will expand for low- and moderate-income families as the ACA is implemented, but, if anything, the complexity of finding the most appropriate and affordable coverage will increase. Consider the following explanation of ACA benefits from the Kaiser Foundation (2012):

> The ACA establishes a new continuum of coverage options that includes an expansion of Medicaid to a national eligibility floor of 138% FPL ($26,334 for a family of three in 2012) and the creation of new Health Benefit Exchanges with tax credits for individuals up to 400% of FPL ($76,300) for a family of three in 2012. These expansions will significantly increase availability of coverage for low and moderate-income populations.... Roughly 60% of nonelderly uninsured Blacks, Hispanics and American Indians/Alaska Native have income below the Medicaid expansion limit of 138% of FPL and over 90% have incomes below 400% FPL. (p. 6)

Then there is the fact that since the 2012 Supreme Court ruling on the constitutionality of the ACA, a number of states are choosing not to participate in the Medicaid expansion under that law. We know that the implementation of Massachusetts reforms similar to the ACA provisions for insurance reduced the number of uninsured significantly, but the ACA has yet to play out fully.

Compromise and Complexity

The political give and take that has marked the development of health care policy in the United States has left us with incredible financial complexity in our health system. **Table 2-3** lists the primary federally financed programs, each of which has its own often-changing set of regulations.

In the Medicaid program, we have more than 50 distinct government health care systems, one for each state and territory, the District of

Table 2-3 Major Federal Programs

Medicaid is the federal health insurance program for the poor and disabled. It can cover pretty much all their medical bills, including nursing home care and drugs. Eligibility levels and services vary by state.

Medicare is the federal health insurance program for those older than 65 years of age, some disabled individuals younger than age 65, and individuals with end-stage renal failure. It consists of three programs:

· Part A is hospital insurance and is covered by payroll taxes. In addition, it may cover hospice care, some home health care, and brief post-hospitalization nursing home care.

· Part B is medical insurance for which the premium due is deducted from one's Social Security check. It pays some parts of physicians' and other providers' fees. It also provides some coverage for home health care, outpatient services, medically necessary physical and occupational therapy, and home health services.

· Part D is insurance for prescription drugs coverage. Most participants pay a monthly premium to a private insurer for coverage under a plan-specific formulary.

Dual eligibles are poor disabled or elderly persons who are eligible for both Medicare and Medicaid. This population accounts for 18% and 16% of the respective beneficiaries of these two programs. Medicare pays for physician, prescription drug, and hospital care, while Medicaid pays the Medicare premiums and cost sharing and covers other health needs, such as long-term care.

Columbia, Puerto Rico, and the Virgin Islands. More than 1,100 current waivers of the rules have been granted to individual state programs to allow expanded coverage and use of managed care approaches. Each state system has its own reimbursement rate, the Federal Medicaid Assistance Percentage, which is based on a complex formula involving income levels in the state. For 2013, the basic federal match ranged from 50% federal payment in a number of wealthier states to 73.43% in Mississippi (see where the states stand in **Table 2-4**). Then there are also additional temporary federal Medicaid subsidies due to the stimulus package, disaster relief, and program expansion under the ACA.

Whether a person is eligible for Medicaid depends on the state in which he or she lives, because income eligibility and some overages vary by state. In 2013, for example, a pregnant woman may have been covered if her family income was at or below 133% of the FPL or 150% or 162% or 185% or 200% or 235% or 275% or 300%, depending on where she is enrolled (State Health Facts, 2013).

Those covered by Medicaid may include the following:

· Categorically needy
  · Families receiving Aid to Families with Dependent Children

Table 2-4 FY 2007 Federal Medicaid Assistance Percentage (FMAP) by State and Territory

Percentage Grouping	States and Territories in Category
50.0	California, Colorado, Connecticut, Delaware, Guam, Illinois, Maryland, Massachusetts, Minnesota, New Hampshire, New Jersey, New York, Virginia, Puerto Rico, Virgin Islands
50.01–50.99	Alaska, Nevada, Rhode Island, Washington, Wyoming
54.00–57.99	Hawaii, Michigan, Nebraska, Pennsylvania, Wisconsin
58.00–60.99	Florida, Kansas, Ohio, Texas, Vermont
61.00–64.99	Georgia, Indiana, Iowa, Maine, Missouri, North Carolina, North Dakota, Oregon, South Dakota, Tennessee
65.00–67.99	Arizona
68.00–69.99	Alabama, Kentucky, Louisiana, Montana, Oklahoma, South Carolina
70.00–73.99	Arkansas, District of Columbia, Idaho, New Mexico, Utah, West Virginia
76.0	Mississippi

Source: Reproduced from: Federal Register 11/20/2011 Doc 2011-30860

- Pregnant women and children younger than 6 years with family income up to 133% of the FPL
- Children ages 6–19 with family or caretaker income up to 100% of the FPL
- Supplemental Security Income (SSI) recipients or aged, blind, and disabled persons whose requirements are more restrictive than SSI
- Individuals and couples living in medical institutions who have monthly incomes up to 300% of the SSI income standard
- Medically needy individuals whose income or assets exceed those of the categorically needy
  - If a program exists, Medicaid must cover pregnant women through a 60-day postpartum period, children under 18, certain newborns for the first year, and certain protected blind persons.
  - The program has the option of covering:
    - Selected groups of full-time students between 18 and 21 years old
    - Caretakers (relatives and legal guardians) living with children
    - Aged persons over 65 years old

- Blind persons
- Disabled persons meeting state or SSI standards
- Persons who would be eligible if they were not enrolled in an HMO
- Special groups
  - Medicare premiums, coinsurance, and deductibles may be covered for Medicare beneficiaries with incomes below 100% of FPL and resources below 200% of the SSI allowable. States can also cover groups up to 135% of that level.
  - States may provide extended Medicaid eligibility while disabled persons learn to work and seek employment and as their conditions improve.
  - Individuals with tuberculosis may be covered for tuberculosis-related treatment costs.
  - Women with cervical or breast cancer may receive time-limited full coverage for cancer-related care.
  - Long-term care (institutional and home health) is covered in all states, but eligibility requirements vary by state.

Until very recently, Medicaid covered prescription drugs, but Medicare did not. Medicare still does not cover long-term care.

LEADERSHIP AT THE STATE AND LOCAL LEVEL

A state is responsible for health insurance regulation as well as for paying up to half the cost of Medicaid. Complexity is increased by the fact that each state has its own system of insurance regulation. Yet this has enabled a wide variety of innovative responses to access and cost issues at the state and local levels. Medicaid is often the largest expenditure category in state budgets and is an open-ended commitment. Jurisdictions that rely heavily on property taxes have major problems dealing with such unpredictable expenditures. State and local governments also end up covering most of the acute care costs of the uninsured. Many of these approaches are discussed in a later chapter.

The ERISA Barrier

Insurance regulation is a strong lever for mandating coverage, access, and high-risk pools. The Employee Retirement Income Security Act (ERISA) of 1974, however, exempted self-insured plans from much of state insurance law because the parent organizations do not have insurance as a primary line of business. Generally, the courts have upheld this law. One exception is a 1995 Supreme Court decision allowing New York State to place a surcharge tax on health premiums, including self-insured plans, to cover uncompensated hospital care. Other states have followed suit.

Park (2000) reported that in 1993 about half the nation's insured workers were enrolled in self-insured plans (also called Section 125 plans), mostly at large employers. The exemption allows companies to offer a consistent benefit package to all of their employees in various states, shelters them from state taxation of premiums and the costs of regulation, and lets them keep any returns on their capital reserves.

A self-funded company takes on the underwriting risk for its own pool of generally healthy employees. These plans were popular in the 1980s and early 1990s, but then lost market share as companies turned to managed care organizations to reduce costs. They are further losing share as companies cut back their benefit costs and offer defined contribution plans or nothing at all. Remember though that when health benefits were part of labor union contracts, workers had opted through their unions to forego part of their wage increases for better health benefits.

ERISA constitutes a barrier to states attempting to achieve universal coverage. It leaves each state with two health care insurance systems, one regulated and one not. Other arguments against the ERISA exemption point to the possibility that unregulated plans might fail because of mismanagement, that they might abuse sick employees, and that they put employees at a disadvantage if employers discontinue their self-funded plans.

There is also a concern that companies trying to wiggle out of the benefit requirements of the ACA will decide to self-insure. Some insurance companies are encouraging this by offering self-insured plans to much smaller companies than before. The *Wall Street Journal* reported in 2013 that 93% of firms with 5,000 or more employees were self-insured, but only 15% with fewer than 200 and 52% with between 200 and 999 (Weaver & Mathews, 2013).

INDUSTRIALIZING STRUCTURES FOR DELIVERY

The terms *industrialization* and *commoditization* keep coming up in discussions of ways to address undesirable health care trends. When applied to manufacturing early in the 20th century, industrialization meant (1) breaking complex tasks performed by individuals down into simple tasks assigned to different members of a team and (2) studying, analyzing, and specifying the best way to do each of those tasks. The result was that work moved from the control and *artistry of the craftsperson* to a systematic process that was perhaps more efficient and less personal. Specialization in the industrialized system can imply *deskilling* for some workers, as well as much higher, but narrower, skill levels for others. Managerial control of the system involves both allocating duties and specifying the right way to do them. Usually management includes two groups: (1) line managers who allocate the work and (2) staff specialists whose job is to specify and improve processes. Where the process is well defined and skill requirements can be reduced, *labor substitution* takes place; that is, routine work is done by less expensive personnel with more limited training and less autonomy.

Despite the monopolies offered by licensure and credentialing, many health care tasks can be done by more than one level of health care worker. For example, both midwives and obstetricians can deliver babies. The practice of midwifery nearly disappeared in the United States but is now undergoing a resurgence. Nurse practitioners and physician assistants now are the first level of care for many patient encounters. In many psychiatric practices, the psychiatrist handles the patient's medications but delegates most other care activities to psychologists, social workers, and other counselors. Pharmacies now use pharmacy technicians as well as pharmacists. Dental practices have their own dental hygienists and technicians working in parallel with the dentists. Primary care physicians perform procedures once limited to specialists. The key to further substitution is whether the alternative workers are qualified for the problem at hand and whether their unit cost is less. Most substitutions were initially proposed to overcome a shortage of personnel in one area, but after the experiment worked, more and more organizations have implemented it on a continuing basis to increase access and reduce cost.

A number of authors (Porter & Teisberg, 2006; Bohmer & Lawrence, 2008; Bohmer, 2009) have identified other aspects of industrialization in health care:

- More physicians employed (under management) rather than partners in practices
- Institutional emphasis on process development, including evidence-based medicine and continuous quality improvement
- External exchange of information on relative experience, outcome quality, and prices and costs
- Emphasis on process conformance and transparency, including pre-authorizations, carve outs, utilization reviews, and clinical pathways
- Development of focused factories that specialize in a limited range of procedures, such as specialty hospitals and ambulatory surgery centers

- Increasing fragmentation of patient care with offsetting efforts aimed at coordination and teamwork
- Increasing substitution of capital for labor
- A more impersonal relationship between the server and the served

Clayton Christensen (cited in Holstein, 2006) expressed the industrializing view most strongly. He believed that rather than continually trying to reproduce the expertise of doctors and major health care institutions, we must treat that expertise as a commodity. This hinges on our ability to diagnose disease precisely using rules-based medicine. Our diagnostic ability, he noted, is evolving rapidly, but our systems for regulation and reimbursement keep us trapped in high-cost delivery models.

Referring to the historical example of pneumonia and consumption, he argued:

> You had tuberculosis there, at least three types, and you had pneumonia. We thought it was all one disease. So the care had to be left with doctors because they were the ones with the training and judgment, but once you could precisely diagnose the cause of the disease, you could then develop a cure. It was so rules-based that you didn't need a doctor any longer. Today a technician can diagnose those diseases and a nurse can treat them.

Managed care has become a major form of organization for care delivery. Practices and institutions have merged or sold out to a wide array of health care organizations. Primary care physicians report frustration with their loss of autonomy and with the pressures for efficiency expressed as a measure of the number of patients seen (Rastegar, 2004). Physician incomes, especially those of specialists, have dropped rapidly. These are all related to the industrialization of what had been a cottage industry organized along craft lines.

Figure 2-2 suggests one way to think about industrialization and the various process requirements that analogy suggests. Two dimensions are identified: type of case, which ranges from simple to complex, and knowledge base, which ranges from science based (codified) to art (tacit). The drivers of industrialization in health care have been the expansion of the science base of medicine and the codification of product definitions and process specifications. For more about art (tacit knowledge) versus science and product and process improvement trajectories in general, see Victor and Boynton (1998). The applicability of their model to health care is discussed in greater detail in McLaughlin and Kaluzny (2006). An example of the trend toward codification by medical institutions and professions is the effort by the Institute of Medicine to support the "learning health care

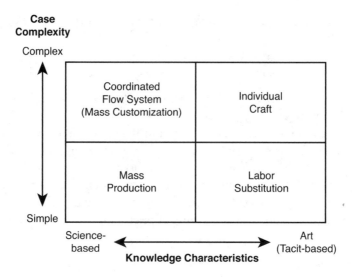

Figure 2-2 Suggested impact of case complexity and knowledge characteristics on process choices in health care.

system." One major output of this effort is the book *Best Care at Lower Cost* (Smith et al., 2012).

Describing medicine before World War II as a craft/guild system implies that medicine was primarily an art lacking decision rules that could be communicated effectively (tacit knowledge) (Ferdows, 2006). With more and more scientific and/or codified knowledge, it was possible to differentiate between cases and processes. Simple industrial activities can be turned into mass production systems that repeat the same process over and over. If the knowledge is still pretty much an art but the task simple, the work can be delegated to less experienced or less trained personnel (as in the *apprentice system*, in which much of the simpler work was delegated to others but the master craftsman maintained control and handled the trickiest parts or the rounding process in the teaching hospital). For example, part of the training process for nurse practitioners is learning what diagnoses not to treat and what to hand off to appropriate experts. Where processes are codified but the cases are complex, and hence varied, patients need to be processed in a coordinated flow between provider subsystems, a process referred to as *mass customization*. The modern hospital can be visualized as a custom job shop process, with a patient moving as needed from the bed tower to the X-ray department to the phlebotomy laboratory to surgery to the intensive care unit to the step-down unit and back to the bed tower. However, we all witness the consequences of matches and mismatches between approaches high in art that fit with craft (e.g., apprenticeship and job costing or fee-for-service) and those high in science that fit with industrialization (e.g., bundled payments, use of clinical pathways, length-of-stay controls).

Mass production exists in areas such as cataract surgery and other "centers of excellence," but in general there is a widespread desire to avoid mass production of medical services. That desire is legitimate given the high inherent variability in patient anatomy, physiology, and psychological needs and preferences. Mass customization is the logical end point for this process. Health care is a mixture of art and science; however, health care differs from industrial production in the sense that patients present themselves with both simple and complex problems (multisystem problems or comorbidities). Problems that have a clearly optimal treatment regimen and those for which medical knowledge is limited can appear simultaneously in the same individual.

What has kept much patient care from being a well-coordinated process has been the very limited amount of process codification that has taken place and inadequate investment in information technology, as well as a lack of provider commitment to share knowledge and to abide by specified process parameters. This is often attributed to lack of sufficiently aligned professional and institutional incentives.

Ownership of Intellectual Capital

As work is industrialized, work methods are specified by the organization rather than the individual artisan. In health care, we have historically assumed that intellectual capital resides with the professional. This stems from an assumed inability of the public (including lay administrators) to understand the technical processes of health care. This notion is the underlying foundation of medicine's claims of professional autonomy, but that autonomy is threatened by recommendations such as those offered by Einthoven and Tollen (2005), who called for reliance on integrated delivery systems for cost control. As advocates of what has since been labeled *administered competition*, they argued against provider-level competition and for system-level competition because integrated delivery systems:

- Can better motivate clinicians to use best practices and hold them accountable.
- Do a better job of achieving coordination and continuity of care, especially for the chronically ill.
- Are more likely to invest in and implement interoperable information technology.

- Are more likely to adopt and successfully implement "large-scale efficiency measures."
- Are more likely to compete directly with each other on quality and price.
- Are more likely to be selective among providers than loose and inclusive provider networks serving most insurers in a community.

These authors urged employers to offer employees a choice of carriers to motivate insurers to avoid providers of low-quality and high-cost care. Haislmaier (2006) argued that a key innovation of the Massachusetts reforms was the "Connector" exchange system, which allowed individuals insurance portability.

As competition increasingly depends on the implementation of evidence-based practices by an institution, and on rapid dissemination and adoption by practitioners, organizational rather than professional learning becomes the focus. That raises new questions about management–provider conflicts (often called *suits versus coats*), the role of continuing graduate medical education, and access to clinical records and research outputs. Professionals must be prepared to take leadership in issues around developing, disseminating, and compensating for intellectual capital or they will lose even more autonomy.

Horizontal Integration

Compartmentalization of services by their separate funding sources contributes to coordination of care problems and to considerable waste of time and treasure. Many efforts are underway with the support of the ACA and professional organizations to integrate care systems involving acute care, preventive care, behavioral health services, public health services, and social services. For example, the Institute of Medicine and others sponsored a Consensus Report by Committee on Integrating Primary Care and Public Health (Association of Territorial and State Health Officers, 2012) that laid out a "strategic map" of steps needed to move both groups out of their silos and into cooperative population health in the community. The five key priorities identified in the map were:

1. Identify and create demonstrated successes.
2. Realign funding to support coordination and sustainability.
3. Disseminate and scale effective approaches and systems.
4. Develop and implement effective measures of population health.
5. Create the infrastructure to support collaboration and sustainability.

A major provision of recent legislation has been the opportunity for the states to integrate services for dual eligibles. Many states have submitted proposals to integrate and enhance their services by combining the Medicare and Medicaid funding. Many have also opted to cover their institutionalized populations with Medicare Advantage Special Needs Plans.

States have also submitted Medicaid waiver proposals that would integrate traditional health services with behavioral health services and social services in community-based programs. Individuals with chronic disease problems, including mental health diagnoses, also tend to be unemployed and have limited social support. A number of states are looking at integrating these services, especially for dual eligibles. We know that readmissions tend to be higher in safety net hospitals due to the lack of community resources. Reliance on emergency rooms is so expensive that some Medicaid programs are providing medical homes and a wider range of community services to keep "frequent flyers" out of hospital settings. In the United Kingdom, the National Institute for Health and Care Excellence (NICE) has been tasked not only with developing evidence-based practices for health care but for social services as well. It remains to be seen whether this trend will result in less medicalization of society or just lead to the medicalization of social services.

The Professions

One interesting aspect of the U.S. medical system is that it did not industrialize under either corporate control, as many other services have done, or government control. Starr (1982) discussed how the medical profession gained control of health care and maintained it in the face of pressures to consolidate into corporate forms of organization. The cover of his book, *The Social Transformation of American Medicine*, states that it is about "the rise of a sovereign profession and the making of a vast industry." Writing in the early 1980s at the height of the interest in HMOs, he foresaw rapid growth in the corporate form of care delivery.

Much of the ebb and flow of employer, insurer, and government attempts to solve health care system issues flows around issues of industrialization and corporate delivery of medical care. Starr (1982, pp. 229–231) cited five structural changes in American medicine before World War II that strengthened the sovereign position of physicians in health care and enabled them to avoid working in a corporate structure:

1. An informal control system based on dependence on colleagues for referrals and hospital privileges.

2. Formal control of labor markets through the licensing process.
3. Transfer of many overheads and investments—those a typical private corporation that provided medical services would make—to societal organizations such as hospitals, public health departments, and educational institutions.
4. A lack of countervailing organizations that could choose to challenge the political and economic influences of the medical profession.
5. Few attempts to develop integrated care organizations that would attempt to rationalize the highly fragmented, but insulated delivery system.

In 1934, the American Medical Society claimed that "all features of medical service in any method of medical practice should be under the control of the medical profession." Elsewhere in the world the response to that assertion is that control should rest with the government. In the United States, we increasingly hear that it should rest on "consumer sovereignty."

Is there something inherently different about health care? The economist and Nobel laureate Kenneth Arrow addressed this question in his influential 1963 article titled "Uncertainty and the Welfare Economics of Medical Care." He argued that some functions, such as insurance, exhibit usual market behavior, but he also observed that the buyer is not a rational optimizer in a perfect market but rather is a vulnerable, trusting patient who seeks information in an uncertain world from a physician who is also dealing with many uncertainties. He emphasized the following elements of uncertainty and market failure:

- Inequality of information (today called *information asymmetry*)
- Inequality of resources, especially income
- Professional ethic demanding that treatment be independent of ability to pay
- Importance of trust to the effectiveness of the care
- Vulnerability and psychological state of patients
- Longer term implications of the ongoing physician–patient relationship

Arrow pointed to a number of unique structural elements of the health care marketplace, such as professional licensure, nonprofit institutions, sliding fee scales, and government intervention, as responses to these elements. He argued that much of the uncertainty could be handled through insurance and government intervention. His postscript concluded:

> The failure of the market to ensure against uncertainty has oriented many social institutions in which the usual assumptions of the market

are contradicted. The medical profession is only one example, though in many respects an extreme one. . . . The logic and limitations of ideal competitive behavior under uncertainty force us to recognize the incomplete description of reality supplied by the impersonal price system. (Arrow, 1963, p. 967)

Criticisms of Arrow and of how this article is interpreted are many, but it remains very relevant and influential. Sloan (2003, p. 58) argued that the article is used by those who oppose markets and that "an alternative approach—in my view, a much more fruitful one is to recognize the market imperfections and devise various interventions to empower consumers. . . . Consumer ignorance should not be taken as a given." Rice (1998) raised 15 questions about the assumptions of the competitive market model applied to health care, such as lack of externalities, fixed preferences, absence of monopoly, complete and accurate information availability, and rational decision making. Henderson (2002, pp. 109, 111) accepted the market failure examples but countered normatively that

> On the other hand, no credible evidence supports government remedies as the answer to the perceived inequities either. Markets may fail, but governments may be just as prone to failure. And correcting government failure is inherently more difficult than correcting market failure. . . . Criticism directed at market failure without at least admitting the possibility of government failure is dishonest, or at minimum naïve.

Starr interpreted many of the social institutions that Arrow cited not as social responses to uncertainty, but as steps that organized medicine used to establish its monopoly control over health care and to stave off industrialization, and he cited examples of them increasing uncertainty.

Why has medicine remained a cottage industry? The medical profession has been very protective of its control over health care. Yet there have been a number of moves in the direction of consolidation and corporate structures. Starr (1982, p. 420) suggested five dimensions likely to change should the practice of medicine move toward a more typical American corporate structure:

1. Change in ownership and control
2. Horizontal integration into multisite organizations
3. Diversification and public restructuring with holding companies and subsidiaries with differing product lines
4. Vertical integration involving multiple stages and levels of care
5. Industry concentration of ownership and control of services

Interestingly, all of these have been taking place, albeit slowly and selectively. Now, however, the government is encouraging it due to perceived waste and lack of coordination of care. In fact, many of the implemented proposals and experiments have accomplished aspects of each of these and have created efficiency, effectiveness, and wealth. They have each had their day, yet they have not stemmed the inflationary trends nor overwhelmed the smaller operators. Hospitals and corporations that bought up physician practices in the 1990s experienced problems in recouping their investments. For-profit hospital chains have had their ups and downs. Integrated health systems do dominate in many specific areas, but they have not been terribly successful in replicating their approach elsewhere.

Status of Professions and Professionals

It may seem odd to think of professional status as a variable to manipulate in establishing health policy; however, professional roles are not immutable. New professions emerge as technology changes and others lose ground. Professions are a combination of knowledge, political power, and custom. Ultimately, the public either accepts or denies one group's dominance over a knowledge domain and the delivery of services.

Health workers existed long before the modern medicine era. Most societies have had shamans, birth attendants, and indigenous healers. Before 1850, physicians did not seem to enjoy any consistent status in the United States. With the advent of modern science and modern medicine, governments became alarmed at the amount of quackery going on. They cooperated with the medical profession and conferred on the profession a near monopoly, which has been buttressed by our system of licensing and credentialing.

Starr (1982) traced in detail the parallel political and social development of monopoly power by American physicians. Freidson (2001) saw the professional model as a third alternative to the hierarchical (corporate) model and to "free market autonomy." In the professional model, the professionals maintain considerable control over (1) the information and (2) the means of delivery in their domain; however, many proposed and implemented health policy alternatives have the effect of weakening the existing status of health professionals. This is a natural result of the emphasis on market mechanisms and an informed consumer, as well as the vastly increased access to information that the public now has, especially through the Internet.

Given that professional status and credentials offer privileges with economic value, health policy analysts must consider how that value and power might be allocated to serve the public interest. The literature suggests a number of concepts related to professional status changes in addition to labor substitution and evidence-based medicine, including:

- Outsourcing
- Rising educational barriers
- Disintermediation
- Consumer-centered care
- Patient-centered care
- Incentive systems for quality, cost, and access

Outsourcing

Outsourcing is a relatively new phenomenon in health care, but it can be driven by the same factors as labor substitution. A shortage of radiologists in rural areas has led to networking arrangements in which radiologists living in urban areas receive digital images produced by technicians in rural hospitals, and the urban radiologists read them offsite (in their offices or homes) without ever going to where the patient is receiving care. Digitized information can be read anywhere in the world, and it is not unusual to find that U.S. imaging and electrocardiograms results are farmed out to Asian locations where salaries are much lower. More and more patients who lack adequate insurance coverage but have reasonable incomes are choosing to have elective surgery done in reputable overseas hospitals where the cost is much lower. Pharmaceutical companies are also moving medical research and clinical trials offshore to reduce costs.

Rising Educational Barriers

A pressure running counter to labor substitution is the tendency of each profession to raise the bar a person must leap to be granted professional status. The biggest suppliers of nursing labor in the United States are the community colleges, which have programs that do not always culminate with a baccalaureate degree; however, nursing leadership has argued for the need to have more, if not all, nurses earn 4-year degrees. At the same time, nursing subspecialists that require master's level degrees are proliferating. Pharmacy schools that once offered pharmacy bachelor degrees now produce Pharm.D. recipients. All of these moves require more training, constrain the supply of personnel in a particular field, and seemingly justify higher wages and greater professional status.

Disintermediation

The term *disintermediation* means removing the person in the middle, the intermediary. One prime example is direct-to-consumer pharmaceutical advertising. Until 1997, companies' selling efforts focused mostly on the prescribing physician. Then the Food and Drug Administration (FDA) eased its regulations on risk reporting sufficiently to allow advertising other than the printed page. Now ad after ad suggests a treatment, syndrome, disease, or risk factor that the patients might not even be aware of (e.g., hypercholesterolemia, acid reflux disease, toenail fungus) and urges them to ask their physician about the branded treatment. This advertising bypasses the physician initially and, given the availability of imported drugs, may bypass the physician entirely. **Table 2-5** provides examples of how physician care is being bypassed when it comes to control of medical information and/or of the means of delivery of care.

The primary care provider is not the only intermediary that can be targeted. The decentralized and disjointed nature of the health care industry has allowed the rise of an array of middlemen who have profited greatly by aggregating the demand of small actors and matching them up with provider organizations with surplus capacity, allowing them to obtain discounts. Middlemen have also achieved at least a temporary knowledge advantage that has enabled them to take advantage of the market (sometimes called *arbitraging*). The *Wall Street Journal* ran a series of articles on these highly profitable intermediaries in 2006, focusing on pharmacy benefits managers, billing consultants, catastrophic case care managers, Medicaid HMOs, nursing home pharmacy firms, and insurers (Wessel, Wysocki, & Martinez, 2006).

Consumer-Centered Care

Quality reporting is relatively new in health care. Diagnosis-related groups (DRGs), introduced in the 1980s, classified hospital services in 467 bundles of care. A parallel relative-value scale system was also developed to evaluate professional fees. It had not been possible to adjust cost data for severity and patient characteristics, nor to maintain quality control records, until those product definitions were established and widely adopted. Once data on costs could be associated with specific diagnoses and compared across

Table 2-5 Disintermediation Activities Affecting the Primary Care Physician

Actor	Activities Affecting Information Control	Activities Affecting Transaction Control
Pharmaceutical companies	Direct-to-consumer advertising (DTCA) websites	Moving patent-expired drugs over the counter (OTC)
Screening centers	DTCA	No referral required
	Direct patient reporting	Direct patient pay
Nurse practitioners/ Physician assistants	Independent practice	Independent practice
Psychologists	Independent practice	Gaining prescribing authority
Insurers	Deep portals for enrollees	Forcing drugs OTC
	Case management	Case management
Case management firms	Taking over patient management	Patient advocacy in community
	Self-care advice	
Pharmacy benefits management firms	Formulary feedback to patients	Multitiered copays
Employers	Educational programs and web portals	Screening programs
Academic medical centers	Newsletters/Web sites Telemedicine programs	Telemedicine programs
Government agencies	Websites/advertising	Preferred drug lists
	Screening recommendations	Screening programs
	Case management	
Patient/disease advocacy groups	Websites/advertising	Screening programs
	Screening recommendations	
Pharmacists	Counseling centers	Screening programs
Hospitals	Protocols shared with patients and their families	Formularies
		Screening programs
	Formularies	

Source: Reproduced from: Table 1, p. 72 from C.P. McLaughlin et al., "Changing Roles for Primary-Care Physicians: Addressing Challenges and Opportunities." *Healthcare Quarterly*, Vol. 8, No. 2, 2005. Copyright © Longwoods Publishing Corp.

cases, providers, regions, and institutions, then the tools began to fall in place for corporate-level analysis, allowing a more industrial approach to health care management. Pressure from employers and patients, the ultimate payers, has led to increased transparency, with more and more information about quality of care becoming available on the Internet. To encourage more careful consumption, more and more plans and employers are offering high-deductible health plans coupled with one or more tax-sheltered saving accounts. We will look at these plans in more detail in a future chapter. For the employer, this approximates the substitution of a defined benefit for a defined contribution plan.

Patient-Centered Care

More recently, emphasis has been placed on involving patients in decisions about health care choices. For example, the ACA calls for "patient-centeredness" to be one of the quality measures for a pilot program, and it has mandated the establishment of the Patient-Centered Outcomes Research Institute. However, the ACA leaves it up to the secretary of Health and Human Services to define what the term means. Don Berwick (2009) has suggested the following definition: "The experience (to the extent the informed, individual patient desires it) of transparency, individualization, recognition, respect, dignity, and choice in all matters, without exception, related to one's person, circumstances, and relationships in health care" (p. w560).

The ACA makes it clear that there is a link to evidence-based medicine, even while it constrains the use of some economically oriented outcome measures by the institute.

Incentive Systems for Quality, Cost, and Access

Once cases could be assessed for process quality, outcomes, and costs, payment could be based on overall experience rather than on the inputs utilized in the specific case (fee for service). We discuss bundling and pay-for-performance later in the text. Many demonstrations of bundling, penalties for readmissions and medical errors, and medical homes are available, and more are contemplated under the ACA.

MEDICALIZATION OF SOCIETY

Looking back over 30 years of sociological research, Conrad (2007) observes that:

> Clearly, the number of life problems that are defined as medical has increased enormously. Does this mean that there is a new epidemic of medical problems or that medicine is better able to identify and treat existing problems? Or does it mean that a whole range of life's

problems have now received medical diagnoses and are subject to medical treatment, despite dubious evidence of their medical nature? (p. 3)

Examples given include erectile dysfunction, sleep disorders, idiopathic short stature, and ADHD.

These definitions of medical conditions impinge on our perceptions of what is tolerable and what is changeable within our society, as well as on our self-perceptions. A 2006 study showed that white, middle-aged British patients reported better health status than Americans, despite spending much less per capita on health care. Some attribute the differences to high U.S. stress levels; however, an alternative point of view is that the high rate of expenditure on medical care, especially the amount of screening taking place and the constant barrage of health care–related advertising, has resulted in a reduced perception of wellness. In essence, the greater the proportion of our economy that goes into health care–related activities, the more "sickness" we experience. According to Welch, Schwartz, and Woloshin (2007), "As more of us are being told we are sick, fewer of us are being told we are well. People need to think about the benefits and risks of increased diagnosis: the fundamental question they face is whether or not to become a patient."

This goes back to the definition that we have heard attributed to any number of sources—that a healthy person is one who has not been sufficiently examined by a physician. Consider, for example, comparisons of high blood pressure and high cholesterol levels in U.S. and British 40 to 70 year olds. Americans self-reported more of these problems; however, measured blood pressures were the same, and Americans had lower cholesterol levels. Some attribute lower levels of reported illness among Britons to the fact that British primary care physicians do much less routine screening (Hadler, 2004; Kolata, 2006). Some see the U.S. screening penchant as a transfer of scarce medical resources from the sick poor to the worried, insured well, and consider it a logical outcome of the medicalization of life together with the industrialization of medicine (Heath, 2005). Some attribute much of the growth of health care costs to screening and treatment of risk factors that are asymptomatic (Hadler, 2011).

Other issues related to the medicalization of U.S. society include the dependence of the economy on the growth of this sector. A 2006 cover story in *BusinessWeek* asserted that two sectors, construction and health care, accounted for all the growth in private sector employment over the preceding 5 years and that growth in health care employment was the greater of the two. "Since 2001, the health care industry has added 1.7 million jobs. The rest of the private sector? None" (Mandel, 2006, p. 55).

Career choices and educational offerings have changed in response to the perceived demand.

Health issues have received increased emphasis in news reporting, television programming, television advertising, and recreation facilities. We have had visitors from other countries ask, unprompted, why we have so much medical and pharmaceutical advertising. There are pluses and minuses to this increasing presence of health care issues throughout our society. We are not arguing that it is good or bad; however, the analyst must take this trend into account when making recommendations. Overall, medicalization tends to increase both the political and economic risks of rapid or radical change to our health care system.

REDISTRIBUTION OF WEALTH

All commerce and most taxation can lead to a redistribution of wealth, but health care in the United States presents some special challenges, including the following:

- Federal Medicaid Assistant Percentage (FMAP) payments to the states are paid out of general revenue and differ from state to state. As a rule, the payments are based on the following formula:

$$FMAP = 1 - .45 \times [(\text{State PCI})^2/(\text{U.S. PCI})^2]$$

  Where PCI is per capita income as computed by the Department of Commerce's Bureau of Economic Analysis. It is subject to a minimum of 0.50 and a maximum of 0.83. This formula was designed to give a greater share to poorer states.
- Medicare Part A is supported by a tax on current earnings of wage earners. This is a transfer from younger working adults to the mostly retired elderly.
- The ACA provides for premium subsidies for low-income workers funded out of a number of tax penalties and excise taxes.
- To the extent that Medicare Parts B and D are not covered by the premiums paid by the elderly or those premiums are subsidized based on income, there is a further transfer of wealth to the elderly.
- Hospitals with a large number of indigent patients (Medicaid, SSI, uninsured) can qualify for Medicare and Medicaid Disproportionate Share payments under complex formulas. The ACA has continued the trend of cutting these payments and tying them more directly to the costs of the uncompensated care. These payments tend to

go heavily to large urban hospitals, especially teaching institutions. There are provisions for special attention to rural hospitals as well.

These transfers create strong special interests and add greatly to the complexity and overhead costs of the U.S. health care system. They also provide plentiful fodder for policy debates, which we hope you will carry over into class discussions.

CONCLUSION

This chapter examines the status of the American health care system in terms of access, technical management, management of interpersonal relationships, and costs. It offers international comparisons of expenditures (both per capita and as a percent of GDP) alongside life expectancy and infant natal mortality. It also outlines possible linkages between these variables, or the lack thereof. With such data, the educated citizen can join the debate about where the United States wants to go. Although the recent legislation overhauling health insurance and patient access has been extensive, it has done relatively little to lower costs, and the policy focus is shifting toward competition, quality and value of care, and increasing efficiency.

Other concerns as the debate continues include the distribution of care and care dollars and the impacts of changes and trends on the professional environment of health care. Two related constructs discussed in this chapter are the industrialization of health care and the medicalization of American society.

Chapter 3

How Did We Get Here?

A history of health care policy making in the United States could well start in 1791 with the passage of the Bill of Rights. The Tenth Amendment to the U.S. Constitution declares that those powers not expressly given to the federal government belong to state and local governments. Health and education were not expressly given to the federal government. In 1910, the Supreme Court ruled that a federal workers' compensation system was unconstitutional. Each state then established its own system. Hadler (2013) cites this as the regulatory template for the U.S. health insurance program as it developed much later. This issue played out again in June 2012 when the Supreme Court narrowly upheld part, but not all, of the Patient Protection and Affordable Care Act (ACA).

With minor exceptions, the federal government has limited its role to financing national programs of health and education, rather than delivering services directly. Federal involvement has been justified under the welfare clause of the Constitution and also through Thomas Jefferson's argument of implied powers. Yet the federal share of health expenditures is fast approaching half the direct cost of care, even without counting individual tax deductions for health care spending and insurance premiums and corporate deductions for employee health insurance premiums. Tax subsidies, health insurance provided to government employees, and public dollars spent on health at all levels of government account for close to 60% of all health spending.

This chapter looks at the coevolution of two separate, but linked, U.S. health systems—one for delivering medical care and one for financing it. Financing, especially the health insurance system, has impacted delivery systems; for instance, it has created incentives for overutilization or underutilization. Separate health insurance systems exist to cover expenses for dental, vision, and long-term care. Public health is financed primarily through state, local, and federal dollars obtained through taxes and fees.

CONTENDING VISIONS OF A SYSTEM FOR DELIVERING HEALTH CARE

Conflicts between different visions of how the health system should operate have dominated U.S. health care policy making. Different ideas have been more or less dominant at different times. Yet there has not been a dominant viewpoint since the 1960s, and all of the contending approaches have remained on the table. Each ideology or philosophy falls along the continuum of alternatives represented in **Figure 3-1**. Five potential characterizations of the health care market are presented. One, a provider monopoly, has been ruled out by our legal system, even though it may best describe the U.S. health system as it existed between World Wars I and II (Starr, 1982). A monopoly occurs when the market for a product or service is controlled by a single provider, and in most cases is illegal. A monopsony exists when a single buyer controls a market. The extreme monopsony position can be represented by the original version of the United Kingdom's National Health Service. This model is not currently a realistic contender for adoption in the United States either.

Oligopolistic competition involves a relatively open market dominated by a few large sellers and is a characteristic of many U.S. industrial sectors. Usually, three or four major sources for goods or services exist, and those sources control at least 40% of the market. In health care, two, three, or four providers often control state or local markets in the absence of a national

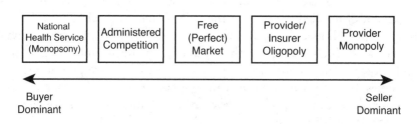

Figure 3-1 Stages of health care market power.

market. National oligopolies appear to exist in many markets, such as pharmacy benefits management, Medicare managed care, replacement joints, imaging equipment, and pharmaceuticals distribution. Two or three hospital groups often control most of the relevant local market. Concentration in hospital markets has been increasing sharply enough to become a concern of the Federal Trade Commission (FTC). Although available studies of hospital concentration can yield conflicting findings (Gaynor, 2006), there can be little doubt that concentration increases pricing power. In many state markets the same is true of health insurance providers. Yet it is widely believed that market power has shifted in recent years from insurers to providers, especially larger hospitals and their associated group practices.

Starr (2011) describes the process leading up to the passage of the ACA as one of reaching a compromise between administered competition and consumer-driven health care, but the legislation was crafted to be minimally invasive to encourage support from interests such as hospitals, pharmaceutical companies, and the insurance industry.

Administered competition implies that there are multiple suppliers but that the market is strongly influenced by a primary (but not exclusive) buyer, usually a government creation. It may involve universal coverage, a single payer, and/or a single underwriter.

Consumer-driven health care is more of a free-market approach that assumes that consumers' choices will help shape the market if consumers have accurate and adequate information and are not subject to perverse incentives.

Perfect (free-market) competition assumes the following conditions:

- There are large numbers of buyers and sellers so that no one controls prices.
- All buyers and sellers have complete and accurate information about the quality, availability, and prices of goods.
- All products have available perfect substitutes.
- All buyers and sellers are free to enter or leave the market at will.

Free-market ideology has been playing out in health care even in the absence of a real free market. It goes by a number of names—consumer-driven health care is one example, as is market-driven health care. Supporters of this approach call for much greater transparency and more consumer choice and responsibility. It has been implemented, in part, through innovations such as health savings accounts (HSAs) and private options for Medicare. Insurance exchanges are another manifestation of this approach and were initially suggested by conservative think tanks that support a free-market approach.

A CHRONOLOGY

Centuries ago, medical care was a religious calling, not a scientific field. The term *hospice* was more representative of health care institutions than *hospital*. Gradually, health care has become a calling *and* an industry. Well into the 20th century, U.S. physicians took whatever people could pay. Teaching institutions provided free care in return for allowing learners to work on those who could not pay. This system of combined fee-for-service and charity care existed before the Great Depression and World War II. From there, one can trace the development and gradual introduction of employment-based health insurance and prepaid group practices, leading to the establishment of health maintenance organizations (HMOs) and the industrialization of parts of the delivery system with the emergence of pharmaceutical giants, hospital chains, pharmacy chains, and large, integrated health care systems.

The Health "Insurance" Approach: Moving from Provider Monopoly Toward Provider/Insurer Oligopoly

Health insurance systems in the United States were implemented during the Great Depression to stabilize cash flows of providers. The concept existed in Europe much earlier (Starr, 1982). Many of the early systems in the United States evolved into the nonprofit Blue Cross/Blue Shield organizations.

Dr. Justin Ford Kimball, the administrator of Baylor Hospital in Dallas, is often credited with starting the U.S. medical insurance movement in 1929. He conceived of the idea of collecting "insurance premiums" in advance and guaranteeing the hospital's service to members' subscribing groups. Furthermore, he found a way to involve employers in the administration of the plan, thereby reducing expenses associated with marketing and enrollment. The first employer to work with Baylor Hospital was the Dallas school district, which enrolled schoolteachers and collected the biweekly premium of 50 cents (Richmond & Fein, 2005).

About the same time, prepaid group practices began in Oklahoma, but they were bitterly opposed by local medical societies. Prepaid group practices, forerunners of today's HMOs and the organizations identified in the ACA as accountable care organizations (ACOs), were also established to provide stable cash flows, but remained a relatively minor factor for decades because of medical society opposition.

State hospital associations controlled the Blue Cross organizations, and medical societies controlled the Blue Shield organizations. Well into the

1940s, laws in 26 states prohibited anyone other than medical societies from offering prepayment plans for physician services. In 1934, the American Medical Association (AMA) set forth conditions that it argued should govern private insurance for physician services (Starr, 1982, pp. 299–300):

- "All features of medical service in any method of medical practice should be under the control of the medical profession." This included all medical care institutions, and thus, only the medical profession could determine their "adequacy and character."
- Patients were to have absolute freedom to choose a physician.
- "A permanent, confidential relation between the patient and a 'family physician' must be the fundamental, dominating feature of any system."
- No form of insurance was acceptable that did not have the patient paying the physician and the patient being the one reimbursed.
- Any plan in a locality must be open to all providers in a community.
- Medical assistance aspects of a plan must only be available to those below the "comfort level" of income.

The Group Health Association of Washington, DC, a prepaid group practice, was established in 1937, but it faced strong opposition. In 1943, the Supreme Court (*AMA v. U.S.*, 1943), hearing a case brought by the FTC, upheld a lower court finding that the AMA and the DC Medical Society were guilty of "a conspiracy in restraint of trade under the Sherman Anti-Trust Act" and had hindered and obstructed Group Health "in procuring and retaining on its staff qualified doctors" and "from privilege of consulting with others and using the facilities of hospitals" (Richmond & Fein, 2005, p. 34).

Expanding Participation

World War II led to the industrialization of all available nonmilitary hands, breaking the Great Depression, inducing migration from rural areas to industrial cities, increasing the power of industrial unions, and inaugurating the era of big science. It also led to an era of optimism that Americans could accomplish anything they wanted if they worked together collectively (Strauss & Howe, 1991).

Many employers had established their own health services to support their employees and the war effort. Some of these services evolved into prepaid group practices. Most notably, Kaiser Industries' medical department became the Kaiser Permanente system, which was opened up to outside enrollees after the war. Similar systems, such as the Health Insurance Plan in New York, which started in 1947, sprang up independently.

The government imposed wage and price controls during World War II. As labor became scarce and the war turned in the Allies' favor, workers pressed for better compensation. The Office of Price Administration held the line on wage increases, but allowed improved benefits through collective bargaining. This led to the rapid expansion of health insurance among unionized industrial and government workers. This trend was also consistent with the provision of medical benefits to the vast military establishment. Unemployment fell from 17.2% in 1939 to 1.3% in 1944, and the real gross national product grew by 75% (Richmond & Fein, 2005). Health insurance costs were not yet a serious concern for corporate managers or the government. In 1948, the National Labor Relations Board ruled that refusal to bargain over health care benefits was an unfair labor practice.

Collective bargaining became the basic vehicle for determining health benefits. Because union officers were elected by their membership, they did not choose catastrophic coverage. Rather, they sought to maximize the visibility of benefits to their rank-and-file (voting) members. This led them to bargain for first-dollar coverage for everyone and to support lifetime limitations on benefits for those who were born with or developed catastrophic or high-cost chronic conditions. It also led them to emphasize employment-related coverage for dependents. They wanted most union members to experience regular payouts from their benefit packages. If the workers were young and healthy, they would still see payment for services such as obstetric and pediatric care for their family members. Employers did not much care how their workers divided the contract settlements among wages, health benefits, and other fringes. Employers saw health insurance as an inconsequential component of the overall labor costs established through collective bargaining. If workers and their families already had individual health coverage, they still gained a tax advantage if the employer paid the premium directly. Blue Cross enrollments tripled between 1942 and 1946, while enrollment in commercial health insurance plans more than doubled (Becker, 1955).

Postwar Responses

Following World War II, most presidential administrations suggested health care reforms of some sort. The Hill-Burton Act of 1946 expanded hospital facilities. President Truman suggested developing a system of universal health insurance based on the report of the President's Commission on Health Needs of the Nation; however, his proposal was opposed by entrenched interests and was ignored when President Eisenhower was elected. In 1950, Congress approved a grant program to the states to pay providers for medical care for people receiving public assistance. Proposals for a Medicare-type system under Social Security appeared in Congress as early as 1957, but it took 8 years of debate for Congress and the White House to reach a consensus.

The 1960 Kerr-Mills Act created a program administered by the Welfare Administration and the states for "Medical Assistance to the Aged," which also covered "medically needy" older persons who did not necessarily need to qualify for public assistance. Richmond and Fein (2005) described Kerr-Mills as an attempt to stave off Medicare-type programs.

The Joint Commission on Mental Illness and Health, formed under Eisenhower, did not issue its final report until 1961, under the Kennedy administration. It led to the passage of the Mental Retardation Facilities Construction Act of 1963 and the Community Mental Health Centers Act of 1963.

Early in his term, President Johnson announced the formation of a Commission on Heart Disease, Cancer, and Stroke. Its recommendations led to the Regional Medical Programs legislation to advance training and research. Congress, however, added a provision that this work was not to interfere in any way with "patterns and methods of financing medical care, professional practice, or the administration of any existing institutions" (Richmond & Fein, 2005, p. 44).

While the Medicare debate continued, Congress passed many health measures as part of Johnson's War on Poverty. Given the highly visible opposition of organized medicine, the health components of these new programs were housed outside of the U.S. Public Health Service. For example, the Office of Economic Opportunity started neighborhood health centers, and its Head Start program provided health assessment and health care components for children.

When the Johnson administration finally secured passage of the Social Security Amendments of 1965, it accommodated AMA concerns by offering three separate programs: (1) Medicare Part A, which provided hospital coverage for most older persons; (2) Medicare Part B, a voluntary supplementary medical insurance program; and (3) Medicaid, which expanded the Kerr-Mills program to help with out-of-pocket expenses such as nursing home care and drugs and extended potential eligibility to families with children, the blind, and the disabled under the Welfare Administration. Starr (2011) cites this set of programs as the beginning of the "policy trap" that haunts us today:

> The key elements of the trap are a system of employer-provided insurance that conceals true costs from those who benefit from it; targeted

government programs that protect groups such as the elderly and veterans, who are well organized and enjoy wide public sympathy and believe, unlike other claimants, that they have earned their benefits; and a financing system that has expanded and enriched the health-care industry, creating powerful interests averse to change. (p. 123)

There were other compromises in the Social Security Amendments. For example, at the time, hospital-based physicians were being placed on salary so that hospitals could use some of their fee revenue to cover the capital costs of their practices. The 1965 Medicare bill specifically required that anesthesiologists, radiologists, and pathologists be paid directly, not through the hospital. That law also stated, "Nothing in this title shall be construed to authorize any federal officer or employee to exercise any supervision or control over the practice of medicine." Some have questioned whether the government's current 1.5% pay-for-performance bonus program violates this provision (Pear, 2006).

Bodenheimer and Grumbach (2005) labeled the years 1945 to 1970 as those of the "provider-insurer pact" (p. 167). Starr (1982) argued that the period before 1970 was characterized by an accommodation between the insurance industry and the medical profession. He noted that it was a period in which most employed Americans were covered because union shops were dominant. "The government supported this private tax system by making employers' contributions into it tax exempt from the government's own taxes. Private voluntary insurance was neither strictly voluntary, nor strictly private, but its compulsory and public features were hardly noticeable" (p. 334). That system, however, left out the poor, the unemployed, agricultural and domestic workers, most farmers, the disabled, and older persons. The 1965 Great Society legislation addressed the needs of some of these uninsured populations.

The Great Society

When implemented in 1965, Medicare mirrored the structure of health insurance in the industrial sector, but without lifetime limitations. It did not provide adequate coverage for drugs or for long-term care (i.e., nursing homes, hospice care, home health), nor did it allocate much for prevention. Many employment-based health plans paid for prescription drugs, but not for long-term care. Medicare did not cover prescription drugs until 2006.

It may be hard to believe today, but before 1965 academic medical centers delivered large amounts of charity care. Local volunteer physicians supervised the clinics, and patients received care at no charge or for a nominal fee in return for letting learners practice on them. Many people covered by Medicare and Medicaid had been receiving charity care, but Medicaid and Medicare paid in full for services once provided free or with income-based discounts. The new coverage also gave the urban poor a choice of institutions, a choice they quickly exercised. Through its association with Social Security, Medicare became viewed as an entitlement earned by years of paying into a system, and something that should be as sacred as Social Security. However, all enrollees received the same benefit regardless of their payment history. Medicaid, although intended to be a comprehensive care plan for low-income families, ended up being primarily a long-term care program, and it did not even cover low-income families without children.

Rapid Expansion of Capacity

The fee-for-service payments for visits once provided for free, or nearly so, increased physicians' incomes without increasing their numbers. At the same time, availability of insurance coverage for underserved populations increased the demand for services. Academic medical centers added new, full-time staff and billed all insurers for their services to subsidize education and research. Heavy investments in medical research increased the variety, cost, and effectiveness of what providers could offer. Hospitals also had to cover the capital and support costs for hospital-based physicians now that they could not bill for these costs directly. That, plus a limited supply of resources, increased demand, and rapid technological advances led to rapid price inflation.

The primary policy response to this increase in demand for health services in the 1970s and 1980s was to increase the supply of resources. For example, Congress launched the Community Health Center and Migrant Health Center programs, which offered subsidized services in underserved communities. In 1970, it established the National Health Service Corps to increase provider supply in underserved areas via scholarships and loan forgiveness. Many new programs provided training for health professionals, and existing ones were expanded with financial assistance from state and federal governments

The Private Sector Responds

At the end of World War II, the health care sector accounted for 4.5% of GDP. By the mid-1980s, its share was up to 11%. With the cash flows from private insurance and Medicare and Medicaid, community hospitals expanded rapidly but no longer relied on philanthropy for capital. Wall Street was happy to finance their expansion by selling bonds. Interest was considered a reimbursable cost by rate setters. Health care attracted entrepreneurs, and for-profit hospital chains grew rapidly. Similarly, the nursing home industry and kidney dialysis centers attracted new capital. The medical establishment, which had fought against corporate control of hospitals and other institutions, was relatively helpless. The AMA's stance against Medicare and Medicaid had cost it credibility, and its constituency was now spread out between the AMA, specialty and subspecialty societies, and the academic medical centers, each of which had its own interests.

Costs and Concerns Mount

As health care costs mounted and the health care sector accounted for a much more significant share of the economy, more and more observers expressed concern about the lack of competition in portions of the industry and began suggesting ways to control costs. One suggestion was to promote prepaid group practices, or HMOs, which share some of the cost risk with the employer, thereby inducing reduced costs. The successes Kaiser Permanente and similar organizations had in delivering care at a lower premium cost without evident diminution of quality drew much attention. This led the Nixon Administration to support the Health Maintenance Organization and Resources Development Act of 1973. Although that legislation had little immediate impact, later amendments opened the way for the explosion of HMOs and other vertically integrated health care systems in the 1980s. That expansion continues today under the rubric of administered competition. In 1974, the Nixon administration proposed the Comprehensive Health Insurance Program, which sought to provide health insurance to all employees. Congress debated this and a similar measure, the Kennedy-Mills bill, but did not enact either. Richmond and Fein (2005), writing before enactment of the ACA, argued that 1974 was the closest the nation ever came to universal health insurance, and that those proposals, although eclipsed by the Watergate cover-up and Nixon's resignation, were the basis for successive calls for congressional action by presidents Carter, Clinton, and Obama.

Charges and Cost Shifting

Over time a provider institution must achieve income sufficient to cover its operating and capital costs. Because of the imperfect market for health care, prices are set by marking up estimated costs or by observing what is charged by others in the same market area. When individuals or insurers pay less than the breakeven price, the institution marks up the prices charged to those it figures can pay more or that lack sufficient bargaining power.

Originally, Blue Cross organizations, which were owned by state hospital associations, were interested in a management cost-finding system that fairly allocated the full costs of services among the users of those services. Because they understood that most costs in a hospital system are (1) fixed and (2) joint,[1] they did not attempt to find out the marginal cost of a service (*marginal cost* is the additional cost of producing one additional unit of a product). They established an estimated average direct cost for each unit of service (e.g., bed day, laboratory test, operating room hour, X-ray) and then allocated the overhead costs on the basis of the number of units consumed by the payer's enrollees. The largest expense in the institution, nursing time, was treated as overhead and not allocated to the individual patient. The resulting charges included all the overhead costs, allowing each institution to break even on its Blue Cross patients. If the patients in a health plan used a quarter of the X-rays produced by the radiology department, the plan paid a quarter of the full costs of that department (including allocated overheads). If hospitals and other health care institutions offered discounts, they tended to favor the Blues, not the other insurers, and certainly not the directly paying patients. This resulted in what is called *cost shifting*.

As more patient care costs went uncovered under insurance contracts, hospitals added the cost of this uncompensated care to the overhead rate and increased charges accordingly. It was easy to manipulate charges to mark up costs and either make a profit or provide deeper discounts to preferred customers. First the Blues and then the federal government exerted pressure on providers, obtaining substantial discounts in return for their business. This shifted the costs of uncompensated care to private insurers and the uninsured. Reinhardt (2006, p. 64) observed, "What prevailing distributive ethic in U.S. society, for example, would dictate that uninsured patients be billed the highest prices for hospital care and then be hounded, often mercilessly, by bill collectors?"

Cost Shifting Hits Private Plans

Bills sent to patients and others were typically based on the official price lists of doctors and hospitals. People with no insurance were asked to pay full charges. Commercial insurance companies had contracts that

---

[1]The cost of a nurse's time is incurred when she or he reports to work; thus, it is *fixed*, regardless of whether there are six patients rounded or three or whether a team approach is used. That time is also *jointly* shared among all the patients the nurse serves. Few systems recorded nursing time by specific tasks.

discounted the charges. The Blues and large HMOs enjoyed even bigger discounts, and the federal government got the biggest discount because it demanded the lowest rate allowed to any customer. Because of the inflated charge figures posted to most bills, the public assumed that unit care costs were a great deal higher than they really were, and that insurers were picking up a higher proportion of the costs of care. Real transfer prices for medical services were kept under wraps. This made deductibles and copayments appear to be a much smaller proportion of actual costs than they really were. Under pressure from the public for greater transparency, this has gradually changed. The public now sees more of what is actually paid and by whom, but real transparency is still lacking. **Table 3-1** shows Medicare charges billed by hospitals and payments made by Medicare and the patients to Miami-area hospitals for a specific procedure type. Making such data available is part of the federal government's efforts to promote price transparency. The payments are the full payments and include added payments such as disproportionate share for the safety net hospitals.

The financial reports of health care institutions offer a picture of the size of these discounts. Many institutions book their full charges as revenue and then deduct trade discounts under discounts and "allowances" and reflect charity care costs under bad debt written off and under "uncompensated care." Tomkins, Altman, and Eilat (2006) reported that the ratio of gross revenue (charges) to net revenue (payments received) had grown from 1.1 to 2.6 over a 25-year period. They also reported that cross-subsidization of services and differential pricing might be difficult to change in the current marketplace. In 2009, markups in Atlanta hospitals ranged from 157% to 702%, and the average had moved from 124% to 319% over the preceding 10 years (Pell, 2011). Because insurance companies and governments negotiate substantial discounts, it is the uninsured or those going out of network who are pressed to pay the full amount. Even then, according to the same article (Pell, 2011), an Atlanta hospital offered an uninsured individual a 40% cash discount. In fact, one for-profit hospital with a markup of 702% reported that no patients paid the full markup.

Currently, every hospital has a price list called a *chargemaster*, which may have as many as 20,000 items. These are the charges that the patient usually sees. Terms are not standardized, and some items are really bundles of services, so patients still have trouble comparing prices between institutions (Brill, 2013). In California hospitals, reported charges for the same procedure at one hospital might be four times that of another, but, on average, hospitals received reimbursements for only about 38% of charges from patients and insurers in 2004. Reinhardt (2006) argued that pricing practices would have to change radically if patients were to be able to make

Table 3-1 2011 Medicare Charges and Payments at Selected Miami-Area Hospitals for DRG 470 (Major Joint Replacement or Reattachment of Lower Extremity w/o MCC)

Hospital	City/Suburb	Number Performed	Average Charge	Average Total Payment
Homestead Hospital	Homestead	22	$96,004	$23,250
North Shore Hospital	North Miami	32	$87,579	$16,112
Doctors Hospital	Coral Gables	105	$85,577	$20,280
Kendall Regional Hospital	Kendall	97	$79,080	$16,533
Univ. of Miami Hospital	Miami	72	$78,553	$16,792
South Miami Hospital	South Miami	68	$77,448	$15,506
Palmetto General Hospital	Hialeah	80	$76,868	$17,197
Aventura Hospital and Medical Center	Aventura	82	$74,628	$13,236
Baptist Hospital	Miami	311	$74,610	$20,610
Mercy Hospital	Miami	146	$74,425	$15,116
Jackson Memorial Hospital	Miami	35	$63,537	$24,467
Good Samaritan Hospital	Miami	31	$63,327	$15,068
Memorial Regional Hospital	Hollywood	66	$60,742	$14,891
Mt. Sinai Medical Center	Miami Beach	108	$58,431	$15,805
Memorial Hospital West	Pembroke Pines	44	$56,876	$14,840
Cleveland Clinic	Weston	168	$47,959	$11,969
Westchester General Hospital	Miami	15	$41,215	$19,761

Source: Reproduced from: Inpatient Prospective Payment System (IPPS) Provider Summary for the Top 100 Diagnosis-Related Groups (DRG). https://data.cms.gov/Medicare/Inpatient-Prospective-Payment-System-IPPS-Provider/97k6-zzx3. Accessed 3/7/2014.

rational buying decisions. He seemed to support the recommendation of Porter and Teisberg (2006) that hospitals post one set of bundled prices per disease entity and charge the same to everyone. However, Altman, Shactman, and Eilat (2006) wondered whether transparent pricing and customer sensitivity to pricing might destabilize the hospital sector, bringing average prices down and forcing some into bankruptcy. The ACA provides for a number of demonstrations of bundled pricing, and the Centers for Medicare & Medicaid Services (CMS) appears to be well on the way to implementing this concept for a number of frequently encountered conditions.

Responding to Cost Shifting

As employers and private insurers became increasingly aware of the effects of cost shifting, they adopted a number of measures to counter it and combat the overall inflation in the costs of care. As early as the 1970s, employers demanded that insurance companies begin to control premiums (Starr, 1982; Mayer & Mayer, 1985). These measures fit under the general heading of *managed care*. Most of these measures spread slowly until the 1980s. Employers moved away from contracts that accepted provider-established fees from any provider, and instead signed up with HMOs. **Figure 3-2** illustrates the roughly 60% decline in market share for traditional indemnity

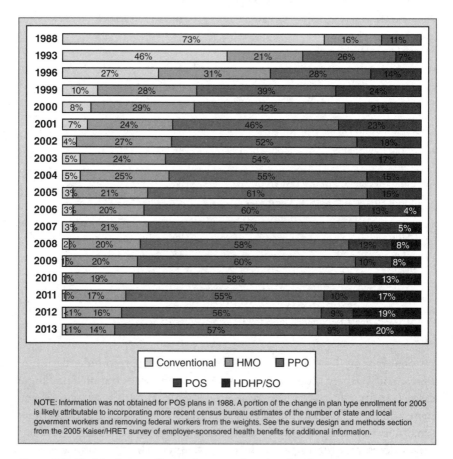

Figure 3-2 Health plan enrollment for covered workers by plan type, 1988–2013.

Source: Reproduced from: Employer Health Benefits 2013 Annual Survey – Chartpack, (8465), The Henry J. Kaiser Family Foundation and Health Research & Educational Trust

plans from 1988 to 1998. The HMO/POS (health maintenance organization plus point-of-service) and PPO (preferred provider organization) plans appeared much better able to control health care costs by exacting their own discounts and by constraining what patients and providers would be able to do.

The Blues began to shed their nonprofit identities and their focus on being community-based cooperative organizations as they competed with the newer for-profit insurers. They often developed their own HMO organizations. The concept of the HMO was no longer a prepaid group practice. It had become an organization that managed the insurance risk and the delivery of care either directly or through a designated provider network. HMOs (for profit and nonprofit) continued to negotiate with individual providers, group practices, hospitals, pharmaceutical companies, and all other types of providers for deeper and deeper discounts.

THE CURRENT "ERA" EMERGES

Fox (2001) described three eras of managed care:

- Pre-1970, the early years
- 1970 to 1985, the adolescent years
- 1985 to 2001, the years when managed care came of age

We would add the following:

- 2001 to present, mixed administered and oligopolistic competition comes of age

Richmond and Fein (2005) described the period 1965 to 1985 as a time of emerging tensions between regulation and market forces and called the period after 1985 the "Entrepreneurial Revolution." Bodenheimer and Grumbach described the 1970s as a period of developing tension, the 1980s as the "Revolt of the Purchasers," and the 1990s as the breakup of the provider–insurer pact. The changeover to managed care slowed the growth of premiums from the mid-1990s into the first years of the new century, but then premiums took off again. In the meantime, both providers and patients expressed displeasure with HMO constraints on treatment choice and provider choice. New state laws sprang up limiting the ability of insurers and HMOs to control professionals and patients. Some thought managed-care control mechanisms had already picked the low-hanging fruit and had stopped the most egregious cases of inappropriate utilization. One control mechanism, *capitation* (a fixed payment per enrollee per time period), had been promoted because it shifted the cost risk from employers and insurers to providers, but it became less fashionable when providers were unable to manage it or lacked sufficiently large risk pools and capital reserves to handle it. Insurers moved toward preferred provider plans that allowed patients and providers more freedom of choice; however, providers gave deeper discounts, and enrollees were subject to higher premiums and greater deductibles and copayments.

Some Movement

Incremental changes in health insurance regulation occurred during the Clinton administration. The Health Insurance Portability and Privacy Act (HIPPA) sought to relieve job lock. More children were covered by Medicaid and the State Children's Health Insurance Program (SCHIP), and more reimbursement became prospective.

A new Republican majority under President George W. Bush passed the Medicare Prescription Drug, Improvement, and Modernization Act (MMA), which had three major components:

- Prescription drug coverage under Medicare Part D, which created major additions to the federal deficit
- HSAs linked to high-deductible insurance
- Privatized and subsidized Medicare plans (now known as Medicare Advantage)

Although the latter two programs were slow to take off, they have become increasingly significant over time. They have allowed the consumer to become more of a decision maker about health insurance. They have also made the ideological landscape more confusing.

The Massachusetts Model

As stalemates in Washington became more intractable, costs mounted and the problems of the working poor got worse. It was clear that many people were being forced to forego necessary care. States were faced with increased welfare burdens, including Medicaid, and providers were supplying more uncompensated care.

Massachusetts had been trying to set up its own universal coverage system since 1988. Finally, in 2006, Massachusetts enacted near-universal health insurance. This was based on a proposal that had come in large part from the Heritage Foundation via Governor Romney's office. The final bill reflected the concerns and proposals of both the Republican governor and the Democratic legislature. It included an insurance exchange, individual mandates, premium subsidies for low-income individuals, and an employer mandate. It did little to try to control costs. Almost half of the uninsured in the state were soon covered, but costs rose and the legislature had to pass cost-control legislation in subsequent years. Public reaction to the program in the state has been generally favorable, but in the 2012 presidential election Governor Romney opposed using it as a national template.

The Obama Administration Makes Reform a High Priority

Once President Obama was inaugurated, he made energy reform and health care reform his highest priorities. As it became clear that energy reform would split the Democrat's narrow congressional majorities, he focused on health care reform. He encouraged Congress to take a much stronger role in formulating the new law than President Clinton had. Many compromises were made on cost control to accommodate interest groups, especially hospitals, insurers, and drug manufacturers. Congress scrapped the "public option," a government-sponsored insurance program that would have been offered through the exchanges. It included increases in Medicaid coverage and voluntary long-term care insurance. The Supreme Court weakened the former, and the administration put the latter off as unworkable.

Although much of the coalition the Obama administration had built ultimately to support the measure fell apart, differing versions of the ACA narrowly passed both houses of Congress in March 2010. The legislation became law after the two houses resolved the differences through the budget reconciliation process. In the wake of the 2012 Supreme Court ruling discussed earlier, a number of states have refused to expand Medicaid with federal money, which means coverage of the uninsured may be less complete than expected.

The ACA does not establish the right to health care. It even allows discrimination in premiums based on age; the oldest workers may have premiums three times higher than those paid by the youngest ones. The effect of this provision is blunted, in part, by income-based subsidies. The law is voluminous and complex, and nearly half has little to do with financing medical care. It would take much of this book just to enumerate the act.

The ACA will not stop experimentation by the states. Oregon and Vermont have sought waivers under the ACA to reallocate state and federal funds to provide a comprehensive coverage system for their resident. Other states, including New York, are working to provide medical homes for chronically ill individuals who are disabled and qualify for both Medicare and Medicaid. These dual eligibles account for a surprisingly large proportion of those programs' costs.

DRGs: The Big Step Toward Industrialization

The lack of common product definitions and labels made it nearly impossible to compare either quality or cost among providers. The introduction of diagnostic-related groups led to *prospective payment* (payment per admission by diagnosis) systems that eliminated some cost *outliers*, first for Medicaid and Medicare and then for the HMOs. Having a uniformly defined cluster of cases to follow allowed for the development of classification and information systems and for internal and external oversight of care. Utilization review became a major activity of insurers, and decisions about whom to retain in the service network could be based on *profiles* of the cases treated by providers and institutions. The intent of the developers of DRGs was to enable quality comparisons, but the system was soon adopted for pricing as well.

EMPLOYERS WANT OUT: BACKING CONSUMER-DRIVEN HEALTH CARE

Throughout the 1990s, observers argued that the United States should move rapidly in the direction of a less regulated national market in health care, as the Reagan Revolution led economists and politicians to seek deregulation and consumer sovereignty in all areas. Commentators, such as Herzlinger (1997), pointed to the disappointing results coming out of managed care contracts and argued that the only way to control health care costs would be to motivate consumers to take more responsibility for their own buying decisions. Management experts noted that neither patients nor providers were fully aware of what things cost, and patient pocketbooks were not affected significantly by the choices made. Providers were likely to benefit from waste and overutilization, which were of no concern to consumers who were not payers. The only way to get costs under control, they argued, was to have as much of a market system in health care as had been developed for other professional services areas. At the same time, the Internet was opening up relatively painless access to medical information for consumers. Payers and insurers established standard sets of provider report cards that purported to rank local providers in terms of their quality of care and costs. They increased deductibles and copayments and launched experiments to test various pay-for-performance schemes that rewarded desired quality and cost-related behaviors. The federal government and some states set up websites to display comparative data on a number of institutions.

Corporations began to assess the impact that high employee and retiree health care costs had on their ability to price goods competitively.

Increasingly, their competition came from countries where the overall tax system supported much of the costs of health care. They began to support strongly the notion of a defined benefit package (a constrained dollar amount) and moves toward a health care market in which employees would take more responsibility for expenditures and for selecting effective care.

Consumer-driven health care insurance contracts fall into two groups: tiered programs and *health reimbursement accounts*. Tiered programs are of two types: (1) tiered premiums and (2) tiered point-of-care cost sharing. The first type gives employees premium benefits in return for accepting higher copayments and deductibles, a less-restrictive network, or less freedom from utilization review. The second type allows cost sharing for those who choose providers deemed to be preferred providers based on cost and/ or quality measures. Media coverage and marketing efforts have focused on the health reimbursement account arrangements, especially tax-sheltered HSAs. Typically, the employer establishes an account for the employee to spend on health care, and then a large deductible comes into play. Insurance kicks in when the total of these two is exceeded. Unexpended money in the initial account often can roll over from year to year. So far, employer payments under these programs seem to be considerably less than under traditional health insurance.

Table 3-2 compares the alternatives available for consumer-managed care, including the tax status and the rollover features of each approach. It is unclear how much of the difference comes from reduced utilization, from higher out-of-pocket payments, or from more knowledgeable purchasing decisions (Rosenthal & Milstein, 2004). Davis (2004) suggested that the success of these innovations will ultimately hinge on whether the public sees them as efforts to shift costs from employers to employees, or whether they motivate provider institutions to "identify, demand and reward high performance, with positive incentives for consumers in a complementary role" (p. 1230). Employers and employees were slow to adopt such policies. However, the enrollment of covered workers in such plans rose from 8% in 2009 to 19% in 2012, and the majority of employers are offering such plans to their employees.

The Law of the Land: The ACA

The ACA means we will likely be living in a transitional period for some time to come. Health insurance will never be the same. However, it is not at all clear what will happen with costs. It is clear that the individual mandate will have to be accepted by the public or it will be undercut somehow. Many states are choosing against signing on for the expansion of Medicaid. They

Table 3-2 What Do HRA, HSA, FSA, and PRA Stand For?

HRA = Health Reimbursement Arrangement

HSA = Health Savings Account

FSA = Flexible Spending Account

PRA = Premium Reimbursement Arrangement

Feature Comparison				
	HRA	**HSA**	**FSA**	**PRA**
Who may contribute	Employer only	Employer or employee	Employee or employer	Employee (final rules pending)
Cost of employer contributions	Only pay for utilization (typically 25–50%)	100% paid regardless of utilization	N/A	N/A
Average cost to cover $2,000/year deductible	$500–$1,000	$2,000	$2,000	$2,000
Maximum annual contribution	No maximum	$3,250 (single) $6,450 (family) for 2013	Determined by employer; capped at $2,500 starting in 2013	Determined by employer; usually total compensation
Eligibility requirements	None or determined by employer	Must have HSA-qualified health coverage ($1,250+ single, $2,500+ family)	None or determined by employer	None or determined by employer
Must each employee open a new bank account?	No	Yes	No	No
Tax treatment	Tax-free	Tax-free	Tax-free	Tax-free
Medical expenses allowed	Health insurance premiums + IRC 213(d) as determined by employer	IRC 213(d) expenses with no employer limitations	IRC 213(d) expenses; but no personal health insurance	Personal health insurance only
Use for nonmedical expenses	None	None	None	None

Table 3-2 What Do HRA, HSA, FSA, and PRA Stand For? (*continued*)

	HRA	HSA	FSA	PRA
Carryover of unused funds to next year	Determined by employer	Yes	No	No
Portable after termination	Determined by employer	Yes	No	No
Administrator	Employer or third-party administrator	Employee	Employer or third-party administrator	Employer or third-party administrator
Cross-compatibility	With HSA* or FSA	Limited-purpose or post-deductible FSA or HRA	With HRA or HSA*	With HRA, HSA, or FSA
Employer reporting	Employer views detailed utilization reports	No tracking possible	Employer views detailed utilization reports	Employer views detailed utilization reports

*HSAs are fully compatible only with certain HRA and FSA administration platforms that enable HSA compatibility.

Source: Reproduced from: Lundquist, R. (2013). HRA vs. HSA vs. FSA vs. PRA Comparison Chart. *Employee Health Benefits and Insurance blog.* Available at: www.zanebenefits.com/blog/bid/143489/HRA-vs-HSA-vs-FSA-vs-PRA-Comparison-Chart. Accessed 12/20/2013. ZaneBenefits, 136 Heber Ave., #308, Park City, UT 84060, tel: 1-800-391-9209

are also refusing to establish state exchanges and are instead relying on the federal exchange. But the attractiveness of the policies the exchanges will offer is uncertain. Employers are moving toward self-insured plans to avoid the generous benefit structures required for exchange offerings. Certainly, trends in premium costs will say a lot about whether employers will cover their employees directly, send them through exchanges, and/or pay the penalties prescribed in the law. Those penalties will likely have to increase sharply to achieve hoped-for coverage rates. Other aspects of the ACA legislation will be covered individually in later chapters.

The Resulting Picture

Currently, the U.S. government and the private sector are operating with a hodgepodge of approaches. Medicare and Medicaid are monopsonistic, government-administered systems. President George W. Bush left a legacy in the form of policies that emphasize consumer-driven health care, particularly a focus on HSAs. Federal health care policy since the Nixon administration has tended to support development of large HMOs, which are examples of oligopolistic competition, and the ACOs envisioned in the ACA could easily go the same way. Consolidation into larger multisite firms continues to take place both locally in hospital markets and nationally in subsectors such as kidney dialysis centers, nursing homes, pharmaceutical distribution, medical oxygen distribution, and rehabilitation centers. Three firms out of 80 in the industry dominated enrollment for Medicare Part D in 2006. At the same time, successive congressional budgets have reduced funding for Medicare and Medicaid, creating new concerns about cost shifting to insurance programs already burdened with the costs of the uninsured and underinsured. The ACA should partially reverse that trend, but future budget battles involving entitlements could reestablish that downward trend in provider payments.

Each of these contending frameworks and philosophies—administered competition, oligopolistic competition, and free-market (consumer-directed) health care—is rooted in our health care system's past and present. It is not clear what role they will play in that system's future.

CONCLUSION

Like any other democracy, the United States has a system of health care that evolved through a political process influenced by trends in culture, technology, demographics, political ideology, and economic development. It also evolved through experimentation. When something did not work or stopped working, the country tried other things. We might take solace in a statement attributed to Winston Churchill, "You can always count on the Americans to do the right thing—after they've tried everything else." But what else is left to try?

Countries that have tried socialized medicine have been moving toward decentralization and allowing more of a private sector. Those that started out with a private insurance system have had to add more and more government funding to deal with aging populations and burgeoning technology. There is little reason to believe that what has worked in one time and place will necessarily work in another, or that what has not worked in one time and place could not be made to work in another. A review of the efforts in many countries shows that there is no magic bullet, that the health care system is the product of a social context, and that many measures and many accommodations are needed to achieve good care at reasonable cost. Where the United States has paid a high price is in its lack of ongoing health policy development with adequate testing of potential interventions and adequate study of new alternatives completed before the political system becomes disappointed and acts, as it often does, without sound, nonideological policy advice.

| Case 3 | **International Comparisons: Where Else Might We Have Gone?** |

It can be useful to consider the roads not taken—the measures that have evolved in other developed countries. This case study briefly reviews the health systems of five developed countries for which data are readily available: Canada, the United Kingdom, Australia, Germany, and Japan. The approaches are amazingly varied, yet all seem to be producing similar results (except costs). Satisfaction surveys for the four English-speaking countries show similar ratings of consumer satisfaction and quality of medical and hospital care; however, self-reported access and expenditures differ widely.

DIFFERENT CULTURES, DIFFERENT SYSTEMS

Canada

Canada's health system initially paralleled the U.S. system, but the country switched to a single-payer system incrementally, beginning with initiatives in two provinces. Federal legislation passed in 1957 offered to pay 50% of costs if provinces provided universal hospital coverage; by 1961, all 10 provinces were participating. The 1966 Medical Care Act extended this cost-share inducement to universal coverage programs, and universal coverage was fully implemented nationwide in 1971.

The following are the key aspects of the Canadian system:

- Universal coverage under provincial health plans is financed through payroll and income taxes. Many Canadians have private insurance to cover costs the government does not pay and to provide rapid access to scarce services.
- Physicians are typically in private practices and are paid per visit according to a government fee schedule. Most hospitals are independent public entities that operate within budgets established by the provincial government. Government regulations also affect the prices of prescription drugs.

Case 3 (*continued*)

- Hospitals finance new technology or facilities through the provincial budgeting system, not capital markets. Adoption of new technology, such as imaging equipment and surgical capacity, is slower than in the United States.
- Rationing occurs through delays in elective services, rather than ability to pay. Lengths of hospital stays have not dropped as rapidly as in U.S. hospitals. Physician visits per person are similar to the United States, but the percentage of GDP devoted to health care has grown much more slowly. Canada has fewer physicians per 1,000 population than the United States (1.98 vs. 2.42) but more nurses (10.43 vs. 9.82).
- Concerns exist about access to specialists and primary care after hours. Canadians' levels of satisfaction with their health care are similar to those of U.S. respondents, but they complain a little more about the shortness of physician visits.
- Although it slowed sharply after 1971, growth in per capita spending has picked up since, despite long waits for scanning procedures and "elective" surgeries such as hip replacements, cataract removal, and cardiovascular surgery.
- Per capita health care spending is somewhat lower than in the United States and health outcomes slightly better. No one is sure how much leakage of services and expenditures takes place across the border between the two countries, with U.S. citizens purchasing pharmaceuticals in Canada and Canadians purchasing scarce physician and hospital services in the United States.

England

The British National Health Service (NHS) became a socialized system in 1948 after a gradual movement through voluntary and then mandatory health insurance. Until quite recently, the NHS was a government program housed in the Department of Health. Ten strategic health authorities (SHAs) implemented national policies at the regional level. Each general practitioner (GP) operated through a local primary care trust (PCTs). PCTs served about 100,000 people each and were responsible for disbursing tax revenues dedicated to health within their service areas. In addition to paying GPs through a system of capitation, allowances, and incentives, PCTs contracted with local consultants (specialists) and the government-owned hospitals. A very small private insurance market was allowed. It has grown in recent years, and some physicians practice outside of the NHS. In London, so-called Harley Street physicians cater to the wealthy.

The Health and Social Care Act of 2012 significantly reorganized NHS. Ostensibly, the reforms were designed to make the system more patient-centric, empower medical providers, increase the focus on clinical outcomes, and provide more local autonomy. The long-term impacts, particularly on the level of privatization, are not immediately obvious.

The following are the key aspects of the British system:

- At the center of the reformed NHS is NHS England, which was established as the Commissioning Board in October 2012. This independent quasi-governmental agency pushes public funds out to local clinical commissioning groups (CCGs), which replaced PCTs on April 1, 2013. It also promotes quality of care and improvements in health outcomes. The role of the national government has been limited to general oversight of the system and combined strategic leadership for the health and social services systems. SHAs were abolished along with the PCTs.
- CCGs are primarily composed of GPs, but nurses and other providers are represented. The CCGs can commission any health services that meet government standards, including NHS hospitals, consultants (who are typically hospital based), mental health services, urgent and emergency care, rehabilitation, and community health services.
- The Health and Social Care Act made several other changes to improve coordination, increase democratic input, improve quality, and address community public health. For example, leaders of public health, adult social services, children's social services, a consumer representative, and an elected community representative comprise health and well-being boards that promote coordination across sectors and advise CCGs. An organization called Monitor has authority to license providers beginning April 2014 and is responsible for overseeing the transition of NHS hospitals from government entities to foundations. Public health has become a local responsibility, but a new government agency,

---

Case 3 (*continued*)

Public Health England, performs a national role similar to the role the Centers for Disease Control and Prevention (CDC) plays in U.S. public health.

- The number of physicians per 1,000 patients is slightly higher in the United Kingdom than in the United States (2.74 vs. 2.42). British nurses do many things physicians would handle in the United States, including delivering babies, and more are available (10.13 per 1,000 in the United Kingdom vs. 9.82 in the United States).

- Rationing has been based on waiting times for treatments for nonacute conditions. These have included cataract removal, hip replacement, and coronary artery bypass surgery, for which patients may wait as much as a year.

- In 2004, the NHS adopted a pay-for-performance system for family physicians that involved 146 quality performance measures. According to Doran et al. (2006), primary care practices met targets for 83% of patients and achieved 97% of the possible points, much more than the 75% anticipated in the budget, resulting in an average of more than $40,000 in additional payments per physician. The result was a substantial budget overrun. Because a major baseline study was not performed, how much of the improvement was due to changed medical care and how much was due to improved documentation is not knowable.

- Long queues were a major political issue in the 1997 elections that brought back the Labour government. That government increased NHS funding, and waiting times dropped. Some management decision making was also decentralized from the regional SHAs to the local hospitals, whose accountability for quality and cost was increased. At the same time, the government established the National Institute for Health and Care Excellence (NICE) to evaluate procedures, treatments, and technologies and to speed their adoption if the evidence is adequate and favorable. This was in response to reliable evidence of differences in treatments and outcome differences among various geographic areas, regional health authorities, and fund-holder groups.

Australia

Australia has a hybrid public–private health care system. A national health care system called Medicare is financed out of taxation. When established in 1984, Medicare supported government hospitals, medical care, and prescription drugs for the indigent. It also provided grants to state and territorial governments to operate hospitals. The 1999 addition of a Medicare levy—1.5% to 2.5% depending on income level—extended these benefits to the general population. Government incentives encourage private insurance, which pays cost-sharing fees and provides access to private hospitals, specialists, and physicians. About 50% of Australians have private insurance, which pays 11% of health care costs.

The following are the key aspects of the Australian system:

- Australians seem to have fewer access problems overall than Canadian and U.S. patients, but they report problems accessing care on nights and weekends and difficulties paying for prescription drugs.
- Australians with insurance entering local public hospitals decide whether to do so as public or private patients. Public patients receive free hospital and physician care. Private patients can choose their doctors; they pay minor charges, but most charges are covered by a combination of Medicare and private insurance.
- Under a program called Lifetime Health Cover, those who join a private health plan before the age of 31 pay a lower premium over their lifetime. Two percent is added to the premium for each year of delay. This is to prevent "hit-and-run" enrollment when people anticipate major expenses and to maintain a larger, healthier risk pool.
- Community rating is mandatory for private health insurance. A "reinsurance" system redistributes the costs of claims among insurers to avoid winners and losers.
- To reduce reliance on public funding, the government provides a 30% rebate on private health insurance costs.
- A government subsidy for the long-term care of older persons includes institutional, community-based, and in-home support. In return, the government controls the supply of long-term beds.

Case 3   (*continued*)

- In 2003, Australia had 2.99 physicians and 9.53 nurses per 1,000 population, compared with 2.42 and 9.82, respectively, in the United States.

Germany

Chancellor Otto von Bismarck is credited with starting the first national health insurance program in the 1880s. Today, it is built around 252 nonprofit sickness funds that negotiate with labor unions, employers, and providers. The various parties interact quite formally.

The following are the key aspects of the German system:

- All individuals must have health insurance. A federal unemployment insurance fund pays premiums for the unemployed (currently a high percentage of the German population). A worker's pension fund pays premiums for retired workers. Workers have choices among funds, but funds tend to be linked to an industry or a locale.
- Funds assess premiums on a graduated scale based on income. Copayments have increased in recent years to cover revenue shortfalls.
- Physician associations receive a fixed amount per person per year, as do hospitals. Hospitals pay hospital-based physicians' salaries from their capitation income. Hospitals are reimbursed under a DRG system similar to the one in the United States except that it includes physician services and aftercare for 30 days post discharge. Ambulatory-care physicians are paid either a fee for service or the physician associations pay them a salary from capitated revenues. They generally cannot follow patients into the hospital.
- Doctor visits are shorter and more frequent than in the United States, and hospital stays are longer; however, the hospital staffing ratios are much lower. The average cost of a hospital stay in the United States is $15,000 versus $5,000 for Germany, despite a 50% longer average length of stay.
- Germany has 3.6 physicians and 11 nurses per 1,000 population compared with 2.42 and 9.82, respectively, in the United States.

- Among developed countries, Germany has the fourth-highest percentage of GDP devoted to health care after the United States, France, and Denmark. Because of cost increases, high unemployment, and an aging population, a 2006 political compromise increased premiums to an average of 14.7% of salaries in 2007. Premiums are pooled, and each insurer receives the same premium per enrollee in an attempt motivate efficiency improvements.

Japan

Employment-based health insurance is the core of Japan's health system, and it continues to produce the best health outcomes of any of the systems mentioned here. However, some ascribe much of the differential outcomes to demographic and lifestyle issues, especially diet.[2] Japan also has a national health insurance program financed with national and local taxes. Premiums are scaled to family income. Households not covered by employment-based insurance must belong to community insurance programs under the national plan. Retirees are covered by their former employers or their community plans.

The following are the key aspects of the Japanese system:

- The government sets fee schedules for physicians at a level much below U.S. rates. Fees are identical for all plans; however, patients often add 3% or 4% "gifts" to their payments. Fee levels are modified based on utilization. If too many of a procedure are done, the fee will be lowered.
- There are both nonprofit and for-profit hospitals, and hospitals may be owned by doctors.
- Most physicians work out of large clinics, some of which are associated with hospitals, and are reluctant to send patients into the hospital because they cannot follow them once they are admitted.
- Specialists are hospital employees and earn less than primary care physicians.

[2]Henderson (2002), while agreeing with this, also cited cultural aversion to invasive procedures and underreporting by at least 1.5% of GDP by excluding medical care preventive services, under-the-table payments for access, maternity care, and private room charges.

Case 3 (*continued*)

- Clinics usually dispense their own drugs.
- Japanese patients have many more, briefer physician visits and many more prescriptions than their U.S. counterparts. They also have many fewer hospital admissions, although lengths of stay tend to be much longer.
- There are fewer doctors per capita in Japan than in the United States, and waiting lines tend to be managed on a first-come, first-served basis.
- Japanese hospitals are considered by many to have somewhat outdated equipment and shabby facilities. Physicians do not seem to be customer oriented or highly motivated to meet patients' affective needs.

Other OECD Countries

Most other Organization for Economic Cooperation and Development (OECD) countries have more physicians and nurses per 1,000 population than the United States. The Netherlands has one of the highest ratios of nurses (13.6 per 1,000) and recently increased the roles of nurses in primary care. France, Sweden, and Spain have high ratios of physicians per 1,000 population (3.4, 3.3, and 3.2, respectively) (Grol, 2006).

SOME REPEATING THEMES

A number of themes recur in the systems of these various countries. Some represent ideas that have been tried in the United States or are being tried as part of the ACA, but all might warrant further consideration as the U.S. system changes over the next 10–20 years.

Universal Coverage

Health care is provided to all. Often it is through a patchwork of public and private funds, but every effort is made to have everyone in the system. General tax revenues (income, payroll, and value-added taxes) are used extensively to fund health care, but in most cases there is a mixture of additional revenue sources, including patient copayments, employment-based insurance, retirement funds, local government revenues, and private insurers. This patchwork of payment mechanisms does not leave large gaps of uninsured or underinsured citizens. Private insurance and private care are available to those who choose to pay more. Where copayments are required, a careful effort is made to make sure that ability to pay does not control access to basic care. In the United States, there have been numerous attempts to expand coverage over the last several decades, with the ACA being the most ambitious attempt to approach universal coverage.

Hospitals Are Budget Constrained

Since the introduction of prospective payment based on DRGs, hospitals in the United States have operated more as cost centers than revenue centers. A number of countries have established global hospital budgets or capitation budgets for hospitals, often administered through local authorities or trusts. Capital investment is constrained to avoid a hospital arms race.

Specialists Are Salaried and PCPs Incentivized

Income of the universal coverage system is used to pay the salaries of specialists, whereas fee-for-service payments reimburse the primary care providers. They serve as gatekeepers for referrals to specialists and hospitals and do not follow patients into the hospital. They are motivated, therefore, to avoid unnecessary hospitalizations. The British experiment with pay-for-performance was sufficiently successful that Epstein (2006) argued that its time has come for the United States. One might also see it as a way to boost the incomes of primary care physicians in the United States sufficiently to attract new practitioners and bolster the currently dwindling supply (Basch, 2006).

Large Premium and Risk Pools Are Maintained

Individuals are compelled to belong to one health plan or another. Young and healthy individuals cannot opt out, or, where they can, incentives are provided to try to keep them in. Trusts serve very large employers, but the needs of small businesses and individuals are met through required community rating, local community health plans,

---

Case 3 *(continued)*

and tax subsidies. Large premium and risk pools are built in to level the playing field and hold down administrative and marketing costs.

Systems Integration

The integration of the system is provided at the governmental rather than the institutional level. Circuit breakers in the system, especially between hospitals, specialists, and primary care practices, keep individuals and institutions from maximizing utilization. Incentives focus on motivating primary care physicians to control costs and improve quality.

Rationalization and Standardization

A trend toward decentralization of health care services is offset, in part, by setting up staff units that analyze and report on current medical technology, evidence about best practices, and evaluation of the cost-effectiveness of common interventions. These recommendations will probably be worked increasingly into pay-for-performance systems.

Labor Substitution

Many countries with lower costs seem to have not only lower professional incomes, but also substitute nurses and pharmacists for physicians and physician generalists for specialists in their delivery systems.

Pharmaceutical Costs

Most countries except New Zealand and the United States constrain or ban direct-to-consumer advertising for prescription drugs (a cost that reached $4.5 billion annually in the United States in 2009) and rely on recommendations to physicians for decision making. The profit margins of pharmaceutical companies are constrained through a number of mechanisms, depending on what alternatives exist for payment in the national system. In a few cases, physicians are allowed to supplement their revenue by dispensing in their practices.

Discussion Questions

We have intentionally omitted some recurring themes from our discussion. We invite you to discuss recurring themes that relate to the following questions:

1. In most of the countries discussed, does universal coverage provide the gold standard of care?

2. Does rationing occur in these countries? If so, how is it different from rationing in the United States?

3. Do revenues used to pay for health care tend to come from a single source or are they derived from many different sources?

4. What steps do these countries take to ensure that payments required of individuals do not become a barrier to access?

5. What other patterns of similarities and differences do you notice?

6. To what extent do you think the crafting of the ACA relied on experiences in other countries? Can you think of examples of policies or countries that may have been influential?

Chapter 4

Where Do We Want to Be?

Even in a country that lacks an overall, cohesive health policy, it is useful to ask: How unhappy are we with our health care, and what do we want to change? Do not expect consistent responses from the American public. When the nation was debating the Clinton health plan, a number of organizations surveyed the public. Respondents reported they believed that the health care system was in trouble. At the same time, they expressed satisfaction with their own largely employer-financed health care programs. Public support for universal coverage was strong, but individuals did not want to pay higher taxes to support it (Peterson, 1995). An *ABC New/Washington Post* poll in October 1993 showed the following (Schick, 1995):

- 51% of the public favored the Clinton health plan.
- 59% thought that it was better than the existing system.
- Only 19% thought that their care would get better under it, and 34% thought worse care would result.
- However, 57% were against tax increases to pay for it, whereas 40% would be willing to pay.

The American public also appears to be split over the Patient Protection and Affordable Care Act (ACA) as a whole. Data about opposition to the act can be misleading, with a significant portion of opposition coming from people who believe the ACA did not go far enough. They would prefer a public option, for example, or a single-payer system. Overall, the public is negative about the individual mandate and the employer mandate, but is much in favor of the insurance changes that have been implemented. People are confused about the insurance exchange provisions of the act as well. An April 2013 tracking poll found that "about half the public says they do not have enough information about the health reform law to understand how it will impact their own family, a share that rises among the uninsured and low-income households" (Kaiser Family Foundation, 2013). The same poll reported that 42% of respondents did not know that the ACA was still the law of the land. Twelve percent believed it had been repealed by Congress, 7% believed it had been overturned by the Supreme Court, and 23% didn't know whether it was still in effect or not.

Americans report being in good health more than any other OECD country. Their complaints are mostly about financial risks and to some extent access and waiting. A 2010 study of six developed countries showed that Americans were satisfied with their doctors and the availability of effective care, but were also more likely to report that the system needed to be completely rebuilt (Papanicolas, Cylus, & Smith, 2013).

ALIGNMENT WITH THE REST OF SOCIETY

The democratic process is likely to generate many policy experiments as we cope with advancing technology, changing demographics, political pressures, and economic fluctuations. These experiments will continue to stir debate about the merits of the many delivery and payment alternatives available in the United States and elsewhere.

For professionals in leadership positions, this is an unpleasant reality that makes it much harder to plan and implement any institutional strategy. Even the most prestigious institutions are affected by these external drivers. For example, the Finnish national orthopedic hospital, the Orton Hospital in Helsinki, had to downsize and reach out to private-pay individuals when the Finnish federal government chose to decentralize its jointly financed government health care program and pass administration on to local governments (Masalin, 1994). These local governments then attempted to control the rising cost of health care by reducing referrals to central specialized hospitals. Orton Hospital was a national resource of high-quality care, but as the referral patterns of the country changed, it, too, had to change the way it functioned in order to survive.

There is no universal, monolithic "we" when it comes health policy. There are interest groups, each of which has a central point of view. Within each group are many individuals with some diversity of views. They may be willing to compromise on some issues, but not on others. In the United States, much progressive legislation has been built by reaching agreement on means rather than on ends.

What Do Providers Want?

Providers are aware of their responsibility to act in the best interests of their patients. They are also inculcated with the "first do no harm" dictum. Even among the "disinterested" parties, some care most about individuals, whereas others focus on populations. This is often a vexing problem for those clinicians who, although committed to the needs of individual patients, are also trained in statistical thinking and population-based approaches.

Provider professionals want professional autonomy, income stability and growth comparable with their peers, successful outcomes for their patients, a sense of mastery of their field, and the respect of the public. They know that they will make some mistakes, but they will work very hard to avoid them. They do not want to put their careers on the line with every decision. They do not want to waste energy on bureaucratic exercises that consume resources and distract them from effective care. They also would like to see provisions to pay for care for the uninsured. They are aware that these individuals often forgo normal care and may end up later with more serious and costly problems. That is why some hospitals and health maintenance organizations (HMOs) have strongly endorsed state plans to cover the uninsured, even when they involve adding a tax on their charges to paying patients.

The American Nurses Association (ANA) has expressed some of these desires in its Bill of Rights for Registered Nurses (ANA, 2014). It addresses not only working conditions for nurses but also the right to provide "services that maintain respect for human dignity and embrace the uniqueness of each patient and the nature of his or her health problems, without restriction with regard to social or economic status." The document says nurses must have the ability to meet their obligations to society and their patients, as well as meet their own needs. In addition, they have a right to workplaces that allow them to meet professional standards, act within their scope of practice, perform their duties in accordance with the ANA code of ethics, advocate for themselves as well as their patients, be safe, keep their patients safe, and negotiate their conditions of employment.

Professional Autonomy

The professional mystique of physicians in the past rested on their control of information. Those who favor a consumer-centric, free-market approach to health care decision making want to maximize the amount of information available to consumers. This has led many physicians to argue for privacy in the conduct of their practices, often in the name of protection of business secrets and personal privacy. Many physicians object, for example, to the fact that a drug company's local sales representative has data on their prescribing behaviors (Saul, 2006). Insurers certainly profile physicians and institutions for costs and outcomes regularly, and aggregated data are increasingly available to employers, the National Committee for Quality Assurance (NCQA), the Joint Commission, the federal government, and the general public. The Centers for Medicare & Medicaid Services (CMS) released physician Medicaid income data in 2014.

Employer representatives want more information to be available to consumers. One thorny issue is information on individual physicians. President George W. Bush called for "transparency in the marketplace" and urged private insurers to disclose data on physician costs and outcomes; however, when the Business Roundtable called on the federal government to make its Medicare databases available, his administration cited a 1979 court ruling protecting the privacy of physicians and prohibiting disclosure of Medicare payments to individual physicians (Pear, 2006).

This is a difficult area. Professionals, like other businesspeople, have some rights to privacy and protections from the prying eyes of competitors, but some observers see the current tensions as the last gasp of a professional monopoly and an attempt to withhold information that bolsters purchaser sovereignty at all levels. Yet the public has difficulty interpreting this information effectively. Current techniques for evaluating case mix and adjusting for risk are crude at best. Measuring the outputs of medical interventions is difficult unless one knows that the inputs are comparable or unless there is a way to adjust the data to reflect differences in inputs, especially the condition of the patient going in.

Other professions fight to overcome the dominance of physicians. In many countries, pharmacists are freer to dispense independently. Nurse practitioners and midwives have fought state by state for the right to practice independently. Psychologists have been fighting some of the same battles with respect to prescribing for the mentally ill, and more and more types of counselors want to be able to bill Medicare, Medicaid, and private insurance.

What Do Patients and Their Families Want?

Patients want to beat the odds. They and their families want the best possible outcomes, and they want to know that everything possible was done to ensure recovery (or a comfortable death) for their loved ones. Some want miracles. All want respect and caring. Most know that they need experts to look after their interests, but still want to be kept informed of what is going on so they can make sense of what is happening and avoid serious medical errors. Again, the issues are complex. Patients and families want to have access to quality information if they have the time and energy to make their own decisions. At the same time, they employ the provider as their agent, and the sicker they are, the more they tend rely on the clinician's judgment.

When they are not terribly sick, they also worry about the cost of their care. They do not want to spend a lot of time in the waiting room or figuring out how to fill out paperwork. That is a nonmonetary cost, but a cost to them, nevertheless. It can also be a monetary cost if they lose work hours or reimbursement opportunities because of it.

They want to know that they were not treated unfairly by any part of the health care system and that their treatment was not affected by their gender, their ethnicity, or the color of their skin. They would like to think that it was not affected by the capacity of their pocketbooks, but probably believe that to be a bit unrealistic.

They also become apprehensive when they believe that profitability concerns or payment mechanisms are influencing which treatments they receive. An example has been the debate over whether the drugs chosen by oncologists for outpatient treatment have been chosen for their effectiveness or their profitability (Abelson, 2006a; Jacobson et al., 2006). Increasingly, patients are aware of the financial incentives affecting providers that in the long run can undermine provider legitimacy (Schlesinger, 2002).

Before passage and early implementation of the ACA, a strong concern of individuals was that they did not want to be denied insurance on the basis of prior medical conditions over which they had little or no control. The ACA specifically prohibits denial of coverage because of preexisting conditions. This provision became effective at the start of 2014.

Some individuals, particularly those sometimes referred to as the "young immortals," have been willing to "go bare" (not carry health insurance) if they perceive a relatively low probability of a significantly costly health care event. This has raised the issue of *free riders* getting emergency care, even though they are not making provision for paying for it ahead of time. This is part of the impetus for the ACA mandate that all individuals obtain health insurance or pay an income tax penalty. An even thornier problem has been the *moral hazard* of those who knowingly indulge in high-risk behaviors for which the general public has had to pick up a share of the costs. The primary rationale for mandatory helmet laws, for example, was not to protect motorcyclists; it was to shelter the public from incurring the tremendous ongoing costs of caring for people with serious brain damage.

Individuals also worry about being bankrupted when they have insufficient insurance coverage for current and future situations. The ACA has dealt with this is a number of ways, including barring lifetime caps on claims. Yet consumers also worry about what the premium costs will do to their disposable income. Again, the ACA tries to deal with that by subsidizing the premiums of low-income workers.

What Do Insurers Want?

Insurers want to stay in business. That is why they fought so hard against any hint of a single-payer system and against the Obama administration proposal for a government health plan that would appear in the exchanges alongside the existing product lines (the public option).

Insurers want to be free to play the odds. They want to be able to make an acceptable level of net revenue whether they are a for-profit or a non-profit organization. They want to be able to compete in the marketplace on a "level playing field." Their customers are the payers—the employers and the group and individual enrollees—and they want to maintain a good reputation with them. In the world of HMOs and preferred provider organizations (PPOs), insurers want the biggest possible discounts from providers to keep their medical loss ratios competitive.

Insurers also want to avoid adverse selection. They want protection against having those who know they have a higher-than-average probability of a claim from joining their system in disproportionate numbers. They also want to be able to attract those with a below-average probability of a claim. They do not want to be in a situation in which they are disadvantaged vis-à-vis other insurers. They would like to continue to compete on marketing skills, on underwriting ability, on investment returns on their reserves, and on their operating efficiencies.

Insurers, however, are very sensitive to market shifts. For example, many are currently developing new insurance products for individuals and small groups as the notion of consumer-oriented care and insurance exchanges increase consumer involvement in choosing products (and as employers reduce their contributions and coverage). They suddenly seem interested in individual subscribers that they ignored a few years ago. They are also interested in offering self-insurance plans to the small employers that they ignored previously.

What Do Employers Want?

Employers want to be able to recruit and retain competent, productive employees, and they want competitive cost structures. They are not in the health care purchasing business for any other reason. They are generally supportive of consumer-driven health care that allows individual consumers, rather than employers, insurers, or provider organizations, to make more decisions than in the past. This effectively shifts more of the costs onto the employees and from the lowest paid employees onto Medicaid. With the exchanges and the play-or-pay provisions of the ACA, they have many more options to consider, and it will be interesting to see what options they gravitate toward and for how long. Because the ACA's employer contribution provisions apply to employers with 50 or more full-time employees, and full time has been defined as an average of 30 hours per week or at least 130 hours in a month, employers may choose to reduce the hours of workers to below 30 hours per week to keep their employee head count below that threshold.

Large Employers and Unions

In unionized firms, premium payments are set through collective bargaining between the company and the union. This bargaining can expand or contract the health care benefits, depending on the wants and needs of the employer and key groups within the union. After a period during which many of our bitterest strikes were waged over health benefit issues, both sides are now recognizing that employment-related health care costs can reduce domestic employment by encouraging companies to shift production to other countries. Employers are rapidly limiting their liabilities to specific dollar contributions toward health care for employees and retirees. Large firms and their unions are increasingly aligned in their desire to hold down costs and maintain coverage.

Small Employers

Because health care insurance bargaining power can be increased by pooling large numbers of beneficiaries, and because administrative costs and insurance prices are very sensitive to the number of individuals covered, small businesses find it hard to provide competitive health benefits to their workers. They need either subsidies or effective ways of pooling their people with others to make a viable enrollee population. Accomplishing this has been a major thrust of the ACA, which includes premium subsidies for small firms.

What Do Governments Want?

They want a satisfied public. They want health care expenditures to be predictable and at a level that does not disadvantage economic growth in both domestic and international competition. The system should work within the parameters of accepted cultural norms of equity and fairness so it does not foment unnecessary voter dissatisfaction. All levels of government want to keep costs down to avoid crowding out other programs or increasing taxpayer discontent. Federal, state, and local governments are also concerned about their longer-term liabilities for the viability of Medicare trust funds, Medicaid costs, and their accrued liabilities for government retiree health benefits.

Federal Government

The federal government purchases health care on behalf of special populations: the poor, older adults, veterans, active duty military, Native Americans, and so forth. It pays for more than 40% of health care purchases (and covers more than 60% of patients in some markets). Children have actually fared better in federally purchased health care since 2000 because of the 1997 startup of the State Children's Health Insurance Program (SCHIP). Federal programs, which are highly sensitive to political pressures, have tended to rely on their purchasing power to garner deep discounts. (Only recently have governments begun to encourage evidence-based medicine and to refuse to pay for avoidable costs such as hospital-acquired infections.) Because of the low federal reimbursement rates, some providers refuse to participate in federal and state programs, further reducing access and availability.

State and Local Governments

The interests of state and local governments are much more limited, involving Medicaid and local programs for the uninsured poor. Their revenue streams are limited and inflexible, often being tied to real property taxes that cannot adapt rapidly to changing economic conditions. However, revenue restraints have encouraged innovation. State and local governments cannot print money to cover deficit spending. Despite all of the rhetoric at the national level, most experimental attempts to control health costs have occurred at the state level. For several years, states such as Maine, Vermont, and Massachusetts have been experimenting with systems to provide universal coverage using a variety of funding sources.

Prior to passage of the ACA, the governors of more than half the states had proposed measures that included one or more of the following approaches:

- Mandated insurance coverage for all citizens
- Mandated employer coverage or payments into insurance pools in lieu of coverage
- Mandated lower premium individual policies from insurers
- State coverage for all uninsured children
- Tax credits and deductions for individual insurance premiums
- Special discounts for prevention and health lifestyles
- Calling for expansion of Medicare to cover the uninsured (Barry & Basher, 2007; Solomon & Wessel, 2007)

Although the ACA institutionalized some of these once-experimental approaches at the national level, state-by-state experimentation is expected to continue.

Governments are also concerned about appropriate access for all of their constituents. The case at the end of this chapter provides the example of the U.S. Department of Health and Human Services standard for Culturally and Linguistically Appropriate Services (CLAS). Some parts of this standard were once mandatory for services paid for with federal funds; since 2013, they are all guidelines. The states developed, and the ACA now supports, simpler portals of entry that allow low-income families to submit one application to determine their eligibility for multiple programs.

What Does the General Public Want?

Members of the general public want to feel that they and their families are safe and that the system will treat them fairly and effectively if and when they need it. This requires access to health care, which means health insurance coverage. They also do not want to feel guilty about the plight of their uninsured fellow citizens. At the same time, they are not enthusiastic about using the tax system to cover the needs of others. They do not want to be treated in a way that marks them as a member of any underclass, but want to be treated as middle class or above.

Americans seem unwilling to pay more than the current proportion of national income (about 19%) for health care, yet the inflation rate in health care continues to exceed the rate of growth in our overall economy (growth in gross domestic product [GDP]). International economic comparisons have shown a close relationship between national income and per capita health expenditures, but with the United States as an outlier. Wealthy nations do spend more per person. This would seem to indicate that part of the cost of health care is related to need, part is related to availability, and part is related to decisions people make as consumers.

Individual Insurance Purchasers

The problems affecting small businesses are even worse for the self-employed seeking coverage. Premiums are highest and rejections frequent. Many end up going without coverage. Yet the self-employed often have an advantage over the working poor who are unable to obtain insurance through their employer—because it is not offered, because they only work part time and are not eligible, or because they cannot afford the added expense.

The exchanges and the premium subsidies for low-income families under the ACA will help with those concerns. It remains to be seen whether the premiums for approved coverage at the minimum cost are financially feasible for those in need.

What Do Policy Wonks Want?

The policy wonks want a system that is efficient, coherent, and rational and that provides effective care to the relevant populace. Health care competes with other services for scarce resources. Money spent on health care cannot be spent on transportation or public amenities; therefore, there must be some calculus for allocating scarce resources to health care and other meritorious causes on a consistent basis. Analysts are sharply divided on many other issues. For example, although many argue for measures to forestall continued growth in health care expenditures, others say, "Don't worry—the U.S. citizenry can afford it and it constitutes economic growth and increasing employment even if it were to approach 25% of our economy." Others say, "Yes, that is growth, but it represents a transfer of assets from the young to the elderly that is not sustainable."

Much care is effective and worth doing, but there is agreement that there is considerable waste and inefficiency, even though waste and inefficiency are income-enhancing for someone. Examples of other areas of concern to policy analysts include the following:

- **Free riders.** As discussed earlier, individuals who could otherwise pay but avoid doing so while still relying on the system for help in case of a catastrophic event are a stress on the system. Some individuals will chose to pay the penalities under the ACA rather that purchase insurance.

- **Overserved and underserved areas.** Not only are health care resources limited by the willingness and ability of governments, firms, and individuals to pay, but available resources can be poorly distributed, resulting in surpluses in some areas and shortages in others. Governments and payers have attempted to regulate the supply of health services as well as the demand. One example of the regulation of supply is *certificate of need* legislation. In an attempt to regulate against an oversupply of health care capital investments, many states have legislation that requires independent review to determine whether additional investments are warranted. If not, the services they provide cannot be compensated for from state and federal funds. Examples of the types of capital investments reviewed include hospital beds, nursing home beds, cardiac catheterization units, and expensive imaging equipment. Legislation has also subsidized the building of hospitals and the posting of health professionals to serve needy populations.
- **Withdrawal of services.** Demand is constrained when payers restrict what they will pay for and how much they will pay for what is delivered. The absence of sufficient demand or reimbursement for services can lead professionals and provider institutions to withdraw from the market, downsize, or file for bankruptcy. Because of high malpractice insurance costs for obstetric procedures, for instance, many obstetricians have stopped doing deliveries and only provide gynecologic services. Many hospitals have reduced their psychiatric beds, shifting the burden to the state institutions. Some withdrawals are responses to overcapacity in an area, but others are the result of decisions that a particular line of services is bound to lose money.

Proposals to solve the access problems seldom mentioned much about the supply of services available or the impact of a large increase in volume on prices and costs. In the minds of many, universal coverage and costs seem to be separable issues. We learned that they cannot be separated when Medicare and Medicaid were introduced and medical expenditures rose rapidly.

CONCLUSION

There are specific things that a majority or a plurality among each set of actors want to see happening in the health care system. For the most part, there are clear majorities on the need for providing insurance for all, controlling the rate of inflation, eliminating waste, improving quality, investing in the most beneficial programs, taking care of children and the older population, and pushing ahead with research to find cures for diseases. Yet there will be a vocal minority on just about every issue—largely people representing special interests and those with strong economic and social ideologies. All of the areas of general agreement are reflected to one degree or another in provisions of the ACA, but these provisions represent compromise, incrementalism, and political pragmatism. There is extensive opposition, and we have much to learn about how theory translates into practice. That is why we believe in the continuing importance of policy analysis as a way toward maximum possible rationality in decision making, fewer ungrounded assertions, and increased ability to deal with new evidence and new opportunities.

Case 4	National Standards on Culturally and Linguistically Appropriate Services in Health and Health Care (CLAS)

In 1997, the Office of Minority Health (OMH) in the U.S. Department of Health and Human Services began work on national standards for culturally and linguistically competent health care. The stated goal was to reduce health disparities. In December 2000, OMH released the standards. Although the standards were primarily directed at health care organizations, OMH encouraged their use by individual providers as well as by policy makers, accreditation and credentialing agencies, purchasers, patients, advocates, educators, and the health care community in general (OMH, 2001).

OMH began reviewing and revising the standards in fall 2010. The National CLAS Standards Enhancement Initiative included three lines of inquiry: a literature review, a public comment period, and consultation with an advisory committee. The purpose was to revise the standards "to reflect the past decade's advancements, expand their scope, and improve their clarity to ensure understanding and implementation." Precipitating factors, according to OMH, were increasing diversity in the U.S. population and rapid growth in the fields of cultural and linguistic competency.

This process culminated in the April 2013 release of a set of enhanced standards (OMH, 2013a). In the supporting documents, OMH explicitly defines health to include physical, mental, and social well-being.

Cultures deserving of appropriate services include those identified by geographic, religious and spiritual, biological, and sociological characteristics, in addition to racial, ethnic, and linguistic groups addressed by the original standards. OMH also expands the target audiences and the target recipients—from "health care organizations" to "health and health care organizations" and from "patients and consumers" to "individuals and groups," respectively (OMH, 2013b).

The original 14 standards included a mix of recommendations, mandates, and guidelines. The 15 enhanced standards are all guidelines of equal weight.

To encourage successful implementation of the enhanced standards, OMH published *The Blueprint*, an extensive implementation guide with explanations of each standard and listings of resources (OMH, 2013b). OMH declared that completion of the enhancement initiative means that for the next decade, the 2013 standard will "serve as the cornerstone for advancing health equity through culturally and linguistically appropriate services" (p. 155)

PRINCIPAL STANDARD

1. Provide effective, equitable, understandable, and respectful quality care and services that are responsive to diverse cultural health beliefs and practices, preferred languages, health literacy, and other communication needs.

GOVERNANCE, LEADERSHIP, AND WORKFORCE

2. Advance and sustain organizational governance and leadership that promotes CLAS and health equity through policy, practices, and allocated resources.
3. Recruit, promote, and support a culturally and linguistically diverse governance, leadership, and workforce that are responsive to the population in the service area.
4. Educate and train governance, leadership, and workforce in culturally and linguistically appropriate policies and practices on an ongoing basis.

Case 4   (*continued*)

COMMUNICATION AND LANGUAGE ASSISTANCE

5. Offer language assistance to individuals who have limited English proficiency and/or other communication needs, at no cost to them, to facilitate timely access to all health care and services.
6. Inform all individuals of the availability of language assistance services clearly and in their preferred language, verbally and in writing.
7. Ensure the competence of individuals providing language assistance, recognizing that the use of untrained individuals and/or minors as interpreters should be avoided.
8. Provide easy-to-understand print and multimedia materials and signage in the languages commonly used by the populations in the service area.

ENGAGEMENT, CONTINUOUS IMPROVEMENT, AND ACCOUNTABILITY

9. Establish culturally and linguistically appropriate goals, policies, and management accountability, and infuse them throughout the organization's planning and operations.
10. Conduct ongoing assessments of the organization's CLAS-related activities and integrate CLAS-related measures into measurement and continuous quality improvement activities.
11. Collect and maintain accurate and reliable demographic data to monitor and evaluate the impact of CLAS on health equity and outcomes and to inform service delivery.
12. Conduct regular assessments of community health assets and needs and use the results to plan and implement services that respond to the cultural and linguistic diversity of populations in the service area.
13. Partner with the community to design, implement, and evaluate policies, practices, and services to ensure cultural and linguistic appropriateness.

14. Create conflict and grievance resolution processes that are culturally and linguistically appropriate to identify, prevent, and resolve conflicts or complaints.
15. Communicate the organization's progress in implementing and sustaining CLAS to all stakeholders, constituents, and the general public (OMH, 2013).

Source: Reproduced from: Office of Minority Affairs, Department of Health and Human Service. (2013). National standards for culturally and linguistically appropriate services (CLAS) in health and health care. Washington, DC: U.S. Department of Health and Human Services. https://www.thinkculturalhealth.hhs.gov/pdfs/enhancednationalclas standards.pdf. Last updated 3/3/2013. Accessed 11/5/2013.

Discussion Questions

1. OMH has said the enhancement initiative followed a decade of successful implementation of the 2000 standards, but the news media have reported on implementation problems, and the 2013 standards were released with an implementation manual almost 200 pages long. What do you think might be some barriers to implementation, and what would you suggest to encourage implementation?

2. What do the expanded definitions of health and culture say in general about the way government framed health in 2013 as compared to 2010? What might have contributed to the change?

3. How do you explain the differences between recommendations, guidelines, and mandates? What are the possible explanations for making all enhanced standards guidelines?

4. Which are the most important standards in your opinion? Which are the least important? Explain your reasoning.

5. What would you change about these standards if you were in charge of the U.S. Department of Health and Human Services?

6. Does it seem unusual to you for a government agency to wait more than 10 years to review and revise standards like these? What might be the reasons for waiting? What arguments could be made for more frequent review?

Chapter 5

What Are the Governmental Alternatives?

The United States has tried an alphabet soup of health policy options: HSAs, HMOs, IPAs, PPOs, POS plans, ACOs, and so on. Health care analysts often must look beyond specific organizational and financial alternatives and address issues at a higher level and deal with the threads of economic and political thought behind different proposals while considering the overall criteria of access, cost, and quality of care.

Politicians and businesspeople from outside the health care sector advocate many alternatives. To offset their tendency to ignore professional issues, in this chapter we discuss alternatives affecting professional status and roles and institutional responses to them. **Table 5-1** presents an array of federal alternatives organized by their primary criteria—access, quality, or cost—and then by the economic philosophies behind them. The items in this array are not intended to be either mutually exclusive or collectively exhaustive; rather, the table provides a framework for looking at both the broad policy picture and specific health care actions taken at various times and places. Later in the chapter, another table (Table 5-3) summarizes policy alternatives added by state and local governments. Many of these alternatives were included as provisions of the Affordable Care Act (ACA).

Table 5-1 Illustrative Federal Government Health Policy Options

Access to Care

· Administered systems
  · Universal coverage
  · Expand or reduce eligibility or benefits
  · Mandate coverage and services
  · Captive providers
  · Control insurance industry practices
  · Mandate employer-based insurance coverage
· Consumer-driven competition
  · Implement insurance exchanges
  · Encourage basic plans with very low premiums for low-income workers and "young invincibles"
  · Mandate individual coverage
  · Allow states flexibility to reallocate federal funds for vouchers
· Oligopolistic competition
  · Expand or contract coverages in entitlement and categorical programs
  · Allow states to reallocate federal uncompensated care funds
  · Eliminate ERISA constraints on the states
  · Expand the capacity of the system

Quality of Care

· Administered system
  · Mandate participation in quality improvement efforts in federal plans and programs
  · Add more pay-for-performance incentives
  · Select providers and programs on the basis of quality excellence
· Consumer-driven competition
  · Encourage or mandate transparency of quality reporting in federal plans and programs
  · Oversee licensure and credentialing of foreign-trained providers
· Oligopolistic competition
  · Work reporting of quality care and adverse events into purchasing specifications for federal programs and disseminate to the public
  · Encourage wider use of health information technology

Cost of Care

· Administered system
  · Use full bargaining power in negotiation of fees and discounts
  · Limit eligibility and covered services in entitlement and categorical programs

Table 5-1 Illustrative Federal Government Health Policy Options (*continued*)

- Consumer-driven competition
  - Change policy on tax-deductible status of employer-paid health premiums and individual health expenditures
  - Support individual medical savings accounts
  - Privatize parts of Medicare, Medicaid, and other federal programs
  - Implement information technology and price transparency in federal programs and promote parallel industrial efforts
  - Support consumer information reporting and database availability
- Oligopolistic competition
  - Expand managed care/disease management
  - Subsidize capacity reductions
  - Constrain anticompetitive practices
- Other interventions
  - Research, development, and deployment
    - Treatment methods (e.g., National Institutes of Health)
    - Delivery system methods (e.g., information technology)
  - Provider quality and availability
  - Health and safety regulation
  - Support malpractice (tort law) experimentation
  - Bundle payments for services
  - Special situations and opportunities

They are still included here, partly because they may be subject to reconsideration in the future.

Governmental alternatives are grouped according to their approach to the health care marketplace: (1) administered systems, (2) consumer-driven competition (assuming near-perfect markets), and (3) oligopolistic competition. These market positions, as reflected in the distribution of buyer versus seller market power and how these have played out through health care policy schools of thought, have been presented elsewhere.

The federal government, especially, has a large number of programs that make indirect investments in health care. Some of these programs, such as the National Institutes of Health (NIH), the Agency for Healthcare Research and Quality (AHRQ), the Centers for Disease Control and Prevention (CDC), the Patient-Centered Outcomes Research Institute, and the Center for Medicare & Medicaid Innovation, focus on research and development. Others focus on education or health care information technology initiatives. State and federal spending programs also influence the supply and training of health professionals and provide for traditional public health services. These have been placed into a fourth section, as they seem to pertain to all alternative economic value systems.

FEDERAL-LEVEL ALTERNATIVES

Access to Care: Administered System Alternatives

The government may try to influence the behaviors of the other actors in the health care arena, but in the end it is patient payments, insurance premiums, and tax revenues that cover the costs of the health care. Much of the financial risk still falls on the taxpayers. Because a national government tends to respond to political pressures, government-administered systems tend to focus on access needs and then on costs. These two issues may take priority over other quality-of-care criteria such as continuity of care (McLaughlin, 1998).

In the United States, the public sector makes very heavy expenditures in health care, even though the private-sector portion is also large. In fact, World Health Organization data indicate that the United States not only spends more per capita on health care than most other countries, but actually spends more public money per capita than Canada and the United Kingdom, which ostensibly have universal public coverage (see **Table 5-2**).

Table 5-2 Comparison of Public and Total Expenditures in Selected Countries, 2012

Country	Health Expenditure as Percentage of GDP	Total Per Capita Health Care Expenditures* ($)	Total Per Capita Health Care Public Expenditures* ($)	Governmental Percentage of Health Care Expenditures
Australia	9.0	3,629	2,529	68.5
Canada	11.2	4,520	3,183	70.4
France	11.6	4,086	3,135	76.7
Germany	11.1	4,371	3,316	75.9
Sweden	9.4	3,870	3,123	80.9
Switzerland	11.9	5,564	3,640	65.4
United Kingdom	9.3	3,322	2,747	82.7
United States	17.9	8,608	3.954	45.9

* Using Purchasing Power Parity adjusted international dollar rate.

Source: Data from: World Health Report 2012. Accessed June 2012 at: http://www.who.int/gho/publications/world_health_statistics/2012/en

Universal Coverage

Most countries operate with a nationally funded, controlled, and administered health care system. In Canada, each province manages its own universal coverage. Although nearly all countries have a policy on paper that promises universal coverage, only the developed countries have the resources to fulfill such promises.

Under a single-payer system, coverage is provided almost exclusively through tax revenues. In reality, there is often a parallel private sector based on private insurance or personal payments and a set of private providers. This allows those who can afford it the option of bypassing any supply constraints. In many less wealthy countries, health professionals work for the government part of the day and see private-pay patients at other times. This is because government revenue is not sufficient to pay health professionals even a middle-class wage for their government service. Even in countries where this private sector is technically illegal, it is usually tolerated as a reality of life. Where the coverage is universal and the resources are not sufficient, the services are just not delivered and/or a rationing scheme is put in place, especially for procedures that can be postponed.

Universal coverage is not synonymous with single payer. It can be financed by direct government payment, by mandatory insurance schemes (with mandates placed on employers, consumers, or both) or vouchers allowing subsidized purchase of insurance directly by the consumer, or by a combination of these. President Clinton's Health Security plan was designed to provide near-universal coverage but preserved the existing system of employer-based coverage. The Obama administration's Affordable Care Act followed a similar path. Alternatives for implementing consumer-centered care tend to favor vouchers because some policy experts think that vouchers lessen the tendency of insured patients to ignore costs and allow consumers a better match between their preferences and the coverage they purchase (Feldstein, 2005). They also favor insurance with high deductibles and coinsurance for similar reasons.

Expand or Reduce Eligibility or Benefits

The U.S. government pays directly or indirectly for more than 45% of health care costs. In recent years, the proportion covered has been slowly increasing as more children are covered each year and the Medicare drug benefit has begun to take effect. Some federal programs are paid from trust funds; others are funded through taxation. A number of optional services can be provided under Medicaid if the states decide to participate. As their budgets dictate, governments may add or subtract from their list of optional services and covered populations. For example, the Trade Act of 2002 created a new category of coverage—displaced workers who became uninsured—in the form of Health Coverage Tax Credits, which paid 65% of the premiums for most COBRA continuation coverage plans of former employers or private health plans arranged by the states. The credits could go directly to the households or be advanced monthly to the insurer. Uptake has been slow, however, because the enrollees facing reduced incomes still have to fund the other 35% of the premium.

The ACA expanded income eligibility for premium subsidies and copay offsets considerably. It also mandated Medicaid coverage for all individuals, including those without children, who earn up to 133% of the FPL. The Supreme Court overturned that mandate, but many states are participating on a voluntary basis and receiving additional federal funding.

Mandate Coverages and Services

One way of moving toward universal coverage is to require that employers provide coverage for their employees and demand that individuals purchase coverage when that is not available. These mandates can come with a wide variety of carrots and sticks, including premium subsidies for individuals with low incomes and firms in sectors where margins have not supported offering benefits. Unless the purchasing pool comprises the bulk of the population, insurers are likely to experience all sorts of adverse selection problems. This issue becomes more serious when barriers to moving in and out of coverage are lowered—for example, by prohibiting preexisting condition exclusions. If people are able to obtain insurance almost instantly when they become sick, why would they maintain coverage when well unless it was mandated? These mandates were implemented in Massachusetts under Governor Romney and in the ACA under President Obama.

Qualifying plans under the ACA must offer a basic benefit package that includes preventive services, maternity benefits, and behavioral health care. The act specifies other plan characteristics that must be met by participating insurers and providers.

Captive Providers

Providers can become captives of the governmental system if they are employed by the government or if they operate in a government-controlled marketplace. Canadian physicians are not employed by the federal or provincial governments, but are unlikely to have much of a practice unless they participate in their province's single-payer system. In the United States, a number of governmental systems employ physicians, including military services, the Department of Veterans Affairs, the U.S. Health Service, and the National Health Service Corps, but, altogether, the federal government employs less than 3% of the nation's physicians. The majority of employed U.S. physicians work in the private sector for hospitals, academic medical centers, HMOs, and other integrated-service organizations. The federal government funds a number of health centers in underserved urban and rural areas. State and local governments participate in supporting the staff of health departments and health centers for low-income patients.

Control Insurance Industry Practices

The provisions of the ACA severely curtailed the flexibility of health insurers to underwrite and otherwise limit their risks. These include provisions requiring insurers to offer coverage for dependent children up to the age of 26, prohibiting them from excluding preexisting conditions or rescinding policies for people with high-cost illnesses, and limiting the waiting periods that can be imposed on new enrollees. These risks still have to be dealt with, especially the issue of adverse selection, which is what necessitated inclusion of the individual mandate.

Mandate Employer-Based Insurance Coverage

Just about every country that has aspirations for universal coverage within a competitive market system relies on employer-based insurance. Some systems also rely, in part, on community-based and affinity-based insurance systems as well. Employers may arrange for the insurance individually or in industry groups.

Access to Care: Consumer-Driven Competition Alternatives

Under this philosophy, the national government's role is to try to mitigate those factors that make the market imperfect. Appropriate government activities would include reducing regulations that influence the market and ensuring that there are adequate numbers of competing providers (the supply side), that buyers and sellers are free to move in and out of the market, and that both buyers and sellers have maximum access to both services and relevant information about price and quality.

Implement Insurance Exchanges

The array of plans available to employees in the United States has usually been shaped by employers' selections. Employers typically choose their offerings from among alternative plans offered by a single insurer. Opting out of company-sponsored plans has meant loss of the benefit. Individuals and small firms have been at a disadvantage unless they could join some kind of pool that was large enough to bargain effectively. Insurance exchanges offer the potential of both wide choices of insurers and pooling for bargaining power. They appear to be a necessary condition for an individual mandate in U.S. markets.

Encourage Basic Plans with Very Low Premiums for Low-Income Workers and "Young Invincibles"

One of the thornier problems in health policy is the free-rider issue. Among the uninsured population are many young, healthy adults who have access to insurance but choose to go without it because their expected health care costs are considerably below the premium levels available. They might be lured back into the insurance market by very low premium plans that cover only their likely health events, such as trauma and infectious disease. This is, of course, a double-edged sword, because such programs might also motivate other healthy workers to leave existing programs, thus exacerbating the adverse selection problem posed by the remaining enrollees. If the individual mandate is repealed, or if the so-called young invincibles, the working poor, or both choose to pay tax penalties rather than purchase insurance, the merits of offering low-cost basic plans will continue to be an area of inquiry for policy analysts.

Mandate Individual Coverage

This serves to force individuals rather than just employers to make insurance and health care service purchasing decisions. It also ensures that younger individuals are paying into the system on a regular basis. However, it cannot work unless people can afford those premiums, and so they have to be accompanied by premium and cost-sharing subsidies. One could also place this intervention under oligopolistic competition because it expands the market for private insurance contracts and should stimulate participation of young individuals in employer-sponsored plans.

The ACA contained both (Kaiser Family Foundation, 2012, p. 2):

Eligibility: Limit availability of premium credits and cost-sharing subsidies through the exchanges to U.S. citizens and legal immigrants who meet income limits. Employees who are offered coverage by an employer are not eligible for premium credits unless the employer plan does not have an actuarial value of at least 60% or the employee share of the premium exceeds 9.5% of income. Legal immigrants who are barred from enrolling in Medicaid during their first 5 years in the United States will be eligible for premium credits.

Premium credit: Provide refundable and advanceable premium credits to eligible individuals and families with incomes between 100–400% federal poverty level (FPL) to purchase insurance through the Exchanges. The premium credits will be tied to the second lowest cost silver plan in that market area and will be set on a sliding scale such that the premium contributions are limited to the following percentages of income for specified income levels:

Up to 133% FPL: 2% of income
133–150% FPL: 3–4% of income
150–200% FPL: 4–6.3% of income
200–250% FPL: 6.3–8.05% of income
250–300% FPL: 8.05–9.5% of income
300–400% FPL: 9.5% of income

Increase the premium contributions for those receiving subsidies annually to reflect the excess of premium growth over the rate of income growth for 2014–2018. Beginning in 2019, further adjust the premium contributions to reflect the excess of premium growth over CPI if aggregate premiums and cost-sharing subsidies exceed 0.54% of GDP.

Cost-sharing subsidies: Provide cost-sharing subsidies to eligible individuals and families annually to reduce the cost-sharing amounts and annual cost-sharing limits and have the effect of increasing the actuarial value of the basic benefit plan to the following percentages of the full value of the plan for the specified income level:

100–150% FPL: 96%
150–200% FPL: 87%
200–250% FPL: 73%
250–400% FPL: 70%

Source: Reproduced from: Kaiser Family Foundation. (2011). *Summary of the Affordable Care Act*, p. 2. Retrieved July 8, 2013, from http://kaiserfamilyfoundation.files.wordpress.com/2011/04/8061-021.pdf

Allow States Flexibility to Reallocate Federal Funds for Vouchers

One recommendation made by those who wish to maximize consumer choice in programs aimed at increasing access is to give targeted individuals vouchers to purchase insurance or services directly. The consumer-choice arguments for this approach parallel those for school vouchers in education. However, such proposals are also often intended to limit the risk to the government by replacing a defined benefit system with a defined and limited payment.

Access to Care: Oligopolistic Competition Alternatives

Oligopolistic competition is the norm in American industry. It is also typical in health care. Many communities have only a couple of hospital groups and a few dominant practices. In the ideological battle between administered systems and consumer-centered care, this fact has gone largely unnoticed.

The federal government's role under oligopolistic competition is limited, but it does have to be concerned about monopolistic practices and enforce its regulations governing open competition in commerce overall and health care in particular. It can also provide incentives for specific corporate responses. For example, the ACA excluded Medicare payments for treatment of some hospital-acquired infections, which will put more pressure on hospitals to reduce their infection rates.

Expand and Contract Coverage in Entitlement and Categorical Programs

Most American health care is delivered on a fee-for-service basis by private providers. The federal government, however, writes or at least approves the regulations that determine eligibility and benefits under programs such as Medicare, Medicaid, and the end-stage renal disease (ESRD) program. It can expand or contract the groups to be covered in those programs, either directly or by approving waivers exempting states from federal regulations.

The federal government has many categorical programs that support local case-finding and service delivery to specific populations and disease groupings, including Native Americans, low-income children, ESRD recipients, and people living with HIV/AIDS. Access could be expanded by adding more such populations or programs.

Allow States to Reallocate Federal Uncompensated Care Funds

Some alternatives being worked on by the states involve the reallocation of federal monies that have been going to the states to fund uncompensated care. The states may be allowed to reallocate these monies directly to purchase insurance or provide services for the uninsured, or pull them back from institutions through special taxes. The ACA has reduced the availability of these funds overall in anticipation of a substantial reduction in the uninsured population.

Eliminate ERISA Constraints on the States

Because the Employee Retirement Income Security Act (ERISA) of 1974 established two employer-based insurance systems, only one of which is under state regulation, a number of promising state and local initiatives have not gotten off the ground. Congress could amend this legislation to remove or weaken this exemption for self-insured employers.

Expand the Capacity of the System

Federal funding can be used to fill in any number of gaps in service programs and facilities. The Hill-Burton program (Hospital Survey and Construction Act of 1946), which funded so many small rural hospitals, is one example. That legislation called for the states to undertake systematic health planning to establish population-based needs for hospital beds and to create a licensing system for hospitals. It then provided construction assistance to bring shortage areas up to a standard level of service. Many newly constructed hospitals had fewer than 50 beds and were situated in rural areas that had completely lacked hospitals. Between 1946 and 1975, when Hill-Burton funding ended, approximately $1 billion of facilities construction had occurred, with about 35% paid for with federal funding. Hospital beds per capita increased by approximately 50%. Hospitals receiving Hill-Burton funding are still mandated to serve the local population with a certain amount of charitable care and care provided on a sliding-fee scale, although government enforcement of that provision has been limited.

More recently, the federal government has provided subsidies for "meaningful use" of electronic health records. It has also made it clear that there will be negative consequences for providers who fail to adopt this technology, which enables efficient billing and will link to shared cost and quality comparisons for payers and consumers.

The ACA did not include much funding for capital investment, which has been well-supported through bonded debt, but it did offer new initiatives to expand the medical and public health workforces.

Quality of Care: Administered System Alternatives

Mandate Participation in Quality Improvement Efforts in Federal Plans and Programs

Increasingly, the Centers for Medicare & Medicaid Services (CMS) has insisted that institutional providers participate in quality improvement programs. These quality improvement requirements often are indirectly enforced through the third-party accreditation procedures of organizations such as the Joint Commission and the National Committee for Quality Assurance (NCQA).

Add Pay-for-Performance Incentives

The federal government has supported a number of pay-for-performance demonstrations and appears to be committed to national implementation of this approach (Epstein, 2007). Not only can its proponents point to the United Kingdom's experience with such a plan, but also there is increasing evidence from the U.S. demonstrations that this may work here. However close this innovation may be to a tipping point, there is still concern that the level of hospital-sector improvement may not be sufficient to warrant the investment (Epstein, 2007; Lindenauer et al., 2007). The ACA expanded the scope of these demonstrations, clearly with the intention of expanding pay-for-performance in the future.

Select Providers and Programs on the Basis of Quality Excellence

Insurers profile providers on the basis of quality, but the federal government has been reluctant to get involved unless fraud and abuse or specified adverse events are involved; opportunities for greater selectivity still exist.

Quality of Care: Consumer-Driven Competition Alternatives

Encourage or Mandate Transparency of Quality Reporting in Federal Plans and Programs

On August 28, 2006, President Bush issued Executive Order 13410, titled "Promoting Quality and Efficient Health Care in Federal Government Administered or Sponsored Health Care Programs." U.S. Department of Health and Human Services Secretary Michael Leavitt interpreted the orders as promoting "value-driven health care." In a letter addressed to employer CEOs, Secretary Leavitt (2006a) wrote, "I am writing to invite you to play a leadership role in the movement toward transparency and value-driven health care." He asked for support of the "four cornerstones" of the executive order:

- Interoperable health information technology
- Transparency of quality
- Transparency of price
- Incentives for high-value health care

The American Reinvestment and Recovery Act (ARRA) and the ACA continued this initiative. Although there is less emphasis on large regional databases, support exists for collecting relevant data directly from electronic medical records and adding Web-based reporting of physician performance in a manner similar to hospital performance reporting.

Oversee Licensure and Credentialing of Foreign-Trained Providers

Graduates of foreign medical schools, whether U.S. citizens or immigrants, must leap a series of hurdles to achieve licensure in the United States. Given the fact that primary care residencies are not being filled by domestically trained graduates and that the ACA should significantly increase the demand for primary care providers, the country will be relying heavily on outsiders for those services for some time to come. These programs will continue to balance the quality aspects of their credentialing process against the need to avoid restricting the supply of providers.

Quality of Care: Oligopolistic Competition Alternatives

Work Reporting of Quality Care and Adverse Events into Purchasing Specifications for Federal Programs

Quality reporting for public consumption was also envisioned in Executive Order 13410 and by the "transparency" efforts of Secretary Leavitt. Reporting of adverse events is required by the Joint Commission and others, and it is also subject to CMS scrutiny.

Encourage Wider Use of Health Information Technology

The same executive order called for government agencies to require in contracts and agreements that whenever a health care provider, health plan, or health insurance issuer "implements, acquires, or upgrades health information technology systems, it shall utilize, where available, health information technology systems and products that meet recognized interoperability standards." Interoperability is a cornerstone of any efforts to collect information on quality of care, costs, and outcomes for reporting to consumers.

Cost of Care: Administered System Alternatives

Use Full Bargaining Power in Negotiation of Fees and Discounts

One bone of contention in the 2006 election was whether the federal government should use its full bargaining power in dealing with the pricing of prescription drugs under federal programs, especially Medicare Part D. Some government programs, such as the Veterans Administration Health System, bargain for and receive much lower prices than Medicare and Medicaid. Federal government policy about use of its monopsony buying power has been very mixed in terms of how strongly federal programs negotiate prices for purchases such as physician services, hospitals, home health services, and pharmaceuticals. It would appear that the lobbying and political power of the affected providers have a lot to do with the intensity of any bargaining. The ACA made further demands for discounting, but that legislation also limited the government's power to bargain.

Limit Eligibility and Covered Services in Entitlement and Categorical Programs

The budget process leads to many year-to-year changes in who and what gets covered in what program. Some of these changes are political, but some can be technologic as well. For example, the ESRD program has added alternatives such as outpatient dialysis centers, home dialysis, and transplantation to its original program of in-hospital dialysis. It has taken steps to encourage less expensive medical technology, including providing national support for organ donation and transportation.

Cost of Care: Consumer-Driven Competition Alternatives

Change Policy on Tax-Deductible Status of Employer-Paid Health Premiums and Individual Health Expenditures

President Bush's 2007 State of the Union message proposed a number of changes in the tax code pertaining to the deductibility of employer-paid and individually paid health care premiums. These proposals would have made individual premium payments fully deductible, just like employer payments, but put a cap of $7,500 per individual and $15,000 per couple on the overall deductibility of premiums. As of 2006, individual health care premiums were included with other health care costs, which could be deducted only if they exceeded 7.5% of adjusted income. The ACA raised the 7.5% hurdle to 10%.

Support Individual Medical Savings Accounts

Market-oriented strategies for controlling costs have gone through a number of phases. In the 1980s and early 1990s, HMOs were encouraged and were temporarily successful in slowing the rise in costs; however, as costs rose again, policy makers looked for alternative approaches. In the late 1990s, the concepts of consumer-centered care gained greater acceptance. More and more companies, faced with increased international competition and increasing inflation in their insurance premiums, felt a need to reduce or eliminate health care benefits. At the same time, there was greater acceptance of a philosophy of defined contribution pension plans replacing defined benefit plans. That made it easier to consider a similar transition for health insurance benefits. Because health care benefits are fully funded annually, the underlying drivers were not quite the same, but that paved the way conceptually for employers to pay a fixed amount regardless of the amount of cost inflation in health care.

There are two basic approaches to structuring limited-benefit plans. The older approach was to fund a basic plan with limited benefits and one or more high-premium plans with the employee responsible for paying the difference. This usually included the option of enrolling one's family and purchasing additional services, such as dental and long-term care insurance. The other approach is characterized by the high-deductible health plans with savings options that allow the consumer to assume more of the risks of health care costs, but to keep some of the winnings if the gamble pays off.

Where the basic plan limits the employee to a preferred-provider panel, one enhanced alternative is a point-of-service (POS) plan under which the employee can go to any provider and pay the difference between the negotiated rate and the provider's bill. This has been a popular option, because American patients strongly value having the freedom to choose their own providers.

Federal tax legislation supports the second alternative, the consumer-driven health plans approach, which often includes the following elements:

- The employer pays a fixed amount toward the employee's health benefit.
- It is paid into the employee's tax-sheltered health account (i.e., the HSA), which the employee controls and uses to pay for care.

- The money in that account that is not spent is allowed to accumulate from year to year.
- The employee is also covered by a high-deductible health insurance policy that provides protection from the worst effects of a catastrophic health event.
- The employee receives online support for health maintenance activities and access to information on provider quality and cost histories, discount programs, and the status of his or her health care account.

Privatize Parts of Medicare, Medicaid, and Other Federal Programs

The George W. Bush administration favored more of a private-market approach to federal programs such as Medicare and Medicaid (Texas Health and Human Services Commission, 2007). For example, private insurance companies were subsidized to offer Medicare Advantage plans that contracted with the federal government to provide Plan A and Plan B benefits to Medicare-eligible employees. The profit margins and executive compensation of many health care insurers rose rapidly. The ACA, however, reduced federal subsidies to Medicare Advantage. The motivation to privatize Medicaid is often the opportunity to capitate payments to contracted providers. The open-ended nature of fee-for-service payments under Medicaid has been a serious budgetary problem for most states, many of which have constitutional requirements for balanced budgets and none of which can print money.

Implement Information Technology and Price Transparency in Federal Programs and Promote Parallel Industrial Efforts

A letter to corporate CEOs from Secretary Leavitt illustrated that administration's vision for consumer-driven health care. In a brochure issued by the U.S. Department of Health and Human Services (Leavitt, 2006b), the secretary outlined the information that each purchaser of health care might need in order to support a major purchasing decision. This is reproduced in **Figure 5-1**. The example provided compares five hospitals on distance, several quality-related variables, and a cost estimate for a hip replacement procedure.

Support Consumer Information Reporting and Database Availability

The combination of health information technology gathering data at the source and the reporting envisioned for individual health care purchasers will have to be based on the development of systems that aggregate data

Surgical Care Consumer Guide
Search Results: **Hip Replacement**   What's included in the cost?

Summary
Average Cost in Network Facility: $11,249–$15,895
Out of Network Facility: $18,889–$23,460

Results sorted by: Distance   Sort by: | Quality   ▼ |

Key
Quality | **** Highest | * Lowest Costs $ Least Expensive | $$$$ Most Expensive Patient Assessment **** Highest | * Lowest

Distance (miles)	Facility Name	Patients per year	Quaity	Cost Estimate	Insurer pays	Patient pays	Patient Assessment of Care
6.2	Clearwater General 14280 Bay Drive Clearwater, FL 22131	400	***	$$ $15,895	85% ($13,511)	15% ($2,384)	**
13.2	All Saints Medical Center 123800 All Saintes Drive Tampa, FL 22122	86	****	$$$ $20,700	80% ($16,560)	20% ($4,140)	***
25.6	Good Samaritan Hospital 11111 E. Samaritan Drive Tampa, FL 22222	232	****	$$ $15,895	90% ($14,306)	10% ($1,590)	****
26.3	Tampa Hip Hospital 1400 East Tampa Boulevard Tampa, FL 22211	170	***	$$$ $20,700	75% ($15,525)	25% ($5,175)	***
27.3	Orthopedic Ciinical Hospital 1444 Goodle Drive St. Petersburg, FL 22113	432	*	$ $11,600	70% ($8,700)	25% ($2,900)	*
33.2	Valley General Hospital 1400 Tampa Bay Way Tampa Bay, FL 22031	310	***	$$ $16,230	85% ($13,796)	15% ($2,434)	***

Figure 5–1 The future.
Source: Reproduced from: M.O. Leavitt (2006) Better Care, Lower Cost: Prescription for Value-Driven Health Care. Washington, DC: Department of Health and Human Services. Retrieved January 30, 2007 from http://www.hhs.gov/transparency

from the providers and present them as needed to the consumers. This will be an expensive proposition, and how it will be financed is uncertain.

Cost of Care: Oligopolistic Competition Alternatives

Expand Managed Care and Disease Management Programs

Although the federal government began with and still maintains a fee-for-service philosophy for Medicare and Medicaid, it has encouraged state efforts to move more and more Medicaid recipients and dual eligibles (covered by both of the programs, mostly the disabled) into managed care programs and adopt disease management programs to control the costs of the 20% of the under 65 population who account for 80% of health care claims. Medicare Part D, the prescription drug benefit, represented a major change for that fee-for-service program; those who want the benefit must enroll in a Medicare prescription drug plan. Furthermore, many large HMOs are working to recruit Medicare patients by offering to waive the Part D premium, at least temporarily, if they also join their Medicare HMO. At the same time, the Medicare program is taxing the states for their share of the drug premiums for some 7 million enrollees, most of whom are active patients whose drugs were previously covered by Medicaid. This tax is a called the *clawback*. In essence, the clawback made the states partially responsible for funding Medicare. States have also been concerned about the drug benefit attracting more enrollees, sometimes called the *woodwork effect*, and about the loss of federal waivers that had allowed some states to receive matching federal funds for their existing pharmacy benefit programs.

Subsidize Capacity Reductions

Some areas and services have excess capacity, and are therefore likely to have high costs and high prices and to deliver unnecessary services. For example, on November 28, 2006, New York State's Commission on Health Care Facilities in the 21st Century recommended closing 7% of the state's hospital beds. This would have involved closing 9 hospitals and reconfiguring 48. The commission operated under a law setting up a process similar to the federal government's procedures for closing military bases. Its entire recommendation had the force of law unless the legislature or the governor turned down the proposal in its entirety by the end of the year. The state would receive $300 million per year for 5 years to defray the transition costs from the Federal-State Health Reform Partnership (Cooper & Chan, 2006). The legislature did not turn down the proposal and, despite court challenges, most of its recommendations were implemented in one form or another.

Constrain Anticompetitive Practices

The Federal Trade Commission (FTC) has been active in overseeing hospital mergers and in stopping constraints on professional service advertising once deemed "unethical" by professional associations. The Food and Drug Administration (FDA) also oversees the truthfulness of drug advertising claims, even those under a patent monopoly; however, much of the action to maintain or constrain the market in professional services is centered at the state level. States make and enforce professional licensure requirements and oversee their local health insurance markets.

Insurers have tended to compete on premium levels because of payer and consumer sensitivity to those payments. They have taken a number of steps to control costs. The easy way to do this is to discourage utilization of services. Ever since the HMO concept became widely accepted in the 1970s, many national and state government efforts have attempted to offset the market power of dominant insurers and providers and to offset any tendency to rely on anticompetitive practices against both payers and providers.

Other Interventions

The federal government also undertakes programs that support health care effectiveness but are not aligned with one political or economic point of view, including investments in medical research, professional education, and information technology. These tend to be individual legislative responses that fulfill generally accepted roles for government. The government at times also invests through public health education programs and screening programs. It may also choose to relax regulatory barriers that in effect reduce the investment requirements of providers, although the tendency has been toward more regulation, which often requires more government investment and more matching efforts by providers and provider organizations. Government also may respond to crisis situations or special situations that arise and gain public support.

Supporting Research, Development, and Deployment

Health care is a service sector with few major players that have enough geographic coverage, and hence enough volume, to amortize the costs of proprietary research programs. Possible exceptions are large insurers, hospital chains, and HMOs. The industry is dependent, therefore, on vendors such as the pharmaceutical industry and equipment suppliers to conduct applied research and product development; however, they, in turn, tend to focus on high-volume, patentable new technologies, often called *blockbusters*. This means there are gaps that government research programs must address:

- **Treatment methods.** These are developed by private industry where patentable and by the government and universities. The U.S. government has maintained world-class research organizations in the NIH and the CDC. AHRQ, a newer player, emphasizes research into treatments that are already in use. Much of the actual research is conducted by universities and contractors, but with the research strategy in the hands of the federal agencies. The ARRA increased the level of effort on comparative effective research with the founding of the Federal Council for Comparative Effectiveness Research with a budget of more than a billion dollars. The ACA founded the Patient Centered Outcomes Research Institute and declared that supporting and disseminating comparative effectiveness research is one of its objectives.

· **Delivery system methods.** Increasingly, the government has become involved in managerial innovations pertaining to the quality and cost of health care. Examples include the National Health Information Network, where the government is also facilitating deployment, and the work of the Institute of Medicine on medical errors and subsequent research to reduce error rates. This trend was recognized in the ACA through the formation of the Center for Medicare & Medicaid Innovation within the CMS.

Provider Quality and Availability

The issue of planning for the supply of health personnel has often been controversial. For example, there has been considerable political pulling and hauling about ensuring residency places for U.S. citizens who graduate from foreign medical schools. In many countries, the ministry of education decides how many professionals of what type will be trained, sometimes in collaboration with the ministry of health and sometimes without. In the United States, neither health care nor education is the responsibility of the central government, and thus the planning is highly decentralized. Individual schools and institutions, influenced by federal, state, and local budgets and local staffing needs, decide how many persons to admit and graduate at each level. Professional associations control supply to some extent by controlling the number of residency and training programs that they accredit, but they must be ever mindful of the possibility of antitrust actions when they try to cut back on the supply. Various nonprofit associations (boards) controlled by the professions handle postgraduate training, testing, and certification; however, the federal government plays a major role by providing grants that support training in shortage areas, such as nursing and pharmacy, and offering loan forgiveness to graduates who agree to work in underserved areas.

The ACA increased the amount and flexibility of funding for graduate medical education (GME) positions in primary care and general surgery. Unused slots will be reallocated with priority for underserved areas. Training for primary care residents and nurse practitioners will be supported in outpatient settings. The ACA included provisions for scholarships, loans, recruitment, grants to states to fund providers, program costs, and so on. The ACA also expanded nursing education at multiple levels. These initiatives are tied in with the ACA's emphasis on medical homes, ACOs, and coordinated management of preventive care and chronic diseases, including mental illness.

Health and Safety Regulation

The FDA is involved in many regulatory programs aimed at protecting the health and safety of the public, including drug and medical device approval, drug advertising, clinical laboratory standards and inspections, drug biologics manufacturing safety, and a host of other programs. NIH policy governs the use and maintenance of laboratory animals. Federal policy also supports a number of voluntary regulatory efforts, such as the activities of the Joint Commission and various professional societies, by requiring certification as a precondition for payments from federal programs.

Support Malpractice (Tort Law) Experimentation

The ACA included a Sense of the Senate paragraph supporting experimentation by the states with various methods of resolving malpractice claims. However, no specific approach was endorsed in that legislation.

Bundled Payments for Services

Porter and Teisberg (2006) have suggested that the United States needs to move to a system in which the full cost of treating a disease entity is made fully transparent by bundling various necessary services into a single price. Although prospective reimbursement systems have accomplished some of this for insurers, including the federal government, they have not translated into transparency for the buying public. It is not clear whether the transparency approach outlined by Secretary Leavitt (2006b) would have captured both physician and hospital and other provider costs into a single figure unless the providers had been integrated into a single billing institution.

The Obama administration provided support for development of the bundling alternative through demonstration projects. These were further authorized through the ACA, which made clear the intent of expanding the number of medical problems bundled and the implementation of a payment system involving bundling.

Special Situations and Opportunities

The federal government intervenes in special situations, such as hurricanes, by picking up the state and local shares of program funding and by offering tax and investment incentives. It is also sensitive to some high-visibility public health concerns, such as preparing for potential pandemics by developing and stockpiling vaccines and treatment supplies. Where the federal government sees an opportunity, such as community funding of access for the uninsured, it can allow allocation of budgeted funds to encourage experimentation and evaluation.

STATE AND LOCAL GOVERNMENT OPTIONS

In fiscal year 2004, Medicaid spending surpassed education as the largest item in state general funds budgets (SCI, 2006). The states have proven to be 50 distinct laboratories for developing health policy initiatives designed to increase access to care, especially for children and the uninsured. States continuously make trade-offs among programs and funding sources. Local governments, with encouragement from Washington, are also adding programs to ameliorate the problems of the uninsured, despite their limited and rather inflexible tax bases. Often they participate as partners with state government, Medicaid, employers, and insurers. A somewhat typical model is the 2005 three-share access program of Muskegon County, Michigan, for low-income uninsured workers (those making less than $11.50 per hour) who are not eligible for existing public programs. The employer pays about a third of the premium, and the worker and the community pay similar amounts. Local government funding comes from federal programs, and care must be delivered locally.

Table 5-3 provides a list of past, current, and proposed state and local government policy initiatives. Again, this is not intended to be exhaustive, as many of the federal government options in the earlier table also can be and are being implemented at these levels.

Access to Care: Administered System Alternatives

Universal Coverage Using Tax Revenues

State governments can attempt to provide universal coverage. States are unlikely to go much further than to reallocate existing federal and state health care funds without further taxation because they have greater financial constraints than the federal government. They cannot print money.

Table 5-3 Illustrations of State and Local Government Health Policy Options

Access to Care

- Administered system
  - Universal coverage using general revenues
  - Expanded/reduced eligibility and benefits
  - Mandated coverages and services
  - Captive providers (e.g., health department clinics)
  - Increase funding to enable full enrollment of eligible populations
- Consumer-driven competition
  - Individual mandate for health insurance
  - Modify medical practice constraints
  - Support cooperative buying arrangements for smaller businesses
- Oligopolistic competition
  - Mandate employer participation/play-or-pay
  - Impose special taxes on providers and insurers to subsidize low-income uninsured
  - Increase primary care provider supply
  - Support pooled insurance risks
  - Make reinsurance more widely available

Quality of Care

- Administered system
  - Encourage "medical home," especially for special needs enrollees
  - Use pay-for-performance approach in state purchased plans
  - Mandate installation and use of health information technology
- Consumer-driven competition
  - Support reporting of quality outcomes and quality survey data
  - Support interoperability and transferability of personal health records
- Oligopolistic competition
  - Support regional consumer information reporting and databases
  - Support pay-for-performance in private as well as public sector
  - Support training of providers in evidence-based practices

Cost of Care

- Administered system
  - Integrate Medicare and Medicaid services for dual eligibles
  - Negotiate program fees and discounts
  - Require disease management for special populations
  - Reduce/enhance primary care provider payments

(continues)

Table 5-3 Illustrations of State and Local Government Health Policy Options (*continued*)

- Consumer-driven competition
  - Strengthen antitrust laws and regulations
  - Remove insurance barriers to medical tourism
- Oligopolistic competition
  - Facilitate exchanges to enable access to more than one insurer's plans
  - Modify medical practice laws and constraints, as necessary, to encourage licensing and credentialing of new providers
  - Use certificate-of-need procedures
  - Encourage managed care and disease management
  - Enforce antitrust laws and regulations

Other Interventions

- Research and development (e.g., embryonic stem cell research)
- Capital investment
- Education of professionals
- Increase primary care provider supply
- Distribution of professionals and services
- Public health functions and departments
- Malpractice (tort law) reform

In Massachusetts, then-Governor Romney and the legislature agreed on a program intended to cover more than 95% of the population by requiring most citizens to carry health insurance or pay into a pool through the state income tax system. This approach also required employers to pay $295 per year per uncovered employee. Governor Romney used his line-item veto to try to strike this play-or-pay provision from the law, but the legislature overrode that veto.

Maine's Dirigo health plan was intended to cover most of the state's uninsured individuals by 2009. It was financed through savings from a series of related cost-cutting moves and provided sliding-scale subsidies to low-income families. At the end of 2013, it was superseded by a state exchange under the ACA.

Expanded/Reduced Eligibility and Benefits

Just as federal agencies can modify eligibility and benefits in their programs, state and local governments can do so in the programs that they fund. They also can apply for Medicaid waivers to reallocate resources in that program toward high-priority needs.

Mandated Coverages and Services

Hawaii has come closest to achieving universal coverage by requiring all employers except for those employing seasonal agricultural workers to provide a minimum level of group health coverage and to pay at least half the premium for all workers working 20 or more hours per week after 4 weeks of employment. Its laws also specify how to meet the needs of children, the disabled, and pregnant women. Other states have not been able to follow suit because the Hawaii plan required a congressional amendment to the ERISA law, and this has not been repeated. In March 2005, Tennessee ended coverage of some 320,000 adults enrolled in the TennCare program. Coverage for some 119,000 children continued. State and local governments can also determine what services are covered in the programs that they administer for their employees and client publics.

Captive Providers

A number of states and municipalities provide primary care services directly through their public health system. Many counties and municipalities also own their own local hospitals, many of which were built with federal government subsidies through the Hill-Burton legislation. Academic medical centers owned by state universities also have their own hospitals and faculty practice plans, often with some expectation of serving the state's population as well as training health personnel. State mental hospitals and other institutions for the disabled are usually the states' largest direct expenditures on health services after Medicaid.

State and local health departments and hospitals can be a source of free care for those without insurance. Often this is seen as a cost-reduction measure that keeps patients from getting sicker and presenting themselves in emergency rooms where care is more expensive. The Healthy San Francisco initiative, for instance, covered low-income individuals up to 500% of the FPL for a small fee and delivered care through health department clinics, health centers, and networked providers who provided a medical home. Individuals were still encouraged to maintain traditional health insurance where possible. The program did not provide for vision, dental, or any care provided outside the city. Many enrollees transitioned to Medi-Cal when it expanded under the ACA.

Increase Funding to Enable Full Enrollment of Eligible Populations

A number of existing programs are not fully funded by the states, and thus some eligible children and adults cannot receive the services intended for them. Governments at all levels could appropriate sufficient monies to cover all eligible individuals and their needs under existing programs.

Access to Care: Consumer-Driven Competition Alternatives

Individual Mandate for Health Insurance

Massachusetts led the way in this, and it has been followed up by the mandate in the ACA. It is still unclear what proportion of the population will choose to pay the tax penalty rather than purchase insurance.

Modify Medical Practice Constraints

Delivery of health care is tightly constrained in the United States by any number of laws and regulations governing medical practice that apply to individuals and institutions. State medical practice acts and reimbursement policies can have a profound impact on the supply of potential providers. There are many possible substitute workers who can perform specific tasks, or pieces of tasks, done by existing professionals: psychologists, psychiatrists, nurse practitioners, and physician assistants for primary care and emergency room physicians, nurse midwives for obstetricians, nurse anesthetists for anesthesiologists, dental hygienists for dentists, pharmacy technicians for pharmacists, and so forth. State governments can step in and expand the allowable roles of substituting professions, increasing the supply of services, and potentially reducing the costs of care.

Support Cooperative Buying Arrangements for Small Employers

A number of states have developed buying cooperatives for small businesses seeking to provide coverage for their employees. State or local governments may or may not choose to pay part of the premium costs for those participating in their buying pools.

Access to Care: Oligopolistic System Alternatives

Mandate Employer Participation/Play-or-Pay

Even before the ACA, states had been experimenting with mandates on employers, usually the large and medium-sized ones, to provide health insurance. Typically, employers that chose not to pay insurance premiums were required to pay a set amount per employee per month to a pool that would cover health insurance purchases for their employees. These payments were seldom sufficient to cover the full premium, and thus additional funding sources were usually needed. Efforts to impose state "play-or-pay" requirements on self-insured firms exempted under ERISA would be of questionable legality. The ACA specifically states that Hawaii's Prepaid Health Care Act (PHCA), that state's employer mandate, is not modified or limited or universally preempted by the ACA. Further experimentation by states is unlikely given the federal employer mandate and continuing ERISA issues.

Impose Special Taxes on Providers and Insurers to Subsidize Low-Income Uninsured

Former California Governor Schwarzenegger proposed a 4% payroll tax that would go into a state insurance fund. Doctors and hospitals would pay 2–4% of their revenues into that fund to subsidize insurance for low-income individuals and increase Medicaid payments to physicians (Fuhrmans, 2007a). Other states have applied variants of this approach.

Increase the Supply of Primary Care Providers

Many states have offices that are trying to expand primary health care services in low-income urban and rural areas. These often work in collaboration with the National Health Service Corps in setting up clinical services in those areas. States may also mandate coverage for alternative and complementary health services. Most states require inclusion of chiropractors as providers. In the State of Washington, health insurance programs must cover acupuncture (the self-insured are excluded).

State educational systems also play a major role in determining the supply of medical providers. When there is a shortage of professionals, state educational institutions are quick to expand their programs; however, it is harder to get them to cut back when there appears to be an oversupply.

Support Pooled Insurance Risks

Most of us are familiar with risk pools in auto insurance, where drivers with poor claims records are assigned to a pool and each insurance company operating in the state must take a proportionate share of those in the pool as an assigned risk at an assigned rate. The same can be done with high-risk patients, forcing the companies that want the lucrative business in a state to take a certain proportion of the chronically ill from specific categories in order to participate. That reduces the likelihood that those sicker patients will be excluded by the insurance-underwriting process. A number of states have pooled-risk programs, but the limitations on underwriting in the ACA may make them less relevant.

One frequently debated option is community rating, in which the whole community is a single pool and the insurer cannot profit by excluding sicker citizens or pricing them out of the market; however, the insurance industry has strongly resisted this concept as unfair to those who take care of their health. The ACA effectively limited the ability of insurers to underwrite, but it did allow limited premium differentials based on age.

States can use their powers to regulate insurance to encourage plans that pool health insurance risks. This can be encouraged in a number of ways, including:

- Barring discrimination through underwriting against high-risk individuals under existing employer programs
- Establishing special pools of high-risk enrollees, a portion of which must be accepted by the insurance companies that want to participate in the state's markets at a special rate (usually with a subsidy from the state)
- Cross-subsidizing the high-risk enrollees through a special tax on all health care premiums that is used to offset their higher premiums

Make Reinsurance More Widely Available

An alternative to or a supplement to risk pools is a reinsurance program. Under that program, the risk of catastrophic cases would be borne by a master policy with other insurers or by a state-financed entity. In New York, the state has offered a reinsurance program since 2001, thereby allowing catastrophic coverage for sole proprietors, small firms, and low-income workers at more reasonable rates. The ACA requires states to establish transitional reinsurance programs in connection with their exchanges in an effort to stabilize prices. If they do not, the U.S. Department of Health and Human Services will step in and do it for them.

Quality of Care: Administered System Alternatives

Encourage "Medical Homes" for Special Needs Enrollees

The American Academy of Pediatrics (2007) has advocated that categorical plans and Medicaid plans require that each covered child with special needs have a medical home; that is, a designated provider who would provide continuity of care, know the family and child's situation, work with the family, coordinate community-based services, and follow up on the case in a timely manner. Many states are working to expand this concept beyond children, and many provisions of the ACA are meant to promote medical homes.

Use the Pay-for-Performance Approach in State-Purchased Plans

Each state and local government is a major regional purchaser of health care, including Medicaid and coverage for its employees and retirees and their families; therefore, these governments can insist that pay-for-performance systems be included in their purchase specifications and care contracts.

Quality of Care: Consumer-Driven Competition Alternatives

Mandate Installation and Use of Health Information Technology

State and local governments can likewise use their buying power to require the expansion and use of health information technology with their clients, including computerized physician electronic order entry and electronic medical records. They can also support economically the development of interoperable community health information networks.

Support Reporting of Quality Outcomes and Quality Survey Data

State and local governments can demand quality transparency for their employee and dependents programs and through funding of surveys and database systems for public use.

Support Interoperability and Transferability of Personal Health Records

State and local governments can encourage the development of local quality reporting systems by supporting requirements for interoperability and transferability of personal health records. The Health Information Technology for Economic and Clinical Health (HITECH) Act has supported this at the federal level with its meaningful use requirements. However, states and local communities will have to work hard to overcome the propensity of institutions to avoid sharing data. One option would be to legislate that patient records are the property of the patient and that they must be made available digitally in a transferable form at low cost.

Quality of Care: Oligopolistic Competition Alternatives

Support Regional Consumer Information Reporting and Databases

Many states already have their own quality-reporting requirements for hospitals, similar to the Medicare requirements. However, states must make sure that their regulations affecting insurance and professional licensure and credentialing motivate and facilitate release and reporting of quality and cost information.

Support Pay-for-Performance in the Private as Well as Public Sector

Federal and state programs can publicize the effects of pay-for-performance plans in public pronouncements and encourage the release of the information to local networks by including such requirements when they contract for coverage of state employees and their dependents, as well as Medicaid contracts. Such a system, once in place, can be a conduit for information to all parties involved.

Support Training of Providers in Evidence-Based Practices

State institutions provide much of the training of providers through universities and continuing education systems. In overseeing and funding such programs, states can have considerable impact on the pace of adoption of evidence-based practices through continuing education courses and academic detailing.

Cost of Care: Administered System Alternatives

Integrate Medicare and Medicaid Services for Dual Eligibles

Individuals with disabilities are often eligible for Medicare and Medicaid and are among the higher cost users of health care. Many have behavioral health issues as well as physical problems. The ACA permits states to undertake an integrated program of care for these individuals after submitting a proposal for coverage to CMS. Many states have already submitted proposals to do so mostly because it is a first step toward capitation and limitation of risk for the state.

Negotiate Program Fees and Discounts

State and local governments can ask for bids from various providers and then select a small number who offer the lowest prices, or more often, the deepest discounts off published prices. Other requirements in the bidding process may also determine the availability of suppliers, such as 24/7 services, access to hospital beds, financial strength, number of years in business, and special certification or licensure requirements.

State and local governments also can enlist suppliers and especially regulated insurers into any number of possible cost-sharing or premium-supplementing arrangements. For example, the governor of Pennsylvania negotiated a deal in 2005 with the state's four nonprofit Blue Cross insurers to contribute 1.6% of their premium revenue over 6 years plus 1% of their Medicare and Medicaid premiums (close to $1 billion dollars) from retained earnings to a state fund that would pay for coverage for low-income and uninsured individuals.

Require Disease Management for Special Populations

State plans have adopted a wide variety of strategies for inducing their enrollees to join HMOs and accept disease management alternatives. They have mandated these approaches in some cases. In others, they have offered a number of inducements for those who elect to accept that type of coverage.

Reduce/Enhance Provider Payments

For a number of years, just about every state has been reducing or freezing payments to providers under their Medicaid programs. Despite inflation controls, a growing caseload and improved access have increased the costs to the states by a rate of almost 9% annually. A significant proportion of the community-based provider population does not take Medicaid patients. States often adjust payments upward where there is a shortage of providers. An example is increasing the compensation of obstetricians because ensuring access to prenatal care providers is likely to offset major preventable costs later.

Cost of Care: Consumer-Driven Competition Alternatives

Strengthen Antitrust Laws and Regulations

States can legislate against specific anticompetitive practices. For example, Pennsylvania law duplicates and supplements a number of the federal anti-kickback and Stark amendment provisions. One section prohibits hospitals from renting clinic or office space to physicians below market. Others require disclosure to patients that their doctor has an economic interest in the facility to which they are being referred and that they are informed of their rights to choose an alternative facility.

Many HMOs require their providers to be board certified. This is a marketing decision that adds another constraint to the local supply of providers. Professional organizations must also approve residency programs in their specialties, thereby exerting some control nationally over the quantity and quality of services available. Large HMO organizations may become dominant in a region and limit the options for other would-be providers.

To offset some of these possible anticompetitive effects, states have countered with antitrust actions and with *any willing provider* legislation. Such legislation often addresses two issues, namely (1) restrictions on the panel of providers that a patient can access within a profession and (2) restrictions across professions as to who can be compensated for a service. Under such a law, for example, if a person has acute low-back pain, the insurer cannot limit the patient to seeing a small number of pain experts and clinics, and it cannot limit payment to primary care physicians and orthopedic specialists. It may also be required to include coverage for chiropractors and acupuncturists. Some argue that such laws hinder institutional cost-control efforts.

Remove Insurance Barriers to Medical Tourism

The primary barrier to medical tourism (individuals leaving the country to seek nonemergency health care at much lower costs plus tourism inducements) is the fact that it has not been covered by many health insurance contracts. Mattoo and Rathindran (2006) suggested that failure to do so is due to the oligopoly nature of the private health insurance industry. These companies operate under the regulatory umbrella of state insurance commissioners. They argue that patients can and do move, making health care an item of international trade, and that quality need not be a problem when certification is available through the Joint Commission International and the U.S. Medical Licensing Examination. They point out that 25% of U.S. physicians, including 20% of medical school faculty, and 14% of U.S. nurses trained abroad and that modern, well-equipped facilities are available.

They and Altman et al. (2006) provided data showing savings of 40–65% and more, even after travel and lodging costs, for procedures such as hip and knee replacements, cardiac and gallbladder surgery, hysterectomy, and rhinoplasty. Foreign providers are increasingly represented by sales organizations in the United States that are negotiating contracts directly with self-insured employers to add foreign doctors and hospitals to their provider networks. More recently, intermediaries have sprung up to support medical tourism within the United States, brokering the capacity of underutilized facilities.

Cost of Care: Oligopolistic System Alternatives

Facilitate the Exchange System to Enable Access to
More Than One Insurer's Plans

One innovation of the Massachusetts legislation to achieve near-universal coverage is the "Connector." There has been some confusion because there are two components under that label. One is the Connector Authority, which negotiates with insurers for basic policies for the uninsured and sets the level of subsidy that the state will contribute for those between the Medicaid upper limit and 300% of FPL. The other is the digital insurance exchange called the "Connector," which allows individuals to compare prices and coverages of all the participating insurers to determine which plan best meets their individual needs. These individuals include the working poor and those with higher incomes whose employers do not offer insurance. This enables them to meet the individual mandate for health insurance required under law in Massachusetts. This innovation became the template for the exchanges in the ACA legislation.

Modify Medical Practice Laws and Constraints, as Necessary, to Encourage
Licensing and Credentialing of New Providers

Most professionals are licensed by state boards, whereas most specialists are certified by national professional boards. All of these represent an opportunity for restricting entry. The FTC has been aware of this issue and has moved decisively against the professions enforcing rules against advertising by their members. Any attempt to introduce a new type of provider that will perform a limited range of services at lower cost has usually been resisted by the entrenched professions. In general, legislatures have had to intervene, citing the needs of underserved areas or populations. Examples include nurse practitioners, physician assistants, and surgicenters.

Use Certificate-of-Need Procedures

Certificate-of-need legislation requires that providers obtain state approval of additional major capital investments in items such as imaging equipment and additional bed capacity if they are to receive reimbursement. It is an attempt to mediate arms races among provider institutions; however, it is typically a highly political process that has often lacked effectiveness, and it is opposed by those who argue that it stifles competition by limiting entry into the field and can be used to stop successful competitors from expanding to meet demand.

Encourage Managed Care and Disease Management

Texas has implemented managed care programs for its Medicaid population targeting a number of chronic diseases. It also had implemented a preferred drug list program for Medicaid requiring a supplemental rebate or special proposal for negotiation (Texas Health and Human Services Commission, 2007). A number of states have continued to follow this trend.

Enforce Antitrust Laws and Regulations

States have their own antitrust laws and regulations that can be applied to mergers of organizations such as hospitals. States can also outlaw anticompetitive practices, which include colluding to set prices for services and attempts by licensing boards and professional societies to limit new entrants.

State antitrust laws can also be used to overcome too much concentration in specific markets, although many major health care markets are clearly multistate, especially those involving complex or specialized referrals.

Other Interventions

Research and Development

Health care research and development have usually been activities of the federal government; however, when the policies of the George W. Bush administration restricted embryonic stem cell research, California acted to set up its own funding.

Capital Investment

Although most states do not fund health care facility construction and renovation directly, many have authority to issue special-purpose bonds on behalf of the state's nonprofit health care institutions. The objective of these agencies is to reduce the funding costs for each borrower by going to the market in larger amounts with a broader risk pool. In most cases, institutions have borrowed at lower rates when the states backed the securities.

Education of Professionals

State-owned technical schools, colleges, and universities are major suppliers of health care personnel. They are often sensitive to the personnel needs perceived by legislatures and local institutions. States frequently have offices and programs that recruit personnel and support services in rural areas. Area Health Education Centers (AHECs) are an example of an extensive support system for dispersed personnel. They provide both training and specialized services to areas of need.

Public Health Functions and Departments

States also administer the traditional public health system in conjunction with local government units. Sometimes these offer primary care to the indigent. Virtually all jurisdictions provide the basic public health services of maternal and child health clinics, infectious disease control, health education, sanitary inspections, and environmental health and safety inspections. Ten essential public health services are frequently cited (**Table 5-4**).

Malpractice (Tort Law) Reform

There is a high level of dissatisfaction with the costs of malpractice litigation and resulting premiums for malpractice insurance and with the costs

Table 5-4 Essential Public Health Services

1. Monitor health status to identify community problems.
2. Diagnose and investigate health problems and health hazards in the community.
3. Inform, educate, and empower people about health problems.
4. Mobilize community partnerships to identify and solve community problems.
5. Develop plans and policies that support individual and community health efforts.
6. Enforce laws and regulations that protect health and ensure safety.
7. Link people to needed personal health services and ensure provision of care.
8. Ensure a competent public and personal health care workforce.
9. Evaluate the effectiveness, accessibility, and quality of personal and population-based health care.
10. Research for new insights and innovative solutions to health problems.

Source: Reproduced from: Centers for Disease Control and Prevention (2013). National Public Health Performance Standards. Retrieved on March 29, 2014 from http://www.cdc.gov/nphpsp/essentialservices.html

of defensive medicine. A number of states have intervened to set health care apart from their usual tort law procedures and remedies. Various remedies have been proposed and many experimented with by states.

Tort law reform usually refers to legislation limiting (capping) the size of malpractice awards caused by negligence, especially the components awarded for pain and suffering and as penalties for gross negligence, and/or limiting the contingent fees paid to lawyers who win such cases. Because the cost of malpractice suits and insurance is much higher in the United States than any other country and legal fees and court costs consume close to half of the awards, a number of alternatives have been proposed, including the following:

- No-fault malpractice insurance similar to that used in some states for auto insurance
- Mandatory arbitration or mediation
- Institutional (enterprise) liability on a no-fault basis

All of these bypass the system of jury trials currently used to prove or disprove negligence and assume that juries and plaintiffs' lawyers are responsible for the size of the awards. Proponents of enterprise liability believe that after an organization sees negligence cases as costing it directly, it will act to reduce such errors in ways that the professions have so far been unwilling or unable to adopt.

CONCLUSION

The U.S. market for health care is very much influenced by governments in their roles as payers, insurers, employers, regulators, and providers of last resort. Much of the public debate is over the possibilities of more reliance on the marketplace. Whatever the ideology adopted, governments must deal with the following concerns:

- Information asymmetry coupled with product complexity
- The conflicting roles of providers as agents for both patients and others
- The tendency of market systems to maximize consumption

Thus we see governments adopting a confusing and seemingly inconsistent array of measures designed to deal with these concerns. For example, resources go out to enhance access to services, expanding the supply of providers and technology, at the same time that other programs seek to constrain consumption. No wonder professionals caught up in this maelstrom sometimes feel discouraged. Still, most professionals persevere and reap the intellectual and personal rewards of their craft. They continue to balance the interests of their patients and their organizations successfully.

All of this reflects the Chinese curse: "May you live in interesting times."

Case 5   Key Features of the Affordable Care Act, by Year (Abridged from HealthCare.gov)

The following time line describes the key features of the ACA and the year of implementation as provided by the HealthCare.gov website (HealthCare.gov, 2013).

2010

New Consumer Protections

- **Putting information for consumers online.** The law provides for sites where consumers can compare health insurance coverage options and pick the coverage that works for them.
- **Prohibiting denying coverage of children based on preexisting conditions.** New rules to prevent insurance companies from denying coverage to children under the age of 19 due to a preexisting condition.
- **Prohibiting insurance companies from rescinding coverage.** In the past, insurance companies could search for an error, or other technical mistake, on a customer's application and use this error to deny payment for services when he or she got sick. The health care law makes this illegal.
- **Eliminating lifetime limits on insurance coverage.** Insurance companies are prohibited from imposing lifetime dollar limits on essential benefits, like hospital stays.
- **Regulating annual limits on insurance coverage.** Under the law, insurance companies' use of annual dollar limits on the amount of insurance coverage a patient may receive will be restricted for new plans in the individual market and all group plans. In 2014, the use of annual dollar limits on essential benefits like hospital stays will be banned for new plans in the individual market and all group plans.

Case 5   (*continued*)

- **Appealing insurance company decisions.** The law provides consumers with a way to appeal coverage determinations or claims to their insurance company and establishes an external review process.
- **Establishing consumer assistance programs in the states.** Under the law, states that apply receive federal grants to help set up or expand independent offices to help consumers navigate the private health insurance system.

Improving Quality and Lowering Costs

- **Providing small business health insurance tax credits.** Up to 4 million small businesses are eligible for tax credits to help them provide insurance benefits to their workers. The first phase of this provision provides a credit worth up to 35% of the employer's contribution to the employees' health insurance. Small non-profit organizations may receive up to a 25% credit.
- **Offering relief for 4 million seniors who hit the Medicare prescription drug "donut hole."** An estimated 4 million seniors will reach the gap in Medicare prescription drug coverage known as the "donut hole" this year. Each eligible senior will receive a one-time, tax-free $250 rebate check.
- **Providing free preventive care.** All new plans must cover certain preventive services, such as mammograms and colonoscopies, without charging a deductible, copay, or coinsurance.
- **Preventing disease and illness.** A new $15 billion Prevention and Public Health Fund will invest in proven prevention and public health programs that can help keep Americans healthy—from smoking cessation to combating obesity.
- **Cracking down on health care fraud.** The new law invests new resources and requires new screening procedures for health care providers to boost these efforts and reduce fraud and waste in Medicare, Medicaid, and Children's Health Insurance Program (CHIP).

Increasing Access to Affordable Care

- **Providing access to insurance for uninsured Americans with preexisting conditions.** The Pre-Existing Condition Insurance Plan provides new coverage options to individuals who have been uninsured for at least 6 months because of a preexisting condition. States have the option of running this program in their state. If a state chooses not to do so, a plan will be established by the Department of Health and Human Services in that state.
- **Extending coverage for young adults.** Young adults will be allowed to stay on their parents' plan until they turn 26.
- **Expanding coverage for early retirees.** To preserve employer coverage for early retirees until more affordable coverage is available through the new exchanges by 2014, the new law creates a $5 billion program to provide needed financial help for employment-based plans to continue to provide valuable coverage to people who retire between the ages of 55 and 65, as well as their spouses and dependents.
- **Rebuilding the primary care workforce.** There are new incentives in the law to expand the number of primary care doctors, nurses, and physician assistants. These include funding for scholarships and loan repayments for primary care doctors and nurses working in underserved areas. Doctors and nurses receiving payments made under any state loan repayment or loan forgiveness program intended to increase the availability of health care services in underserved or health professional shortage areas will not have to pay taxes on those payments.
- **Holding insurance companies accountable for unreasonable rate hikes.** The law allows states that have, or plan to implement, measures that require insurance companies to justify their premium increases will be eligible for $250 million in new grants. Insurance companies with excessive or unjustified premium exchanges may not be able to participate in the new health insurance exchanges in 2014.
- **Allowing states to cover more people on Medicaid.** States will be able to receive federal matching funds for covering some additional low-income individuals and families under Medicaid for whom federal funds were not previously available. This will

Case 5   (*continued*)

make it easier for states that choose to do so to cover more of
their residents.

- **Increasing payments for rural health care providers.** The law
  provides increased payment to rural health care providers to help
  them continue to serve their communities.
- **Strengthening community health centers.** The law includes
  new funding to support the construction of and expand services
  at community health centers.

2011

Improving Quality and Lowering Costs

- **Offering prescription drug discounts.** Seniors who reach the
  coverage gap will receive a 50% discount when buying Medicare
  Part D covered brand-name prescription drugs. Over the next
  10 years, seniors will receive additional savings on brand-name
  and generic drugs until the coverage gap is closed in 2020.
- **Providing free preventive care for seniors.** The law provides
  certain free preventive services, such as annual wellness visits and
  personalized prevention plans, for seniors on Medicare.
- **Improving health care quality and efficiency.** The law establishes a new Center for Medicare & Medicaid Innovation that will
  begin testing new ways of delivering care to patients. Additionally, by January 1, 2011, the Department of Health and Human
  Services (HHS) will submit a national strategy for quality
  improvement in health care, including by these programs.
- **Improving care for seniors after they leave the hospital.**
  The Community Care Transitions Program will help high-risk
  Medicare beneficiaries who are hospitalized avoid unnecessary
  readmissions by coordinating care and connecting patients to
  services in their communities.
- **Introducing new innovations to bring down costs.** The
  Independent Payment Advisory Board will begin operations to

develop and submit proposals to Congress and the president aimed at extending the life of the Medicare Trust Fund. The board is expected to focus on ways to target waste in the system and recommend ways to reduce costs, improve health outcomes for patients, and expand access to high-quality care.

Increasing Access to Affordable Care

- **Increasing access to services at home and in the community.** The Community First Choice Option allows states to offer home and community-based services to disabled individuals through Medicaid rather than institutional care in nursing homes.

Holding Insurance Companies Accountable

- **Bringing down health care premiums.** The law generally requires that at least 85% of all premium dollars collected by insurance companies for large employer plans are spent on health care services and health care quality improvement. For plans sold to individuals and small employers, at least 80% of the premium must be spent on benefits and quality improvement. If insurance companies do not meet these goals, because their administrative costs or profits are too high, they must provide rebates to consumers.
- **Addressing overpayments to big insurance companies and strengthening Medicare Advantage.** Today, Medicare pays Medicare Advantage insurance companies over $1,000 more per person on average than is spent per person in traditional Medicare. This results in increased premiums for all Medicare beneficiaries, including the 77% of beneficiaries who are not currently enrolled in a Medicare Advantage plan. The law levels the playing field by gradually eliminating this discrepancy. People enrolled in a Medicare Advantage plan will still receive all guaranteed Medicare benefits, and the law provides bonus payments to Medicare Advantage plans that provide high-quality care.

Case 5 (*continued*)

2012

Improving Quality and Lowering Costs

- **Linking payment to quality outcomes.** The law establishes a hospital value-based purchasing (VBP) program in traditional Medicare. This program offers financial incentives to hospitals to improve the quality of care. Hospital performance is required to be publicly reported, beginning with measures relating to heart attacks, heart failure, pneumonia, surgical care, health care–associated infections, and patients' perception of care.
- **Encouraging integrated health systems.** The new law provides incentives for physicians to join together to form ACOs. These groups allow doctors to better coordinate patient care and improve the quality, help prevent disease and illness, and reduce unnecessary hospital admissions. If ACOs provide high-quality care and reduce costs to the health care system, they can keep some of the money that they have helped save.
- **Reducing paperwork and administrative costs.** The new law will institute a series of changes to standardize billing and requires health plans to begin adopting and implementing rules for the secure, confidential, electronic exchange of health information.
- **Understanding and fighting health disparities.** To help understand and reduce persistent health disparities, the law requires any ongoing or new federal health program to collect and report racial, ethnic, and language data.

Increasing Access to Affordable Care

- **Providing new, voluntary options for long-term care insurance.** The law creates a voluntary long-term care insurance program—called CLASS—to provide cash benefits to adults who become disabled. [Note: On October 14, 2011, Secretary Sebelius transmitted a report and letter to Congress stating that the department does not see a viable path forward for CLASS implementation at this time.]

2013

Improving Quality and Lowering Costs

- **Improving preventive health coverage.** To expand the number of Americans receiving preventive care, the law provides new funding to state Medicaid programs that choose to cover preventive services for patients at little or no cost.
- **Expanding authority to bundle payments.** The law establishes a national pilot program to encourage hospitals, doctors, and other providers to work together to improve the coordination and quality of patient care. Under payment "bundling," hospitals, doctors, and providers are paid a flat rate for an episode of care rather than the current fragmented system where each service or test or bundles of items or services are billed separately to Medicare.

Increasing Access to Affordable Care

- **Increasing Medicaid payments for primary care doctors.** The act requires states to pay primary care physicians no less than 100% of Medicare payment rates in 2013 and 2014 for primary care services. The increase is fully funded by the federal government.
- **Open enrollment in the health insurance marketplace begins.** Individuals and small businesses can buy affordable and qualified health benefit plans in this new transparent and competitive insurance marketplace.

2014

New Consumer Protections

- **Prohibiting discrimination due to preexisting conditions or gender.** The law prohibit(s) insurance companies from refusing to sell coverage or renew policies because of an individual's preexisting conditions. Also, in the individual and small group market, the law eliminates the ability of insurance companies to charge higher rates due to gender or health status.

Case 5   (*continued*)

- **Eliminating annual limits on insurance coverage.** The law prohibits new plans and existing group plans from imposing annual dollar limits on the amount of coverage an individual may receive.
- **Ensuring coverage for individuals participating in clinical trials.** Insurers will be prohibited from dropping or limiting coverage because an individual chooses to participate in a clinical trial. Applies to all clinical trials that treat cancer or other life-threatening diseases.

Improving Quality and Lowering Costs

- **Making care more affordable.** Tax credits will become available for people with income between 100% and 400% of the poverty line who are not eligible for other affordable coverage. (In 2010, 400% of the poverty line comes out to about $43,000 for an individual or $88,000 for a family of four.) The tax credit is advanceable. It is also refundable. Individuals may also qualify for reduced cost-sharing (copayments, coinsurance, and deductibles).
- **Establishing the health insurance marketplace.** If your employer does not offer insurance, you will be able to buy it directly in the health insurance marketplace. Individuals and small businesses can buy affordable and qualified health benefit plans in this new transparent and competitive insurance marketplace. The marketplace will offer you a choice of health plans that meet certain benefits and cost standards.
- **Increasing the small business tax credit.** In this phase, the credit is up to 50% of the employer's contribution to provide health insurance for employees. There is also up to a 35% credit for small nonprofit organizations.

Increasing Access to Affordable Care

- **Increasing access to Medicaid.** Americans who earn less than 133% of the poverty level (approximately $14,000 for an individual and $29,000 for a family of four) will be eligible to enroll in

Medicaid. States will receive 100% federal funding for the first 3 years to support this expanded coverage, phasing to 90% federal funding in subsequent years.

- **Promoting individual responsibility.** Under the law, most individuals who can afford it will be required to obtain basic health insurance coverage or pay a fee to help offset the costs of caring for uninsured Americans. If affordable coverage is not available to an individual, he or she will be eligible for an exemption.

2015

Improving Quality and Lowering Costs

- **Paying physicians based on value not volume.** Physicians will see their payments modified so that those who provide higher value care will receive higher payments than those who provide lower quality care.

Source: Modified from: Key Features of the Affordable Care Act by Year. U.S. Department of Health & Human Services. http://www.hhs.gov/healthcare/facts/timeline/timeline-text.html

Discussion Questions

1. The material presented in this case was abridged from a document provided by the Obama administration on the HealthCare.gov website. Does it fairly represent the key issues in the law?

2. What do you think was behind the phasing in of the various provisions of the law? Would you have phased them in differently?

3. How do these provisions represent the three visions of how health policy should work?

4. How has the implementation of this time line changed over time:
   a. After the Supreme Court ruled on the constitutionality of various provisions of the ACA in 2013,
   b. As the Administration experienced problems with the computer systems it had put in place, and
   c. As various groups requested temporary or permanent relief from the law's implementation requirements?

Chapter 6

Alternative Responses and Initiatives of Institutions and Professions

Nongovernmental health care organizations provide most medical services and handle the financing of much of the system. For-profit and nonprofit institutions operate side by side, often competing directly for the same business.

This chapter identifies a number of strategies that individuals and organizations adopt in response to governmental programs or initiate on their own to influence health policy. We start with **Table 6-1**, which outlines the actors and the alternatives for responding to government actions and the marketplace. Where alternatives have been addressed and terms defined in earlier chapters, we try not to repeat that information.

COMMON RESPONSES

All of the players listed in Table 6-1 employ strategies to influence the marketplace and its regulators. These can be classified into three main types of interventions:

- Public relations
- Marketing and education
- Lobbying

Table 6-1 Responses and Initiatives of Institutions and Professions

Common Approaches

· Public relations
· Marketing and education
· Lobbying

Payers

· Employers
  · Eligibility
  · Subsidy offered
  · Plans offered
  · Relationship with insurers/self-insurance
  · Worker education and training
· Insurers
  · Method of organization
  · Method of payment
  · Plans offered
  · Case management/carve-outs
  · Utilization constraints
  · Consumer education

Providers

· Professionals
  · Organization of practice
  · Services offered
  · Incentives
  · Pricing
  · Patient relationships
  · Primary versus specialty care
  · Efficiency
· Institutions
  · Organizational structure
  · Scope and scale of services
  · Pricing/discounts
  · Efficiency
  · Quality improvement
  · Consumer information
  · Credentialing decisions
  · Involving payers in change processes

Table 6-1 Responses and Initiatives of Institutions and Professions (*continued*)

· Professions
  · Quality improvement
  · Provider education
  · Consumer education

Consumers

· Plan selection
· Provider selection
· Self-help

Each player manages its relationships with the media and with politicians and regulators directly, and each acts indirectly through trade associations and professional groups. You will see illustrations of this throughout the cases included in this text and in subsequent chapters dealing with political feasibility and values. The focus of each intervention changes depending on the nature of the specific market. Lobbying is particularly intense in administered markets such as Medicare and Medicaid, especially when new legislation is under consideration. Lobbying also goes on continuously with the relevant executive branch agencies. Public relations and education are used more assertively when regulators are considering changes, and marketing, especially advertising, is most intense where the market is less regulated. The term *education* can apply to the many different types of efforts to influence behavior. Government antismoking campaigns can be characterized as education, for example, but the term can also be used as one of the rationales behind highly commercial interventions, such as direct-to-consumer advertising of prescription drugs.

PAYERS

Customarily, the term *payers* refers to the financial entities, usually insurers, who pay the bills; however, they are only intermediaries for the true payers, those who sign the contracts for care, who are usually employers and the government. In an increasing number of cases, insurers will cover individuals who purchase their policies directly or through state and federal insurance exchanges, if they choose to participate in them.

Employers

Employment-based health care benefits have changed markedly since the 1950s. At first, employers were very passive about whether their unions took collective bargaining settlements as wages or as benefits and how those benefits were distributed. All that they cared about was the immediate cost per hour of the total contract agreement. Health care costs were low, and the workforce was young; however, these defined benefit packages took on a life of their own as costs in both pensions and health care began to rise much faster than prices or productivity. Now employers have to deal with both rising costs and the reactions of employees, retirees, and the public when they reduce benefits. A number of U.S. steel and airline companies, for example, have gone through Chapter 11 bankruptcy proceedings in part to free themselves of these "legacy" liabilities for their employees, even the unionized ones.

Employers compete for the best workers, especially the highly skilled ones, in every labor market. They want their health benefits for workers and their families to be in line with those offered by competing employers. If benefits are too low, better employees will go elsewhere. If they are too high, the employer will attract those with high health care costs or health risks in their families (adverse selection) and become saddled with higher costs than their competition.

With the passage of the Affordable Care Act (ACA), employers with more than 50 full-time employees that have not offered a health insurance benefit or that are considering dropping it have to factor in the cost of the penalty, which is $2,000 to $3,000 per uncovered employee. This is, of course, well below the average nonpublic employer contribution for individual premium coverage, which was about $4,500 in 2012.

Eligibility

Employers can decide who gets health care benefits and when they start. New employees usually have a waiting period before they are eligible for health care benefits. Full coverage is typically limited to full-time, directly employed individuals and their families. This is one reason why contract employment and outsourcing have become so attractive. Contracting relieves the employer of the direct expense of health care and pension benefits, although some of those costs are probably reflected in higher wages paid to skilled contract employees and in the bids from prospective domestic suppliers. Under provisions of the ACA, however, federal regulations will determine who is considered a full-time employee for penalty purposes (initially,

30 hours or more of service per week or 130 hours in a month), and employer working hours and benefit policies will tend to align with that.

Subsidy Offered

The proportion of employees' health insurance that the employer pays is fixed by contract in unionized settings and by company policy elsewhere. The employer negotiates for an array of plans, marketing them to employees, collecting premiums, and funding much of the cost of the basic plan. More recently, employers have moved toward pledging a defined contribution (a fixed dollar amount). Coverage for dependents is usually much cheaper under the employer's plan than anything available independently. This is due to the purchasing power of the group and the reduced costs to the insurer of marketing and administering the plan. Employers may also offer additional health insurance products not normally included in health insurance, such as dental insurance, long-term care insurance, and vision insurance. Here employers most likely do not subsidize the care, but pass along the advantages of group purchasing.

Many employers have traditionally offered new employees plans that do not exclude preexisting conditions, offering coverage not usually available on the open market prior to the ACA. Some employers, however, do require a pre-employment physical. Under the Americans with Disabilities Act, the use of this information must be limited to the ability to meet specific job requirements, but it may still have a chilling effect on the job-seeking behaviors of those who have severe health problems.

Plans Offered

Most employers offer multiple plans so that they do not bear the onus of forcing their employees to participate in a specific plan. Because of the antipathy among Americans to plans that do not allow a choice of providers, most offer a point-of-service (POS) plan as well as the basic plan and plans with alternative tiers of deductibles and copayments. The exchanges under the ACA also offer choices of plans with various levels of benefits.

Some employers also offer *cafeteria plans*, which allow employees to select customized sets of benefits that best meet their individual needs, including or excluding health care benefits. Cafeteria plans are also called flexible benefit plans or Section 125 plans after the applicable section of the Internal Revenue Code.

Employers, especially those with self-insured plans, can also provide incentives to their employees to participate in wellness programs, pay only the prices negotiated with local centers of excellence for specific procedures, or limit risk through reference pricing. The latter puts a cap on what the plan will pay based on prices of services available in the community. For example, grocer Safeway found that prices for a colonoscopy in the San Francisco area ranged from $898 to $5,984. The company determined that it could provide reasonable coverage with practices charging $1,500 or less in 2009, and limited its payment to that. This was reduced in 2010 to $1,250 (Robinson & MacPherson, 2012). A number of European countries use reference pricing for prescription drugs. Using it in the United States requires careful attention to both federal and state regulations.

Relationship with Insurers/Self-Insurance

Employers offering insurance have the option of bargaining with insurers or of self-insuring. A self-insured plan may be administered by the employer or by an insurance companies or *third-party administrator*, but regardless of who administers it, the employer takes the risks and rewards of the resulting underwriting loss ratios. Usually the employer also purchases stop-loss insurance against any string of unexpected adverse events. This alternative is used mostly by large employers. More than half of all covered U.S. employees work for self-insured employers. This proportion of firms that choose self-insurance is particularly high among firms with more than 1,000 employees and in multistate companies. Small employers are showing greater interest in self-insured plans to avoid the benefit levels required for the exchanges under the ACA.

Worker Education, Disease Management, and Worksite Wellness

Increasingly, employers are providing wellness and disease management programs directly or through their insurers. Most commonly, they provide wellness promotion through Web-based portals. Some employers provide personal interventions. Company nurses who in the past were mostly responsible for treating acute problems often now play a proactive role in identifying high-risk employees and helping them change their behaviors. Some employers also provide incentives for healthy behaviors, such as not smoking or joining and using a health and fitness club. Some are changing the workplace environment to promote health—for example, placing parking lots away from the building, publishing walking maps and holding walking meetings, installing exercise equipment on site, and replacing high-calorie, high-fat food and drink in lunchroom vending machines with more healthy fare. The Centers for Disease Control and Prevention

(CDC) decorated its stairwells with art and piped in music to make them more enticing to employees who might otherwise take an elevator.

Employers have a strong interest in promoting medical savings accounts, which shift more of the costs of routine medical care to the employees while still providing catastrophic care insurance.

Insurers

Insurers are intermediaries between payers and patients. Many insurers provide a wide array of insurance products and work to sell employers on the economics of one-stop shopping for all of their insurance needs. Others offer only or primarily health insurance products. Some are for-profit, and some are nonprofit. They all compete in the same market with similar products offered under the same state regulatory requirements. Insurers compete with each other based on price (driven by costs), their ability to keep enrollees happy, and their ability to come up with creative solutions to perceived problems.

Historically, insurance has been described as "driving through the rearview mirror." Premiums are based on experience rating, namely the past claims experience of one's employees or similar employee groups. If claims were high in one year, losses could be recouped by raising premiums the next. Even when changing insurers, one cannot necessarily run away from a costly claims history. Underwriters examine past data and the composition of the workforce and decide whether to take on a group and, if so, at what premium level. Their analyses are backed by statistical analysts, called actuaries, who estimate trends in costs and claims and forecast outcomes.

Method of Organization

The insurer can provide insurance only, or it can provide health care services as well. Organizations that combine both insurance and care management functions tend to be called health maintenance organizations (HMOs). If the company is only an insurer, it negotiates the terms of contracts (policies) with providers and with the enrollee. It collects a premium up front and invests it in reserves until claims are filed. Corporate profits are a function of claims history, operating efficiency, and investment earnings. If the investment income is sufficient, premiums can be less than the combined costs of operating and paying claims. If a company provides coverage at sites where it does not maintain much of a presence, that company may use a third-party administrator to process claims and provide other services locally.

Reinsurance

Insurance is a business of taking risks. If the insurer decides that the risk is too great to take on alone, it may purchase reinsurance against unacceptable losses (also called stop-loss insurance) from one or more other insurers.

Method of Payment

The payer wants to motivate providers to look after its interests. In economics this is called an agency issue. For health care providers, agency is a major issue because the physician is already an agent for the patient; thus, if the provider is also expected to be an agent for the payer or the insurers, this sets up a potential conflict of interest. To exert some influence over clinical decision making, insurers have experimented with a number of alternative ways of paying for care. **Table 6-2** lists various contract options used by insurers and also identifies the dominant organizational form associated with each payment method and the degree of control that each method exerts on providers.

Health insurance companies historically paid for care on a fee-for-service basis, with the provider establishing a fee schedule and billing accordingly. Then large payers, especially the Blue Cross and Blue Shield organizations, began to take discounts, and Medicare and Medicaid took even greater discounts to the tune of 40–60%. Some payers contract with their key network providers, usually primary care gatekeepers, to assume some of the risk and allow a withhold from their payments until a certain settlement date, at which time each provider receives some or all of the withheld funds depending on their cost performance. Today, a number of payers have pay-for-performance clauses built into their contracts that offer additional compensation for meeting certain quality criteria, especially in the areas of prevention and following evidence-based practices. Ultimately, payers want to pay for outcomes, but such compensation systems depend on integrated information systems that can capture more than just an episode of care.

Capitation involves giving the provider so much per enrollee per time period and leaving the provider to take the profit or loss on the actual transactions for the period. For example, a primary care provider might be given a certain amount per member per month to cover primary care and diagnostics. Sometimes the costs of subspecialty referrals are included, which puts the primary care provider at even greater risk. Provider organizations may choose a staff-model HMO structure as well. Where state medical practice acts allow, physicians may be employed directly. Otherwise, they

Table 6-2 Compensation Arrangements for Physician Health Care Services

Type of Fee Arrangement	Associated MD Organization	Cost Risks Borne By	Payer Control	Comments
FFS	Independent partnership	Insurer	Weak	Rapidly disappearing
Discounted FFS	PPO	Insurer	Relatively little, some through review process	Includes Medicaid and Medicare under assignment
Discounted FFS with withhold	PPO or IPA-type network	Mostly insurer	Relatively weak	Often associated with gatekeeper roles
Discounted FFS with performance incentives	PPO or IPA network, heavy concentration in one payer	Mixed	Some through incentive structure	Frequently related to quality and not quantity
	ACO partnership			
Mixed capitation FFS	HMO network	More to provider	Some through structure of payments	May include hospitalists and other specialists
	ACO partnership			
Capitation	HMO contract	Provider	Must review quality	Few providers can tolerate risks for long
	ACO partnership			
Salary and bonus	Staff model HMO or ACO	Mixed	Potentially high	Medical practice acts often limit control

FFS = fee for service. PPO = preferred provider organization. ACO = affordable care organization.

form a separate partnership entity that contracts (sometimes exclusively) with the HMO to deliver services. In such cases, the arrangement may offer additional compensation to the physician group if it meets certain targets.

HMOs

HMOs started out as providers that integrated prepayment and service delivery into a managed care system, usually with a closed panel of providers. Over time, that distinction has blurred. Today, HMO is virtually synonymous with a managed-care organization, one that does more than pay claims. It takes responsibility for the quality and content of care over a period of time.

The HMO–provider relationship can be set up in a number of ways:

- **Staff model.** Physicians are employed or in a captive group with physicians on salary, with or without performance bonuses.
- **Group model.** A physician group accepts capitation from the HMO and allocates the capitation payments among its members.
- **Network model.** The HMO contracts with groups and individual physicians to take care of its enrollees. Providers may be paid by capitation or on a discounted fee-for-service basis.
- **Individual practice association (IPA) model.** A group of practices contract as a whole for payment under either capitation or discounted fee for service.

The ACA promoted a similar organization called an Accountable Care Organization (ACO). An ACO is not dominated by an insurer, but allows for partnerships among providers (i.e., doctors and hospitals), with the providers sharing in the savings rather than passing most of them on to the insurer. Therefore, the standards of care are under the control of the providers rather than the insurer, and the potential antagonism between doctors and hospitals that bundling threatens to create is reduced by having a common incentive system.

Plans Offered

Insurers usually offer an array of plans to meet employer demands. Most corporate benefits managers would prefer to leave the choices up to employees rather than risk a backlash from dissatisfied employees who believe the company is forcing them unfairly to use a specific plan or specific provider. The dominant type of plan in recent years has been the POS plan, which gives employees more choice among providers but at additional cost. The most recent rapid growth has been in high-deductible health plans.

Case Management/Carve-Outs

Many of the problems in patient care occur because of a lack of coordination. For example, a patient may stay in the hospital extra days because the family cannot arrange for care at home or facilities in the area lack the capacity for aftercare. Payers have responded by employing case managers for costly cases. Where there is better expertise outside the organization, the insurer may carve out a set of cases, such as diabetes or congestive heart failure, for a specialized contractor to manage. This is also typically done where mental illness is covered (carrying the dubious name "behavioral health") because the insurer's professionals may be familiar only with medical/surgical cases. In many markets insurers will have contracts with most established acute-care providers. Case managers often oversee services provided after hospital discharge and may act as patient advocates within the hospital. In some situations, they may recommend providers who are especially qualified to deal with rare situations; however, there are concerns about a payer representative directing someone to a provider because of cost rather than quality. In 2002, the American Case Management Association (2009), whose members are predominantly nurses and social workers, defined its field as follows:

> Case Management in Hospital/Health Care Systems is a collaborative practice model including patients, nurses, social workers, physicians, other practitioners, caregivers and the community. The Case Management process encompasses communication and facilitates care along a continuum through effective resource coordination. The goals of Case Management include the achievement of optimal health, access to care and appropriate utilization of resources, balanced with the patient's right to self determination.

Utilization Constraints

Precertification and preauthorization are devices widely used to control hospital and drug costs. The provider must obtain authorization before admission for common procedures and usually is told how many inpatient days are allowed. If the admitting physician wishes to keep the patient longer, he or she must notify the insurer and get reauthorization for the additional costs if the insurance company is to pay. Certain procedures and prescription drugs must be preauthorized because they are expensive, of limited value, or experimental, so the insurer's medical staff must agree beforehand that the intervention is medically necessary.

Although most providers object strongly to these measures, they are not as draconian as they appear. If the provider pushes back hard enough, the insurer usually lacks a scientific reason for rejecting the physician's definition of medical necessity and ultimately gives in. Much of the cost reduction seems to come from the *sentinel effect*—providers change their behavior just because they know that someone is watching.

Insurers have experimented with a number of ways to reduce inappropriate utilization of health care resources. They profile providers to identify outliers in terms of cost per diagnosis, consumer satisfaction, and appropriateness of treatment, and they cancel contracts with those who appear too much out of line. The federal government has profiled physicians on the basis of their distribution of codes used for office visits, using the data to search for indicators of "fraud and abuse."

Consumer Education

Insurers have partnered with employers to provide consumer education materials, guidelines, and events. They advertise their skill at this type of information dissemination and are continuously upgrading their online portals for more and better customized information for each enrollee, from the worried well to the chronically ill.

PROVIDERS

Professionals

For many years, most physicians and dentists were in solo practice or a simple partnership. These entities have gradually been replaced by ones that mix the partnership and the corporate form under the titles of professional association (PA) or limited liability partnership or corporation (LLP or LLC). Such entities enable the professionals to maintain control, but offer tax advantages, greater access to capital, and/or protection from some liability claims other than malpractice. Which entities are acceptable depends on each state's corporate practice of medicine act and its medical licensing board's interpretation of that act. Essentially, a medical practice act restricts the practice of medicine to an individual licensed practitioner and forbids others from exercising such privileges. The Medical Board of California stated in 2006 that the existing legislation "is intended to prevent unlicensed persons from interfering with or influencing the physician's professional judgment" and governs the following:

- Determining what diagnostic tests are appropriate for a particular condition
- Determining the need for referrals to, or consultation with, another physician/specialist
- Responsibility for the ultimate overall care of the patient, including treatment options available to the patient

- Determining how many patients a physician must see in a given period of time or how many hours a physician must work
- Ownership is an indicator of control of a patient's medical records, including the contents thereof, and should be retained by a California-licensed physician
- Selection and hiring/firing (as it relates to clinical competency or proficiency) of physicians, allied health staff, and medical assistants
- Setting the parameters under which the physician will enter into patient care services
- Decisions regarding coding and billing procedures for patient care services
- Approving the selection of medical equipment and medical supplies for the medical practice

Similar boards and distinctive regulations govern other health care providers, including nurses, pharmacists, dentists, and physical therapists. However, with more than half the physicians in the country employed, and with the continuing trend of consolidation of individual practices into larger organizations, the complete autonomy visualized in that legislation has gone by the boards.

With such restrictions, how can HMOs, hospitals, and physician practice management firms (PPMs) buy physician practices and merge them into a horizontally or vertically integrated care system? Kaiser Permanente, a long-standing and respected integrated system with much of its operations in California, has been able to do this by separating the medical practice component from everything else. After 1955, Kaiser Permanente split into three organizations: two nonprofits, one for the health plan (insurance and administration) and one for the owned hospitals, and a for-profit organization for the physicians. Subsequently, to meet the requirements of the medical practice acts, the physician groups have become separate entities in each state. The Kaiser health plan contracts with the local medical group for physician services. Kaiser physicians tend to self-select on the basis of values other than income maximization, but negotiations have been contentious at times.

Emergency departments are an area where there are conflicting concepts of professional practice responsibilities. At least half the emergency rooms in the country are staffed under contracts with PPMs that specialize in staffing and operating these 24/7 activities, which are not of much interest to other community physicians. The PPMs and the American Academy of Emergency Medicine have been at odds over due process for their contract physicians, the proportion of professional fees going to them, job opportunities for board-certified individuals, and physician access to billing and economic data on their worksites (McNamara, 2006). Most health care professionals other than physicians can be employed directly. Some states require supervision by a physician in some situations, whereas others do not.

These examples illustrate the balancing act the political system goes through to maintain professional accountability for services and enforce licensure requirements, yet avoid sustaining the old professional monopolies and not interfere too much with appropriate labor substitution and the development of integrated health delivery systems.

Practice Ownership

As physician incomes dropped in the 1990s, many physicians chose to sell their practices to new organizational entities or to form associations to deal from a position of strength with payers and the hospitals. These numerous and sometimes complex relationships led to the alphabet soup of the 1980s and 1990s. Alternatives have included the following:

- Selling out
  - To HMOs that were developing integrated service organizations, often without ownership of the hospital component.
  - To hospitals that were attempting to develop integrated delivery systems and capture patients through their physicians.
  - To academic medical centers that also were attempting to develop integrated delivery systems.
  - To publicly traded PPMs, which were in vogue in the 1990s, but then ran into profitability problems due to their inability to increase physician productivity.
  - To others.
- Taking greater risks in return for greater rewards (ideally)
  - Accepting capitation, which involves a fixed payment for providing care to an enrolled population for a defined set of services per member per month. It has tended to be too risky for all but the largest integrated practices and IPAs.
  - Joining IPAs, which contract with the managed care organization, usually for capitation, and then allocating the work and the revenue to their members.
- Partnering with institutions
  - Physician-hospital organizations, usually formed to contract with managed-care plans.

- Medical service organizations, often owned by hospitals that provide management and support services to independent practices and may purchase certain practice assets in the process, presumably at a fair market price.
- Withholds, which are usually associated with a gatekeeper role and involve the payer holding back some portion of the negotiated fee as a risk pool in case of cost overruns.
- Community hospital, often by seeking more board representation in hopes of influencing the impact of cost cutting on providers.
- The ACOs encouraged by the ACA presumably would align incentives between physicians and hospitals in a more nuanced way to encourage effective coordination of care and reduced cost.
- Pricing
  - Negotiating the fees paid under managed care contracts. Practices' bargaining power varies widely. If a practice is large, provides a scarce resource, or includes a substantial number of the payer's enrollees, it can and should bargain. If the practice is small and has many competitors, it can do little more than accept the discount structure offered. In large urban areas, a practice may contract with many payers. In rural areas, options for either or both parties may be limited.
  - Refusing to accept insurance or specific plans such as Medicaid or Medicare. If a provider believes enough paying patients would be willing to pay directly, the provider may refuse to accept insurance payments entirely. The patient can either pay directly or file directly for insurance, usually based on paperwork supplied by the physician's office. The risks of reduced payments, denials, and deductibles then rest with the patient.
  - Offering boutique or concierge medicine, in which the provider, usually a primary care provider, agrees to provided outpatient care for a fixed annual fee, taking many fewer patients and having more time to devote to the concerns of each one. Some practices meld both insurance and an annual fee for personalized service.
  - Refusing to accept assignment from Medicare, perhaps on a patient-by-patient basis. Providers who accept assignment from Medicare agree to charge patients no more than the Medicare approved amounts. This includes copayments and unmet deductibles. Money is paid directly to the physician by the Medicare Part B intermediary. Physicians who do not accept assignment receive somewhat less (about 5%) from Medicare, but are allowed to bill

the patient for an additional amount (called balance billing), capped at 15% above the lower schedule. The Medicare intermediary writes the check to the patient, who must then write a check for the full amount due to the nonparticipating physician.

Services Offered

Physicians can organize by specialty or join a multispecialty group. Solo practice is an option for some, but most prefer a group partnership to deal with issues of after-hours coverage, efficiency of operation, economies of scale, contract negotiation, collegiality, and intellectual stimulation. Group stability tends to vary widely depending on personalities and the degree of agreement on lifestyle and work–life objectives, which, of course, change over time. Academic medical centers tend to be organized along rigidly specialized lines, whereas the multispecialty group practice is more prevalent in the outside community.

Dividing lines between specialists and generalists often are fuzzy. Primary care providers may perform procedures often left to specialists. Examples include radiologic exams and sigmoidoscopies in primary care practices and automated neurologic testing in primary care offices. Some insurers offer incentives to primary care providers to perform outpatient services, such as sigmoidoscopy, that otherwise would require a specialist referral.

Incentives

The health policy literature devotes ample attention to the misalignment of incentives in the health care system. Providers are encouraged by fee-for-service payment systems to promote overutilization, whereas payers and HMOs might provide incentives that encourage underutilization. The issue is how to define and incentivize right-utilization based on scientific knowledge and expert assessments. Free-market capitalism is fueled by ever-increasing consumption, and health care is no exception.

Pay-for-performance, also known as pay-for-quality, is a current hope of many interested in health policy. It involves providing incentive payments (usually as a percentage of the usual negotiated fees) to those provider network members who conform to certain process requirements, such a computerized prescription order entry, computerized billing, and meeting targets for preventive services. For the most part, it does not mean achieving specific clinical outcomes because of the difficulty of recording and then effectively risk-adjusting them. What payers do not want to do is motivate the better clinicians to avoid difficult or high-risk cases just to improve their numbers.

Plan managers who want to encourage provider participation can also enhance the rates they are paying to a desired group. Medicaid plans in a number of states, for example, have raised obstetrical fees to get pregnant women into care earlier, even while holding down or reducing other fees for other services.

Disincentives for utilization are numerous and varied. We all hear litanies of the numbers of calls a practice makes in a day to obtain prior approvals and to reverse denials. Some insurers seem to use denials as a hurdle the office staff must clear in order to get paid, but paid late. Providers also have to keep in mind that their decisions might be reviewed by the insurer's utilization review staff, by Medicare and Medicaid's data-mining fraud and abuse computers, and by the hospital's quality audit staff. Any one of these may cost future business income. Porter and Teisberg (2006) offered an alternative view of incentives. They argued that the current competition in health care is based on an inappropriate zero-sum mentality that causes providers (1) to provide the broadest range of services to avoid movement to other providers or locations and (2) to reduce utilization through hurdles, barriers, copayments, and deductibles.

They suggested a somewhat utopian alternative mindset in which the focus of all payer and provider decisions would be on maximizing the value of health care for the patient. We revisit some of their proposals later on.

Patient Relationships

Individual providers and provider organizations are becoming increasingly sensitive to their service reputations with patients they want to keep. This is due in part to the widespread use of consumer satisfaction surveys by payers and employers. Consistent negative evaluations can affect their access to patient revenues, but an even more important reason is the increasing competition for the patient's attention, especially as more and more commercial entities try to disintermediate traditional patient–provider relationships. For example, emergency room waiting times, which had averaged 38 minutes in 1997, increased 25% from 46.5 minutes to 58 minutes between 2004 and 2009 (Hing & Bhuiya, 2012). This has prompted development of alternative systems for delivering acute care on a low-cost, rapid-access basis, especially as insurers take measures to discourage using hospital emergency rooms as dispensaries. Urgent care centers and clinics staffed by nurse practitioners and physician assistants are appearing in chain stores such as Wal-Mart and Target. They charge less and offer shorter waiting times, and their longer hours help patients and family members avoid lost wages. Their efforts seem focused on the needs of uninsured families. It is interesting to speculate how this system might develop as the number of individuals without insurance increases or decreases. Another example is Wal-Mart and other pharmacy chains offering a low fixed price for a month's supply of a broad array of generic prescriptions.

Traditional primary care practices have responded by setting aside a larger portion of their day for same-day acute care visits. This has meant longer waits for those needing routine physicals and checkups. Available software has enabled practices to handle more prescription renewals and patient inquiries without telephone calls and visits and to schedule same-day visits effectively. Some insurers also compensate physicians for responding to patients via the Internet.

Primary Versus Specialty Care

In most countries, the gatekeeper role of the primary care physician is critical to the efficient functioning of the health care system. In the United States, however, there is considerable confusion, much of it purposely created, about the role of primary care and how it is delivered. Most U.S. patients do not hesitate to self-refer to a specialist based on their personal assessment of the problem. Specialists encourage this by advertising themselves as primary care providers for specific populations. An example would be a sports medicine clinic. It would likely be part of a specialized orthopedic practice.

A male patient who uses an academic medical center and has a chronic heart problem might select any of the following as a primary care physician:

- A physician in a family medicine department
- A physician in the general internal medicine division of the internal medicine department
- A physician in the cardiology division of the internal medicine department

His children could go to either pediatrics or family medicine and their mother to either OB/GYN or family medicine. For vision care, the family could go to an ophthalmologist or an optometrist, unless tertiary care is required. The family also has similarly confusing choices among physicians in the community, not to mention additional choices among chiropractors, urgent care centers, and community health centers.

There was once great hope for integrated health systems built around multispecialty groups linked to one or more community hospitals;

however, that has not proved as successful as hoped for and is threatened by the development of specialty hospitals and ambulatory surgery centers.

Efficiency

Providers work hard to increase the number of patients seen. Visits have been continually shortened. More and more practices have added not only nurses and nursing assistants, but also nurse practitioners, physician assistants, and certified nurse midwives. Physicians have resisted computerized systems that fail to speed up their work processes, but they have added such systems where they anticipate improved efficiency. For example, one of the drivers for same-day appointment systems is that they tend to eliminate no-shows and increase practice throughput.

Physicians have also embraced electronic claims filing.

The subsidies for "meaningful" use of electronic medical records under the Health Information Technology for Economic and Clinical Health (HITECH) Act of 2009 are significant, but it will take time for providers to smooth out the workflow to the point where it pays off in terms of efficiency. A key element in the success of these new systems is the involvement of the clinical staff in their design and implementation.

Distribution of Specialties

Over time, the availability of physicians in specific fields reflects perceptions of income potential. Average physician income in constant dollar terms has fallen in recent years. Increasingly, medical students have chosen to avoid primary care training (family medicine, pediatrics, and general internal medicine) and have instead chosen specialties that produce fees for performing procedures. An orthopedic surgeon could expect to earn roughly twice the income of a primary care physician after expenses. Yet, a primary care physician may bring in almost as much revenue from visits, lab tests, and procedural fees, but not including referrals (about $2 million). Primary care physicians are now in short supply and high demand. This increased demand is causing salaries for primary care physicians to rise faster than those for many specialties, but overall physician salaries have not risen as fast as overall medical care costs.

The experience of other countries and studies of small area differences in practice patterns indicate that the prevalence of specialists and other resources often seems to influence the amount of care delivered, some of which is of questionable value to patients, even at the medical centers with the most prestigious reputations (Fisher et al., 2004).

Institutions

The dominant actors among health care institutions have been the general hospitals, especially community hospitals, and academic medical centers. The array of institutions delivering care, however, includes community health centers, specialty hospitals, large integrated systems, large multisite practices, state and local government hospitals, pharmaceutical companies, and other vendors.

Relationship to Providers

Much of the time, an institution's key objective is to capture a large population for its services. If one accepts the primary care provider as a gatekeeper, the way to increase activity is to capture referrals from local gatekeepers, especially if insurers constrain self-referral. This is one reason why hospitals, academic medical centers, and others have bought so many primary care practices and have worked to put satellite centers in shopping centers and continuing care retirement communities. They want the referrals, together with the ancillary revenues in their laboratories, operating rooms, and imaging centers. Their behaviors epitomize the zero-sum mentality Porter and Teisberg (2006) cited as a core problem behind the growth in health care costs.

Despite extensive regulations designed to prevent institutions from buying referrals, there is a continuous effort to bind referring providers to the institution. Hospitals build office buildings on site or in high-traffic areas, offer physicians seats on hospital boards, and give them influence over the capital investments the hospital makes.

Pharmaceutical companies donate samples, provide educational lunches and speakers, and support technical society meetings. Some even make large donations to charities controlled by private-practice physicians that fund research and medical residency programs (Abelson, 2006b). Many institutions have taken steps to curb some of these activities, and federal regulations now require much more transparency concerning these potential conflicts of interest.

Efficiency

Institutions, including large medical practices, have to decide how to configure their staff and facilities for the efficient use of all their resources. They must conform to all sorts of regulations and restrictions and still come up with an efficient and effective delivery system. Especially sensitive areas include staffing and labor substitution. Because these institutions are loosely coupled organizations, most departments try to operate as independently as possible and tend to emphasize growth over reduced use of resources. Interest in saving resources tends to focus on scarcity situations. Efficiency is more of a slogan than a goal in many provider environments.

Staffing

Perhaps no debate rages as long or as loudly as whether an institution is staffed adequately. Health professionals usually see themselves as overworked because there is always more that could be done for the patient. The demand for their services is highly variable, and thus there are peak periods when they are under pressure to go faster. This is not without risks, but staffing only for peak demand results in considerable lost value the rest of the time. There is usually a dynamic tension, therefore, between professional leadership and institutional management over whether more staff is warranted.

Staffing shortages have been critical in some areas, such as nursing and child psychiatry. An increasing body of evidence suggests that adverse hospital events, such as hospital-acquired pneumonias and urinary tract infections, are associated with low levels of nurse staffing and nursing staff education (Stanton, 2004). The market response is to raise wages, and most institutions try that. It does work over time. Nursing education programs are expanding as potential students are increasingly attracted by rising wages and plentiful employment opportunities; however, institutions are also sensitive to the increased salary costs. The pressure to develop and license substitutes is great.

Labor Substitution

Current areas of contention related to labor substitution include the educational requirements for registered nurses, substitution of other nursing staff for registered nurses, the degree of independent practice allowed nurse practitioners and physician assistants, substitution of anesthesiologist assistants for nurse anesthesiologists, and granting prescribing authority to psychologists. These battles differ from state to state, but it is not unusual for the health committees of state legislatures to devote a significant amount of their time to scope of practice issues. The currently dominant professional group usually objects strongly to substitution. The training and licensure of substitutes is usually justified at first on the basis of workforce shortages. After a new group gains a foothold in some states and establishes an acceptable safety record, its members push for privileges in other states as well.

Institutions see these substitutions as having potential for leveraging expensive staff members and for allowing flexibility in work team composition. A secondary issue is sometimes control. In a hospital, for example, nurse practitioners usually report to the director of nursing, whereas physician assistants report to a different administrative unit or to the medical staff directly. Medical staffs often prefer the latter.

Scope and Scale of Services

Institutions can add or drop programs. Many hospitals are dropping services that do not appear to pay for themselves. The risk is that patients and providers will go somewhere else to access a missing service and not come back.

Pricing/Discounts

Hospitals do not offer meaningful price lists and try to deal with payers individually. Monopsonistic federal and state programs arbitrarily set their own payment levels, but there is room to negotiate with large insurers. The individual consumer usually lacks reliable information on which to compare costs or quality, the cornerstone comparisons of any consumer-driven health care system. Regulators and legislators understand the issue and are taking action bit by bit. The public is increasingly aware of the issue, especially after the federal government made comparative data readily available in 2013 and the issue was highlighted in the popular press (Brill, 2013).

Quality Improvement

Institutions are the key to quality improvement. They have the data and operate on a corporate model that can support improvement and change. Accreditation requires that they show that quality improvement efforts are under way. The main problem remains provider involvement. Institutions that have effective programs, however, have achieved major outcome improvements. As quality is increasingly reported, these programs should begin to pay off in improvements in patient volumes and increased reimbursements under pay-for-performance initiatives.

Consumer Information

Institutions, just like insurers, woo consumers with Web portals and informational advertising. They advertise "ask a nurse" lines to capture self-referrals and increase patient loyalty. They work with primary care providers to stimulate referrals and establish centers of excellence to enhance visibility in the marketplace for profitable procedures.

Credentialing Decisions

Many physicians cannot serve Medicare and Medicaid patients without hospital privileges, even if they have predominantly outpatient practices. Hospitals can award or withhold these privileges through their credentialing processes. Credentialing is intended to ensure quality of care and patient safety, but there are also opportunities for *economic credentialing*— rewarding physicians who bring in profitable patients and penalizing those who own competing organizations.

Involving Payers in Change Decisions

The impact of changes may benefit others rather than the institution. One strategy is to involve the payers in the change process so that they can explain to staff where the costs of the institution are out of line with competing providers and also see how the bottom line of the provider is affected by process changes. For example, Virginia Mason Medical Center in Seattle teamed up with Aetna and Starbucks to look at the cost of treating back pain cases. It found that it was not responding rapidly enough, and that many cases could be referred directly to physical therapy without expensive magnetic resonance imaging. Those cases that appeared complicated were sent to specialists for workup, but those that were acute without sciatica were treated promptly at much lower cost. After a review of the finances by Aetna and Starbucks, Aetna agreed to increase the payments for physical therapy to offset some of the lost income (Fuhrmans, 2007b).

Professions

Professional societies and their representatives can have a major influence on the cost, quality, and access dimensions of health care. Starr (1982) documented the American Medical Association's long and strong opposition to universal health insurance as a primary reason we do not have it today. Because the societies test and credential their members, they also have a major potential to influence the quality of the care provided.

Quality Improvement

Two physician leaders of the quality movement, Lucent Leape and Donald Berwick (2005), pointed to their profession's need for autonomy and authority as a major barrier to the implementation of many quality improvement measures. They argued that a climate devoted to safety would require acknowledgment of errors and additional teamwork to reduce them. They suggested a number of interventions, including parallel and coordinated enforcement of standards by the Joint Commission, the Centers for Medicare & Medicaid Services (CMS), and the National Committee for Quality Assurance (NCQA) and a system of incentives for implementing safe practices and disincentives for the continuation of unsafe ones. In 2003, the Joint Commission began to require hospitals to implement 11 safety practices and added more in 2005. The error-rate reductions reported at specific institutions were quite impressive:

- 62% reduction in ventilator-associated pneumonias
- 81% and 90% reductions in medication errors
- 15% reduction in cardiac arrests
- 66% and 78% reductions in preventable adverse drug reactions (Leape and Berwick, 2005)

Reporting of preventable events has broadened, and events that were once considered routine side effects, such as hospital-acquired pneumonias and central line infections, are now considered reportable medical errors and not worthy of reimbursement.

Provider Education

Most professions have continuing education requirements linked to certification and licensure. Providers must maintain proficiency in their field and retake professional examinations at prescribed intervals. Given the data on regional variability in care, one must question how up-to-date and evidence-driven these courses tend to be. Some subspecialty groups have added requirements for participation in quality improvement programs as part of their recertification process.

Consumer Education

Professional societies also undertake consumer education programs designed to persuade potential patients to use their members. Often it is difficult to differentiate between consumer education and advertising in defense of professional turf. Societies often lend their names and data to other advertising campaigns acceptable to their professional ethics. There is considerable risk in doing this because new data might show that they supported a policy or product that later turned out to be counterproductive.

CONSUMERS

The choices consumers make involve their preferences and the options available to them. Until recently those choices were limited to a few offered by their employers. Now their choices are expanding.

Plan Selection

During the managed care revolution of the 1980s and 1990s, plans were quite restrictive in their efforts to keep members within their provider networks. After consumers rebelled, insurers expanded their networks and offered POS options. Enrollees also had to decide what gambles to take in terms of deductibles and copayments, balancing premium costs above the basic employer plan against anticipated out-of-pocket costs during each enrollment period. The implementation of state and federal exchanges under the ACA added additional choices for many, but there remains a strong need for more consumer education and support in decision making.

Retirement Planning

Middle- and upper-income families also have to plan for their health care needs during retirement, especially given the increasingly shaky status of employment-based coverage plans for retirees. They must make decisions about coverage during retirement, long-term care insurance, and specialized insurance and income needs.

Provider Selection

Individuals want to continue their provider relationships if they are satisfactory. They have made their preference for not changing providers clear.

Most of those forced to change providers have been members of Medicaid managed care or retiree benefit programs with restricted choices. Patients' quality concerns seem to center on the affective relationships with their providers and are the focus of most consumer quality assessment questionnaires. Technical proficiency or outcome measures may be available, but, where they exist, consumers have to be alerted to their availability and taught how to interpret them. Bedside manner still is important, especially as interactions with providers have been shortened by productivity and income pressures.

Self-Help

Increasingly, plan members are being steered to online self-help sites. Many large insurers, including HMOs, provide customized Web portals for their insured, which build on diagnoses reported by network providers. These portals provide information on treatment and prevention as well as links to lower cost providers of complementary services and supplies. Experiences with these sites may encourage enrollees to search further on their own and study available quality information on potential providers.

Insured with Low Likelihood of Use

Many of the insured have little likelihood of using services during a particular time period. Some 20% of the population under 65 account for 80% of that group's expenses. Given the recent imposition of increased deductibles and copayments in many plans, even those seeking acute, episodic care will not file claims except to build their deductibles, just in case. Members of this group would be the candidates for medical savings accounts and high deductibles, that is, consumer-driven health care. If they remain healthy, there are no claims, and their premiums go down further, but if they have major claims, they are covered for amounts for catastrophic events above the large deductible.

Under the individual mandate of the ACA, they also face the possibility of a penalty, or "tax," by the IRS for failing to secure coverage. The penalty will be phased in over time, and once it is completely phased in it will be adjusted for inflation. The 2016 amount is set at $695 per person for up to three people in the household (or $2,085). Households with higher taxable income levels would pay 2.5% of household income above the filing threshold, but the penalty cannot exceed the average cost of a basic (or "bronze") plan through the exchanges. There are real questions as to whether that penalty will be sufficient to motivate compliance even with the premium tax credits offered to low-income individuals. Also consider that individuals up to 100% of federal poverty level (FPL) in some states and 130% of FPL in others are eligible for Medicaid.

Prevention is an important arena with this healthier group. If their insurer, their employer, or the media keep them informed of risks of chronic and acute disease and they follow valid advice, they should benefit like everyone else. The question still to be answered is whether they will behave differently from the untreated population in general and whether efforts to reach them will induce changes. A number of factors are pushing in both directions. On the one hand, physicians are known to be a strong force for change when they have a bond with the patient, but these individuals might not visit a primary care practice regularly or form a bond with the provider staff. On the other hand, they will have the financial motivation to stay healthy.

FOR-PROFIT VERSUS NONPROFIT

We noted at the start of this chapter that for-profit and nonprofit firms operate side by side in many health care sectors. One policy choice is whether to encourage one form or the other in the private sector or to ignore the issue. Hansmann (1996) noted that the nonprofit portion of the economy has grown steadily. He suggested that nonprofit firms come into being when consumers are not in a position to determine the quality or quantity of what they are purchasing without unreasonable cost or effort. This means the consumers could be seriously exploited by a for-profit firm. "The solution is to create a firm without owners—or, more accurately, to create a firm whose managers hold it in trust for its customers. In essence, the nonprofit form abandons any benefits of full ownership in favor of stricter fiduciary constraints on management" (Hansmann, 1996, p. 228).

Many of the same issues are cited as the sociological grounding of professional status and autonomy for health care providers. Somehow accountability must be established to protect the interests of the patients when only highly imperfect information is available to the individual at risk.

THE VALUE-DRIVEN CARE INITIATIVE

What if we were to make the value offered to the patient the basis of competition in the health care marketplace? This is the objective suggested by

Porter and Teisberg (2006). To achieve this focus, they recommend the following:

- Mandating participation in health insurance by all, with subsidies for low-income participants
- Focusing on the complete disease management process at the level of specific medical conditions (such as coronary artery blockage) to optimize process coordination and efficiency and information flow
- Providing reliable and relevant information at the medical condition level on total cost and outcome
- Organizing systems of care to compete on the basis of maximum patient value, which they believe would result in narrower product lines in community hospitals, more referrals of complex and rare cases to centers of excellence, and more organization into multisite (horizontally integrated) systems
- Reporting all process steps electronically, producing reports that give bundled costs of care across providers and institutions, and providing more extensive follow-up and reporting of outcomes
- Creating extensive incentives to reduce duplication and waste and improve quality for each medical condition at all process stages

Porter and Teisberg's analysis has attracted considerable interest among employers because it is easy to understand in terms of the industrial model for marketing and operational improvement, appears likely to support new forms of oligopolistic competition, and draws parallels from consumer experiences with the rationalization of other professional services where the consumer was once considered unable to make decisions (such as travel, insurance, and financial services). The impact on the professions and health care delivery institutions of such a major shift in emphasis would be profound. Just what would drive it over the opposition of entrenched interests is hard to contemplate, although the ACA is a start.. That is why we referred to it above as being somewhat utopian. However, it would make great sense if we were building our health system from scratch.

The authors have discussed elsewhere the notion of a continuum of market power ranging from a market dominated by a single buyer (a monopsony such as the U.K.'s National Health Service) to one dominated by single seller (a monopoly), with other forms along the continuum being administered competition, a free market, and an oligopy comprising insurers and providers. **Figure 6-1** places value-driven health care on this continuum. Despite the emphasis on competition, we have included it as an administered system because it is going to have to be buyer-driven at the onset.

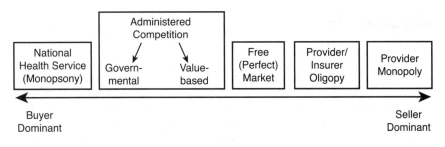

Figure 6–1 Modified stages of health care market power.

CONCLUSION

The health care marketplace is very complex. Many actors and many alternatives merit consideration as the system tries to strike a balance between overutilization and underutilization and as the commercial aspects of health care become increasingly apparent.

| Case 6 | **Global Medical Coverage** |

BACKGROUND

Blue Ridge Paper Products, Inc. (BRPP) in Canton, North Carolina, is a paper company whose predominant product is food and beverage packaging. It was the largest employer in Western North Carolina in 2006, with 1,300 covered employees in the state and 800 elsewhere. Started as the Champion Paper plant in 1908, it was purchased by the employees and their union (a United Steelworkers local) in May 1999 with the assistance of a venture capital firm. Today it operates under an employee stock ownership plan (ESOP). To purchase the plant, the employees agreed to a 15% wage cut and frozen wages and benefits for 7 years. From the buyout through the end of 2005, the company lost $92 million and paid out $107 million in health care claims. It became profitable in 2006. Maintaining health benefits for members and retirees is a very high priority with the employees and the union, although retiree medical benefits have been eliminated for salaried employees hired after March 1, 2005. The venture capital firm that financed the ESOP retained 55% ownership with 40% going to the employees and 5% to senior management. Profitability varied from year to year as the company

Case 6 *(continued)*

expanded capacity and improved productivity of its single-serving drink carton lines and was caught up in a number of suits over water pollution problems at its Canton, North Carolina, plant.

The majority of BRPP employees are male, older than age 48, and have several health risk factors. Most employees work 12-hour, rotating shifts, making it extremely difficult to manage health conditions or improve lifestyle (Blackley, 2006). The ESOP has worked hard to reduce its self-insured health care costs. Health insurance claims for 2006 had been estimated at $36 million, but appeared likely to hold near $24 million, which is still 75% above the 2000 numbers. A volunteer benefits task force composed of union and nonunion employees worked to redesign a complex benefit system. After 2 years of 18% health care cost increases, the rate of growth dropped to 2% in 2003. It was 5% in 2004 and –3% in 2005.

Programs initiated in 2001 included a plan offering free diabetic medications and supplies in return for compliance, and a tobacco cessation plan with cash rewards. In 2004, the company opened a full-service pharmacy and medical center with a pharmacist, internist, and nurses. In 2005, it began a population health management program. Covered employees and spouses who completed a health risk assessment were rewarded with $100 and assigned a "personal nurse coach." The nurse coach assisted those who were ready to change to set individual health goals and to choose from among one or more of 14 available health programs, which included reduced copays on medications, free self-help medical aids/equipment, and educational materials.

Where BRPP could not seem to make headway was with the prices paid to local providers. Community physicians refused deeper discounts. Even banding together in a buying cooperative with other companies could not move the local tertiary hospital to match discounts offered to regionally dominant insurers. This hospital was not distressed and had above-average operating margins.

Articles on "medical tourism" in the press and on television attracted the attention of benefits management. Reports were of high-quality care at 80% or less of U.S. prices with good outcomes. BRPP contacted a company offering services at hospitals in India, IndUShealth in Raleigh, North Carolina, and began working on a plan to make its services available to BRPP employees.

INDUSHEALTH

IndUShealth provides a complete package to its U.S. and Canadian clients, including access to Indian superspecialty hospitals that are Joint Commission International accredited and to specialists and supporting physicians with U.S. or U.K. board certification. It arranges for postoperative care in India and for travel, lodging, and meals for the patient and an accompanying family member—all for a single package price. For example, it represents the Wockhardt hospitals in India, which are Joint Commission International accredited and affiliated with Harvard Medical International. Other Indian hospitals boast affiliations with the Johns Hopkins Medical Center and the Cleveland Clinic.

MITRAL VALVE REPLACEMENT

One of the first cases considered was a mitral valve replacement. IndUShealth and BRPP sought package quotes from a number of domestic medical centers and could get only one estimate. That quote, from the University of Iowa academic medical center, was in the $68,000 to $98,000 range. The quote from India was for $18,000 and included travel, food, and lodging for the patient and one companion. Testifying before the U.S. Senate Special Committee on Aging, Mr. Rajesh Rao, IndUShealth's CEO (2006), cited the following costs:

Procedure	Typical U.S. Cost	India Cost
Heart bypass surgery	$55,000 to $86,000	$6,000
Angioplasty	$33,000 to $49,000	$6,000
Hip replacement	$31,000 to $44,000	$5,000
Spinal fusion	$42,000 to $76,000	$8,000

EMPLOYEE PARTICIPATION

To encourage employee participation, BRPP prepared a DVD on its medical tourism initiative, which it called Global Health Coverage. It outlined the opportunities and described the Indian facilities and credentials. The next step was to be a trip by an employee "due diligence" committee to India to inspect facilities and talk with doctors. Then they would discuss how to handle the option in the next set of union negotiations.

Case 6   (*continued*)

SENATE HEARINGS

On June 27, 2006, the U.S. Senate Special Committee on Aging held hearings titled "The Globalization of Health Care: Can Medical Tourism Reduce Health Care Costs?" Both BRPP and IndUShealth testified for the committee. When testifying to the Senate subcommittee, Bonnie Grissom Blackley, benefits director for BRPP, concluded:

> Should I need a surgical procedure, provide me and my spouse with an all expense-paid trip to a Joint Commission International-approved hospital, that compares to a 5-star hotel, a surgeon educated and credentialed in the U.S., no hospital staph infections, a registered nurse around the clock, no one pushing me out of the hospital after 2 or 3 days, a several-day recovery period at a beach resort, email access, cell phone, great food, touring, etc., etc. for 25% of the savings up to $10,000 and I won't be able to get out my passport fast enough.

BLUE RIDGE PAPER PRODUCT'S TEST CASE

The test case under the new arrangement was a volunteer, Carl Garrett, a 60-year-old BRPP paper-making technician who needed a gallbladder removal and a shoulder repair. He reportedly was looking forward to the trip in September 2006, accompanied by his fiancée. A 40-year employee approaching retirement, he would be the first company-sponsored U.S. worker to receive health care in India. The two operations would have cost $100,000 in the United States, but would cost only $20,000 in India. The arrangement was that the company would pay for the entire thing, waive the 20% copayment, give Garrett about a $10,000 incentive, and still save $50,000.

However, the United Steel Workers Union (USW) national office objected strongly to the whole idea and threatened to file for an injunction. The local district representative commented, "We made it clear that if healthcare was going to be resolved, it would be resolved by modifying the system in the U.S., not by offshoring or exporting our own people." USW President Leo Gerard said, "No U.S. citizen should be exposed to the risk involved in travel internationally for health care services." The USW sent a letter to members of Congress that included the following (Parks, 2006):

> Our members, along with thousands of unrepresented workers, are now being confronted with proposals to literally export themselves to have certain "expensive" medical procedures provided in India.
>
> With companies now proposing to send their own American employees abroad for less expensive health care services, there can be no doubt that the U.S. health care system is in immediate need of massive reform.
>
> The right to safe, secure, and dependable health care in one's own country should not be surrendered for any reason, certainly not to fatten the profit margins of corporate investors.

The union also cited the lack of comparable malpractice coverage in other countries. The company agreed to find a domestic source of care for Mr. Garrett, but may continue the experiment with its salaried, non-union employees. Carl Garrett responded unhappily. "The company dropped the ball . . . people have given me so much encouragement," he said, "so much positive response, and they're devastated. A lot of people were waiting for me to report back on how it went and perhaps go themselves. This leaves them in limbo too" (Jonsson, 2006, p. 2).

Discussion Questions

1. What difference did it probably make that BRPP is an ESOP owned by the union members or that the national union is busy recruiting health care workers as members?

2. What are the ethical implications of a reward of up to $10,000 for the employee to go to India for a major procedure?

3. If you were a hospital administrator, how would you react when a number of patients and companies began to ask to bargain about prices, including presenting price quotes from companies like IndUShealth?

4. What would be the difference in the bargaining position of an academic medical center and a large tertiary community hospital system?

5. How might state and national governments respond to this increasingly popular phenomenon?

Part II

THE POLICY ANALYSIS PROCESS

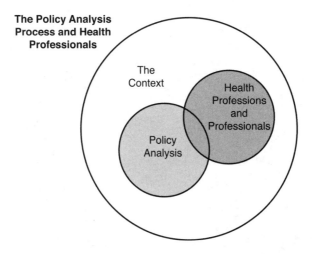

The Policy Analysis Process and Health Professionals

The Context

Health Professions and Professionals

Policy Analysis

This section describes policy analysis processes applicable to health care. It begins in Chapter 7 with the need to develop an appropriate definition of the issues to be analyzed and then presents three major areas of analysis: technology (Chapters 8 and 9), political feasibility (Chapter 10), and economic viability (Chapter 11). This is followed in Chapter 12 by a review of values issues that impact many analyses and the presentation process and in Chapter 13 by consideration of implementation issues. Although each chapter covers a discrete topic, in the real world these are usually intertwined and are often addressed iteratively or in parallel.

Chapter 7

The Policy Analysis Process: Identification and Definition

In a December 1, 2005, talk at Duke University, Dr. Julie Gerberding, then director of the Centers for Disease Control and Prevention (CDC), suggested three important concepts to consider when looking at recent public health crises (e.g., epidemics, terrorist attacks, and natural disasters) and preparing for future threats:

- Imagination
- Connectivity
- Scale

She argued that we have to do a better job of imagining problems if we are to prepare for them. The connectivity issues—the ease and speed with which information, people, and diseases move around the world, bringing clusters of individuals into contact—are widely understood. These issues are often cited in descriptions of globalization (Friedman, 2005; Naim, 2005). Scale relates to the fact that when critical events happen, they happen on a scale of considerable magnitude. Citing the response to Hurricane Katrina in New Orleans, Dr. Gerberding noted that the lack of preparedness was not due to a failure of imagination. The tragedy was widely forecast. Connectivity worked favorably, as rescuers and support resources quickly arrived from all over the United States and Mexico. To her, much of the problem was one of scale. The governments involved were not prepared to deal with events of that scale. However, Admiral Thad W. Allen, the U.S. Coast Guard commandant who took over the federal response, reported at least one failure of imagination. There were procedures to deal with a hurricane and its storm surge, and there were procedures to deal with a flood; however, there were not procedures to deal with both occurring in the same place only a day apart.

When it comes to preparing for or responding effectively and imaginatively to any major health care event or pressing health policy issue, defining the problem is critical. Imagination involves calling on more than what is already known and experienced. There are a number of adages about how well generals are prepared to fight the last war. Learning from experience is a good thing, but only when it is relevant experience.

Identifying and defining the problem may be only the first steps. When experienced individuals who deal regularly with an issue are unable to resolve it, one or more of the following conditions likely pertain:

1. There is not a shared understanding of the nature of the problem.
2. There is a shared understanding, but it is not appropriate to the situation.
3. There is a realistic and relevant understanding, but it is not in some people's interest to resolve it.
4. There is an appropriate understanding and a shared desire for a solution, but there are not sufficient resources to implement the solution:
    a. There are inadequate facilitation and leadership skills to reach the necessary compromises.
    b. There are inadequate levels of skilled personnel to implement the preferred solution.
    c. There are insufficient financial resources to implement the preferred solution.
    d. The implementers cannot focus the political process on the problem or the solution sufficiently to move ahead.
    e. Some combination of the above.

In this chapter, we deal primarily with the first two conditions—making sure that there is an accurate and appropriate definition of the problem that is understood by all involved. The other conditions relate to technological assessments, political feasibility, economic feasibility, implementation, and leadership and are addressed elsewhere.

GETTING THE SCENARIO RIGHT

Assessing the Impact of a Health Policy

A World Health Organization (1999) report, the *Gothenberg Consensus Paper*, defines a *health impact assessment* as, "A combination of procedures, methods and tools by which a policy, programme or project may be judged as to its potential effects on the health of a population and the distribution of those effects within the population." As we shall see later, the distributional effects may take these studies well beyond the population at immediate risk, especially in a market system like the United States.

If we are to reach agreement about the scope of potential and existing problems, possible alternatives, and desired outcomes, we have to reach some agreement on several key areas (University of Birmingham, 2003):

1. The relevant definition of health
2. Identification of the target population
3. The current or likely future status of the health of a targeted population
4. The factors that determine the health status of concern with that population
5. The methods realistically available to change that health status
6. The responsibilities of the various actors in dealing with the identified issues
7. The societal values that are to govern the selection of alternatives and the acceptability of alternative outcomes

A health policy analysis seldom starts with a clean slate. The starting point is usually a recent major event. Often that leads to overcorrecting for earlier mistakes, rather than taking a fresh look at the situation. Complex systems are full of problems in search of solutions, but they are also full of solutions in search of problems. A policy proposal is often put forward by someone with a specific solution already in mind. It is important, however, to ask whether a broader range of alternative solutions should be considered. One secretary of defense used to complain that the Joint Chiefs sent up the requisite three alternatives, two of which did not count. It is a waste of scarce resources to evaluate alternatives that do not count. Screening for additional alternatives, however, can be enlightening. The following box describes an actual situation in which this occurred.

Finding an Alternative Definition

The administrators and the board of trustees of a large academic medical center were at an impasse over the design of their new facility. At issue was whether to purchase a new and relatively untried monorail system for the distribution of supplies, laboratory samples, paperwork, and so forth. The investment would be large, and the risk was relatively high. Finally, one of the senior medical staff asked a consultant to meet with them. After listening to the arguments on both sides, the consultant asked, "Why are you in a hurry to make a decision now?" They replied, "The architect for the first building needs to know how big to make the passageways and utility channels in the plans which are nearly complete." After listening to the various concerns, the consultant asked, "How much additional would it cost to design the building to take either the new or the old technology?" Here was a new alternative. It turned out the additional cost was not much when compared with the uncertain gamble on the new technology. Both sides quickly agreed on that new alternative.

Defining Health

Table 7-1 presents the view of health and health care espoused in the constitution of the World Health Organization. Although the United States is a U.N. member state, one would be hard put to find consensus in the United States on a number of the points that it cites as basic principles.

Asking people in the United States if health is more than the absence of illness or infirmity could produce a host of different responses. Some respondents might come down on the side of physical and mental well-being but have a problem with trying to address social well-being under the heading of health. Indeed, the fact that we have millions of uninsured and do not provide mental health care to a large proportion of the population would seem to indicate a lack of commitment to physical and mental well-being.

Those analyzing or deciding on a policy need to understand the differences in the operational definitions of health that are represented around the table. In the best of all possible worlds, those seated at the table would agree on that definition and move on, but sometimes the art of politics depends, in part, on knowing when to try to agree on principles, or on actions, or on both, and whether to use limited political capital to try to bring them into alignment publicly.

Table 7-1 Excerpts from the Preamble of the Constitution of the World Health Organization

. . . the following principles are basic . . .

· Health is a state of complete physical, mental, and social well-being and not merely the absence of disease or infirmity.

· The enjoyment of the highest attainable standard of health is one of the fundamental rights of every human being without distinction of race, religion, political belief, or economic or social condition.

· The health of all peoples is fundamental to the attainment of peace and security and is dependent on the fullest cooperation of individuals and States.

· The achievement of any state in the promotion and protection of health is of value to all.

· Unequal development in different countries in the promotion of health and control of disease, especially communicable disease, is a common danger.

· Healthy development of the child is of basic importance, and the ability to live harmoniously in a changing total environment is essential to such development.

· The extension to all peoples of the benefits of medical, psychological, and related knowledge is essential to the fullest attainment of health.

· Informed opinion and active co-operation on the part of the public are of the utmost importance in the improvement of the health of the people.

· Governments have a responsibility for the health of their peoples which can be fulfilled only by the provision of adequate health and social measures.

Source: Reproduced from: Constitution of the WHO, Basic Documents, 45th Ed. Supplied 2006, October at www.who.int/governance/eb/who_constitution_en.pdf

Defining the Target Population

Just what population are we talking about? The history of community mental health centers illustrates how difficult—and critical—it can be to answer this question. A system designed to help the developmentally disabled and severely and persistently mentally ill morphed into a general mental health treatment system in which many practitioners avoided the original target group and concentrated on the more rewarding (professionally and financially) cases (Torrey, 1997). As more and more states now focus more intently on the original target population, many of those previously served must rely more on private payment or insurance or go without.

An analyst in charge of developing a maternal health program policy who wanted to determine the health status of the target population might start by looking at the health of all females of childbearing age. But what constitutes childbearing age when 8-year-old girls and women in their 50s can give birth? An analyst would have to put both an upper and a lower limit on the age range in order to get a count of the target population.

Identifying the Health Status of the Target Population

The next step after defining the target population is to assess its health status. Many data sources are available for this task, but sometimes they do not match up exactly with the target population that has been identified. The CDC demonstrated the complex connection between defining the target population and assessing its health status using available data in 2000 when it reported on changes in serum foliate levels in noninstitutionalized women ages 15–44 who participated in the National Health and Nutrition Examination Surveys from 1991 to 1994 and in 1999 (CDC, 2000). It did not conduct a special study of pregnant women or women of childbearing age, the recommended target group. Instead, it segmented the data in the existing surveys and analyzed that. There certainly are women bearing children after age 44, before age 15, and in institutions; however, the age range covered most of the potential recipients, and the differences in outcomes were so great that the analysts did not feel the need for further refinements.

Looking at the health status of the target population in the aggregate can often obscure differences between subgroups. One frequently hears about the millions of people in the United States who lack health insurance. Does their health status suffer because they lack insurance? Sometimes and sometimes not. Historically, many of the uninsured have been young people who have made a calculated trade-off between the cost of health insurance and the fact that they are young and healthy (a group sometimes referred to as "the young immortals"). Yes, they are more likely to have severe auto accidents than an older population, but until one happens they are not part of the 20% of the population that accounts for 80% of health care costs. They are transferring the risk of low-probability events to the public at large because they would probably receive care anyway. Others may want insurance and need it, but are simply unable to afford it. The point is that there is plenty of room to talk at each other rather than solve problems. One can talk about the issue by discussing the uninsured as a bloc or about the needs of specific segments. The important thing is that analysts define clearly whom they are talking about.

Identifying the Factors Determining the Health Status of Concern Within That Population

Causation is the bane of the policy world. Politicians and polemicists would have us think that the right policy is certainly this or definitely that. If it were that simple, however, there would be little need for analysis. The conclusions of studies seeking causation are seldom as clear as obvious results of taking the handle off the local water pump and watching the cholera epidemic stop. Most policy problems support the characterization by the Danish mathematician and poet Piet Hein, who wrote, "Problems worthy of attack prove their worth by hitting back." Inference is one thing, and causation is another.

If we return to our historical population of uninsured individuals as a target (it will take years to understand the full impact of the ACA), we find that they have poorer health than the average population, and data show that they are more likely to postpone care and not fill a prescription because of cost and have an avoidable hospitalization. One might counter that some lack coverage because they are in poor health and cannot find employment. Also, when one deals with a policy issue of uninsured populations, one probably needs to address issues of the underinsured as well. Problems of definition and causation are also thornier because so many studies and analyses rely on information entered into the claims data bank, which does not include information on the underinsured because they do not generate claims.

Identifying Methods Realistically Available to Change Health Status

With all the alternative solutions being offered for health policy changes, the analyst needs to identify the few that are most realistic economically and politically. By politically realistic, we mean acceptable to those who are likely to fund and use the analysis and implement its findings. Many potential actors may express a preference for specific alternatives *a priori*. The analyst must respect these preferences and still keep the process simple enough that decision makers are not likely to ignore the work or be confused by it.

Defining the Methods Operationally and Optimally

In an industry with a recognized high degree of waste like health care, one has to add the step of defining the alternatives operationally by answering the following questions:

1. Has the alternative been in use?

   a. If so, determine how it could be improved prior to applying it in this context.
   b. If not, define it in more detail to establish operational feasibility.

2. For the more promising, feasible, and relevant alternatives, determine optimal methods and procedures for delivery.

3. Use these optimal processes to determine costs and effectiveness where relevant.

HIDDEN ASSUMPTIONS

Other assumptions, often dealing with values, can impinge on an analysis. They may get addressed, or they may be left implicit or tacit to maintain organizational civility or political compromise. They include professional perspectives and personal conceptions of equity, due process, decision-making methods, and rights. This is not an exhaustive list. It does not include many value issues, such as the value of a human life.

If the group doing the analysis seems to be agreeing on most things but cannot reach closure, look for hidden assumptions that might be holding up the process. If the problem persists, it may be necessary to bring in a skilled process observer who will listen carefully to what people are saying and identify the stumbling blocks. It is unlikely that the team's leadership can push successfully toward closure until hidden assumptions have been addressed.

Professional Perspectives

Social science disciplines have built-in assumptions about how societal and personal decisions are made, and these underlie known differences between each discipline's jargon, research methods, and notions about things such as cognitive processes, equity, and appropriate governance. These assumptions also support aggregate assumptions (sometimes called visions) of institutional roles and how effective change takes place in a society.

Each discipline appears to redefine issues in its own terms and research approaches. MacRae (1976, pp. 109–110) used his background in public policy research to characterize how social science disciplines approach decision making. He noted that disciplines talk to themselves, try to emulate the physical sciences, like to believe that they engage in "value-free" activities, and reward research that conforms to existing theory. He characterized four policy-related disciplines, as follows:

- "Economics deals with the satisfaction of existing individual preferences."
- "Psychology—especially in its relations with education and psychotherapy—is concerned with the changes that may be produced in preferences and their structures in individual personalities."

- "Sociology is concerned with social norms, and a related emphasis is on joint action undertaken to change them."
- "Political science, insofar as it escapes from the economic perspective, deals with those roles and institutions in which responsible citizens and public officials may be expected to consider the general welfare."

In business education, most decisions are assumed to be individual rather than social outcomes. Marketers usually see preferences as malleable. Decision theorists usually assume that they are a given. The assumptions cited by MacRae, although subject to challenge, still seem to dominate today, and the disciplines differ in their approaches to common issues of our society involved with ethics, markets, social change programs, political regimes, and social norms.

Implications for Problem Solving

Think about a meeting called to consider chronic local underemployment and homelessness. One participant cites educational differences, whereas another mentions disparities in educational opportunities. Then another speaks of imperfections in the local labor market. Oops! By now, the meeting is ready to derail. Some consider the term *labor market* to be dehumanizing. Others see it as jargon. What is a concrete, defined concept to one discipline may have a strong negative valence for another.

Multidisciplinary groups will be better able to work together cooperatively if they discuss the following early on in their work:

1. How can we express our personal assumptions and vision and incorporate them into intellectual discourse that respects others' points of view? This includes acceptance of the sensitivities of those with other approaches.
2. What notions of social equity and social change processes do we hold?
3. What is a reasonable objective for social change?
4. If we cannot agree on those assumptions and visions, how can we best cooperate on limited objectives that are compatible with our disparate viewpoints?

Is it unrealistic to expect any ad hoc group of busy professionals to spend the time necessary to achieve this level of trust and understanding? Yes, but without that level of investment, the group may be wasting its time by convening in the first place. Without that trust and understanding, participants are unlikely to respond effectively. At a minimum, thinking about one's own assumptions and visions and their topic-specific and temporal inconsistencies is a prerequisite for a personal commitment and contribution to interdisciplinary work. Sowell (2002, p. 254) suggested that "an analysis of the implications and dynamics of visions can clarify issues without reducing dedication to one's own vision, even when it is understood to be a vision, not an incontrovertible fact, an iron law, or an opaque moral imperative." All too often visions are unexamined after years of immersion in one's profession, and becoming aware of them in one's self and in others is probably half of the uphill battle toward successful interdisciplinary problem solving.

Professional Conflicts

Similar problems are of concern among the physical and medical sciences, according to the National Academy of Sciences and the Institute of Medicine (IOM, 2000a). When working with a multidisciplinary group, you have to be sensitive to these professional visions. If you are including health professionals in the group, you also have to deal with the animosities between professions that have existed for years, especially those relating either to status differentials (such as nurses' anger at their treatment by physicians) or conflicting economic interests (such as between academic and community-based physicians). People will bring those experiences and attitudes into the meeting room.

Equity

Discussion aimed at defining a situation may stall because individuals have not reached consensus about the definition of equity to be applied. People's assumptions about equity are seldom on the table unless the group is very homogeneous in terms of value structures. If it is homogeneous, then the group faces the problem of all of the members seeing things the same way, sometimes called *group think*. In almost any health care policy analysis, the issue arises of how the costs and benefits are distributed. Then follows the issue of what is fair. Individuals in a policy group can define equity at least five ways: (1) equal payment, (2) equal inputs, (3) equal risk, (4) equal satisfaction of demand, or (5) equal process (McLaughlin, 1984).

Equal Payment

In legal terms, equity requires equal payment for equal services. This concept is written into a number of requirements of government programs; however, that notion of equity omits two important conditions:

externalities and ability to pay. Externalities can be illustrated by the fact that you cannot go to school with a case of measles even though you are not going to catch measles again. In other words, the costs of your actions are external to your frame of reference. A neighbor may not inoculate her children because she cannot pay for the vaccine. The county health department may provide the service for free because it is in the public interest to avoid the spread of the disease and the permanent injury that might result from additional cases. The health department has a number of policy choices in providing the vaccine from tax revenues. It could provide it to all comers as a free *public good*. It could subsidize the process and charge less than private-sector providers to encourage participation, or it could use a sliding-fee scale based on ability to pay.

Equal Inputs

A communicable disease program might choose to allocate its resources to provide so many service resources per capita throughout the counties of a state. That way there would not be any hassles over whether any one section of the state is being shortchanged.

Equal Risk

If illegal drug use is high in a particular section of a city, prevention programs are likely to be concentrated in that area. This is likely to increase productivity, but one might object to some versions of that approach as trying to equalize risk across the whole community. If I live in a neighborhood that has a relatively low incidence of crack cocaine use, I still may want it stopped in my neighborhood. Residents of upscale neighborhoods might be arguing that they are entitled to less risk because they are paying more in taxes.

Equal Satisfaction of Demand (or Need)

Many health care organizations start out allocating resources on the basis of need, as professionally determined. After a while, need may or may not turn into consumer demand, even when the resources available are adequate. Staff will ultimately be assigned to clinics in proportion to the number of patient visits, and ambulances will be assigned to various sections of town based on the frequency of emergency calls.

Equal (Due) Process

People want the same access to health care, regardless of whether they use it. They want to be treated with the same respect regardless of ability to pay, and they do not want unreasonable waiting times. These desires are relatively independent of the equality of inputs, risks, and so forth. They are related to what one would call equal process (Drucker, 1974).

Decision Making

A team also has to address the members' hidden assumptions about how the group reaches decisions. It is unlikely in policy analysis that decisions would be reached by majority vote; however, the group does need to think about the concept of consensus and how to determine when and whether it has been reached. The group also has to decide how to handle dissent. In some settings, a dissenting report or note is appropriate, whereas in others it would not be acceptable. Sometimes sensitivity analysis can be used to address disagreements over numerical values.

Rights

Paradoxically, no hidden assumption gets more attention than whether health care is a right. A yes or no answer gets us nowhere. Is one talking about antibiotics for a serious illness, cosmetic surgery, or in vitro fertilization? Again, there is a need to try to define what one is arguing about rather than repeating assertions based on undefined assumptions. What about the example of a patient's right to see his or her medical record? What if there are comments on it about the patient or the patient's family being uncooperative? To what extent is the health record a business asset of the physician, the hospital, or the health maintenance organization (HMO)? Again, state laws may differ on this, but, increasingly, the patient is gaining more access, a sign of the waning dominance of the medical professions.

In some cases, issues of rights may be extremely contentious, but those situations are usually politicized well beyond the domain of the policy analysis team. Certainly, this has been the case with Levitt and Dubner (2005) and their assertion that the passage of abortion rights laws by the states and then the *Roe vs. Wade* decision are closely associated with a decline in serious crime rates some 20 years later. Both liberals and conservatives have been left unhappy by that finding.

Collective Versus Individual Responsibility for Health

Social welfare versus individual welfare is the elephant in the room in health care policy. Garrison (2009) makes this point in looking at the ways that the United Kingdom and the United States look at utility in allocating public resources. The United Kingdom clearly has come down in fovor of having experts determine utility using quality-adjusted life-years (QALY) and cost data, whereas the United States has pretty much limited discussion of the concept to academic papers.

Garrison (2009) noted that these choices are determined by the following economic approaches:

- Monoposony (U.K. position): Experts use QALY and cost-utility analyses to maximize social benefit.
- Administered system competition: Experts determine minimal benefit package and use comparative effectiveness and cost for decisions at the margin.
- Consumer-driven (free market): Buyers (patients and payers) are provided with effectiveness and cost data and are then left to let them trade off utilities.
- Oligopolistic competition: Vendors prove effectiveness and let payers determine utilities.
- Monopoly: Providers and insurers maximize profitability.

Garrison suggested that defining a minimum benefit package (called an essential benefit package in the ACA) is a compromise between the two contending approaches—meeting a socially acceptable minimum for care, but leaving marginal choices up to the individual. Garrison (2009) and Nord, Daniels, and Kamlet (2009) also pointed out a more subtle difference in the approaches: experts tend to use average *ex-ante* utilities, whereas patients tend to use experiential ones based on their current state of health.

DEFINING WHAT IS A MEDICAL PROBLEM

One medical care debate concerns the medicalization of so much of human experience. How much is this improving our quality of life, and is it worth paying for individually or collectively? Increasingly, we are expanding the conditions that can be treated, especially with biochemical treatments, yet all of these treatments have negative impacts beyond costs. They introduce side effects, some hazardous, especially when combined with other treatments. Because treatment effects vary from individual to individual, what is the dividing line between:

- Those who would benefit from treatment and those who would not?
- Those who need treatment and those who do not?
- Those whose treatment should be covered by a society and those for whom treatment is a "lifestyle" choice?

Table 7-2 Strategies Attributed to Disease-Mongering Campaigns

- Develop a drug effective with a small segment of the population that is heavily impacted by the symptoms.
- Redefine the disease in terms of the symptoms that the drug treats.
- Inflate disease prevalence rates.
- Encourage academic specialists to promote new disease definitions in seminars and articles.
- Advertise to create anxiety about the symptoms, which may be quite normal.
- Promote the drug as an aggressive, first-line treatment for the symptoms.
- Promote treatment of measurable risk factors, especially if their status is measurable.
- Promote the drug widely to all physicians rather than specialists handling problematic cases.

Increasingly, the debates over where these limits should be are moving into the realm of discussions about permissible marketing, advertising, and commercialization and charges of outright disease mongering. Much of this debate centers on the role of direct-to-consumer advertising and other marketing efforts, particularly by the pharmaceutical industry. **Table 7-2** outlines promotional steps that seem to lead to the development of new, highly advertised treatments or screening policies. One example is the recommendation that all pregnant women be screened for herpes, which is not supported by the CDC or the U.S. Preventative Services Task Force, but rather has been advocated by continuing medical education instructors in programs supported by the suppliers of screening tests and treatment drugs. A very small portion of children born to infected mothers will experience blindness, cerebral palsy, and/or death, but there is inadequate evidence of the extent to which screening and subsequent treatment for asymptomatic women whose sexual partners do not have the disease would avoid these adverse outcomes, and there are risks of significant side effects. Study results on the cost effectiveness of such screening vary widely as well (Armstrong, 2006), yet providers of tests and treatments are free to go ahead paying for presentations that support their positions.

CONCLUSION

Defining the problem and the process appropriately is critical to effective analysis. That is not to say that there will not be learning along the way. Policy analysis is a learning process, and there must be sufficient cognitive flexibility among the actors to allow for learning. At the same time, it is a step in a political process. Some may view policy analysis as a purely political process and may even object to the notion of analysis. The policy process must be open to inputs from a variety of viewpoints and attempt to deal with objections as they arise. Groups may even go so far as to reveal and explore hidden assumptions among the participants when it is essential to achieving a product that is acceptable to the working group and, hopefully, to the users of the analysis.

Key issues that are likely to arise include the operational definition of health to be used, the definition of the problem, hidden professional and personal values, and the assumptions of those participating in the policy process. Key decisions relate to how much time, effort, and political capital to expend in attempting to bring recommendations and values into alignment.

Case 7   **Small Area Variations**

BACKGROUND

One of the ways to examine the efficiency and efficacy of different approaches to medical care is to study variations in the types of care delivered in different areas and then compare the outcomes. The Dartmouth Atlas Working Group at Dartmouth Medical School uses Medicare data to conduct this type of "small area analysis."

In 2006, the group reported that residents of Elyria, Ohio, received angioplasties at four times the national average. Angioplasty is an invasive, nonsurgical procedure widely utilized for treating heart attacks and alleviating symptoms of heart disease. It is also used in cases of severe heart disease in hopes of possibly preventing future heart attacks. The procedure involves pushing a collapsed balloon into the coronary artery and then expanding the balloon to press plaque against the arterial wall. Often a stent is left behind in an effort to keep the artery open. Other approaches to heart disease include drug therapy, lifestyle changes, and coronary artery bypass grafts. The latter procedure requires open heart surgery.

Elyria has a population 54,533 (2010 census) and is the county seat of Lorain County. In 2003, the rate of angioplasties in Elyria was 42 procedures per 1,000 Medicare enrollees. By comparison, the rate for all of Ohio that year was 13.5, and the national rate was 11.3. All but 2 of the 35 cardiologists in Elyria at the time belonged to the North Ohio Heart Center, which relied heavily on angioplasties. The center performed 3,400 angioplasties in 2004 (Abelson, 2006c).

Case 7 *(continued)*

There is considerable controversy about different treatment options for blocked coronary arteries. Some experts, according to an August 2006 *New York Times* article on the Dartmouth findings, "say that they are concerned that Elyria is an example, albeit an extreme one, of how medical decisions in this country can be influenced by financial incentives and professional training more than solid evidence of what works best for a particular person" (Abelson, 2006c). .

According to medical historian Dr. David S. Jones, neither angioplasty nor coronary bypass surgery have been shown to prolong life except in cases of severe disease. Risks associated with bypass surgery include infections and brain damage resulting in memory loss and cognitive impairment. One of the concerns with angioplasty is that most heart attacks stem from tiny, often invisible lesions, and angioplasties tend to target the larger lesions that show up on angiograms. He argues for a greater focus on prevention through medicines and lifestyle changes (Park, 2013).

Angioplasty and coronary bypass surgery are highly profitable, and together they make up a $100 billion a year industry in the United States. At the time of the Dartmouth study, Medicare was paying Elyria's community hospital $11,000 for angioplasty with a coated stent, and the cardiologist performing the procedure received about $800. Bypasses, however, were performed by surgeons from the Cleveland Clinic who had privileges at the community hospital. Those surgeons received up to $2,200 per operation, and the hospital would receive up to $25,000.

OUTCOMES

The founder and president of the North Ohio Heart Center responded to the Dartmouth findings by telling the *New York Times* that the center had good results with its patients and attributed the high use of angioplasty to early diagnostic interventions and aggressive treatment of coronary heart disease and to concerns about patient safety. Because of safety concerns, the center treats many of its patients in stages, doing more than one admission and procedure. Other cardiologists might perform multiple procedures at the same time. Thirty-one percent of the Elyria center's patients underwent multiple admissions and procedures, about three times the rate in Cleveland. Insurers report that the hospital's results are good, and UnitedHealth has named it a center of excellence for heart care.

Discussion Questions

1. What do you think about using small area studies based on large Medicare databases, such as the one presented here, to identify outliers?

2. Salaried cardiologists at Kaiser Permanente in northern Ohio used drugs more often and performed cardiac procedures at slightly below the national rate. What role might different financial incentives be playing here?

3. If you were Anthem Blue Cross and Blue Shield in Ohio, what studies would you conduct to attempt to explain and/or deal with these striking local differences in treatments and costs?

Chapter 8

The Policy Analysis Process: Health Technology Assessment

Health technology assessment involves multiple disciplines because in the end it must take into account the usual variables of cost, efficacy, safety, and effectiveness, together with organizational and individual adoption, ethical and legal issues, and societal impacts. It is an important aspect of health care planning, and the accelerating rate of technological change in health care will make it even more important in the future. This is due to the following:

- Increasing investments in medical research at the molecular level, leading toward breakthroughs in molecular biology and genetics
- Applications of information technology to medical research and epidemiology
- Globalization of health research and health delivery, which reduces costs and increases market competition
- Increased will to enhance dissemination and application of new knowledge and acknowledged evidence-based practices

Advances in technology, its adoption, and its implementation are a mixed blessing to policy planners. They present new possibilities for intervention and improvement, but each new possibility comes with new issues and uncertainties about future costs, efficacy, financing, and ethical decision making. Reliable technological forecasts are important in health care for the following reasons:

- Long lead times for testing and approval of new technology
- Slowness of adoption of new technology due to bureaucracy, decentralized decision making, and diffusion of power
- Impact of new technology on delivery and costs of health care (McLaughlin & Sheldon, 1974)

TERMINOLOGY

When the Washington State legislature established the Health Technology Clinical Committee to review the evidence basis for up to eight medical technologies a year, the authorizing legislation, House Bill 2575, defined *health technology* as "medical and surgical devices and procedures, medical equipment, and diagnostic tests." The definition specifically excluded pharmaceuticals, but the state already had established a separate process for evaluating pharmaceuticals and establishing a preferred drug list. For most of us, when we use the word *technology* we are often referring to highly sophisticated machines, computers, and networks, such as the Internet. In the context of health care, however, we should think about the term more broadly. In this chapter, we include pharmaceuticals and medical procedures within the definition of health and medical technologies, regardless of whether they are considered high tech.

At the same time, issues related to computerized storing, processing, and exchanging of information—in other words, information technology—play a major role in the current evolution of health and health care. It is critical that they play an even larger role in the immediate future. In the application of information technology, the health care sector lags behind other industries.

Key terms related to the discussion of health information technology (HIT) include the following:

- **Health information network (HIN).** A computer network that connects provider offices, hospitals, and other places where health care information is generated or used in order to allow the secure exchange of electronic information.
- **Electronic medical records (EMR) or electronic health records (EHR).** These are databases or other software applications used

for electronically storing and retrieving family histories, diagnoses, treatment records, laboratory results, digital images, prescriptions, and other elements of a patient's medical record.
- **Personal health record.** Patients can use Web portals or other technological interfaces to gain access to their own medical records. Robust personal health records are interactive and include health information other than just medical treatment records. The patient may own the record, but at the least should be able to maintain and add information to it and share it with the patient's entire care team, which could include family members and other sources of support as well as medical providers.
- **Regional health information organization (RHIO).** An organization, often a nonprofit, that promotes and coordinates the use of HIT within a given region.

This chapter looks concurrently at medical technology used to provide care and information technology used to document and coordinate care.

TECHNOLOGICAL FORECASTING

Some new health care technologies were immediate successes. Others failed at first and then succeeded, or they succeeded and then failed. There are even cases of technologies that succeeded, failed, and then succeeded again. Our ability to forecast adoption rates and outcomes with new technology is limited at best; however, we have no choice but to try because it is an important input into rational decision making. Many of our recent health crises are described by able thinkers as failures of vision. We cannot be prepared, given the scale of many events, unless we have predictive scenarios with which to work.

Aiming at a Moving Target

One problem with forecasting technology as part of analyzing policy options is that we are always moving ahead with limited knowledge, despite our admittedly cumbersome systems to avoid unnecessary uncertainty, such as the Food and Drug Administration's (FDA) new drug clinical trial and licensing procedures. Forecasts differ based on the forecaster's particular vision of how society works. Other differences in forecasts may be driven by tunnel vision, self-interest, or by one's general outlook on life (e.g., optimistic or pessimistic). The forecasting process has to accept the context of the analysis, yet avoid being biased completely by that context.

Forecasting Costs

The ability to forecast costs is important. In the United States, Centers for Medicare & Medicaid Services (CMS) actuaries are responsible for making long-range forecasts about the costs of Medicare and Medicaid. Some trends, such as inflation rates, are relatively predictable. Many critical cost estimates, however, require assumptions about where technology is headed. Around 1990 when the Oregon Health Services Commission was attempting to set up a utility ranking for medical conditions and treatments, it gave a very low utility to the treatment for AIDS, because at that time there was a very low chance of survival. Today, the utility ranking would most likely be very different considering that we have far more effective treatment resources for AIDS. The drug costs of treating those living with AIDS have now become a significant component of current and future health costs and have to be addressed in planning.

Forecasting Efficacy

One important component of most health care forecasts is how well an alternative will treat a given medical problem. Is the alternative safe, and is it effective? This is why new drugs and devices undergo FDA safety approval before they enter the market. The effectiveness of most surgical procedures seems to be improving as less invasive methods have been developed and become part of the standard of care. In 1932, a member of our family required a subtotal thyroidectomy. The patient's survival was doubtful, and he was laid up so long that he lost his job. The long-term prognosis was not encouraging. Some 50 years later another family member, born in 1932, needed a subtotal thyroidectomy (for a different diagnosis). He was hospitalized a couple of days, was back in the office within a few more days with the sutures still in his neck, and his prognosis was excellent. Contemporary experience with infectious diseases is less consistent. Antibiotics have worked wonders, but we face a continuing battle over whether we will stay ahead of microbes' ability to develop resistance. Serious diseases such as HIV, hepatitis, and influenza evolve, and unknown ones may cross species to create new diseases, like SARS and bird flu, and potential pandemics. These kinds of shifts in efficacy complicate our forecasting efforts.

LEVELS OF TECHNOLOGICAL FORECASTING

Sometimes it is important to forecast the effect of a given technology; other times it is adequate to forecast a specific system variable. Gilfillan (1952) visualized six systematic levels of "future causality." They were as follows:

1. A specific invention
2. Alternative inventions for the same purpose
3. Technical accomplishment
4. Social and economic effects possible with a set of technical accomplishments
5. Social and economic effects predicted to flow from a set of accomplishments
6. Secondary and indirect effects of the predicted technology

All too often we focus on the invention or the technical accomplishment and not on the latter three levels of prediction. Consequently, we face surprises and unintended consequences.

Sterman (2006) referred to these unintended consequences as policy resistance. He argued that many complex systems cannot be understood without some modeling of their behavior, including feedback loops that allow simulated system adaptation to the planned intervention. He suggests that this is true when the systems have the following characteristics:

- Constantly changing, adapting, and evolving
- Tightly coupled
- Governed by feedback
- Nonlinear
- History dependent
- Characterized by trade-offs
- Counterintuitive

Tight coupling implies that one actor reacts strongly in response to the actions of another actor. Weick (1976), however, suggested that it is also difficult to predict the behavior of systems when the actors are loosely coupled. History-dependent processes are ones that are very slow to change in response to the forecast interventions. Coye and Kell (2006) noted that barriers to adopting new technology are built into hospital budgeting processes. They classified them as fragmentation barriers and funding barriers. They also argued that there is a need for an umbrella organization in the United States to evaluate the evidence base behind new technologies and advise hospital decision makers. One concern they expressed is the resistance in the fragmented system to any disruptive technology, especially technology that physician groups find threatening. On the funding side, they argued for revolving loan funds and other new financing vehicles to support the adoption of new technology.

Selecting the Right Level

Addressing technological forecasting at the right level is important. All too often we are overly focused on the first and second levels of Gilfillan's typology (specific interventions and their alternatives) when others are the really critical ones. Two historical examples are Moore's Law and the Polaris missile program. In 1965, Gordon Moore, cofounder of Intel, observed that the number of transistors per square inch on integrated circuits had doubled every year since the integrated circuit was invented. He predicted that this trend would continue for the foreseeable future. Although the technology has changed greatly, data density has doubled approximately every 18 months. This is the current definition of Moore's Law, and it has held for decades. This has been a useful predictor at the third level (technical accomplishment), which is not tied to any specific invention. Today one has to factor in cloud computing as an alternative to more circuitry.

In 1957, the Soviet Union launched Sputnik, the world's first artificial satellite. In response, President Eisenhower called on the armed services to develop the capability for a deterrent nuclear ballistic missile. Admiral William Radford analyzed the trend in the size and weight of atomic warheads developed by Atomic Energy Commission contractors. He decided that over the period of time given for the task, the navy could not develop a missile to lift existing warheads, but it could develop one that would lift a warhead of the size that he forecast the contractors could make available by the end of that period. He proposed the Polaris program on this basis, and the gamble paid off. He did not have to know which technical breakthroughs would be achieved by the contractors. He looked at the overall trends in the specific design parameters that affected his forecast and his planning. Often this result can be conceived of as an envelope encompassing the results of a succession of innovations over time, as illustrated in **Figure 8-1**.

NOT JUST *WHAT*, BUT ALSO *WHEN*

To forecast the flow rates implied at the fifth level of Gilfillan's typology (predicted social and economic effects), one has to understand the

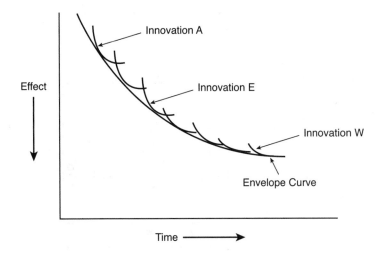

Figure 8-1 Using an envelope of innovations' effects to estimate a technology trend over time.

influence of several interacting processes that may affect the timing of the predicted outcome, including the following:

- Regulation (in many cases)
- Dissemination
- Adoption/compliance

It is not enough for the technology to be effective or even cost effective. It must also be pushed and guided through these additional processes, and policy analysts must be aware of their importance and their likely impact on the timing of adoption.

Regulation

Health care is one of the more heavily regulated sectors of our society. Proponents of a new technology must often prove to both regulators and potential users that it is safe and cost effective. The FDA process for dealing with potential new prescription drugs is a well-known example. It is outlined in **Table 8-1**. There are really two submission processes: one for an investigational new drug, and then another for new drug approval after clinical trials have been completed. Both of these processes can be very slow and costly but are in place to protect the populace against unsafe drugs.

Health care is also governed by many voluntary regulatory bodies that set standards and then administer professional licensure and certification,

Table 8-1 The Drug Discovery, Development, and Approval Process

It takes 12–15 years, on average, for an experimental drug to travel from the lab to U.S. patients. Only 5 in 5,000 compounds that enter preclinical testing make it to human testing. One of these five tested in people is approved.

	Discovery/Preclinical Testing	Phase I	Phase II	Phase III	FDA	Phase IV
Years	6.5	1.5	2	3.5	1.5	15 Total
Test population	Laboratory and animal studies	20–100 healthy volunteers	100–500 patient volunteers	1,000–5,000 patient volunteers		
Purpose	Access, safety, biological activity and formulations	Determine safety and dosage	Evaluate effectiveness; look for side effects	Confirm effectiveness, monitor adverse reactions from long-term use	Review and approval process	Additional postmarket testing required by FDA
Success rate	5,000 compounds evaluated		5 enter trials		1 approved	

File IND at FDA (between Discovery/Preclinical Testing and Phase I)

File INDA at FDA (between Phase III and FDA)

Source: Modified from: Pharmaceutical Research and Manufacturers of American. Phrma.org

inspect and certify facilities, and test and certify products and equipment. These are both collaborative and competitive settings where interest groups are represented and able to present their points of view. Most of the time compromise solutions are reached.

Dissemination and Adoption/Compliance

After a product or process is deemed effective by regulators and evaluators, it is available for use, but that does not mean it will be used. News about the safety and effectiveness of the new technology has to reach potential adopters. Many experiments have been conducted to determine how to introduce change into clinical practice. Clinical experts asked about adoption rates will often vastly overestimate the speed with which the change will take place. Adoption depends on the impact of experiences that build up to shared perceptions of technology's utility and ease of use (Davis, 1989; Tornatzky & Klein, 1982). Even when the criteria for use are met, it still takes a great deal of time to work through the various groups of potential adopters, starting with the risk takers and then the early adopters and then the late adopters and so forth (Rogers, 1983).

Where patients and providers are concerned, the adoption issue often centers on *compliance*; that is, the use of a prescription or a routine as directed. Compliance often starts high but then slacks off, particularly with chronically ill patients. An example is providers' low rates of compliance with rules about hand washing and use of antibacterial aids. In a hospital these can bring the rate of central line infections to close to zero, yet hospitals and payers have had only mixed success with sanctions, even when they are unusually strong for the health care environment.

The Interactive Adoption and Startup Processes: An Example

The much anticipated introduction of interoperable HIT systems is an example of the complexity of introducing new technology into the health care system. Despite the highly favorable cost-effectiveness estimates and the vast transformations that information technology has produced in other professional services, the adoption of HIT has been agonizingly slow.

Development and implementation of interconnected health care networks and EMRs requires a process characterized by six basic steps (Kibbe & McLaughlin, 2004):

- Acceptance of the need for the technical capability
- Alignment of interests and actions
- Feasibility demonstrations

- System blueprints (e.g., standards, protocols, and specifications)
- Configuration of operating systems, including certification of components
- Capital availability and financing

In recent years, the federal government has taken several proactive steps to promote more rapid deployment of HIT. The Health Information Technology for Economic and Clinical Health (HITECH) Act of 2009 memorialized the Office of the National Coordinator for Health Information Technology, which had been created by executive order in 2004. The office is charged with coordinating national efforts to promote the use of HIT and to develop systems for securely exchanging health information. Interoperability is a major focus of the office. HITECH, which was part of the American Recovery and Reinvestment Act (ARRA; that is, the "stimulus package") earmarked $25–$35 billion to promote HIT adoption. It included financial incentives for Medicaid and Medicare providers to purchase EMR systems and required the creation of phased-in "meaningful use" standards to ensure minimum capabilities for EMR systems.

Incentives for HIT adoption also are woven throughout the Affordable Care Act (ACA). Provisions addressing value-based care, evidence-based medicine, accountable care organizations (ACOs), medical health homes, independence-at-home demonstration projects, and many other initiatives were written to leverage HIT. HIT integration is a requirement for federal funding of many initiatives.

Acceptance of the need for interoperable health information capability is virtually universal now that more and more organizations are demanding computerized physician order entry (CPOE) as a safety measure and look to EMR systems to reduce waste and improve care. In addition, backers of consumer-driven health care and pay-for-quality see the availability of EMRs as a key to ongoing quality-of-care reporting and evaluation.

Alignment and Demonstrations of Feasibility

Providers and vendors have been busy aligning their efforts to produce systems that have considerably more interoperability and integration than in the past; however, two competing approaches arose, leading to multiple sets of standards. The vendors of large, complex, legacy systems recommended expanding their systems as intranet-based community networks. Advocates of Internet-based systems, such as the American Academy of Family Physicians, launched several demonstration projects involving implementation of an Internet-based application service provider system and an open standards technology infrastructure. The debate over the two approaches—expansion of proprietary systems versus reliance on the Internet and open standards—continues after more than a decade, and the idea of a national system of networks has still not been proven to be technically or economically feasible.

The Internet-based alternatives probably meet the description of a disruptive technology offered by Christensen, Bohmer, and Kenagy (2000)—simple, inexpensive, but capable of expanding across a boarder range of applications once it enters the marketplace. Christensen et al. observed, "Health care may be the most entrenched, change-averse industry in the United States. The innovations that will eventually turn it around are ready, in cases—but they cannot find backers" (p. 102). HIT was one of their primary examples, and the health care industry's implementation of this type of technology has lagged behind virtually all other information-intensive service sectors. Now there is agreement that the time for HIT has come.

Christensen et al. (2000) made a number of recommendations that would support disruptive innovations in health care, including the following:

- Less investment in high-end technology and simplification of complex problems
- Creation of new organizations to do the disrupting
- Overcoming regulatory barriers
- Leadership favorable to change

The technological forecaster must be alert to the possible emergence of disruptive technologies and be able to extrapolate the use of more sophisticated and expensive technologies into the future.

FORECASTING METHODS

Methods of forecasting include the following:

- Gathering expert opinions
- Time-series analysis
- Surveying and sampling
- Correlational and causal modeling
- Simulation and system modeling

Gathering Expert Opinion

When a technology is new, few individuals have sufficient experience to estimate trends or identify causal relationships. In such cases, a panel of experts in the field can be assembled to provide the best estimates of likely events and outcomes. If there are concerns about the dominance of one or two individuals in the forecasting process, a number of approaches, such as the nominal group or Delphi techniques, can be used to gather and feed back information while avoiding the undue influence of any one person. One major Delphi study of the future of health care consisted of three rounds of questionnaires. The first round asked the experts to suggest significant medical events that were likely to occur in the time period 1969–1999. These suggestions were then edited by the researchers to define 62 specific events. They were both technological and societal. For example, one event was defined as follows: "Solution of the histocompatability problem in transplantation, or the means around it." Another was, "We now have a legal precedent for the right of the terminally ill patient to determine his (or her) own time and method of death." A second questionnaire asked respondents to estimate for these 62 events a date of occurrence (in 5-year periods), a priority classification (high, low, or none), a current level of action category (much, little, or none), and the respondent's own level of expertise on this item (some or none). The third round reported back on 33 items where there was lack of agreement and asked the experts to refine their date estimates in light of the feedback. They were also asked to comment on why they selected a specific alternative. The third questionnaire also included scenarios that indicated interactions among them and their overall impact, and the respondents were asked to give their feelings about the acceptability of that overall possible outcome (McLaughlin & Sheldon, 1974). The resulting time estimate for the histocompatability question was 1980–1989; for determining the time and methods of death it was 1990–1994. Generally, the respondents were biased toward the optimistic side in their estimates. For example, these experts forecast that "A computer-based medical record bank covers 80% of the United States population and gives ready, accurate access to full medical records" would be in use by 1987.

Time-Series Analysis

If data are available, one can plot a trend line and extrapolate it to estimate a value in the future. This can be done visually or by using regression analysis. The model can weight the more recent data more heavily using one or another form of exponential smoothing. If there are multiple variables in the estimating equation, these can be adjusted for time lags where applicable (Gardner & McLaughlin, 1980). The examples of Moore's Law and the Polaris system both involved identifying and extrapolating technology trends over time. Software is readily available for applying alternative models to time-series analysis and selecting the one that fits the historical data most closely.

Surveying and Sampling

One can also ask the affected individuals about their anticipated behavior in response to a forecast scenario or analyze their past and current behavior by gathering survey data. Unfortunately, such surveys are useful only if the participants already have experience with the same or similar technology. A clinical trial is one form of surveying and sampling. A set of patients receives the new technology, and the results are observed and compared to the results of those who did not experience the change. This approach is likely to provide good forecasting information, but it is very expensive to develop and administer, and thus it is employed only if the stakes are very high. In the corporate world, this is called market research, and many consultative resources are available to help with these predictions.

Correlation and Causal Modeling

Life is simplest when we know how a given action causes a reaction. To figure that out, we often turn to regression analysis with time-series data, which tells us over time what is likely to happen to the dependent variable as independent variables change over time. One example is the assessment of survival rates for surgical procedures at an institution over time as experience mounts. For open heart surgery, survival rates increase with reduced pump time. Pump time decreases with experience, and experience usually increases more rapidly with greater volumes of procedures. In industry, this is called the *learning curve* or *progress function*. It has been shown to apply in health care, as well; however, one should be aware that most statistical models only show relationships that may or may not indicate a cause. Sometimes the relationships are temporally related so cause and effect are evident, but most of the time one can only say the degree to which two effects are correlated, leaving the issue of causation open to argument.

Simulation and System Modeling

As the picture of relationships becomes clearer, it does not necessarily become less complex. The complexity often calls for computer modeling of the system to see how the variables interact with each other. Four approaches to modeling seem to be in general use for prospective studies of technology (Homer & Hirsch, 2006; Jones et al., 2006):

- **Spreadsheet models (including those derived from regression models).** These involve the simple mathematical manipulation of estimates to provide projected results into the future.

- **Probabilitistic (Monte Carlo) simulations.** These add uncertainty to the model by including the distributions of random variables in the process and then projecting out the results of a large set of runs of the model that include both deterministic and stochastic elements. This approach has been used to support sensitivity analysis in a wide variety of analyses.
- **Feedback models (also known as *systems dynamics models*).** These are based on causal analysis and use an interlocking set of differential and algebraic equations to model complex systems, which may combine physical and societal elements.
- **Markov models.** These add one or more elements in which there are time-dependent transition probabilities from one state (e.g., getting better, staying the same, or dying) built into the model. The steady-state outcomes of patient disease progression can be determined analytically by some Markov models.
- **Scenarios.** These involve taking individual predictions and putting them into a story that assumes their coexistence and their interactions, the kinds of interactions that so often lead to unintended negative consequences of otherwise desirable plans.

Integrated Approaches

A major study can combine a number of these techniques. For example, a RAND Corporation study of the health status and medical treatment of the future elderly for CMS used the following:

- Expert panels were used to identify key technologies, their time of availability, and their impact (Shekelle et al., 2005).
- A representative sample of 100,000 Medicare beneficiaries' histories was drawn from the Medicare Current Benefit Surveys and a forecast was made of the health of future entrants based on the National Health Information Survey.
- A demographic and economic probabilistic simulation model was performed that moved participants ahead through time, changed their health status, estimated their survival patterns, and added a new cohort each year. This digital simulation was used to ask "what if" questions about the cost of Medicare under varying conditions of health status, medical innovation, and changes in chronic disease patterns (Goldman et al., 2004, 2005).

The RAND study showed that future costs would be quite sensitive to the implementation of certain new technologies and to the health status of the incoming cohorts, especially if obesity trends continued.

Appropriate Skill Sets

Technology assessment for health policy analysis relies on a combination of clinical assessment skills, data analysis skills, and technology evaluation skills to assess and implement medical technology, including the following:

1. **Identifying populations affected by the technology.** The affected population must be carefully defined so that data on it can be mined from available databases or collected appropriately. It must be the population specifically affected by the technology under consideration. After the affected population is identified, it must be segmented for measurement purposes. An example is segmentation of HIV/AIDS cases by ranges of T-cell counts to estimate the resources necessary to treat that population.

2. **Identifying the impact of the technology on the treatment of those populations.** This usually requires a detailed process analysis, including the identification of the process changes induced by the new technology. This may or may not require developing detailed protocols for the application of that technology. These details may be needed to estimate the impact of an innovation on the relevant costs. These costs are not only monetary, but also convenience costs of use by providers and patients.

3. **Projecting clinical outcomes under a representative cross section of payment and reward systems.** Because we have a mixed payment system, we are likely to see mixed effects from adopting a new technology unless it clearly dominates existing technology on the dimensions of cost, convenience, and health outcomes. Currently, improved costs are a hurdle any technology must pass unless there is a significant and obvious improvement in outcomes and/or quality of life. Adoption rules for new technologies are likely to differ considerably, depending on whether providers are compensated via capitation (cost minimization) or fee for service (revenue maximization).

4. **Projecting degree of adoption and/or compliance with the proposed innovation.** Projections should take into account the motivation for adoption in both the provider and patient communities. Health professionals can help by identifying the drivers that will lead to adoption of a specific protocol by the relevant provider community.

5. **Comparing results with existing methods of delivery and competing new alternatives.** If the multidimensional results are mixed, as they often are, determine the trade-offs among cost, convenience, and outcome quality.

6. **Recommending whether to adopt a proposed technology, how best to implement it, and how best to arrange for its adoption and diffusion**. Making a recommendation is only the start of the process of technological change. Health care organizations are notoriously slow to change. Given the risks to patients of any change, this resistance is not irrational. There has to be either a significant improvement in cost or outcome and/or a strong understanding of the scientific causation behind the change if the technology is going to be adopted quickly or on a wide scale.

Segmentation

Health care practices and institutions provide a wide variety of products. Current practice using diagnosis-related groups (DRG) categories identifies almost 500 products, and that differentiation is often too coarse for effective technological planning. This leads to two requirements for technology management: (1) methods to identify the affected population segments and (2) simplicity in approach to allow application to multiple product lines. Not only does one need to have large clinical databases to identify enough cases affected by a specific technology, but one must also deal with ever-shifting definitions of disease states as medical knowledge accumulates and the technology itself affects the nature and distribution of what is to be treated. An example is the treatment of AIDS. Initial classification schemes differentiated between patients with T-cell counts of 200 or more CD4 cells per mm^3 and those with 100 or fewer; however, Portela (1995) found the economic impact of AIDS to be greatest in the population with T-cell counts below 50 and recommended a different segmentation for treatment planning and costing. Since then, the success of the drug "cocktails" involving expensive sustained treatment for a much larger population—HIV-infected people who are symptomatic, have T-cell counts below 350, or have viral load greater than 55,000 copies/mL—has changed the approach to fighting the disease from one of avoiding overwhelming infections to one of fighting drug toxicity and drug resistance. Each approach brings much different technical requirements, morbidity patterns, and survival rates.

CHANGING BUSINESS MODELS

The management of technology in health care has a number of requirements that differentiate it from most industrial decision making. It does not just deal with dollars and cents; it incorporates a number of aspects of well-being and occasionally matters of life and death. Furthermore, health care is undergoing a rapid transition, one in which the basic units for analysis have been shifting from the cost of a visit or a day in the hospital toward the cost of an episode of care or cost per person per period of time. Future analyses will have to take such shifts into account.

ORGANIZATIONS DEVOTED TO HEALTH CARE TECHNOLOGY ASSESSMENT

Federal agencies, such as the Centers for Disease Control and Prevention (CDC), the Agency for Healthcare Research and Quality (AHRQ), the FDA, and the National Institutes of Health (NIH), play an important, albeit fragmented, role in technology assessment. However, they are not the only actors involved. Numerous other organizations are engaged in health care technology analysis and assessment at the state and local levels. And of course, the private sector is heavily involved as well.

The Role of States in Technology Assessment

From 1972 to 1995, the focus for technology assessment in the United States was the Office of Technology Assessment (OTA), an arm of the U.S. Congress that was overseen by six senators and six representatives equally representing both political parties. It was a small agency with a professional staff of about 140, and it provided reports on a number of scientific areas, including health care, global warming, telecommunications policy, nuclear defense, and transportation. It published a 1980 study (OTA, 1980) of how benefit/cost analysis should be applied to health that is still widely cited:

> Between 1975 and 1980, another OTA group set the stage for today's booming industry in the technology assessment of health care by demonstrating the inadequacy of information on which decisions about technology were made; laying out the strengths and weaknesses of methods to evaluate technology; and crystallizing the process by which economic trade-offs could be incorporated into decisions. (Houghton, 1995, p. E1968)

The booming industry that Representative Houghton described includes what is referred to as *pharmacoeconomics*. The OTA had a reputation for being professional and balanced in its reports, even though that meant many of its reports were not conclusive and were cited in debate by both sides addressing an issue (Morgan, 1995). For a while, there was a hope that state agencies, such as the Oregon Health Resource Commission, would take over much of that effort (Mendelson, Abramoff, & Rubin, 1995). The charge of the Oregon Health Resources Commission is presented in **Table 8-2**. The ACA significantly expanded the role of the federal government in technology assessment, albeit

Table 8-2 Charge to the Oregon Health Resources Commission

The Health Resources Commission was created as part of the Oregon Health Plan to help it achieve its goal of assuring all Oregonians access to high quality, effective health care at an affordable cost, whether that care is purchased by the state or by the private sector. Its role is to encourage the rational and appropriate allocation and use of medical technology in Oregon by informing and influencing health care decision makers through its analysis and dissemination of information concerning the effectiveness and cost of medical technologies and their impact on the health and health care of Oregonians. Through its activities, the commission can contribute to reducing the cost and improving the effectiveness of health care, thereby increasing the ability of public and private sources to provide more Oregonians with financial access to that care.

The Health Resources Commission is directed to

· Conduct the medical technology assessment program (MedTAP) that it has developed, which performs assessments of selected technologies, develops advisory health resources, plans that address the introduction, diffusion, distribution, and use of assessed technologies, and disseminates the assessments and associated plans to public and private health care decision makers and policy makers

· Serve as a statewide clearinghouse for medical technology information

· Monitor the use, costs, and outcomes associated with selected medical technologies in Oregon, using available data

· Identify information that is needed but lacking for informed decision making regarding medical technology and fostering mechanisms to address such deficiencies

· Provide a public forum for discussion and development of consensus regarding significant emerging issues related to medical technology

· Inform health care decision makers, including consumers, of its findings and recommendations regarding trends, developments, and issues related to medical technology

In carrying out this program, the commission is encouraged to

· Seek the advice of the Health Services Commission, medical directors of health plans, and practicing physicians in identifying for assessment those technologies with the highest likely impact on the health and health care of Oregonians, particularly on the cost of that care

· Achieve an appropriate balance between the cost, access and quality of the medical technology available in Oregon, containing its costs while enhancing its quality and accessibility

· Develop cooperative public–private partnerships with health care providers, payers/health plans, purchasers, manufacturers and suppliers, consumer and community groups, and academic research centers, as well as with other government agencies

· Solicit the cooperation of health care providers and payers in the appropriate allocation and use of medical technology

· Strive for scientific credibility, timeliness and responsiveness, public accountability, and independence from but collaboration with health care stakeholders and constituencies

Source: Reproduced from: Oregon Health Resources Commission at http://www.oregon.gov /oha/OHPR/HRC/pages/about_us.aspx

with some severe constraints on the use of the information. The result of all of this is that we have a patchwork of federal agencies (e.g., CDC, AHRQ, FDA, NIH, and others), state agencies (such as Oregon's commission and Washington's Health Technology Clinical Committee), and private industry (to justify inclusion in formularies and health plan reimbursement) that still tend to focus on new technology rather than on existing treatment practices. AHRQ has, however, supported considerable evaluative effort on high-volume, high-cost problems, such as acute low-back pain, where new technology may not be involved.

Technology Assessment in the Private Sector

Developers of new technologies understand that they cannot get their products approved and sold until the professionals consider them safe and effective and the payers deem them cost effective. This trend accelerated as HMOs began entering into disease management and hospitals became more aggressive in limiting drug formularies. Private-sector activity has grown to the point where most pharmacy schools now have departments, professorships, or centers with the word *pharmacoeconomics* in their titles, often together with the terms *disease management* and *outcome studies*. Houghton's forecast of a boom came true in the private sector, but was delayed in government until the stimulus legislation and then the ACA pushed it forward.

Technology Assessment Internationally

A number of countries with more centralized health systems have their own government units responsible for technology assessment. The United Kingdom requires rigorous cost–benefit analysis for new technologies and drugs prepared by its National Institute for Clinical Excellence (NICE). It also offers advice about use and safety of existing technology. It has been known to recommend very expensive but effective procedures despite the budgetary limitations of the National Health Service (Bradshaw & Bradshaw, 2004). It also is supported by the National Coordinating Center for Health Technology Assessment at the University of Southampton, which commissions and supervises needed studies at independent academic centers.

The Canadian Coordinating Office for Health Technology Assessment publishes brief reports on new drugs and technologies that include references about them and comments on their use, cost, and evidence of effectiveness. Its *Health Technology Update* also identifies recent assessments by other agencies in Canada and in other countries. The health technology assessment field has at least one international journal, and there is also an international association of health technology assessment centers.

Technology Assessment and Staffing Requirements

Knowing where technology is going could also help us in developing the workforce that will be needed in the future. Although the United States lacks a central policy on the supply of professional personnel, there is concern about potential shortages and surpluses of trained personnel in the job market and in the educational pipeline. The most widely publicized effort to address this was the Graduate Medical Education National Advisory Committee report of 1980, which predicted a major physician surplus by 2000. It forecast a surplus of 70,000 physicians and recommended reducing the number of trainees in residency programs in a number of areas. That forecast seems to have been very wide of the mark. Still other reports suggested a shortage of physicians as the population has aged and new technologies have been added. They have been more accurate, but the predicted shortage has not materialized because of in-migration of large numbers of foreign-born physicians, the return of U.S. citizens educated in foreign medical schools, and the expanded supply of trained nurse practitioners and physician assistants to carry much of the primary care caseload. In 2005, the Association of American Medical Colleges (AAMC) announced that it was moving from a neutral position to one favoring expanding medical school enrollment based on the Council on Graduate Medical Education's estimates of a shortage of 90,000 physicians by 2020; however, the AAMC website noted that "there are many unknowns that make forecasting future supply and demand very difficult such as medical advances and changes in organization and financing" (AAMC, 2005, p. 2).

Yes, it is difficult, but we certainly need to try to forecast the impact of medical advances and possible changes in organization and financing care on health care.

CONCLUSION

Calculating the benefits of a technology starts with the science, with the measurement of its effect on the health of a population. Usually that involves a comparison between an existing technology and a new approach about which much less is known. Rules and regulations mandate trials of some new technologies to determine their safety and efficacy. Although such trials are often conducted under ideal conditions and on limited populations, they are usually sufficient to estimate the benefits in non-monetary terms; that is, their impact on quality of life and patient survival. Because the results are so important for the developers of the technology, a great deal of money and effort goes into those trials and into measuring the technology's effects at each stage of development; however, there is still a great deal that is not known about treatments that have been around a long time. Even with the results of the trials in hand, it is necessary to estimate the impact of the new technology on the health care system when used under field conditions.

Several techniques are available to forecast the progress of technology and the overall effects of technology for the purpose of health planning. Some, such as expert opinion, are necessary when the general public has no experience with the technology. As experience develops, users and consumers can be consulted and surveyed. Where experience is extensive, time-series and causal-modeling methods can be applied. It is important to recognize, however, that in the real world there is a great deal of interaction among factors. Therefore, more complex modeling techniques often are necessary to estimate the adaptation of the system to multiple factors and to assess whether resulting adaptations are acceptable. That is why relatively sophisticated organizations are needed to conduct health care technology assessment and advise decision makers and the public on which measures to choose. Before the investment is made, society should be thinking about not only the direct effects but also the indirect effects of major technology decisions.

| **Case 8** | **Comparative Effectiveness: Avastin Versus Lucentis** |

Imagine that you are going to clean the windows of your home and you discover that your spray bottle of commercial glass cleaner is empty. You are about to go to the store to buy more when your neighbor points out that the main ingredient is vinegar and that it is far, far cheaper to buy vinegar and dilute it with water. You try your new homemade cleaner and find that it seems to work just as well as what you were using before. What would you do in the future?

This scenario is similar to the choice now faced by many people with age-related macular degeneration (AMD), as well as their providers and insurers, but with one wrinkle: What if you discovered that your homemade cleaner could be more toxic than the commercial product if mixed incorrectly?

AMD is a debilitating eye disease that is the leading cause of blindness for older Americans, with 200,000 new cases diagnosed annually. In the more severe "wet" form (wAMD), blood and other fluids leak from abnormal blood vessels into the macula, a yellow oval at the center of the retina.

Case 8 (*continued*)

A common, effective treatment for wAMD is injections with ranibizumab, a drug that Genentech, a division of Roche, sells under the trade name Lucentis. Chemically, Lucentis is almost identical to bevacizumab, a cancer drug that Genentech calls Avastin. The same active component found in both drugs inhibits the function of vascular endothelial growth factor (VEGF), which stimulates the growth of blood vessels. For cancer patients, that means less blood flow to support cancer growth; for wAMG patients, it means fewer vessels to leak fluids into the macula.

To turn Avastin into Lucentis, Genentech made the molecules smaller; in theory, smaller molecules would be better able to penetrate the macula. Genentech also raised the price dramatically. The cost to Medicare of a Lucentis injection is about $2,000. Injections can be given on an as-needed basis or on a monthly schedule. With a monthly schedule, the annual cost per patient per year comes to $24,000. Genentech maintains that it specifically formulated and tested Lucentis for administration in the eye, and that the higher cost is necessary to recover the company's investment in research and development.

While waiting for the FDA to approve Lucentis, doctors discovered they could take Avastin, have compounding pharmacists repackage it into smaller vials, and then treat their patients for around $50 an injection. Not surprisingly, Avastin is used in more than half the injections to treat wAMD in the United States, and ophthalmologists do not observe any difference in patient outcomes. This has huge financial implications for Medicare, which funds care for 95% of patients with wAMD. If all Medicare patients were treated with Lucentis, the annual cost would be $1 billion to $3 billion, but if Avastin were used instead, the cost would be less than $1 million (Martin et al., 2010).

Genentech has maintained that repackaging by compounding pharmacies raises safety concerns. It announced in October 2007 that it would no longer sell Avastin directly to compounding pharmacies. Angry doctors and professional associations argued the move would limit supply and create affordability problems for low-income patients. Genentech relented somewhat; it said it would sell directly to physicians who could then send it to compounding pharmacies if they wished. The International Academy of Compounding Pharmacists claimed that Genentech was motivated by money, not reasonable safety concerns.

The Lucentis versus Avastin controversy would appear to be low-hanging fruit for supporters of comparative effectiveness research

(CER). If one treatment costs $600 a year and another costs $24,000, and they produce the same results, why would the CMS or any other fiscally responsible payer facilitate the use of the more expensive option? But as part of CER, someone would have to conduct a robust, head-to-head clinical trial to compare the effectiveness of the two drugs. The problem is that such trials are usually funded by manufacturers trying to prove their product's effectiveness to win FDA approval.

Avastin's history provides a useful example of how clinical trials, which provide the foundation for CER and evidence-based medicine, typically occur in the United States. Avastin is approved for treating colorectal, lung, kidney, ovarian, and other metastatic cancers. It is approved for treatment of breast cancer in other countries, but not in the United States. The FDA had provisionally approved it for treating advanced breast cancer in 2008, pending further study. Genentech funded the additional studies. The findings showed the drug slowed progression of the disease, but because the studies failed to demonstrate that Avastin extended patients' lives or improved their quality of life, the FDA withdrew its approval.

But off-label use of Avastin to treat wAMD is a quite different and highly unusual case. Genentech has no interest in testing a cancer drug for treating wAMD when it already has an effective (and more profitable) wAMD-specific drug on the market. It does not want Avastin approved for wAMD, and the FDA had no standing to demand Genentech conduct a trial.

Instead, funding for a head-to-head trial, called the Comparison of Age-Related Macular Degeneration Treatment Trials (CATT), came from the National Eye Institute (NEI), which is part of the NIH. In 2006, NEI agreed to provide $1 million to purchase, repackage, and distribute the Avastin. Researchers initially assumed Medicare would pay for Lucentis as routine care for clinical trial participants, but it turned out that existing CMS policy did not allow for that. This changed with the adoption of new policies in 2007.

That left the question of how to handle copayments for the 15% of Medicare recipients who did not have supplemental insurance and were on the hook for 20% copays. Ultimately, NEI was able to cover copays under the special circumstances provisions in the NIH guidelines. The complicated system of obtaining and billing for commercially purchased drugs, however, made it hard to devise a system for masking the identity of study participants. Resolving this issue required amendments to the Medicare Improvements for Patients and Providers Act of 2008.

Case 8   (*continued*)

Martin et al. (2010) noted that the ARRA provided $1.1 billion for CER, but after describing all of the roadblocks encountered by the CATT Research Group, they concluded that the infrastructure for implementing federally sponsored CER trials is inadequate. They called on the insurance industry to facilitate CER trials and on the government to develop a comprehensive policy to cover the drug-related costs of trials without relying on existing billing and payment mechanisms. The ACA requires most insurers to pay "comparative effectiveness research fees" to fund a new Patient-Centered Outcomes Research Institute to conduct research into comparative effectiveness of medical treatments, along with their risks and benefits.

The CATT Research Group published its 2-year results in 2012 (Martin et al., 2012). The group found no statistical difference between the gains in visual acuity produced by the two drugs. There was no evidence that Genentech's "smaller molecule" approach made Lucentis a more effective treatment. The study did find that the rate of serious systemic adverse events was higher for participants treated with Avastin (40%) compared to those treated with Lucentis (32%). "The interpretation of the persistence of higher rates of serious adverse events with bevacizumab is uncertain because of the lack of specificity to conditions associated with inhibition of VEGF" (p. 1388), the authors wrote. Monthly treatment had better outcomes than treatment as needed, although this must be weighed against costs and the risks associated with each injection. The authors concluded, "The choice of drug and dosing regimen for patients must balance the comparable effects on vision, the possibility of true differences in adverse events, and the 40-fold difference in cost per dose" (p. 1397).

Concerns about possible contamination when compounding pharmacies repackage Avastin have proven to have some basis. In 2012, U.S. Representative Edward J. Markey (D-Massachusetts) introduced legislation to clarify and strengthen the FDA's role in regulating compounding pharmacies. The bill was a response to a fungal meningitis outbreak that sickened hundreds of people and killed 64. The outbreak was tied to contaminated injected steroids produced by New England Compounding Center in Markey's district. That same year, the FDA reported 12 cases of blindness in Miami following injections with bacterially contaminated Avastin from a single compounding pharmacy. Other cases were reported in Nashville, Tennessee, and Los Angeles, California. The American Society of Retina Specialists subsequently published a set of guidelines to help providers identify high-quality compounding pharmacies. In March 2013, the FDA announced it was recalling 40 lots of syringes containing Avastin. Five reports of eye infections had reached Clinical Specialties of Martinez, Georgia, a compounding pharmacy that had supplied the syringes to doctors in four states. A revised version of Markey's bill was enacted in November 2013.

In late 2011, a third treatment, Eylea from Regeneron, which uses a different molecule, was approved by the FDA. It costs about the same as Lucentis. In 2012, the sales of the three drugs for AMD were estimated at $1.66 billion based on Medicare claims data and distributed as follows (Whoriskey & Keating, 2013):

	Percent of Market (%)	Percent (%) of Total Spent on AMD Drugs
Avastin	55	4
Lucentis	34	73
Eylea	11	33

Source: Data from: Whoriskey, P., & Keating, D. (2013, December 26). Medicare rules create a booming business in hospice care for people who aren't dying. *The Washington Post*. Retrieved from: www.washingtonpost.com/business/economy/medicare-rules-create-a-booming-business-in-hospice-care-for-people-who-arent-dying/2013/12/26/4ff75bbe-68c9-11e3-ae56-22de072140a2_story.html

Clinical trials are underway for additional treatments, including one involving drops rather than injections.

Discussion Questions

1. If you were a retina specialist, how would the data in this case affect your drug procurement processes, your clinical practices, and your recommendations to patients? (You are currently allowed a 6% markup on outpatient injectable drugs.)

2. If you had AMD, what treatment choices would you make after reading this case? Would your choice depend on whether you had significant copays or other out-of-pocket expenses related to eye injections?

3. If you were a CMS official, what coverage-related policies would you promote?

4. If you were a legislator with oversight of a state Medicaid program, how would you respond to this case?

5. If you were a policy analyst, what would you recommend and to whom?

6. What policy changes might be needed to support government-sponsored initiatives related to CER and evidence-based medicine?

7. If you were an insurer, how would you respond to the recommendation that insurers facilitate CER research? What forms might such facilitation take?

Chapter 9

The Policy Analysis Process: Evidence-Based Medicine

Evidence-based medicine is not a new concept, but its use is increasingly widespread. The concept has many labels, including *evidence-based practice* and a more recent offshoot, *translational medicine*. The term has been attributed to Dave Sackett and his clinical epidemiology colleagues at McGill University, who presented it in a series of 1980 articles in a Canadian journal. In a 1996 article, they presented a revised definition, stating that evidence-based medicine is "the conscientious, explicit, and judicious use of current best evidence in making decisions about the care of the individual patient. It means integrating individual clinical expertise with the best available external clinical evidence from systematic research" (Sackett et al., 1996).

Evidence-based medicine can be implemented as a top-down or bottom-up approach, and this difference can lead to considerable confusion. With the top-down approach, experts form a consensus based on strong empirical evidence, and that consensus is then disseminated as standard guidelines and protocols. With the bottom-up approach, a provider deals directly with the patient, identifying the problem and searching for the best evidence about what to do next. Even when strong, evidence-based protocols are available, the bottom-up process can take into account patient variability, patient preferences and situational factors, and the provider's expertise.

The provider's expertise may be based on evidence or experience, but usually a combination of both leads to the better outcomes.

Resistance to evidence-based medicine often stems from providers' fears that the top-down approach will deprive them of their autonomy. A further concern is that the top-down approach may be based on statistical analyses involving homogeneous populations and will not be aligned with the needs of the specific patient. For example, randomized clinical trials may select a homogeneous population without secondary diagnoses, whereas many patients typically presenting in a practice will have multiple conditions. Sackett et al. (1996) addressed these concerns by stating:

> Evidence-based medicine is not "cookbook" medicine. . . . External evidence can inform, but can never replace, individual clinical expertise, and it is this expertise that decides whether the external evidence applies to the individual patient at all, and if so, how it should be integrated into a clinical decision. (p. 317)

Some providers also are concerned about requiring evidence-based practices for diagnoses, procedures, technologies, and professional settings when there is not an adequate body of research from which to draw conclusions. In medicine, research is often funded by drug and device manufacturers, but it is much more difficult to find funds for research in areas such as mental health, public health, and social services. Policy makers are reluctant to pay for unproven interventions and often are tempted to mandate that programs be evidence based. Such requirements can tie the hands of service providers who must rely on expert opinions unless and until robust research becomes available. Public health, for example, has long believed in the importance of inspecting food establishments, but because foodborne illnesses largely go unreported and public health research is poorly funded, it is difficult to measure the overall effectiveness of restaurant inspections, much less compare the value of different regulatory practices.

REDUCING VARIATION AND SAVING RESOURCES

Reducing variation in the way clinicians in an organization approach frequently encountered diagnoses clearly has benefits. Standardizing treatment protocols results in less waste of resources and more consistent outcomes. Clinical guidelines are widely available from prestigious organizations as well as local management. However, provider resistance to the top-down approach is common. Farias et al. (2013) reported on locally developed standardized clinical assessment and management plans

(SCAMPs) that offer more flexibility when applied to varied and complex patients. With SCAMPs, providers work with clinical guidelines, but the clinicians are free to deviate, provided they report their reasons for doing so. After about 200 patients are treated using a particular SCAMP, provider comments, related cost data, and the most recent literature are reviewed, and the SCAMP is revised. Such a process can be managed locally or applied to a professional network. The authors report that physician compliance is greatly increased by this process.

CROSSCURRENTS INVOLVED

The rise to prominence of evidence-based medicine is a result of several factors:

- Rapid generation of new and revised scientific information
- Pressures on clinicians to conserve time
- Payer and patient concerns about the rising cost of care
- Concerns of all parties about the relatively high rate of medical errors
- Long lead times needed to adopt new information and change practice behaviors
- Commercial free speech and the viral movement of information and misinformation on the Web, which means more information—good and bad—in the hands of the public

Both biased and unbiased information is available to practitioners and to the public. One sees advertisement after advertisement, especially about newly defined health problems and new treatments. These are almost all paid for by someone who wants to change provider and patient behaviors. Before changing a clinical practice, however, the provider has to vet all these sources of information and revise his or her script for dealing with that clinical situation and with the questions put forward by patients and their families in the face of those pressures. Providers could spend all their time following the literature and do little else. However, both the downward pressure on fees and the second-guessing of providers by payers forces the provider to pay attention to secondary information sources to discover the latest consensus and assess what is clinically appropriate for the patient at hand. In some cases, such as central line infections, what was once an acceptable risk is now considered a medical error, and the provider has to bear more of the risk. The individual practitioner's judgment is less and less likely to be free from scrutiny, and yet that practitioner must operate in an environment where information can seldom be taken at face value.

The plight of the policy analyst is not much different. He or she will have to rely more on medical experts for interpretation and recommendations. However, the information coming in is likely to be transmitted by individuals with distinct points of view, if not distinct financial interests. Policy analysts, too, are visited by lobbyists and consumer advocates. They have access to the same journals and press reports and have to make evaluations with respect to scientific merit and economic impact. Boden and Epstein (2006) warn about the fallacies of "policy-based evidence" where the advocates (political or social) conduct or cite research that begins with a policy solution and generates only arguments supporting that alternative.

THE PROCESS OF EVIDENCE-BASED ANALYSIS

Evidence-based medicine has its roots in clinical epidemiology. It is analysis based on:

1. A problem definition, which enables the analyst to focus on clinical questions and clinical information.
2. An effective search of the available, relevant information for evidence concerning the clinical question.
3. Assessing the level of the evidence and its validity, and selecting the best available answer for implementation.
4. Trying the approach in one's clinical practice.
5. Evaluating the performance of the new or revised clinical response, and consciously incorporating positive results into one's expertise set.
6. Adapting this knowledge to the needs of the specific patient.

Not surprisingly, this parallels the approaches used for continuous quality improvement. Evidence-based medicine rests on continuous personal, professional, and/or organizational learning. Obviously, it is very much dependent on the participation of the provider, although chronic disease patients also can become very good at it in their area of interest.

Clinical Decision Making

When a clinician and a patient are searching for the best treatment for a particular situation in real time, they will want to consider only treatments that are efficacious. They will most likely select those that are sufficiently effective and offer sufficient value to warrant their use. The tragedy of American medicine is the tendency to want to do something, and often the most technologically advanced and most expensive thing (Hadler, 2013). Hadler (2013) noted that much of American medicine incorporates treatments that have proven efficacy, but that do not have a proven significant effect on clinical outcome. They often relate only to risk factors or to a very limited segment of the population with a specific diagnosis, and yet they are widely applied.

Levels of Evidence

The evidence tools used by analysts are often presented as an evidence pyramid or hierarchy of evidence. Anyone who goes on an Internet search engine looking for images related to "levels of evidence" will be deluged with graphical representations, mostly pyramidal, expressing pretty much the same rankings. The top of the pyramid represents the most reliable studies, which are the fewest in number. At the bottom are the least reliable ones, the anecdotes, personal opinions (expert or otherwise), and case reports, which are greatest in number. The pyramid may have anywhere from 4 to 10 levels. What is counterintuitive about these pyramids is that expert opinions are at or near the bottom and randomized controlled trials (often referred to as the "gold standard") are in the middle. At the top are systematic studies that integrate findings from multiple studies. An example would be a Cochrane Collaborative Review. Below that would be meta-analyses involving multiple studies, followed by synthesis of a limited number of studies. Then come randomized controlled trials. Below that would likely be cohort studies, followed by case-control studies. The Agency for Healthcare Research and Quality (AHRQ) has boiled this down to three categories of strength of evidence (**Table 9-1**).

Some representations include clinical guidelines, which tend to be reliable but vary in their underlying levels of evidence. They have been known to come from reviews and meta-analyses, as well as from a process known as GOBSAT, which stands for "Good Old Boys Sitting Around Talking." A useful classroom exercise would be to call up the available set of pyramidal images and pick one for use in future class discussions.

Example of the Preventive Services Task Force

The U.S. Preventive Services Task Force (USPSTF) has developed its own methodology for evaluating proposed recommendations. Preventive services have a long-term and substantive impact on the cost of care. They represent an area where guidelines are helpful because most clinicians have to rely on them rather than clinical experience. However, the guidelines can be controversial, as demonstrated by the recent debates over recommended reductions

Table 9-1 Three Categories for Rating the Strength of Evidence at AHRQ

Drawing on elements of these established systems, the Innovations Exchange uses three categories to provide meaningful distinctions in assessing the strength of the link between the innovation and the observed results:

Strong: The evidence is based on one or more evaluations using experimental designs based on random allocation of individuals or groups of individuals (e.g., medical practices or hospital units) to comparison groups. The results of the evaluation(s) show consistent direct evidence of the effectiveness of the innovation in improving the targeted health care outcomes and/or processes, or structures in the case of health care policy innovations.

Moderate: While there are no randomized, controlled experiments, the evidence includes at least one systematic evaluation of the impact of the innovation using a quasi-experimental design, which could include the nonrandom assignment of individuals to comparison groups, before-and-after comparisons in one group, and/or comparisons with a historical baseline or control. The results of the evaluation(s) show consistent direct or indirect evidence of the effectiveness of the innovation in improving targeted health care outcomes and/or processes, or structures in the case of health care policy innovations. However, the strength of the evidence is limited by the size, quality, or generalizability of the evaluations, and thus alternative explanations cannot be ruled out.

Suggestive: While there are no systematic experimental or quasi-experimental evaluations, the evidence includes nonexperimental or qualitative support for an association between the innovation and targeted health care outcomes or processes, or structures in the case of health care policy innovations. This evidence may include noncomparative case studies, correlation analysis, or anecdotal reports. As with the category above, alternative explanations for the results achieved cannot be ruled out.

If the available qualitative and quantitative information is insufficient to place the innovation in one of the three categories above, the activity fails to meet the minimum inclusion criterion for evidence, and therefore is not eligible for inclusion as an Innovation Profile in the AHRQ Health Care Innovations Exchange. It may, however, qualify for inclusion as an Innovation Attempt.

in early breast cancer screenings and the PSA test for prostate cancer. The Task Force recommendations also carry a great deal of weight with payers who are expected to include those specific services in their coverage.

Table 9-2 presents the example of the system the Task Force uses to grade recommendations. There are two categories of grades: one for "Suggestions for Practice" and one for "Certainty of Net Benefits." Note the introductory paragraph about the change in the definition of Grade C.

Biases in Evidence Gathering

The gold standard for gathering new evidence is the randomized, controlled clinical trial, which uses a specifically selected population randomly divided into a control group and a treatment group. The control group,

Table 9-2 U.S. Preventive Services Task Force Recommended Grade Definitions

What the Grades Mean and Suggestions for Practice

Describing the strength of a recommendation is an important part of communicating its importance to clinicians and other users. Although most of the grade definitions have evolved since the USPSTF first began, none has changed more noticeably than the definition of a C recommendation, which has undergone three major revisions since 1998. Despite these revisions, the essence of the C recommendation has remained consistent: at the population level, the balance of benefits and harms is very close, and the magnitude of net benefit is small. Given this small net benefit, the USPSTF has either not made a recommendation "for or against routinely" providing the service (1998), recommended "against routinely" providing the service (2007), or recommended "selectively" providing the service (2012). Grade C recommendations are particularly sensitive to patient values and circumstances. Determining whether or not the service should be offered or provided to an individual patient will typically require an informed conversation between the clinician and patient.

Grade	Definition	Suggestions for Practice
A	The USPSTF recommends the service. There is high certainty that the net benefit is substantial.	Offer or provide this service.
B	The USPSTF recommends the service. There is high certainty that the net benefit is moderate or there is moderate certainty that the net benefit is moderate to substantial.	Offer or provide this service.
C	The USPSTF recommends selectively offering or providing this service to individual patients based on professional judgment and patient preferences. There is at least moderate certainty that the net benefit is small.	Offer or provide this service for selected patients depending on individual circumstances.
D	The USPSTF recommends against the service. There is moderate or high certainty that the service has no net benefit or that the harms outweigh the benefits.	Discourage the use of this service.
I Statement	The USPSTF concludes that the current evidence is insufficient to assess the balance of benefits and harms of the service. Evidence is lacking, of poor quality, or conflicting, and the balance of benefits and harms cannot be determined.	Read the clinical considerations section of USPSTF Recommendation Statement. If the service is offered, patients should understand the uncertainty about the balance of benefits and harms.

(continues)

Table 9-2 U.S. Preventive Services Task Force Recommended Grade Definitions (*continued*)

Levels of Certainty Regarding Net Benefit

Level of Certainty*	Description
High	The available evidence usually includes consistent results from well-designed, well-conducted studies in representative primary care populations. These studies assess the effects of the preventive service on health outcomes. This conclusion is therefore unlikely to be strongly affected by the results of future studies.
Moderate	The available evidence is sufficient to determine the effects of the preventive service on health outcomes, but confidence in the estimate is constrained by such factors as: · The number, size, or quality of individual studies. · Inconsistency of findings across individual studies. · Limited generalizability of findings to routine primary care practice. · Lack of coherence in the chain of evidence. As more information becomes available, the magnitude or direction of the observed effect could change, and this change may be large enough to alter the conclusion.
Low	The available evidence is insufficient to assess effects on health outcomes. Evidence is insufficient because of: · The limited number or size of studies. · Important flaws in study design or methods. · Inconsistency of findings across individual studies. · Gaps in the chain of evidence. · Findings not generalizable to routine primary care practice. · Lack of information on important health outcomes. More information may allow estimation of effects on health outcomes.

* The USPSTF defines certainty as "likelihood that the USPSTF assessment of the net benefit of a preventive service is correct." The net benefit is defined as benefit minus harm of the preventive service as implemented in a general, primary care population. The USPSTF assigns a certainty level based on the nature of the overall evidence available to assess the net benefit of a preventive service.

Source: Reproduced from: U.S. Preventive Services Task Force Grade Definitions (2008, May). Retrieved from www.uspreventiveservicestaskforce.org/uspstf/grades.htm

which may receive a placebo or other sham intervention or the current normal treatment, is compared to the treatment group. The design objective parallels the economist's holy grail of "all other things being equal." Concerns about bias are likely to be related to the relevance of the sample for clinical decision making or the reporting of the results. Only a very limited number of variables can be controlled directly in such a study.

More recently, there has been support, usually governmental, for comparative effectiveness studies, which tend to be observational in nature. They attempt to compare treatments under field conditions. However, the inputs and conditions of such studies are not as tightly controlled as in randomized, controlled clinical trials. They are considered suitable for hypothesis generation, but not as proof of efficacy. In the case of pharmaceuticals that have already been tested for efficacy, they are perhaps more meaningful than they are in the case of new procedures and other interventions. Comparative effectiveness studies have the advantage of being able to use large, relatively available databases, lowering the cost and duration of the study. Potential sources of bias include sample variety; practice variation; and unknown, uncontrolled variables. Because they use data that can be associated with charges, payments, and costs, as well as safety outcomes, they are critical to the measurement of that currently fashionable construct—*value*.

Clinician experience enters into decision making as well. However, a clinician's experience has likely been influenced by past training, marketing efforts, event importance, recency effects, payer contracts, and perhaps even personal economic interests. Off-label use is often based on clinician experience, and it often is influenced by both legal and illegal promotion efforts.

Patient observation is important, but it is also subject to some of the same biases as clinician experience. There is also the lack of observational training and less experience (often based on a sample of one). Patients living with long-term major chronic problems often become very good observers and tie into observational networks that amplify their limited experience. They may even have more experience than the average clinician. They are certainly an important source for socioeconomic and psychosocial support information that is crucial to effective community-based care. Marketing efforts can shape patient attitudes and expectations in ways unsupported by effectiveness evidence.

CONSTRAINTS ON VARIABLES USED IN ANALYSIS OF EVIDENCE

Congress has constrained the use of certain economic and outcome valuations. These exclusions are presented in the case at the end of this chapter. However, the USPSTF continues to specify the following outcome measures as analysis inputs:

- Deaths, where relevant
- Important health outcomes, such as strokes avoided or cancers caused

- Quality-adjusted life-years, if possible
- Harms (adverse events/states)

The Task Force's experiences show the ambivalence and contentiousness that surrounds the rigorous use of evidence in the health sector. Remember here that one person's waste is another person's income.

THE EXAMPLE OF NICE

The National Health Service (NHS) in the United Kingdom has long had a process for assessing evidence and developing guidelines through its independent National Institute for Health and Clinical Excellence (NICE).

"We are internationally recognised for the way in which we develop our recommendations, a rigorous process that is centered on using the best available evidence and includes the views of experts, patients and caregivers, and industry," notes the institutes's website. "We do not decide on the topics for our guidance and appraisals. Instead, topics are referred to us by the Department of Health. Disease burden, resource implications, practice variations, and other factors are considered when determining topics to address. Our guidance is then created by independent and unbiased advisory committees." (NICE, 2013a)

Other countries have equivalent organizations.

DECISION AIDS

Evidence-based medicine uses guidelines and protocols, but it also strives to ensure that patients are part of the decision-making process. Current information technology can be used to support the dissemination of decision aids for both patients and caregivers. Sooner or later these applications will become part of the national information technology standard for meaningful use, which is being defined and implemented in stages.

Section 3506 of the Affordable Care Act (ACA) authorizes a program under the new Center for Medicare & Medicaid Innovation to develop decision aids that will:

> . . . facilitate collaborative processes between patients, caregivers or authorized representatives, and clinicians that engages the patient, caregiver or authorized representative in decision-making, provides patients, caregivers or authorized representatives with information about trade-offs among treatment options, and facilitates the incorporation of patient preferences and values into the medical plan.
>
> The term "preference sensitive care" means medical care for which the clinical evidence does not clearly support one treatment option such

that the appropriate course of treatment depends on the values of the patient or the preferences of the patient, caregivers or authorized representatives regarding the benefits, harms and scientific evidence for each treatment option, the use of such care should depend on the informed patient choice among clinically appropriate treatment options. (p. 469)

States can support this movement through mandates or incentives for the implementation of decision aids (King & Moulton, 2013).

This movement is driven, in part, by discomfort with the authoritarian nature of the clinician's typical role and, in part, by the knowledge that when patients are given information and choices the observed outcomes are better and the costs of care are often lower (Hibbard, Greene, & Overton, 2013; Veroff, Marr, & Wennberg, 2013). Cost is a major driver of patient-driven health care.

The February 2013 issue of *Health Affairs* was partly devoted to the themes of patient engagement and patient activation. The previous quote from the ACA highlights patients' twin roles as active and informed consumers and as involved clinical decision makers. The patient may be involved as an individual, in collaboration with the payer, or in collaboration with the physician. **Table 9-3** provides examples of activities associated with each of the roles.

Table 9-3 Examples of Engaged Patient Activities

Engaged Patient Roles	Informed Consumer	Clinical Decision Maker
Independent	Use Hospital COMPARE	Access:
	Use consumer satisfaction databases	· PatientsLikeMe.com
		· Guideline databases
	Do comparison shopping	· Advocacy sites
	Ask local friends and experts	· General information sites
		Ask others about experiences
With payer	Get data on in-network providers	Access Web portals
	Discuss with case managers	Discuss with case managers
	Compare on exchanges	Review literature and brochures
		Make inquiries about coverage
With provider	Agree on appropriate entry mode	Study journal literature
	Discuss rates and fees	Review guidelines together
	Observe and/or discuss philosophy and attitudes on cost and aggressiveness of treatment	Use joint decision aids
		Talk through behaviors and preferences

Source: Reproduced from: *Patient Outcomes Research Teams (PORTS): Managing Conflict of Interest*. (1991). Institute of Medicine, Washington: National Press, p. 21. Courtesy of the National Academies Press, Washington, D.C.

Patients acting alone, or family members or other advocates acting on their behalf, can engage in information searches and decision making by consulting any number of sources of information. Comparative databases on quality and cost for hospitals and other providers are available. Patients can talk to their neighbors, professionals, or local experts.

Many websites are available that are devoted to specific symptoms and diagnoses, such as the American Diabetes Association (www.diabetes.org) and PatientsLikeMe (www.patientslikeme.com), as well as the medical literature and databases of governmental and professional guidelines (domestic and international). These can provide access to reports backed by evidence that falls along the evidence hierarchy, including reports from sources with major potential biases, such as television ads and vendor websites.

Then there are information providers fulfilling the role of honest broker, such as the insurance exchanges authorized under the ACA and administered either by the states or the federal government. Many payers maintain Web portals where enrollees can find tips on certain diagnoses and conditions, and they may also provide case managers for patients with certain chronic diseases or catastrophic illnesses. Again the validity and level of evidence can vary a great deal.

The collaborative relationship between the provider and the patient envisioned in this movement is relatively new. So far, demonstration efforts have identified major barriers to widespread adoption, especially the drain on provider time, lack of payment for the time used, physician perceptions about patients' ability to understand evidence, lack of relevant information, and patients' preferences for a provider who acts as an authority figure (Lin et al., 2013; Yergian et al., 2013). A study of the use of Web-based decision aids in the NHS indicated that "clinicians did not feel the need to refer patients to use decision support tools, web-based or not, and, as a result, felt no requirement to change existing practice routines" (Elwyn et al., 2012). A review of the literature about the advantages and disadvantages of shared decision making and its effects on outcome in mental illness services is provided in SAMHSA (2011).

An interesting finding in the research on this change in the health care culture is that although physicians have the greatest influence over patient behavior, other clinic staff and off-site personnel can contribute successfully to the support of shared decision making (Veroff et al., 2013; Courneya, Palattao, & Gallagher, 2013).

To support collaboration, the patient and the physician must have an understanding of how, when, and where the patient will receive services, such as by telephone, email, in the physician's office, or at an alternative service site. They must have a discussion of their philosophies and attitudes toward issues such as aggressiveness of treatment and costs of care. Some patients will want to control costs, whereas others will be uncomfortable when clinicians focus on costs in clinical decision making (Sommers et al., 2013). However, cost will play an increasingly important role in informing consumer behavior in the future.

DETERMINING VALUE

Most randomized, controlled clinical trials are conducted on proposed prescription drugs for which patent protections provide a potential monopoly. In such trials, U.S. researchers only need to establish a pharmaceutical's safety and efficacy. By comparison, medical devices can piggyback on the testing of similar devices and procedures that do not require licensing. Manufacturers usually support studies in which a placebo is the control. This implies that the product being tested just has to be better than doing nothing at all. Determining whether a new product has value greater than that of existing products requires a comparative effectiveness study that includes cost comparisons. Because of the reluctance of manufacturers to conduct such studies, the government has had to step in. This is a relatively recent development. In 1989–1990, the predecessor to AHRQ issued a series of contracts for Patient Outcomes Review Team (PORT) studies that were quite controversial. A list of the initial studies is shown in **Table 9-4**. These studies tended to evaluate high-volume and/or high-cost interventions, and the concept was not popular with the

Table 9-4 Patient Outcomes Research Teams Funded as of October 1990

Title of Project	Principal Investigator or Institution
Assessing Therapies for Benign Prostatic Hypertrophy and Localized Prostate Cancer	John E. Wennberg Dartmouth College
The Consequences of Variation in Treatment for Acute Myocardial Infarction	Barbara J. McNeil Harvard Medical School
Back Pain Outcome Assessment Team	Richard A. Deyo University of Washington
Variations in Cataract Management: Patient and Economic Choice	Earl P. Steinberg The Johns Hopkins University
Assessing and Improving Outcomes: Total Knee Replacement	Deborah A. Freund Indiana University

(*continues*)

Table 9-4 Patient Outcomes Research Teams Funded as of October 1990 (*continued*)

Title of Project	Principal Investigator or Institution
Outcome Assessment Program in Ischemic Heart Disease	David B. Pryor Duke University
Outcome Assessment of Patients with Biliary Tract Disease	J. Sanford Schwartz Stanford University
Analysis of Practices: Hip Fracture Repair and Osteoarthritis	James I. Hudson University of Maryland
Variations in the Management and Outcomes of Diabetes	Sheldon Greenfield New England Medical Center
Assessment of the Variation and Outcomes of Pneumonia	Wishwa N. Kappor University of Pittsburgh

provider community. Some of the issues addressed by these studies are still open to debate. In fact, after the publication of a study showing that it did not matter what type of provider treated acute (without sciatica) low back pain, surgeons almost succeeded in getting Congress to defund the agency. By 2008, however, concerns about value had become so great that the American Recovery and Reinvestment Act (ARRA) contained significant funding for comparative research, and the ACA established the new Patient-Centered Outcomes Research Institute (PCORI).

TRANSLATIONAL MEDICINE: ADOPTION, ADAPTATION, AND COMPLIANCE

Many are concerned with how slowly the results of basic research make their way into practice and the amount of time it takes for practice innovations to be evaluated and adopted. In addition, some experts suggest that clinician compliance with suggested guidelines is only about 50%. No one knows what the right figure actually is, because many patients do not duplicate the conditions envisioned by the guidelines and protocols. Because adoption rates affect both the quality and cost of health care, there has been increasing interest in more effectively linking basic science and clinical practice. The attempt to build a bridge between the silos of research and practice is called *translational research*, and medical researchers involved in such multidisciplinary work have defined their new field as *translational medicine*. Interest in this interface increased sharply after the National Institutes of Health began funding such efforts through the National Center for Advanced Translational Sciences.

The field of translational medicine is still loosely defined. A consensus report from the Evaluation Committee of the Association for Clinical Research Training proposed a definition of translational research. According to the report, translational research seeks to improve the public's health by supporting the multidirectional integration of three types of research: basic, patient oriented, and population based. The definition specifies three types of translational research:

> T1 research expedites the movement between basic research and patient-oriented research that leads to new or improved scientific understanding or standards of care. T2 research facilitates the movement between patient-oriented research and population-based research that leads to better patient outcomes, the implementation of best practices, and improved health status in communities. T3 research promotes interaction between laboratory-based research and population-based research to stimulate a robust scientific understanding of human health and disease. (Rubio et al., 2010)

Current efforts in translational medicine range from analyzing gene sequences associated with treatment outcomes to methods of improving patient compliance. The multidisciplinary teams may involve a wide array of members. It remains to be seen how this type of research will be accepted in academic medicine because it often involves observational studies and critical inputs from many disciplines. Observational studies involving expanding registries and clinical databases show great promise but face a number of barriers (Lauer & D'Agostino, 2013; Fleurence, Naci, & Jansen, 2010).

CONCLUSION

The policy analyst will rub elbows with team members with skills in clinical epidemiology and experience with care delivery. The use of evidence-based medicine is increasing, and the analyst must be knowledgeable about its concepts and terms. The trained analyst will recognize that it follows the logical paradigm adopted by systems analysts, industrial engineers, and quality and safety improvement managers—that is, the scientific method. Much of the actual research and analysis will be carried out by health professionals in the burgeoning cottage industry of providing meta-analyses, summary reviews, protocols, and guidelines. It is important to know and understand the hierarchy of evidence and stay current with the rapidly expanding development of decision aids and with studies about how to activate and engage patients in clinical decision making. Although political and economic interests will try to seize the process of policy analysis and warp it in their favor, the antidote is to maintain high standards for validity and quality of evidence throughout. Policy makers in the United States are increasingly demanding such professionalism behind the scenes, if not in their public discourse.

Case 9   **Constraints of the ACA on Evidence-Based Medicine**

The ACA expanded the emphasis on developing evidence-based medicine in the 2009 stimulus act and established the Patient-Centered Outcomes Research Institute (PCORI) within the Centers for Medicare & Medicaid Services. However, the same legislation limited the ways the Institute's research could be used within the Department of Health and Human Services. There clearly was a concern among federal lawmakers that these research findings would find their way directly into the workings of the even more controversial Medicare Advisory Payment Commission.

Pearson and Bach (2010) noted:

> Under current law and because of years of precedent, Medicare generally covers any treatment that is deemed "reasonable and necessary," regardless of the evidence on the treatment's comparative effectiveness or its cost in relation to other treatments. Likewise, with only rare exceptions, Medicare does not use comparative effectiveness information to set payment rates. Instead it links reimbursement in one way or another to the underlying cost of providing services. (p. 1796)

This is quite different from the way comparative effectiveness research is used in other counties at various regulatory stages, such as new drug approvals and approved protocols.

Congress maintained this status quo, in part, by placing a number of constraints on the use of comparative effectiveness research. Section 6301 amended Section 1181 of the Social Security Act to establish the Institute with the following purpose:

> The Institute is to assist patients, clinicians, purchasers, and policymakers in making informed health decisions by advancing the quality and relevance of evidence concerning the manner in which diseases, disorders, and other health conditions can effectively and appropriately be prevented, diagnosed, treated, monitored,

and managed through research and evidence synthesis that considers variations in patient subpopulations, and the dissemination of research findings with respect to the relative health outcomes, clinical effectiveness, and appropriateness of the medical treatments, services, and items described in subsection (a)(2)(B).

ADDING CONSTRAINTS

However, the ACA went on to specify:

SEC. 1182 o42 U.S.C. 1320e–1. (a) The Secretary may only use evidence and findings from research conducted under section 1181 to make a determination regarding coverage under title XVIII (Medicare) if such use is through an iterative and transparent process which includes public comment and considers the effect on subpopulations.

(b) Nothing in section 1181 shall be construed as—

(1) superceding or modifying the coverage of items or services under title XVIII that the Secretary determines are reasonable and necessary under section 1862(l)(1); or

(2) authorizing the Secretary to deny coverage of items or services under such title solely on the basis of comparative clinical effectiveness research.

(c)(1) The Secretary shall not use evidence or findings from comparative clinical effectiveness research conducted under section 1181 in determining coverage, reimbursement, or incentive programs under title XVIII in a manner that treats extending the life of an elderly, disabled, or terminally ill individual as of lower value than extending the life of an individual who is younger, nondisabled, or not terminally ill.

(2) Paragraph (1) shall not be construed as preventing the Secretary from using evidence or findings from such comparative clinical effectiveness research in determining coverage, reimbursement, or incentive programs under title XVIII based upon a comparison of the difference in the effectiveness of alternative treatments in extending an individual's life due to the individual's age.

The law further restricted use of the findings in other sections:

(d)(1) The Secretary shall not use evidence or findings from comparative clinical effectiveness research conducted under section

---

Case 9   (*continued*)

1181 in determining coverage, reimbursement, or incentive programs under title XVIII in a manner that precludes, or with the intent to discourage, an individual from choosing a health care treatment based on how the individual values the tradeoff between extending the length of their life and the risk of disability.

(2)(A) Paragraph (1) shall not be construed to—

(i) limit the application of differential copayments under title XVIII based on factors such as cost or type of service; or

(ii) prevent the Secretary from using evidence or findings from such comparative clinical effectiveness research in determining coverage, reimbursement, or incentive programs under such title based upon a comparison of the difference in the effectiveness of alternative health care treatments in extending an individual's life due to that individual's age, disability, or terminal illness.

(3) Nothing in the provisions of, or amendments made by the Patient Protection and Affordable Care Act, shall be construed to limit comparative clinical effectiveness research or any other research, evaluation, or dissemination of information concerning the likelihood that a health care treatment will result in disability.

(e) The Patient-Centered Outcomes Research Institute established under section 1181(b)(1) shall not develop or employ a dollars-per-quality adjusted life year (or similar measure that discounts the value of a life because of an individual's disability) as a threshold to establish what type of health care is cost effective or recommended. The Secretary shall not utilize such an adjusted life year (or such a similar measure) as a threshold to determine coverage, reimbursement, or incentive programs under title XVIII.

Additional constraints in the law included:

- Section 6301 (d)(8)(iv), which states: "The Institute shall ensure that the research findings . . . do not include practice guidelines, coverage recommendations, payment, or policy recommendations."

- Section 6301(j), which addresses the rule of construction, includes this language concerning coverage: "Nothing in this section shall be construed . . . to permit the Institute to mandate coverage, reimbursement, or other policies for any public or private payer."
- Section 6301 adds a Section 937 on Dissemination and Building Capacity for Research to Title IX of the Public Health Service Act, which states: "Materials, forums, and media used to disseminate the findings, informational tools, and resource databases shall . . . not be construed as mandates, guidelines, or recommendations for payment, coverage, or treatment."

Discussion Questions

1. What do you think are the interests that are being protected here?
2. How effective are these constraints likely to be?
3. Why is the United States constraining these analyses while other countries are using them?
4. What will be the impact of these constraints in the long run?

Chapter 10

The Policy Analysis Process: Evaluation of Political Feasibility

Evaluating political feasibility can be one of the most challenging steps in the policy development process. Policy choices are proposed, considered, adopted, and implemented in sociopolitical contexts that are complex, subjective, and dynamic. They are difficult to quantify or to analyze within a structured, systematic, rational framework, especially because politics can be quite irrational when factors such as emotions, ambitions, egos, disputes, personalities, allegiances, relationships, and deeply held value systems come into play.

This makes reliable prediction of whether policies have a realistic chance of being adopted and successfully implemented virtually impossible (Dror, 1969). It also helps explain why explicit discussions about political feasibility are often absent from policy debates and why literature specific to political feasibility is sparse. Oberlander (2003) observed that "political calculations are often a footnote in health care reform proposals" (p. 392). There has been some increase in the use of structured political feasibility analysis, particularly using a framework called *stakeholder analysis*, in the last decade, but as Gilson et al. (2012) noted, "there remains surprisingly few published accounts of the use of stakeholder analysis in health policy development generally, and health financing specifically, and even fewer that draw lessons from experience about how to do *and* how to use such analysis" (p. 164).

Yet no policy analysis is complete if it avoids the issue of political feasibility, and there are some systematic techniques that can help predict political feasibility.

TERMINOLOGY

Brown (2006) described *political feasibility* as "the right fit between bright ideas and the values and interests that animate stakeholders with crucial pieces of power" (p. W163). Oberlander (2003) noted, "Feasibility analysis deals not with policy ideals but with what is more or less adoptable given policy constraints" (p. W3-392).

Dror (1969) identified three characterizations of political feasibility:

1. For a political actor, political feasibility is a measure of the actor's ability, within a given period of time, to influence various activities, specifically policy adoption and implementation. He used the term *political leverage* to describe the actor's influence and *political leverage domain* to describe the setting or range of activities within which an actor can exercise political leverage effectively.
2. For a specific policy alternative, political feasibility is a measure of the likelihood that an alternative will be adopted and implemented within a specific time period.
3. For an issue area, political feasibility is a measure of the range of policy alternatives that could potentially be adopted and implemented within a specific time period. Dror referred to the range of politically viable alternatives as the *political feasibility domain*.

Dror also described four sets of "variables" for thinking about political feasibility:

1. The main actors—who they are and what they intend.
2. Other inputs into the policy arena—the political climate, the state of the economy, public opinion, technological capabilities, and so forth.
3. The interplay of the first two—how actors come together and interact, taking the other inputs into account. Those interactions are governed by laws and informal "rules of the game." Some actors

may join to form a *required coalition* with enough combined political leverage to move a policy forward.

4. The threshold for adoption—in the House of Representatives, for example, the threshold for passage is a simple majority, but the threshold changes if Congress has to override a presidential veto, which requires a two-thirds majority. An actor or a coalition may have considerable aggregated policy leverage, but whether it has enough will depend on the threshold that has to be met.

In Dror's model, the actors, influenced and informed by various inputs, interact with other actors and seek to combine political leverage to achieve a mass of critical leverage.

Health care has traditionally been a *political feasibility domain* in which the range of political feasible policies is severely limited. Taking other *inputs* into account, the *actors* supporting change have not been able to create enough *aggregate political leverage* to meet the *threshold for adoption*. Therefore, it has been a domain marked by incrementalism, compromise, and failure. Starr (2011) has attributed this to a policy trap—the health care system is unwieldy and dysfunctional, yet enough people are satisfied by the current arrangement that they are unwilling to support disruptive changes. Even the Affordable Care Act (ACA), as sweeping as it may appear, is a product of this dynamic.

Another set of variables involves factors that induce actors to become concerned about a particular issue or attracted to a particular policy strategy or solution in the first place. If an issue is not on anybody's radar, there are no actors, and thus no actor interactions.

In the fields of political science and public affairs, the process by which political parties and government entities decide to address a particular problem or consider a particular policy approach is called *agenda setting*. A prerequisite, of course, is that a set of circumstances be identified as a problem whose time has come. A number of factors influence when a problem is identified, how it is defined, and whether politicians choose to address it. These include public opinion, the national political mood, media coverage, emerging social movements, interest group mobilization, voter attitudes, arising risks and threats (real or perceived), new research findings, critical evaluations of program performance, economic changes, the level of sympathy for the affected populations, and the availability of potential policy solutions (Hacker, 1997; Oliver, 2006). Action on an agenda item may be either *ceremonial* or *intentional*. Ceremonial action means going through the motions for public relations reasons or political leverage, but does not imply a strong will to address the underlying issues.

OVERVIEW

To assess political feasibility, one needs to turn to the fields of political science, public administration, economics, and business management. The first part of this chapter focuses on the *authorizing environments* in which policy is made. By mapping an authorizing environment (a process also referred to as *stakeholder mapping*), we identify the major actors that populate the political stage. These are all policy makers to some extent, even if they are not elected officials, bureaucrats, or judges, because they all can influence political feasibility. Next we discuss the players' roles and briefly describe some inputs they typically take into account, some factors that influence what gets onto their agendas, some formal and informal rules they operate under, and some ways they push a policy toward adoption. The oft-repeated word in the preceding sentence is *some*, because there is no room in this work for more than a very cursory overview of U.S. political science.

The second part of this chapter focuses on methods for analyzing political feasibility. These include various techniques, some dating back to the 1950s, as well as the most widely used contemporary methodology, stakeholder analysis, which is a framework that incorporates many of the older techniques.

Finally, we examine some of the ways political feasibility analysis can be used, for good or ill, to drive political decisions and policy adoption.

Although this chapter focuses primarily on government policy making—the adoption and implementation of policies through legislation, budgets, executive orders, rules, or court decisions—many other channels for implementing policy exist. Organized community-based activities that are designed to change attitudes, beliefs, and individual norms also can be considered policies (Lamson & Colman, 2005). Individual private nonprofit and for-profit organizations are also political environments in which policy alternatives have to be evaluated for political feasibility (Hansmann, 1996).

AUTHORIZING ENVIRONMENTS

The term *authorizing environment* comes from the field of public administration and refers to a list of the actors from whom a public manager must receive authorization in order to survive and be effective. It applies equally well to an institution, and, in a pluralistic society, it is relevant to the development, adoption, and successful implementation of a policy.

Consider the authorizing environment experienced by one of the authors while employed by the Washington State Board of Health. The board's authorities include the ability to make rules for the environmental health and safety of schools. When the board decided to update its school environmental health rules, it had to operate in a crowded and contentious authorizing environment.

The primary authority for schools rests with local school districts, and school board members are accountable to voters. Washington laws grant local jurisdictions considerable authority. The state, however, pays 69% of public schools' operating costs and most construction costs. The legislature imposes numerous mandates on the districts.

School health and safety inspection programs, where they exist, reside with local public health jurisdictions governed by local boards of health comprised wholly or in part of county commissioners. They work closely with the state Department of Health. Local governments and local boards of health can enact their own ordinances, as long as they are not less stringent than state statutes and rules. They have limited authority over school districts; however, they can adopt and enforce building codes.

The governor appoints 9 of the state Board of Health's 10 members to 3-year terms and is the supervisor of the 10th member, the secretary of health.

The legislature granted the board its regulatory powers and could repeal them or cut the board's budget. It also could overrule board action through preemptive legislation, and a special committee can investigate whether any agency's rules exceed its authority.

Other state agencies have authorities and programs related to health and safety.

- The Office of the Superintendent of Public Instruction operates a "coordinated school health" program and has sustainability standards for school construction.
- The Department of Health is a partner on the coordinated school health project, provides technical assistance to schools and local public health agencies, regulates drinking water systems, and administers money for schools to test for lead.
- The Department of Labor and Industries protects employees' workplace safety.
- The Department of Ecology addresses contaminated soils on school grounds.
- The Department of Agriculture regulates pesticide use on and near school grounds.
- The Building Code Council establishes the statewide building code.

At the federal level, the U.S. Environmental Protection Agency regulates drinking water, although a standard for lead in school drinking water has been invalidated by the courts. It also runs a voluntary program to help schools ensure a healthy environment. The Centers for Disease Control and Prevention administers the coordinated school health program.

In Seattle and other communities, parents are active and organized. They have concerns about other drinking water contaminants, indoor air quality, and mold. These issues have been the subject of extensive media coverage. The Washington State PTA is an influential political player in the state.

Often aligned with parents are teachers and their Washington Education Association (WEA). School employees attribute many ailments to school environmental conditions. The WEA is a major actor in state politics.

The State Board of Health is committed to basing decisions on science, but the science is incomplete, inconclusive, and evolving.

The state, the schools, and the WEA all consulted with lawyers during rule making, and school districts have frequently challenged state policies in court.

On this one rule alone, the board's authorizing environment included schools, school boards, local government, local public health jurisdictions, the governor, the legislature, several state agencies, two federal agencies, parents, students, teachers, researchers, the courts, labor, the media, contractors that provided service to schools (such as architects), and the general public (see **Figure 10-1**).

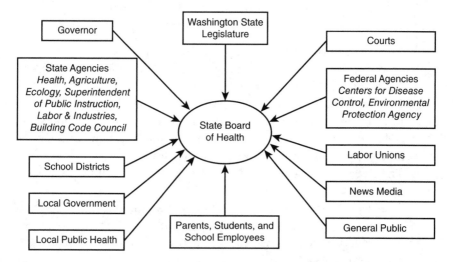

Figure 10-1 Washington State Board of Health authorizing environment for school health and safety rules.

Nearly all health policy making operates in similarly complicated authorizing environments. Each actor has its own agenda, its own constituencies, its own set of inputs to consider, and its own idiosyncrasies. That complexity is one of the main reasons that political feasibility is so difficult to predict.

KEY GOVERNMENT ACTORS

Many important governmental actors are active at the federal level, and in this section we consider factors that determine how they behave within their niches. This will be followed by a discussion of key actors at the state and local level and some of the ways they may differ from their federal counterparts.

Federal Government Actors

The drafters of the U.S. Constitution were wary of a government that put unrestrained power in the hands of one individual or institution. The Constitution that took effect in 1789 created a stronger national government, but it established three branches—legislative, executive, and judicial—and a system of checks and balances to ensure that no one branch would dominate. This basic framework also exists down through lower levels of government. At the federal level, the strengths of these branches relative to one another have waxed and waned over the years, but the separation of powers has survived intact.

Congress: The Legislative Body

Assessments of the relative power of the three branches of government in the modern era tend to conclude that Congress is the most powerful. This is largely because only Congress has the power to make laws and create budgets, whereas bureaucracies implement them and courts interpret them. The relative power of Congress has grown over the past few decades as its members have expanded their capacity to act as policy entrepreneurs. In this they are supported by personal and committee staffs that grew after World War II and expanded dramatically in the 1960s and 1970s. The larger staffs have freed Congress from reliance on the executive branch to generate major policy proposals. According to Oberlander (2003), "Congress, measured in terms of its political independence, administrative capacity, and ability to pursue policies that diverge from the executive, may be the most powerful legislature in the world" (p. W3-394).

The Senate and the House of Representatives have different makeups and personalities. Each plays by its own rules. Senators are elected by a statewide vote—two from each state—which means that the least populous states have the same representation as the most populous. House members represent congressional districts that are roughly equal in population and are redrawn after every census.

Committees are where the bulk of the work in Congress gets done. When legislation is introduced, it is referred to one or more policy committees. They may hold hearings, mark up a bill, and refer it to the floor for action. Committees have subcommittees with policy expertise in certain areas. Major policy subcommittees for health care issues are the Subcommittee on Public Health of the Senate Committee on Health, Education, Labor, and Pensions and the Subcommittee on Health of the House Energy and Commerce Committee. If the policy has budgetary implications, it will also have to go through one or more of the six powerful fiscal committees—Appropriations and Budget committees in both houses, House Ways and Means, and Senate Finance. The latter two have tended to be bottlenecks for major health care legislation. In the House, another powerful committee, the Rules Committee, directs the progress of legislation and establishes the rules of debate.

If related but different legislation passes both houses, one house may ask the other to reconsider, or leadership from both houses may appoint a joint conference committee that will develop compromise legislation and send the new iteration back to both houses for adoption. Legislation can perish from neglect in a conference committee. Committee members can also add major policy changes with little fanfare. Just 10 days before the 1974 passage of the Employment Retirement and Income Security Act (ERISA), conferees slipped in language that restricted states from regulating the health benefit plans of self-insured companies. This "ERISA exemption" severely limited the ability of states to enact significant health care reforms such as play-or-pay laws.

Congress will sometimes authorize a new program but not provide an appropriation. In 1998, for example, Congress passed the Ricky Ray Hemophilia Relief Fund Act, which authorized payments of up to $100,000 to hemophiliacs and their partners (or their survivors) infected with the human immunodeficiency virus. Congress, however, did not appropriate money for the payments until 2001.

Another part of the budget process that can undermine policy committees is the reconciliation bill. Congress can adopt a budget, and then committees can go back and recommend changes to existing laws to conform to the budget instructions. These recommendations are compiled into a reconciliation bill that requires no hearing and often passes with little scrutiny. Anything vaguely related to the budget can be thrown in. Most major health legislation during the 1980s took this route (Starr, 2011).

The two houses passed different versions of the ACA. Resolving the differences typically would have meant sending the bill to a conference committee, then having both houses vote on a compromise version. But after Democratic Senator Ted Kennedy of Massachusetts died in office, Republican Scott Brown won his seat in a special election. Senate Democrats no longer had the 60 votes needed to survive a filibuster if the ACA came back to the Senate (it was doubtful they had the votes even before Brown's victory because the House insisted on changes that were unpalatable to some Democratic senators). In an unprecedented move, the House passed the Senate version despite reservations, then included negotiated changes in a reconciliation bill. On the Senate side, the reconciliation bill was not subject to a filibuster, so proponents needed only 50 votes (the vice president would have been the tiebreaker).

Before major legislation can take effect, then, it may have to wind its way through a maze of committees and subcommittees, be scheduled for a floor vote, receive a majority vote in both houses (and perhaps 60 votes in the Senate), survive a conference committee, have a budget appropriation, and be signed by the president or have enough votes for a veto override. It is hardly surprising that major reform initiatives are easy to derail. Oberlander (2003) identified the fragmented structure of Congress as a significant barrier to health care reform.

The President: The Chief Executive Officer

The U.S. president is often referred to as "the leader of the free world." The phrase perhaps overstates the importance of the office, given the relative strength of Congress. The day after the 2006 midterm elections, Representative John P. Murtha told National Public Radio, "The president has no power. The president has perception of power." That phrase is very apt in some ways because while a president has limited authority to *make* policy, he or she has tremendous ability to *influence* policy. A president is more likely to become a policy maker because of leadership than any direct authority.

The president can and does craft major legislative initiatives—the annual State of the Union address is often full of new policy initiatives—but only Congress can introduce them. The president must find a sponsor to introduce legislation, and after a bill is in the hands of Congress there is no guarantee it will pass or if it does pass that it will resemble the original proposal. In health care, perhaps the greatest example of the limits on a president's ability to ensure a bill's passage is the 1993 Health Security Act proposed by Bill Clinton, which is the subject of the case at the end of the chapter.

The federal government passes a new budget for each fiscal year. The president initiates the budget process, but the budget that emerges from Congress may be significantly different. In 2006, for example, George W. Bush proposed a fiscal year 2007 budget that would have eliminated the Urban Indian Health Program. Legislative committees marking up the Department of the Interior, Environment, and Related Agencies Appropriation Bill restored the funding and even proposed an increase in the program's budget.

A president's ability to push a measure through Congress depends in large part on his or her *political capital*. For presidents, political capital primarily comes down to two things—popularity and their party's strength in Congress. For a recently elected president, popularity can be judged by the electoral margin of victory. For a president well into her or his term, popularity can be assessed by opinion polls.

The 1965 passage of Medicaid and Medicare has been attributed to Lyndon Johnson's phenomenal political capital. He clearly had a mandate, as he was elected with more than 61% of the popular vote, a feat unsurpassed since. The first Gallup poll of his term showed an 80% approval rating. He was a Democrat, and his party had a two-thirds majority in both houses. This gave him authority to push the agenda that had gotten him elected and a Congress unified enough, despite a North–South split in the Democratic Party, to tackle even the most divisive issues.

In a sense, the president is a stand-in for the body politic, the most visible official in the country. Presidential words can carry considerable moral authority. Presidential messages reach the public through numerous vehicles—the State of the Union address, press conferences, speeches, fireside chats, photo opportunities, public appearances, and more. This gives the president unequalled ability to elevate issues onto the national agenda, propose strategies, and bring public pressure to bear. The president's leadership role involves working to build coalitions, broker negotiations, and develop compromises. When Congress balks at a presidential proposal, the president can engage in education, persuasion, and horse trading. Extreme arm-twisting by a president, however, is rare.

Presidents do have authorities they can use to leverage policy. One is veto power. The president has 10 days after enactment to sign or veto legislation. Congress can override a veto by a two-thirds vote in both houses.

Another policy tool at the president's disposal is the ability to issue executive memoranda, which provide direction to agencies. If they are published in the *Federal Register* and not challenged by Congress, they become executive orders, which have the force of law. Because they can address almost any policy area provided that they are supported by some constitutional administrative authority or congressional directive, they can be legislative in nature. A 1999 executive memorandum required the Federal Employee Health Benefits Board to provide mental health parity (coverage for mental illnesses equivalent to that for physical ailments) by 2001.

In theory, most bureaucracies are line agencies under the control of the executive, but the truth, as usual, is more complicated. For one thing, the president's reach is limited. Although a president fills some 2,400 positions, appointees occupy only the top layers of a bureaucracy's management ranks. It is not unusual for career bureaucrats further down in the organization to try to subvert a president's agenda. How much attention a given president pays to the management of executive agencies varies.

Bureaucracies serve two masters. Senior appointments may require congressional confirmation. Congress establishes the agencies' budgets, authorizes their programs, and enacts the laws under which they must act. Congressional committees and subcommittees oversee agencies under their purview.

Bureaucracies and bureaucrats can draft legislation, and their expertise may be called on to craft amendments at various stages of policy deliberations. Weisert and Weisert (2002) described the role Wilbur Cohen, then assistant secretary of Health, Education, and Welfare and the leading expert on Social Security, played in the 1965 passage of Medicare and Medicaid:

> Cohen helped draft the administration bill on Medicare, consulted with members on proposed bills, and was asked to summarize various proposals to the key committees. When Wilbur Mills decided to combine several proposals into a "three-layer cake" (the layers were later known as Medicare Parts A and B and Medicaid), he asked Cohen to draw up legislative language to pull the pieces together, along with an analysis of the costs, within 12 hours. (p. 154)

Many bureaucracies generate data, information, and research as part of their regular activities, and these work products can inform the policy development process. Examples in health care include the research produced by the 25 centers and institutions that make up the National Institutes of Health and the data on the cost and quality of personal health services generated by the Agency for Healthcare Research and Quality.

Bureaucracies have their own networks and constituencies. They can mobilize outside groups to support or oppose legislations and work with them to convince them of the merits of a particular proposal or to at least minimize resistance, or pull together stakeholders early in the policy-making process to craft a policy alternative that has broad support. They can also use their outside contacts to try to assess political feasibility.

Finally, bureaucracies with regulatory authority are policy makers in their own right. Although legislatures make law, regulatory agencies make administrative law in the form of rules and regulations.

At the federal level, most agencies with health-related portfolios are part of the Department of Health and Human Services (DHHS). **Table 10-1** offers a list of DHHS agencies. **Table 10-2** lists some of the agencies that operate health-related programs but are not part of DHHS.

The Judiciary: The Federal Courts

The federal courts most often play a critical role when it comes to issues of federal preemption, constitutional protections, and interstate commerce. In the federal system, district courts oversee most civil and criminal trials, although there are separate court systems for bankruptcy, international trade and customs issues, and claims for monetary damages against the federal government.

Table 10-1 U.S. Department of Health and Human Services Program Divisions

Administration for Children and Families
Administration for Community Living
Agency for Healthcare Research and Quality
Agency for Toxic Substances and Disease Registry
Center for Faith-Based and Neighborhood Partnerships
Centers for Disease Control and Prevention
Centers for Medicare & Medicaid Services
Food and Drug Administration
Health Resources and Services Administration
Indian Health Service
National Institutes of Health
Office for Civil Rights
Office of Global Health Affairs
Office of Health Reform
Office of the National Coordinator for Health Information Technology
Substance Abuse and Mental Health Services Administration

Source: Data from: the U.S. Department of Health and Human Services. (n.d.). HHS organizational chart. Accessed on December 11, 2013, at www.hhs.gov/about/orgchart.html.

Table 10-2 Federal Agencies with Health-Related Duties (Excludes HHS Divisions)

Department of Agriculture
· Animal and Plant Health Inspection Service
· Cooperative State Research, Education, and Extension Service

Department of Defense
· TRICARE
· Army Medicine Department
· Navy Medicine
· Air Force Medical Service

Department of Homeland Security

Department of Labor
· Mine Safety and Health Administration
· Occupational Safety and Health Administration
· Employee Benefits Security Administration
· Benefits Review Board

Department of Veterans Affairs, Veterans Health Administration

Environmental Protection Agency

Federal Bureau of Prisons, Health Services Division

Federal Mine Safety and Health Review Commission

Nuclear Regulatory Commission

Occupational Safety and Health Review Commission

Uniformed Services University of the Health Sciences

Source: Data from: the Office of the Federal Register, National Archives and Records Administration, & U.S. Government Printing Office. (2013). United States Government Manual. Retrieved on December 11, 2013, from www.usgovernmentagency.gov.

When Maryland enacted a play-or-pay law requiring that any company with more than 10,000 employees spend at least 8% of its payroll on employee health care or pay into a state fund for covering the uninsured, the Retail Industry Leaders Association filed suit in federal court. U.S. District Court Judge Frederick Motz overturned the law on July 19, 2006, finding that ERISA preempted state authority.

All districts belong to one of 12 regional circuits, each of which has its own U.S. Court of Appeals. The federal appeals courts hear appeals to decisions reached by district courts, the Court of International Trade, the Court of Federal Claims, and federal agencies.

The U.S. Supreme Court picks from among the cases brought before it and chooses which it will hear. It seeks out cases involving important issues related to the Constitution or federal laws and hears cases where the rulings of the district courts appear to be in conflict. The court ultimately decided the lawsuit filed by Republican attorneys general that argued the ACA was unconstitutional. The justices upheld the constitutionality of the law's individual mandate but ruled that a requirement that states expand Medicaid was unconstitutional because it was overly coercive.

State Governments

States play a leading-edge role in formulating health policy and are major purchasers of health insurance and health care. Health care is the most critical cost driver for state government. Medicaid spending alone accounts for 24% of spending across all states (National Association of State Budget Officers, 2012). States are major local employers and also manage and fund public health and mental health services, authorize public hospital districts, regulate health insurance, license and discipline health care providers, and oversee health care facilities. They also serve as test markets for reform efforts.

States are organized on the surface as smaller versions of the federal government. The governor plays a role akin to the president. All have legislative bodies that correspond to Congress, and all but Nebraska have a bicameral legislature. States apportion legislative seats in both houses on the basis of population—the result of a Supreme Court decision in the early 1960s affirming the "one man, one vote" doctrine. States also have their own courts system, including their own supreme courts.

One of the most profound policy changes in terms of health outcomes for this country came solely through the courts and started at the state level. Attorneys general from several states sued tobacco companies to recover the costs of caring for publicly insured individuals with smoking-related illnesses. In 1998, the 5 largest tobacco companies and 46 states, plus 6 commonwealths and protectorates, signed the Master Settlement Agreement (4 states settled previously). The agreement called for payments of $206 billion over 5 years. Several of the states used the money to fund anti tobacco programs that have contributed to lower smoking rates. Although the states filed the suits in state courts, the cases might have been consolidated in federal court if the parties had not settled.

To describe states as miniature replicas of the national government would not do them justice. Their different powers, authorities, and organizational structures need to be taken into account. For example, most states allow the governor to veto line items in the major budget bills or sections of legislation. The president does not have line-item veto authority. Fifteen states also have term limits. The only federal term limit is Article 22, ratified in 1951, which restricts presidential terms. State legislatures have their own rules and customs as well.

Bureaucracies are also organized differently from state to state. Some states have combined public health, social services, and health care purchasing into a single huge agency. Some have split off public health into a separate department so that it does not get overshadowed. Some states have health care–purchasing agencies that may or may not include federal entitlement programs. Something as simple as state boards of health provides an example of the high variability in organizational structure among states. The Washington State Board of Health (2003) identified entities fitting the definition of a state board of health in 30 of the 50 states. Eight were advisory only, whereas 22 made policy in addition to providing advice. Eight of the 22 policy-making boards had direct oversight of the state health agency.

Weissert and Weissert (2002) have identified three key differences between states and the federal government that directly affect health care policy making:

- Budget limitations: States are not able to run at a deficit (although technically, Vermont is not prohibited from doing so), and they are generally prohibited from borrowing to cover operating expenses.
- Direct democracy: Twenty-four states allow initiatives—voters can pass statutes directly by voting on them on the ballot or indirectly by submitting them to the legislature. Twenty-four states (mostly the same 24) allow referenda. A legislative referendum is when the legislature puts something to public vote. A popular referendum is when, as a result of a petition, voters can confirm or repeal a legislative action. Eighteen states allow voters to recall officials.
- Media coverage: State governments receive less news coverage. Fewer reporters cover the state houses, and legislators are less adept at generating media attention.

Local Government

Local government bodies can be even more diverse. Generally speaking, each state has two levels of local governments: counties (parishes in Louisiana and boroughs in Alaska) and municipalities (cities, town, villages, and boroughs). Typically, these exist side by side, but there are examples of combined cities and counties (San Francisco is one), and, in Virginia, some large cities operate outside of the county structure. Hawaii has four counties and no municipalities, except that Honolulu is a consolidated city–county.

Such entities typically have a chief executive, a legislative body, and a court system. Depending on the level of government, the state constitution,

state statutes, and the charter for the political subdivision, officehold-
ers may have different titles, and institutions may have different names.
Municipalities typically use one of two basic structures:

- The council–manager system: A city council, board of alderman, city
  commission, or other legislative body handles policy. The mayor
  (who may be a member of the council) is largely ceremonial, and a
  city manager hired by the council performs most day-to-day administrative functions.
- The mayor–council system: A legislative body works with a separately elected mayor. How much executive authority the mayor has
  depends on whether the municipality has a "strong mayor" or "weak
  mayor" system.

County government is often structured like the council–manager system, and the legislative body is often called the board of commissioners.
Counties are typically responsible for providing services such as fire, police,
public health, criminal justice, garbage and recycling, and roads in unin-
corporated areas.

Just as states have despaired at looking to the federal government to
address access-to-care issues and other problems linked to the nation's system of health care finance and delivery and have tried to find solutions on
their own, so, too, have local governments and local communities. Some
local community efforts have experienced significant government involvement, whereas others have relied on grassroots efforts. One example of an
effort driven by local government began in the early 1990s in Hillsborough
County, Florida. In response to the strain placed on the local budget due to
the rising costs of providing services to the disadvantaged at the local public hospital, voters approved an increase to the county property tax to purchase health coverage for low-income residents ineligible for other public
health insurance programs. Through a network of local hospitals, clinics,
and providers, the Hillsborough County Health Care Plan would provide
case-managed care to an initial 30,000 beneficiaries. Part of what made the
plan politically feasible was a commitment that it would in time lead to a
reduction in property tax levies.

POLITICAL INPUTS

Being able to identify the actors and describe their interactions is only
part of the challenge of assessing political feasibility. It is also important to understand another set of variables—inputs that influence actor

interactions. There are many such inputs, but key ones include elections, constituent relations, campaign fund-raising, party agendas, the economy and its impact on government budgets, political trading, and idiosyncratic personal factors. This section discussed these types of inputs and provides examples of how these inputs have influenced public health and health care financing. Many of the examples are from Washington State because one of the authors spent several years as an agency executive for the state.

The Election Cycle

Elected officials, unless they are planning to retire or face term limits, must be concerned with reelection. The timing of elections can profoundly influence their willingness to take on controversial issues. If an issue is likely to interest the electorate favorably, it might rise to the top of a politician's or party's agenda preceding an election. Such instances often provide examples of ceremonial agenda setting. If an issue or policy is likely to alienate or confuse voters, politicians might put the issue off until after the election. Lawmakers are reluctant to raise taxes during an election year, for example. Presidents typically focus on reelection throughout most of their first term, but tend to demonstrate more independence during their second. When assessing political feasibility, it is important to consider the timing of the next election and the mood of the electorate.

Constituent Relations

For politicians concerned about reelection, one of their top two concerns is likely to be constituent relations. The nature of constituent relations activities will differ depending on the geographic area and population represented. Generally, the smaller the direct constituency, the greater the importance given to grassroots activities such as addressing service clubs.

One of the jobs of a politician is to bring home benefits, such as state and federal funding for capital improvement projects. A member's focus on these activities could make it difficult to get other issues onto his or her agenda, or a policy proposal that makes sense on a national level may conflict with the interests of folks back home. Efforts to ban tobacco sampling in Washington State were tied up for years by an influential state representative who said he opposed sampling bans because giving tobacco to kids was already illegal, and for adults, tobacco is a legal product; however, he also represented a district that is home to many small rodeos that are supported by tobacco companies and are major sites for tobacco giveaways (Callaghan, 2006).

Campaign Fund-Raising

The second major concern for politicians looking to be reelected is campaign fund-raising. Like constituent relations, fund-raising can vary in scope depending on the office. The bigger the constituency, the more it costs to campaign. The need to raise money continually influences the behavior of elected officials in many ways. When one of the authors covered politics as a reporter in California during the 1980s, legislators jockeyed aggressively for appointments to so-called juice committees—those that regulated industries and professions where a lot of money was involved, such as horse racing. These regulated entities could be counted on to make generous campaign contributions to ensure access to committee members.

Discussions of the role of money in U.S. politics tend to focus on campaign fund-raising and often include the axiom that money buys access, not votes. That can be said of various gifts and junkets, as well as cash campaign contributions. Jesse "Big Daddy" Unruh, the powerful speaker of the California Assembly in the 1960s, once said of lobbyists, "If you can't take their money, drink their booze, eat their food, screw their women, and still look them in the eye and vote against them, you don't belong here." There are, however, numerous examples, some recent, of contributions and gifts, as well as outright bribes, influencing government decisions, or at least creating the appearance of a conflict of interest. North Carolina's Speaker of the House, Jim Black, helped push through a bill in 2005 requiring comprehensive eye exams for children during the first 6 months of kindergarten. These exams would earn optometrists $75–100 per exam. Black was an optometrist and accepted $59,750 in campaign money from his professional peers that year.

Party Agendas

Candidates' ability to bring their own money to the table or to raise funds independent of the political party they represent has weakened party control in U.S. politics. Oberlander (2003) argued that the weakness of political parties in the United States is one of the political obstacles to health reform in this country. Of late, though, party politics has become more polarized and policy positions have more closely followed ideological lines. Moderate Republicans who have broken ranks to work with Democrats on health care and other issues have been defeated in their primaries by more conservative candidates. Historically, members have crossed the aisle to form bipartisan coalitions in support of health legislation, but the votes on the ACA followed strict party lines.

The Economy and the Budget

The state of the economy and the revenues flowing into government coffers can determine a politician's willingness to create new programs or retain or expand existing ones. When Washington's Governor Gregoire took office in 2005, one of her first acts was to roll back health care–related changes instituted under her predecessor that had reduced the number of children enrolled in government health insurance programs. After the September 11, 2001, attacks and the economic downturn that followed, the previous administration and the legislature had needed to cut $1–2 billion a year from the state budget for a few years running. By 2005, the state economy had begun to rebound, which left Gregoire with a projected surplus and allowed her to allocate an additional $140 million to provide coverage to an estimated 70,000 more children.

Political Trading

Lawmakers will not infrequently leverage their votes, pledging to vote a certain way in return for obtaining something else they are interested in. Leadership and committee chairs can also hold a bill hostage until some kind of quid pro quo is negotiated. In Washington State, one Senate committee chair refused to release a bill to reduce commercial sources of environmental mercury, including methylmercury, which is found in fish, unless an agency withdrew its opposition to her bill banning vaccines for children and pregnant woman that have more than trace amounts of thimerosal, a preservative that contains ethylmercury. Methylmercury is a persistent toxin that accumulates in the environment and is extremely harmful to humans, whereas ethylmercury appears to be metabolized quickly and cleared by the body. Yet the committee chair saw the two mercury bills as linked. Public health advocates had to weigh their concerns that the thimerosal bill, which was largely symbolic, would reinforce unsubstantiated fears about vaccine safety against the very real threat to human health posed by environmental releases of elemental mercury.

Adjournment

In states whose legislatures do not meet year-round, the end game can become very important. Bills can languish and appear to be dead, when in fact they may be being saved for the wheeling and dealing that invariably happens as the end of session approaches. On the other hand, a bill may pass in one chamber and be kept bottled up in another until the session ends, thwarting its passage. Sometimes a bill passes both houses quickly; however, the money to implement it may not be appropriated before the session ends, and it effectively dies, although the legislators can claim credit for having voted for it.

Personal Issues

In the fields of public administration and public policy, rational decision making is held out as the ideal. Decision makers are expected to weigh the costs and benefits of various policy options and make reasoned choices that maximize the gains to themselves, their constituents, or society as a whole, but personal preferences, relationships, irrational behaviors, and unanticipated events often influence political feasibility. In the case of the thimerosal legislation, for example, the chair of the senate committee who sponsored the bill was the grandmother of a child with autism, and family members believed that the autism was linked to an immunization the mother received when pregnant. Few analysts trying to assess the political feasibility of the environmental mercury legislation would have anticipated that its fate might be tied to a personal tragedy. In the case of the tobacco sampling bill, sympathy for the bill's sponsor, who was terminally ill and wheelchair bound, may have contributed to the bill's eventual passage.

Sometimes a bill does not move because one party does not want the other to get the credit, because one house does not want the other house to have credit, or because one member does not want another member to have credit. Committee chairs have been known to bottle up legislation in response to a sponsor's behavior before their committee.

Unexpected Events

An unanticipated event that many believe influenced the outcome of health legislation occurred in Washington State during the 2004 legislative session. Senator Rosa Franklin, an African American Democrat, sponsored a bill to establish the Joint Select Committee on Health Disparities. Many observers doubted the resolution would pass because of a lack of enthusiasm among Republicans who held a majority in the state senate. As part of an unrelated discussion of health policy, however, the chair of the senate health committee called the minority leader of the house health committee a "nigger in the woodpile." Both men were white Republicans. Franklin defended the senate committee chair (although not his choice of words) and tearfully accepted his apology on the floor of the state senate. There was never any public discussion of a deal, but few political observers were surprised when Franklin's resolution passed unanimously.

NONGOVERNMENTAL ACTORS

The Public

Politicians are constantly attempting to read the prevailing winds of public sentiment as they chart their policy courses. This is commendable up to a point. In a representative democracy such as the Unites States, elected officials presumably have some autonomy to pursue the policies and advance the values that got them elected without polling the electorate before every vote, but there is also an expectation that their actions will reflect the views of the majority of their constituents. At a baser level, focusing on public opinion can be about winning the next election, and subservience to public opinion polls can work against elected officials providing leadership, consistently pursuing long-term strategies, or taking risks. Politicians often focus on determining and responding to the opinions of likely voters more than those of their entire constituency. This is relevant in the context of health care reform, where a significant number of the uninsured are socially disenfranchised and generally not a powerful voting bloc. Additionally, older people are more likely to vote and are less likely to support significant changes to the health care system (Starr, 2011).

Individuals can make a difference. Politicians can be very sensitive to a small number of contacts from constituents expressing an opinion on an issue (they are less influenced by individuals they do not represent). The type of contact also matters. Elected officials are more likely to be influenced by a unique, personalized visit, telephone call, letter, or email than by something obviously generated by an organized letter-writing or email campaign. Furthermore, efforts to sway public opinion often are targeted to sets of individuals who are well informed and engaged in public issues. These are people who have a "big picture" view of the world and help form other peoples' opinions and can bring issues to the attention of the media and policy makers (Goddard, 1998).

Public opinion polls consistently show that at most points in time a majority of people in the United State have favored health care reform. Historically, however, public support for major reforms has been "soft." The public can easily be talked out of supporting a reform through the use of carefully crafted messages. In 1993 and 1994, polls repeatedly showed that Americans supported universal access to health care. Public support continued, and even seemed to be growing as the Clinton plan moved forward, even though people seemed confused about exactly how the plan would work or what it would do. That supportive trend began to reverse itself in late 1993, about the same time that the Health Insurance Association of America began running its famous Harry and Louise advertising campaign (Goldsteen et al., 2001). These ads were targeted at informed members of the public who could serve as opinion leaders (Goddard, 1998). By April 1994, only 43% of the country supported the proposal (Blendon, Brodie, & Benson, 1995).

One useful construct for understanding the vulnerability of public support for health reform is the notion of frames. The FrameWorks Institute defines a *frame* as, "The way a story is told—its selective use of particular values, symbols, metaphors, and messengers—which, in turn, triggers the shared and durable cultural models that people use to make sense of their world" (Gilliam, 2005). Essentially, people use predictable story elements to help them sort information; they respond to metaphors, plots, and values and other familiar aspects of the story. When communication is inadequate, says Gilliam, people rely on the pictures and stories already in their heads, but effective communication can allow them to see things from new and different perspectives. Health care reform efforts, if not understood, are subject to attack by arguing within certain frames and appealing to certain closely held values. For example, many Americans are skeptical about government and opposed to too much direct government involvement in their lives. Designers of the Harry and Louise ads conducted research that told them the public did not want a massive government program and tailored their campaign accordingly (Goddard, 1998). In other words, they told a story within a "big government" frame.

According to Gilliam (2005), frames, or value-based messages, that move people toward supporting health care reform (i.e., increase political feasibility) include interdependence, the need for practical management, and the importance of prevention. They suggest that advocates of health reform promote the need for a health coverage infrastructure akin to a utility or transportation infrastructure. **Table 10-3** provides an example of the kind of language that might have framed the issue effectively.

Interest Groups

When individuals and corporations with common social and political goals form alliances and influence policy in support of those goals, they comprise an interest group. Weissert and Weissert (2002) argued, "Next to Congress, interest groups may well be the most important actors in health policy" (p. 117). The use of the term *the third house* to refer collectively to the

Table 10-3 Sample Frame for Promoting a Health Coverage Infrastructure

In the last 50 years, the United States has built a series of modern networks that are essential to our economy and our quality of life—our power grid, phone systems, water systems, interstate highways, and the Internet; however, with health coverage we are stuck in the 1940s because we never built a modern health coverage infrastructure. Instead, we still have job-based insurance, which has become an increasingly hit-or-miss, inefficient, and unreliable approach. What we have is the equivalent of scattered wells, individual generators, and county roads but no health coverage infrastructure we can rely on, no system for making sure that people have health coverage.

Source: Modified from: Gilliam, F. D. (2005, December 6). Framing health care reform for public understanding and support. Presentation delivered at Health Legislative Conference, Seattle, WA. © 2006 Frameworks Institute; and Making the Public Case for Improving Health Care: A Frame-Works MessageMemo. 2009. Washington, DC: FrameWorks Institute.

lobbyists that represent interest groups before the legislative branch is no misnomer.

Interests groups do more than just attempt to sway votes in their favor; they can be critical partners with government actors in policy development from inception to implementation. They generate proposals, provide expertise that can improve others' proposals, offer channels for testing the feasibility of proposals with their members, broker deals, and help mobilize public opinion. After a policy is adopted, their support, apathy, or opposition can determine whether it succeeds or fails. Much of the legislation introduced by lawmakers is initially drafted by interest groups.

Interest groups also lobby the executive branch and may resort to lawsuits to assert their policies. Some narrowly focused industry or consumer groups work almost exclusively with regulatory agencies. Others, such as the Sierra Club Legal Defense Fund in the environmental policy arena, work almost exclusively through the courts.

Hundreds of interest groups are involved in health care issues. A majority of them represent either occupations or health-related companies. Major, longstanding examples of these, respectively, would include the American Medical Association (AMA) representing physicians and the American Hospital Association (AHA) representing health care facilities. The last few decades have witnessed a splintering and proliferation of these groups. Each medical specialty, for example, is likely to have its own professional association that engages in some form of political lobbying. Nurses, midlevel professionals, home health aides, and providers of alternative and complementary medicines also have their own groups. In addition to the AHA, there are associations representing smaller, more specific groupings of health care facilities, such as specialty hospitals, rural hospitals, and public hospitals, as well as associations of other types of facilities that provide care, such as long-term care facilities and adult family homes. Then there are the insurance companies and their associations and the manufacturers of pharmaceuticals, other health care technologies, and durable medical equipment. Associations of businesses and labor unions also lobby on health care. There are also several interest groups organized to represent consumers, specific subsets of consumers, and the uninsured. These include groups formed to combat a certain disease or class of diseases and to represent the interests of those afflicted. One of the most powerful consumer groups in the country, the AARP, represents people older than 50 years of age and is a major player in discussions related to Medicare, retiree health benefits, and other health policy issues. Oliver (2006) stated that the proliferation of groups "has led scholars to conclude that political influence is more generally dispersed across loosely organized 'issue networks' or 'policy communities'" (p. 209).

Interest groups have multiple tools at their disposal for influencing policy, including the following:

- Political action committees: Fund-raising committees that can make contributions to candidates, parties, or issue campaigns.
- Direct democracy: Sponsoring voter initiatives and referendums, hiring signature gatherers, and funding campaigns.
- Grassroots lobbying: Organizing the general public (or voters) to appeal directly to lawmakers or to make their positions known at the ballot box.
- Cross lobbying: Convincing other groups to support a particular policy or change an existing position that runs counter to that policy.
- Coalition building: Increasing political leverage by forming coalitions to work on a specific issue or policy, often for a limited time.
- Research: Conducting studies, compiling data, and producing reports that influence policy choices, often focusing on the evidence basis and economic and technological feasibility of policy options.
- Framing: Using public opinion research, message development, and other communications techniques to "tell the story" about a policy in a way that changes the public discourse.

The Media

The news media play a critical role in shaping policy debates and outcomes in this country. Media outlets exert their influence in three principle ways:

- Setting the frame: The news media tell stories to interest their readers and viewers, and the way those stories are organized helps establish the frames that people use to interpret both the coverage and the underlying social issue. Media provide the context people use to help form opinions on an issue, and even a set of often subtle cues to guide them to their decision.
- Sorting and delivering data and information: Decision makers rely on data and information; however, their time is limited, and we live in an era of information overload. They are not able to sort and process all of the relevant information that emerges in a constant stream of studies, reports, and journal articles, and thus they tend to rely on media to sort information and identify what is relevant. Opinion makers tend to rely on facts to shape their opinions or buttress them—facts they often gather as news media consumers.
- Setting the agenda: The role of the *New York Times* in promoting the Jackson Hole Group's managed competition model, described in the case at the end of the chapter, provides a clear example of how the media can set the political agenda.

Here is how Goddard (1998) explained the role the media plays in U.S. public opinion formation and agenda setting:

> The media communicates with opinion leaders . . . about an issue. "Hey! Here's something that's important" . . . What's really critical is that the opinions that "informed" Americans form after exposure to them are then communicated to policy makers. And all of a sudden the policy makers say, "Wait a minute! All these people out there who I count on for support are concerned about this issue." (p. 1)

Scientists and Other Experts

The notion of rationality in decision making presupposes that there is sufficient information and resources to understand fully the implications of each policy alternative. Although this rarely occurs in practice, most policy makers try to understand what the research tells them about the value of various policy proposals. This gives researchers who generate data and informed analysis considerable influence over political feasibility.

Research and data can come from a variety of sources. Generally, the most credible sources are academic researchers who publish their findings in peer-reviewed journals. Policy makers also turn to raw data from primary sources (especially from government agencies) and to reports and studies from think tanks, advocacy groups, pharmaceutical firms, university centers with narrowly defined missions, and a variety of other sources whose work may reflect an ideological or financial bias.

The push toward evidence-based medicine has heightened the focus on making policy based on data, as government policy makers have realized that it is becoming increasingly common for state governments to fund research centers that evaluate the comparative evidence basis for certain drugs and other medical technologies. Oliver and Singer (2006) found that research conducted by the California Health Benefits Review Program, which relies on university-based researchers to analyze the evidence basis for requiring that health insurance plans cover certain types of care, played a significant role in shaping legislative decision making around mandated benefits in that state.

METHODS FOR ANALYZING POLITICAL FEASIBILITY

Dror (1988) confessed that he had become skeptical about formal modeling. Almost by default, political feasibility prediction tends to rely on seeking out expert informants and asking them how key players are likely to respond to the policy or policy alternatives.

Identifying the actors by mapping the authorizing environment, as we did in the example earlier in this chapter, is often a key early step. A subsequent step would likely involve determining the amount of support or opposition that each actor is likely to generate, either by soliciting information from the actors themselves or from some other set of experts. One could also solicit the experts' opinion on how much influence each actor is likely to have over the outcome. It also is important to identify other inputs likely to influence the outcome of a specific policy debate. This would involve addressing a variety of questions, such as the following:

- Is the economy expanding or contracting? What is that likely to mean for government revenues? How expensive is the policy alternative?
- What other focusing events are likely to demand the attention of the public and decision makers?

It may be useful to tease apart the different factors that contribute to political feasibility. Kingdon (1984) suggested that there are three streams to the policy process. He argued that change will be incremental unless these three streams converge favorably, typically as a result of a crisis that redefines a problem or a change in who controls the government that creates a window of opportunity. The three streams are:

- The problem stream: People need to agree there is a problem, their understanding needs to be supported by basic science, and they need to share a common definition of what the problem is.
- The policy stream: Credible scientific, technological, and/or policy solutions must be available.
- The political stream: The problem needs to be on the agenda, and there needs to be political will to address it.

Another useful concept for thinking about political feasibility is force field analysis, a decision-making tool developed by psychologist Kurt Lewin that provides a way of examining the forces working for or against a particular decision. Lewin (1951) argued that issues were held in balance by driving forces (those promoting change) and restraining forces (those favoring the status quo). These included both strong and weak forces, as represented in **Figure 10-2**. As a decision-making tool, force field analysis is often represented with a chart. In a box in the middle is the decision, or in our case, the policy. On the left side is a set of arrows representing the forces for change, and on the right side is a set of arrows representing forces against change. In political feasibility analysis, those arrows would represent actors and inputs.

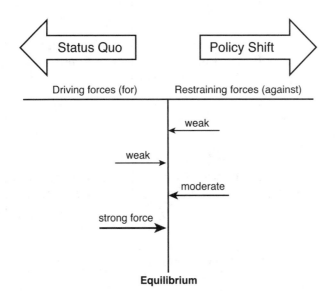

Figure 10-2 Force field analysis diagram.

Source: Modified from: Lewin, K. (1951). Field theory in social science. New York: Harper and Row.

After you have identified the forces bearing on the policy, you can assign them a score from 1 (weak) to 5 (strong) and tally to create a combined score for the forces for and against.

In their analysis of the political feasibility of mandated health insurance benefits, Oliver and Singer (2006) used a framework that examines whether the costs and the benefits are concentrated among a few or diffused among many (see **Figure 10-3**).

The most politically feasible solutions are those involving "client politics" where there are strong advocates who would reap the concentrated benefits but little opposition because the costs are minor or are spread broadly among many interests or individuals. The least politically feasible are those involving "entrepreneurial politics" where the benefits are shared so broadly that there are no impassioned, self-interested advocates and yet there is great opposition from interests that would bear the concentrated costs. Incrementalism, according to Oliver (2006), is a natural byproduct of "interest group politics" that occurs when both benefits and costs are concentrated. "With clear winners and losers, the level of conflict is high and the outcome of any single proposal is highly unpredictable" (p. 211).

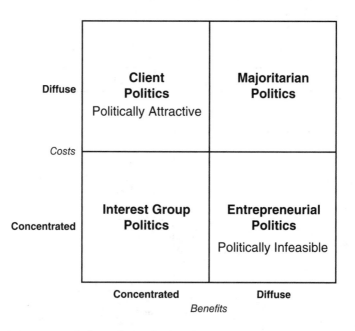

Figure 10-3 Framework for analysis of policy design and political feasibility.

Source: Reproduced from: Oliver, T. R. (2006). The politics of public health policy. Annual Review of Public Health, 27: 195–233. Reproduced with permission of ANNUAL REVIEWS in the format Republish in a book via Copyright Clearance Center.

Dror (1969) proposed a framework for political feasibility analysis that relies on the Delphi method. He recommended that prediction panels consist of senior executives, politicians, and political observers:

> While politicians are the ideal panel members for political feasibility prediction studies, this itself may be politically and personally non-feasible, especially if such studies become widespread. Therefore, main reliance may have to be put on politics-observing persons, such as political aides, political correspondents, political science scholars, senior civil servants, etc. (pp. 12–13)

Dror suggested that panelists be asked to complete three different types of questionnaires. One form would ask the panelists to rate the probability that specific policy alternatives might be adopted across different time frames. Another would ask whether various alternatives were feasible within a specific time frame and solicit information about barriers to adoption and what conditions would have to change to make adoption possible. These two forms are displayed in **Tables 10-4** and **10-5**. The third one would solicit opinions about the various actors—how much leverage they have, what their intentions are, and what actions they are likely to take alone or in combination with other actors. He also recommended that the informants be divided into three panels that get the surveys at different times. This would allow the coordinator to test for consistency. A number of researchers and analysts over the years have proposed or employed numerous variations on both the Delphi technique in general and the framework proposed by Dror. Turoff (1970), for example, has proposed a variant technique called the Policy Delphi that can be used to identify the

Table 10-4 Scheme 1: Direct Political Feasibility Estimation

	Political Feasibility Estimate			
Policy Alternatives	**Next X Years**	**Next Y Years**	**....**	**Next N Years**
Alternative 1				
Alternative 2				
....				
Alternative N				

Each cell to be filled out with a probability, or probability distribution, or alternative probabilities with explicit assumptions—depending on the capacities of the predictor.

Source: Reproduced from: Dror. (1969). The prediction of political feasibility. Santa Monica, CA: The Rand Corporation.

Table 10-5 Scheme 2: Political Feasibility Conditions

Policy Alternatives	Is politically feasible during next X years?	If not, what changes in conditions are required to make it politically feasible?
Alternative 1		
Alternative 2		
....		
Alternative N		

Depending on interest and on capacities of the predictor, the scheme can deal with various time spans, different feasibility probabilities and probability changes, and various combinations of conditions and assumptions.

Source: Reproduced from: Dror. (1969). The prediction of political feasibility. Santa Monica, CA: The Rand Corporation.

universe of policy options, estimate the impact and consequences of those options, and assess their acceptability.

In the past couple of decades, stakeholder analysis has emerged as the most common methodology for analyzing political feasibility. It has been employed across many disciplines, including political philosophy (Gilabert & Lawford-Smith, 2012), public health (AusAID et al., 2004), business management, development, environmental and natural resource management, and health care finance (Brugha & Varvasovszky, 2000). Spreadsheets, manuals, software systems, and consulting services can be purchased online to help people conduct such analyses, and several governments have published guides.

There are many ways to structure stakeholder analysis, but the process generally involves three steps: (1) stakeholder identification; (2) stakeholder mapping or prioritization; and (3) gathering information from stakeholders. Each of these we have already discussed, just not within the context of stakeholder analysis. Though anyone conducting a stakeholder analysis will want to start with stakeholder identification, these steps are iterative and not necessarily sequential. Key informant interviews, say, might identify stakeholders that researchers would not have included otherwise, or they might cast new light on the relative power of organizations or interest groups.

Stakeholder identification is basically the same process as developing a map of an authorizing environment. This can be the product of brainstorming, or asking experts and readily identified stakeholders to identify the players. When Vermont was researching policy options for a statewide health care system after the implementation of the ACA, researchers conducted a "political landscape analysis" that included conducting a literature review to gather information of the history of health policy in the state and the organizations involved in shaping health policy (Hsiao, Kappel, & Gruber, 2011).

Stakeholder mapping or stakeholder prioritization typically involves placing the identified stakeholders on a grid, such as the one developed for expert interviews by Oliver (2006), or the "stakeholder matrix" proposed by the Victoria state government in Australia (see **Table 10-6**) to identify how influential they will be and how much effort should be put into encouraging their support.

A stakeholder analysis for a project to improve universal health care coverage in South America and Tanzania expanded on this concept by

Table 10-6 Stakeholder Analysis (Stakeholder Matrix)

Description

Stakeholder analysis is an essential part of developing a useful Engagement Plan. A common method of stakeholder analysis is a Stakeholder Matrix. This is where stakeholders are plotted against two variables. These variables might be plotting the level of 'stake' in the outcomes of the project against 'resources' of the stakeholder. Another is the 'importance' of the stakeholder against the 'influence' of the stakeholder. The concept is the same, though the emphasis is slightly different.

		Importance of Stakeholder			
		Unknown	Little/No importance	Some importance	Significant importance
Influence of Stakeholder	Significant influence	C			A
	Somewhat influential				
	Little/No influence	D			B
	Unknown				

Boxes A, B, and C are the key stakeholders of the project. The implications of each box is summarized on the next page:

(continues)

Table 10-6 Stakeholder Analysis (Stakeholder Matrix) *(continued)*

Box A

These are stakeholders appearing to have a high degree of influence on the project, who are also of high importance for its success. This implies that the implementing organization will need to construct good working relationships with these stakeholders, to ensure an effective coalition of support for the project. Examples might be the senior officials and politicians or trade unions.

Box B

These are stakeholders of high importance to the success of the project, but with low influence. This implies that they will require special initiatives if their interests are to be protected. An example may be traditionally marginalized groups (e.g., indigenous people, youth, seniors), who might be beneficiaries of a new service, but who have little 'voice' in its development.

Box C

These are stakeholders with high influence, who can therefore affect the project outcomes, but whose interests are not necessarily aligned with the overall goals of the project. They might be financial administrators, who can exercise considerable discretion over funding disbursements. This conclusion implies that these stakeholders may be a source of significant risk, and they will need careful monitoring and management.

Box D

The stakeholders in this box, with low influence on, or importance to the project objectives, may require limited monitoring or evaluation, but are of low priority.

Method

1. Make a list of all stakeholders.
2. Write the name of each stakeholder on a sticky note or index card.
3. Rank the stakeholders on a scale of one to five, according to one of the criteria on the matrix, such as 'interest in the project outcomes' or 'interest in the subject.'
4. Keeping this ranking for one of the criteria, plot the stakeholders against the other criteria of the matrix. This is where using sticky notes or removable cards are useful.
5. Ask the following questions:
   · Are there any surprises?
   · Which stakeholders do we have the most/least contact with?
   · Which stakeholders might we have to make special efforts to ensure engagement?

Source: Reproduced from: State of Victoria. (2013). Effective Engagement: Stakeholder Analysis (Stakeholder Matrix). Victoria, Australia: State of Victoria. Last updated on April 26, 2013. Retrieved from www.dse.vic.gov.au/effective-engagement/toolkit/tool-stakeholder-analysis-stakeholder-matrix. Courtesy of Department of Environment and Primary Industries, State Government of Victoria.

producing a "force field analysis map" that was similar to the one depicted earlier in this chapter, but it included more categories for measuring both the political power and the degree of support of each stakeholder (Gilson et al., 2012, p. 1174). This is comparable to determining whether the arrows in a force field diagram should be represented as strong, weak, or moderate.

The third step, gathering information from stakeholders, can take several forms, including use of a Delphi technique or key informant interviews. For the Vermont study, researchers interviewed 120 people representing at least 60 organizations (Hsiao et al., 2011). They then determined the key interests and concerns of different sectors and identified policy options that would not be politically feasible because of strong opposition from highly interested and engaged groups with significant economic and political power; for example, "stakeholder analysis shows that hospitals would mobilize all their political strength and support to oppose any reduction in the total amount paid to hospitals" (p. 7).

CRITIQUES OF POLITICAL FEASIBILITY ANALYSIS

The highly qualitative nature of such techniques makes their results subject to human error. Dror (1988) cautioned that "experts may easily be emotionally biased when hot political issues are touched upon and may be overconservative in underestimating possibilities of changes and jumps in political situations" (p. 273). Oberlander (2003) pointed out that the headlines about health reform in 2003 were reminiscent of those that appeared in 1993 and 1973. The disturbing statistics and the comprehensive reform proposals designed to address them were eerily similar. The problem, he argued, is not a lack of good ideas but a consistent failure to realistically assess political feasibility. People confuse feasibility with desirability and tend to argue that their favorite solution is the most feasible, he stated, or they can be predisposed to accept a flawed feasibility analysis that supports their position. He added that a "beltway mentality" leads people to assume that whatever appears in the *Washington Post* or has caught the imagination of Washington insiders is most politically feasible.

Both Dror and Oberlander raised concerns about the use of political feasibility predictions. Dror pointed out that such predictions assume that no unexpected occurrences would take place—and they often do. Bill Clinton ran for president on a campaign built around a central premise: "It's the economy, stupid." The economic downturn that hit at the end of George H. W. Bush's term not only doomed his reelection bid, but it also produced a great deal of public anxiety about people losing their health insurance.

That was in 1992, however. By the time Congress was seriously considering the Clinton Health Security Plan in late 1993 and early 1994, the economy had greatly improved, and the public was less inclined to see health insurance as an immediate crisis.

It should be noted that frameworks like stakeholder analysis can lead to an almost exclusive focus on the actors, which may contribute to inadequate analysis of inputs such as economic changes. To effectively analyze political feasibility, it is important not to be satisfied solely with identifying and consulting with stakeholders. It may also be important to consult with experts on various inputs—economists, historians, futurists, political pollsters, organizational psychologists, and other experts.

Something akin to the Heisenberg uncertainty principle of quantum physics also operates in the realm of feasibility prediction. Efforts to measure something can influence the thing being measured and change the measured result. Feasibility analyses can actively influence the outcome of a political debate— they can be merely self-fulfilling or conflicting analyses can cancel each other out. Oberlander (2003) stated that "feasibility analysis does not merely play a passive role in the political process as an objective judge of what will or can happen. Rather, policy analysis itself can influence the course of events and is often deployed as a political weapon" (p. W3-393). As an example, he pointed to the number of policy analysts that opponents of the Clinton health plan brought forward to explain why the plan was irredeemably flawed.

Dror (1969) cautioned that "care must be taken to avoid a mistake widespread in practice and sometimes supported by theory, that 'feasibility' becomes a dominant criterion of a preferable alternative, in the sense of 'the more feasible the better'" (p. 2). He suggested that political feasibility analyses should be seen as challenges, not constraints. He noted that:

> . . . every political feasibility prediction tends to ignore the capacities of human devotion and human efforts to overcome apparently insurmountable barriers and to achieve not only the improbable but the apparently impossible. A good policy may be worth fighting for, even if its political feasibility seems to be nill [sic], as devotion and skillful efforts may well overcome political barriers and snatch victory out of the mouth of political infeasibility. (pp. 18–19)

CONCLUSION

Policy analysts may tend to avoid political feasibility assessments because they are highly qualitative in nature and subject to a great deal of uncertainty. We have discussed how medicine has become increasingly industrialized, but politics will likely remain more of an art than an industry. To address political feasibility at all, an analyst must understand the authorizing environment, the key political actors, the various inputs into the political process, and how they are likely to interact. Techniques such as force field analysis, independent looks at the three streams of policy that can create windows of opportunity, and assessments of whether the benefits or costs of a policy are concentrated or diffuse can be useful. Systematic approaches to assessing political feasibility typically rely on surveys of stakeholders but can also include surveys of experts who are not direct stakeholders. The Delphi technique provides one structure for such inquires. It is important, however, to select informants with care. This includes reaching out to a broad, diverse range of stakeholders, or in the case of academic or technical experts, being aware of the experts' biases and limitations. Finally, political feasibility analyses can become self-fulfilling prophecies if not used wisely. Analysts should be wary of abandoning good policy ideas because they seem unfeasible or settling on a poor idea because it would be an easy sell.

| Case 10 | The Politics of the Clinton Health Plan |

BACKGROUND

A premature death helped set in motion the events that ultimately pushed health care reform to the fore of the U.S. political agenda in 1993, but it was not the early demise of a child whose insurance company refused life-saving treatment or the death of a heart attack victim turned away from the closest emergency room because of lack of insurance. The precipitating event was the April 4, 1991, plane crash that killed Henry John Heinz III, a Republican Senator from Pennsylvania. On November 5, Harris Wofford, the Democrat appointed to replace Heinz, won a special election to complete the term by upsetting frontrunner Richard Thornburgh with a campaign built almost entirely around health care reform. Politicians and pundits of all stripes quickly agreed: Major health care reform was just a matter of time.

Bill Clinton's election to the White House a year later reinforced that belief. Clinton recruited many of the campaign consultants who had advised Wofford, and he pledged during the campaign to reform health care. He set about delivering on his pledge within days of taking office.

Case 10   (*continued*)

On September 22, 1993, before Congress and a national TV audience, he outlined his plan to "fix a health care system that is badly broken." A little more than a year later, however, another unexpected death occurred. The deceased was President Clinton's plan for "Health Security." The plan's collapse doomed any hopes advocates had of passing significant health care reforms in the 1990s and was credited by some with inducing the electoral tsunami that gave Republicans control of both houses of Congress in the 1994 elections.

BUILDING TOWARD REFORM

A confluence of events put health reform on the top of the agenda in the early 1990s, not just the bellwether Senate race. The Clinton-era reform effort was not a unique event but rather part of a chain of efforts that spanned much of the century. What seemed to set the 1990s apart, however, was the variety of stakeholders prepared to support some kind of reform. Most came to the table because of the spiraling cost of health insurance and the growing number of uninsured:

- Businesses that covered their workers were spending as much as 25% of their earnings on health insurance.
- Organized labor was seeing business shift more and more of the costs of health care onto workers.
- Providers were frustrated by insurance companies managing their professional decisions and monetary losses when patients did not pay up.
- Hospitals were concerned about the increases in uncompensated care.
- State governments had watched the share of their budgets going to health care climb from 9% to 14% in the 1990s.
- Large insurers were concerned about small insurers siphoning off younger and healthier customers, leaving them to cover more high-risk populations.

Less certain going into the 1991 election was where the electorate, particularly the middle class, stood. As the sign at Clinton's campaign headquarters noted, "It's the economy, stupid." The United States was in the grips of a recession, and the middle class was worried—about unemployment, about medical bankruptcy, about jobs that offered no health insurance, or about insurance that required high out-of-pocket expenses or covered only catastrophic events. Wofford's and Clinton's elections had seemed to settle the issue—it seemed the electorate was prepared to support a major overhaul of the health care system.

THE MENU OF OPTIONS

Even before the 1991 and 1992 elections, several health care proposals were in the hopper. There were basically three concepts under consideration:

- Many congressional Democrats were pushing play-or-pay. Businesses that did not provide employee insurance would pay more in taxes, and government would use that money to provide health care to uncovered employees. Some were concerned that this strategy would lead businesses to decide to pay, not play, effectively creating a government health care system.
- Progressive Democrats were pushing for a single-payer system modeled on Canada's. Government would replace insurance companies, but would not run the health care delivery system itself. Under a variant, which Hacker (1997) referred to as "the liberal synthesis," the government would purchase universal capitated coverage from a mix of competing public and private insurance plans.
- Many congressional Republicans and President H. W. Bush supported various packages of market-oriented reforms that would regulate insurance company practices, provide tax credits or subsidies for people unable to afford insurance, offer tax incentives for business to cover employees, establish industry-wide insurance purchasing pools, reform malpractice litigation, and support expansion of managed care.

In the late 1980s, Alain Enthoven and Richard Kronick began developing their "managed competition" approach. Their first proposal included a pay-or-play system. People who could not obtain employer coverage could acquire coverage through a "public sponsor." Plans would have to offer standardized types of coverage and set premiums based on risk. Employers and the public sponsor would only pay a fixed

Case 10   (*continued*)

percentage (they initially proposed 80%) of the cost of a plan that provided a basic set of standardized benefits. If employers or individuals wanted to purchase more comprehensive coverage, it would come out of their pockets. Tax reform would ensure that this additional money was not tax exempt.

Enthoven and Kronick believed health care inflation was driven mostly by the fee-for-service system, which provided no incentive for providers to provide better health outcomes at lower costs. They were also concerned about the effects of risk selection on health insurance affordability. They believed their plan would encourage people to purchase basic, lower cost plans appropriate to their level of actuarial risk and priced accordingly. They also believed it would drive people toward managed care plans.

Enthoven and Paul Ellwood invited health policy experts, government officials, and reform-minded executives from health care organizations and large health insurance companies to a meeting in Jackson Hole, Wyoming, in February 1990. The group anticipated that government would play a greater role in regulating health care unless someone put forward a successful market-oriented proposal. They sought to reform the system while minimizing government regulation and using managed competition as a starting point.

The group met throughout 1990 and 1991 to refine ideas and seek consensus. Ellwood and health policy consultant Lynn Etheridge drafted four papers that collectively articulated the Jackson Hole proposal. Much of the Enthoven–Kronick framework remained. An independent health board would certify health insurance plans and establish the basic services those plans would cover. Employers would be required to provide coverage to their full-time employees. They would also pay a business tax to fund coverage for part-time employees. The public-sponsor notion evolved into something called health insurance purchasing cooperatives (HIPCs)—regional organizations that would contract with certified insurance plans to purchase coverage for the employees of businesses with fewer than 100 employees and for people not covered through work or federal entitlement programs. HIPCs would subsidize coverage up to the cost of the least expensive plan. People who chose more expensive plans (or businesses that provided employees with additional coverage) would make up the difference. Only the cost of the least expensive plan would be tax deductible.

Initially, the Jackson Hole Group considered the proposal to be an academic exercise, but then Michael Weinstein at the *New York Times* picked up on the plan. The paper ran dozens of articles that mentioned "managed competition" and endorsed the Jackson Hole Group's framework on its editorial page. Thus, when Wofford won his election in November, the idea had public legitimacy and was known to members of Congress and congressional staffers as a policy to champion. In particular, the idea attracted considerable interest from the conservative wing of the Democratic Party, although the Conservative Democratic Forum rejected the idea of an employer mandate.

During the 1992 presidential primary campaigns, many health care reform proposals emerged, including one by Paul Tsongas that emphasized managed competition. Clinton, a centrist with ties to the conservative wing of his party, promoted a play-or-pay strategy, but after winning the nomination began moving toward a plan that combined managed competition with regulatory reforms designed to drive down costs. He formally unveiled this plan at a September 24 speech delivered at the headquarters of Merck & Co., a major pharmaceutical company.

DEVELOPING THE CLINTON PROPOSAL

Clinton took office in January 1993, and for about the first 8 months his administration focused primarily on developing a budget that might grow the economy and reduce the deficit; however, he did try to deliver early on his promise to reform health care. Within days of his taking office, Ira Magaziner, an old family friend and business consultant, completed a work plan for an interagency health care task force that would oversee working groups charged with conducting analyses related to topics such as financing, economic impacts, controlling costs, and delivering preventive care. Acting on Magaziner's framework, Clinton established the President's Task Force on Health Care Reform, made up mostly of cabinet members. Magaziner would coordinate the effort, but the chair would be the First Lady, Hillary Rodham Clinton.

A ballooning number of working groups set about defining their respective pieces of the elephant. Participants, mostly executive agency employees, numbered more than 500. As they identified preferred policy options, they then took them to the task force leaders for a protracted,

Case 10 (*continued*)

sometimes days-long vetting process called "tollgates." The task force also held hearings to solicit input from stakeholder groups.

The task force's initial meetings were not open to the public or the press—a fact that prompted a *Washington Post* story saying that the private meetings violated the Federal Advisory Committee Act. The act is meant to prohibit committee members who are not part of the government from having undue and undisclosed influence over government policy making. It technically applied because Hillary Rodham Clinton did not draw a paycheck and was not a "government employee." On March 10, a judge ordered that all task force meetings be public. Critics of health care reform exploited the brouhaha. "It was a deft political move," Hillary Clinton wrote in her autobiography, "designed to disrupt our work on health care and to foster an impression with the public and the news media that we were conducting 'secret' meetings" (2003, p. 154).

In May, the task force handed a thick set of recommendations to the White House and disbanded. Work continued as small White House teams began the next phase, which included tasks such as converting the task force output into legislative language, working up budget projections, and developing political and communication strategies. Most of this work was done behind the scenes while the president focused his efforts, and the public's attention, on the budget. Very few decisions were put on paper, and high-level meetings were avoided from the end of May through August.

It wasn't until September 7 that copies of a "Working Group Draft" went to key members of Congress and from there leaked to the public. Full bill language was not available until October—after Clinton's September 22 televised address to Congress.

THE HEALTH SECURITY PROPOSAL

Clinton's Health Security proposal owed a lot to the Jackson Hole Group, but also borrowed from existing proposals on both sides of the aisle. It relied on the employer-based system by mandating employer coverage. To help small businesses and those with low-wage employees, the government would offer subsidies. It would also provide payments to help the poor cover the costs of premiums and out-of-pocket expenses. The self-employed would be able to deduct their premium costs fully. Annual premium increases would be capped, but as a cost-control measure, this was a backup to the core of the Clintons' plan—the creation of regional "health alliances," much like the Jackson Hole Group's HIPCs. Under the oversight of a national health board, they would pool individual and business premiums and collectively bargain with insurance companies.

The proposal had to be revenue neutral, and thus there had to be a way to offset the estimated $331 billion cost. Some of that money, according to the administration, could come from a cigarette tax and a 1% tax on corporations with more than 5,000 employees that did not participate in the regional alliances. Because health care costs would presumably go down, tax revenues would increase. Nearly $200 billion could be trimmed from Medicare and Medicaid budgets because of cost savings and decreasing caseload. Critics scoffed at the savings potential, pointing out that cutting Medicare and Medicaid would be politically difficult and arguing that increased coverage would lead to greater utilization of health care services, driving costs up, not down.

THE BEGINNING OF THE END

On October 27, the Clintons handed off their brainchild to the U.S. Congress. It suddenly had to compete for attention with more than 20 cousins. These included a single-payer bill supported by more than 200 liberal House Democrats, another version of managed competition supported by centrist Democrats that stopped short of an employer mandate and would not have limited premium increases, a Republican proposal that would have required individuals to purchase insurance and used resulting Medicaid savings to help low-income individuals and families pay their premiums, and another Republican proposal to introduce insurance industry reforms that would help chronically ill people obtain and retain health insurance and allow for the creation of health savings accounts (called medisave accounts).

Not only were there competing proposals, but there were competing fiefs. Health care as an issue did not belong exclusively to any one committee in either house. Arguably, five different committees had jurisdiction. Each committee and its chair had its own personality and its own perspective on the issue. The Clintons' plan quickly bogged

Case 10   (*continued*)

down in jurisdictional disputes. Congress was becoming increasingly polarized and partisan, making it difficult to move any kind of major initiative. Breaking this gridlock would have required a coordinated, unified approach from the party leadership, but many Democrats were still drawn to the simplicity of a single payer. Many Republicans, meanwhile, were drawn to a strategy advanced most strongly by the Project for a Republican Future—refuse any temptation to compromise and defeat any Clinton proposal outright, at any cost. Democrats did not seem to have a clear strategy for moving the bill through the various committees without Republican cooperation.

As the Health Security proposal took a tedious, contentious, and messy path through committee hearings and markups, external stakeholder support, which had seemed so solid at the start, began to crumble. The plan's greatest nemeses proved to be the Health Insurance Association of America (HIAA) and the National Federation of Independent Business (NFIB), which vehemently opposed any employer mandate. In addition to lobbying policy makers, NFIB engaged in what Michael Weisskopf, a *Washington Post* reporter, labeled "cross lobbying"—targeting other stakeholder groups to change their positions. One of the first targets of cross lobbying was the AMA. The AMA had expressed several reservations about the Clinton plan, but had reversed its decades-long opposition to any employer mandate and was on record as supporting health system reform. At the urging of NFIB, the AMA House of Delegates voted December 7, 1993, to rescind its support for an employer mandate.

Big business also broke ranks. Medical inflation seemed to be slowing in late 1993, and President Clinton had failed to deliver on his promise to reduce domestic spending. In February 1994, the Business Roundtable endorsed a competing plan, and the National Association of Manufacturers and the U.S. Chamber of Commerce followed quickly by repudiating the Clinton proposal.

That same month, the Congressional Budget Office announced that it could not support many of the budget assumptions the Clinton working groups had used to argue that the plan would help reduce the deficit. It would not even agree the plan was budget neutral. Instead, it argued the plan would add $74 billion to the deficit.

The White House, meanwhile, was losing ground in the court of public opinion. Polling immediately after the proposal went public was strongly favorable. A Harris Poll conducted in March 1993 found strong support for short-term price controls (76%), caps on premium increases (78%), an employer mandate (82%), and regional purchasing cooperatives (86%), but early polling also disclosed that people did not understand these concepts. Early response to the Clinton proposal released later that year was also favorable according to the polls, but some of the same surveys demonstrated that the public did not really understand what was being proposed in the highly complex 1,342-page draft legislation. The public also had some major concerns.

An ABC News/*Washington Post* poll conducted in early October 1993 found that 51% supported the Clinton plan and 59% thought that it was better than the current system; however, 57% opposed new taxes to pay for it. More people thought health care would get worse under the plan (34%) than thought health care would improve (19%). Many were worried about having less choice in providers (72%), increasing costs (70%), a loss of access to expensive services (69%), and a host of other issues.

These concerns gave the plan's opponents very effective points of leverage. In particular, HIAA focused in on them with its Harry and Louise campaign, which featured a worried couple discussing concerns about the plan. These campaigns made good use of polling information. The first advertisement focused on worries that health insurance plans would be less comprehensive and there would be fewer types of plans from which to choose. The couple concluded its conversation with the exchange, "They choose. We lose."

Congress struggled with the proposal through the first half of 1994, trying different solutions and searching for some kind of compromise that had a chance of success on the floor; however, none of the proposals appeared to have enough support to survive a filibuster. At one point, Republican Senator Phil Gramm announced that Congress needed to "stop carrying around this corpse, changing its clothes, and putting more powder on its face."

When Congress returned from summer recess, it was prepared to consider less-ambitious reforms. By this time, 57% of the public favored more incremental steps according to a *New York Times* poll published September 13, although 50% said the president should veto anything that did not cover everyone. Even modest reform bills were considered too risky by this point because they could serve as stealth vehicles for comprehensive reforms, expanding at the last minute into some kind of universal coverage legislation. In late September, congressional leaders delivered a demand to President Clinton—if the president expected action on the General Tariffs and Trade Treaty, there could be no more discussion of health care legislation. On September 26, a year after Clinton said he would fix a broken system, Senate Majority Leader George Mitchell took health care reform off life support. The "corpse" was now officially dead.

Discussion Questions

1. Theda Skocpol (1996) described two approaches that critics argue Bill Clinton should have used to develop his proposal: (1) ask a small group to develop broad outlines for reform and then ask Congress to work out the details and (2) establish a prestigious blue-ribbon commission that might have achieved buy-in from business groups, congressional leaders and other policy makers, and stakeholders. What might be some of the pros and cons of the three different approaches? (The third was the Clinton approach.)

2. What would a map of Bill Clinton's authorizing environment for health care reform look like?

3. Discuss how the three streams of policy making identified by John Kingdon—policies, politics, and problems—opened a window of opportunity for health care reform in 1993 and what had changed in those streams by the time that window had closed in 1994.

4. What would a force field analysis of the Health Security plan look like?

5. Where would the Health Security proposal fall on Oliver's framework for analysis of policy design and political feasibility? What were some of the concentrated costs and benefits and to whom did they accrue? Now answer the same question of diffuse costs and benefits.

6. Who would you have surveyed if you were using the Delphi technique to analyze the political feasibility of the Clinton proposal at the time?

Chapter 11

The Policy Analysis Process: Evaluation of Economic Viability

Policy analysis involves the allocation of scarce resources. This chapter focuses on economic and financial aspects of the allocation process. Both affect the economic viability of a proposed policy alternative, which likely turns on the following questions:

- How much will it cost?
- What value will we be getting for the money?
- How does that value compare with other alternatives under consideration?
- If it is something we want to do, how will we pay for it?

To address these questions, the analysis team needs to undertake the tasks outlined in **Figure 11-1**. The team also needs to consider the points of view or interests of whoever commissioned the study. However, a fine line exists between pleasing the "customer" and maintaining a group's professional integrity. One way to address this is by "changing hats." The analysts can say, "When we put on Hat A, we get X, but when we put on Hat B, we get Y." All of us wear many hats in health care, including patient, payer, parent, spouse, professional, and citizen.

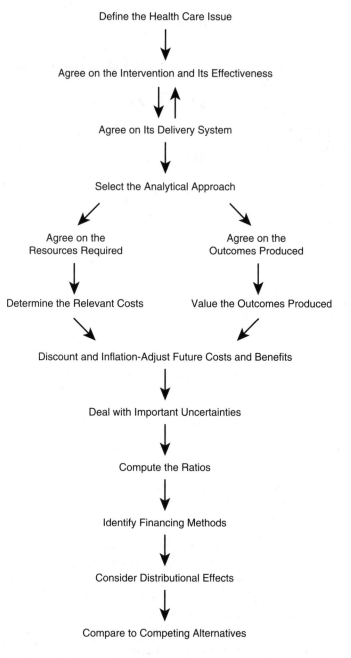

Figure 11-1 Steps in the cost-benefit analysis (CBA)/cost-effective analysis (CEA) process.

The team can then proceed to subsequent steps. The first is to define the health issue that is to be addressed, including population, diagnosis, incidence, and impact, and then study the relevant intervention technologies. Then the group must agree on the effectiveness of the current and proposed interventions and, if necessary, conduct research to establish an acceptable range of effectiveness values for the analysis.

DEFINING THE HEALTH CARE PROCESS INVOLVED

The team should conduct a detailed process analysis to ensure agreement on how the intervention is delivered, especially if there is little field experience with it. It is often well worth the effort to step back and visualize how a new or modified process will work and how its detailed implementation will go forward. Otherwise, the team may be making a stab in the dark about the resources required.

The feedback arrow in Figure 11-1 indicates that sometimes the process analysis produces a revised estimate of the expected effectiveness as the team learns details about possible barriers to adoption and implementation. Many more feedback loops could be added because at any point in time the team can uncover a need to revise its earlier estimates.

AGREEING ON ITS EFFECTIVENESS

Clear evidence on the effectiveness of a proposed policy is a rarity. Much evidence is contestable even as to its science. Clinical trials may be limited, or in a few cases may not even be feasible. The populations involved in clinical trials and demonstrations may have been small or somewhat different from the one that will be affected by the policy. Often professional groups, having differing interests, cite studies that support their viewpoint and ignore those that do not. For example, in an analysis of folic acid supplementation, those who favored it cited its effects on neural tube defects (NTDs), whereas those opposed cited its ability to mask other metabolic deficiencies.

Where the evidence is unclear or disputed, one way to proceed is through sensitivity analysis. For example, after an analysis is done using the efficacy estimate that the analysis team thinks most valid, the calculations are repeated with alternative efficacy values to determine the range of values over which the conclusion holds. Many times the conclusion is not affected despite the heat generated by the differing estimates, but where the solution is sensitive to the choice of high- or low-end parameter values, it is necessary to make the decision makers aware of the applicable range. Perhaps they will authorize a study to narrow that range further. Sensitivity analysis is relevant to other variables besides efficacy, including costs, the population affected, and inflation rates.

The relevant change in effectiveness associated with an intervention is the *marginal change*. For example, in 2005, the Washington State Legislature directed the Washington State Institute for Public Policy to report on the benefits and costs of "evidence-based" approaches to the treatment of alcoholism, drug addiction, and mental illness. The institute performed a meta-analysis based on a review of 206 studies in the literature that met a specific set of criteria for quality of experimental design and measurement, such as use of a control group. This was an unusually complex analysis, because the legislature specifically mandated the study of the effects of treating individuals with substance abuse disorders and/or mental illness disorders in terms of their fiscal impact and "the long-run effects on statewide education, crime, child abuse and neglect, substance abuse, and economic outcomes." There were already systems in place for dealing with these disorders, thus the researchers calculated the benefits based on marginal changes in costs and outcomes from expanding the existing services to provide evidence-based and consensus-based services to those not yet served. Few mental illnesses are currently cured, and many who stop abusing drugs and alcohol relapse over time. The study team had to estimate the reduced incidence or severity from implementing best practices. It estimated the number of people in the state with each disorder and subtracted out the number already receiving services. Then they assumed that about 50% of the untreated populations would accept services if they were made available. The analysts did not try to estimate the impact of having existing services move from their current modes of operation to the evidence-based approaches. Because the available studies were all short-term studies, the institute's staff estimated a "decay rate" for each disorder to represent the loss of participants and program impact over time, and it also included a factor in the modeling for those individuals who would recover on their own without treatment.

The institute's meta-analysis of the suitable studies concluded that the expansion of services would achieve a 15–22% reduction in incidence or severity of these disorders, resulting in a savings of $3.77 for each additional $1 invested. Taxpayers would see direct savings of $2.05 per additional $1 invested, or $416 million per year in net payer benefits, if fully implemented (Aos, Mayfield, & Yen, 2006).

AGREEING IN DETAIL ON THE DELIVERY SYSTEM INVOLVED

Analysis team members may have differing assumptions about how the intervention is to be delivered in the field. Reaching a common description of that process is an important early task. Discussing the process and drawing up a detailed process map are ways to get at that reality. Doing so leads directly to a description of the resources required. Team members may choose to revise their estimated effectiveness after the process is better defined and they better understand the problems of implementing the process in the field.

SELECTING THE ANALYTICAL APPROACH

A number of types of economic analysis can be performed. One key question will be, "What impact will a proposal have on the supply and demand for services?" Payment, access, and quality issues affect the perceived price and demand for services as well as their costs. Given an analysis of changing demand and supply, the team must decide how to analyze the most promising approaches. Rychlik (2002) suggested a hierarchy of analytical approaches for comparison and decision making:

- Establish the cost (burden) of the illness, usually including quality-of-life impacts of the problem.
- If the assessment shows little difference in impact from the relevant interventions or between the intervention and the status quo ante, conduct a cost-minimization study.
- If the comparison is among similar types of outcomes but there are significant differences in benefits and costs, conduct a cost-effectiveness study.
- If there are significant differences among the programs being considered, such that a common metric is necessary for benefits and costs, do a cost–benefit study.
- If quality of life after survival is an important parameter, then consider a cost-utility study, in which differing quality measures are compared using market research techniques such as conjoint analysis.

Sometimes public agencies focus on whether a proposed outlay is cost neutral or whether it is cost effective. To be cost neutral, the proposal must not increase the overall costs to the agency. To be cost-effective, the proposal must be the least costly method for reaching a predetermined level of total benefits to the public. In the medical literature, however, the term *cost-effectiveness analysis (CEA)* has acquired its own specialized meaning as an analysis in which the benefits are measured in nonmonetary units, such as lives saved or quality-adjusted life-years (QALYs). Such analyses, however, do not allow for comparisons of proposals that express outcomes in different units.

At higher policy levels, health care investments must be compared with other public investments, including those outside the health sector. When a common metric must be used to value both costs and benefits of the full set of proposals being analyzed, it almost always turns out to be dollars. This is known as cost–benefit analysis (CBA). Private-sector organizations use the same techniques but often with a different terminology, employing terms such as *return on investment (ROI)* and *internal rate of return (IRR)* when they evaluate and compare investment opportunities.

Hacker (1997) suggested that concerns about health care as an economic marketplace emerged forcefully in the 1970s following the introduction of Medicare and Medicaid and the resulting cost inflation. With the nation's access problems significantly addressed, government and industry turned toward issues of efficiency and effectiveness. This concern for efficiency and effectiveness in the federal government extended well beyond the health sector. The Bureau of Management and Budget issued Circular A-94, currently titled *Guidelines and Discount Rates for Benefit-Cost Analysis of Federal Programs*, in 1972 (OMB, 1972). It was and still is intended for use across most federal government agencies and programs.

Since then there has been an explosion of studies and methodologies coming out of the subfield of pharmacoeconomics. These have been developed to meet the expectations of managed care organizations and government regulators for expanded justification for authorizing use of yet another new drug or device. Safety alone is less and less their only concern.

BASIC TOOLS

The basic tools of economic analysis, including supply and demand analysis and benefit and cost analysis, are frequently bypassed by health care professionals because of measurement difficulties. These measurement problems pertain primarily to demand and benefit estimation, but also to costs.

Supply and Demand Concepts

Much of the health policy literature is concerned with aligning incentives properly through payment mechanisms, such as copayments, withholds, discounts, and reimbursement rates. All of these really refer to changes in perceived prices and the effects these perceptions will have on the supply and demand for services. What really complicates health care is that some demand is generated by the consumer and some by the consumer's agents, the health professionals.

The policy analysis team will have to estimate the impact of those perceived price changes on the activity levels that they can expect to see in the service system. These estimates are not easy, even where a program is budget constrained. Take, for example, the situation in which a program is budget constrained and a budget increase is proposed. **Figure 11-2** illustrates a simple demand analysis relating to a budget constraint:

Given: Initial Budget = $B_0 = C_0 \times Q_0$
Where initial cost = C_0, clients served = Q_0
Increased Budget = B_1, where $Q_1 > Q_0$ and $B_1 > B_0$

In panel A, the new larger budget is fully consumed, but no cost change is assumed ($B_1 = C_0 \times Q_1$, where Demand = D_0 still is > Q_1).

In panel B, the budget is increased to B_2, but this enhanced availability of services exceeds the demand (D_2) at the current perceived cost ($Q_1 > D_1 > Q_0$), and the budget is underexpended ($C_0 \times D_2 < B_2$).

In panel C, the program management proposes responding by making the services more accessible (available more conveniently at more sites). This reduces the perceived cost of the service to the clients and the demand increases ($D_3 > D_2$), but at an added cost, which increases the average cost ($C_2 > C_0$). Given this situation, the program management and the policy analysts must make new estimates (C_2, D_3) and see whether the demand will be greater than, less than, or approximately equal to the new budgeted level of activity, which is B_3 divided by C_2. This will again determine the programmatic resources required.

Yes, this is complicated, but it is the way life goes.

If the prices charged are modified by a proposal, then the analyst must investigate supply and demand relationships further, including the following:

- The rate of change in demand with a given change in price (price elasticity)
- The rate of change in supply with a given change in price

Where data are available, these relationships can be estimated through regression analysis.

Panel A – Demand Greater than Budgeted

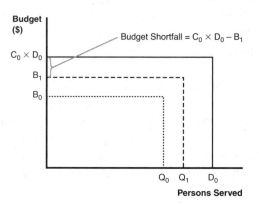

Panel B – Demand Less Than New Budgeted Quantity

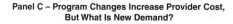
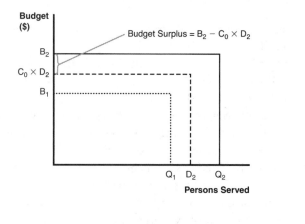

Panel C – Program Changes Increase Provider Cost, But What Is New Demand?

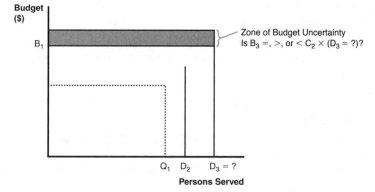

Figure 11-2 Supply and demand over time in a constrained budget setting.

Utilities and Preferences

Health policy analysts use the terms *utility* and *preference* somewhat inter-changeably. The latter sounds admittedly subjective; however, public policy has no objective tool for measuring utility or for comparing utility across individuals. This creates an enormous challenge. Without the capacity to measure welfare, how do we maximize it? (Wheelan, 2011).

We also know that in health care people's utilities differ based on their health status. One has to be very careful to articulate whether the utilities asserted come from the general population or from the population affected by the relevant diagnosis. It is also important to know what stage of the disease progression they are in, if they have the disease.

A number of methods are used to try to get at preferences and utilities, including:

- Direct measures:
    - Standard gamble: What probability of success would be necessary to get you to choose a proposed outcome over the status quo or some other alternative(s)?
    - Time trade-off: How many months of life would you be willing to give up to achieve the more desirable outcome?
    - Rating scale (visual analogue scale): Pick a spot on a line from 0 (worst possible outcome) to 1 (best possible outcome) that represents each alternative being considered.
- Indirect measures:
    - Generic utility instruments: Use value weightings set by the general public with off-the-shelf questionnaires. For example, in the U.K., NICE uses the EQ-5D instrument; in the United States, the FDA seems to favor the SF-6D. The Health Utilities Index (HUI), the Quality of Well-Being (QWB) scale, and the 15 dimension (15D) instrument also are used.
    - Disease-specific instruments: The attributes and weights are tailored to the diagnosis and observed attributes.
    - Mapping the attributes from a validated disease-specific instrument onto a generic instrument.

Each approach has its strengths and weaknesses. For example, the standard gamble approach is sensitive to a person's risk tolerance. In addition, each presents its own problems in terms of comprehension and representation (Tolley, 2009).

Valuing Costs, Benefits, and Outcomes

Analysts crossing over from other sectors will find some very specific problems in applying their usual evaluation methods in health care. Effective cost and benefit analysis in health care often requires understanding the nomenclature and diagnostic coding systems used in this sector. Furthermore, market failure in this industry often makes it necessary to measure separately the consumer satisfaction and benefit/cost impacts of specific technological alternatives. Analysts can also expect to encounter a lack of cooperation because of fear of loss of autonomy, accounting systems biased toward revenue rather than cost finding, high levels of inherent variability, compartmentalization of information systems, and poorly aligned reward systems.

The role of benefit–cost analysis in health care was investigated thoroughly in the 1960s and 1970s (Baker, Sheldon, & McLaughlin, 1970; Bunker, Barnes, & Mosteller, 1979; Office of Technology Assessment, 1980; Weinstein & Stason, 1977). During that period, the problems of benefit measurement seemed so insurmountable that most health care professionals doing analysis preferred to rely on CEA. Weinstein and Stason (1977) described the difference as follows:

> The key distinction is that a benefit–cost analysis must value all outcomes in economic (e.g., dollar) terms, including lives or years of life and morbidity, whereas a cost-effectiveness analysis serves to place priorities on alternative expenditures without requiring that the dollar value of life and health be presented. (p. 717)

The basic problem is not one of using dollars, however, but one of expressing all of the relevant factors in any single metric. The alternative approach is to express the outcomes as a vector, but because one alternative vector seldom dominates the other, one must still deal with trade-offs among variables. The vector representation gets one into all the complexities of multidimensional scaling.

Further problems arise from the following:

- Determining the relevant costs, especially supply and demand estimation and resulting price levels.
- Incorporating values of nonmedical outcomes, including the way benefits and costs are distributed.

Pauly (1995) suggested that CBA and CEA are used because the better normative measure, willingness to pay, is hard to assess in the real world. He defined a personal benefit as an informed individual's willingness to pay for a program, whereas a programmatic benefit is the sum of the willingness to pay of all informed persons affected by the program, including those making altruistic contributions but not directly affected by the service process. In a few situations, willingness to pay can be imputed from what individuals are paying for insurance against an event or to mitigate the risk of an event, such as installing seat belts or highway crash barriers. As Pauly (1995) noted, "Such concepts as addition to measured gross national product associated with a health program, the additional wages to beneficiaries and providers, or addition from investment now and in the future have validity only to the extent that they proxy willingness to pay" (p. 103).

WHOSE WILLINGNESS TO PAY?

A study to determine the need for a third London airport, as well as its location, found that a preferred location would displace a 12th-century Norman church that was still in use. One group contended that the willingness-to-pay valuation of the church should be based on the value the current parishioners were insuring the building for against fire. A second group, however, argued that the Normans had incurred an opportunity cost for the last 8 centuries for the £100 that they invested to build it. They had foregone the opportunity to loan the money to the local usurers at a reasonable rate of interest; therefore, the church should be valued at the willingness to pay of the original parishioners, which would lead to a valuation of £100 plus compound interest for more than 800 years. Using this calculation, it would be worth more than the construction cost of the entire new airport.

A proxy is something that stands in for the real thing. In one analysis, for example, the costs of the early loss of a mother because of breast cancer were estimated by the value of replacement family care services plus a proxy for the emotional losses. The proxy chosen was the estimated cost of the amount of psychotherapy used by those who lost a mother early in life (Bunker et al., 1979).

Indicators also are used to substitute for direct measures. "Good indicators are easily measurable and highly correlated with the underlying variable of interest, which is usually impossible to measure" (Wheelan, 2011,

p. 145). We cannot agree whether a population is healthy or not, but we often use measures to indicate success or failure, such as visits to the emergency room or hospitalizations.

Pauly (1995) opposed two other approaches often cited in the literature: (1) the human capital approach, which emphasizes the economic cost to society, such as a worker's daily wage multiplied by the number of work days lost, or some other measure of lost productivity (assuming full employment), or (2) the friction cost approach, which measures the loss in productivity until the system resumes full productivity with a trained and experienced new worker or with the ill worker restored to full capacity.

Benefit-Cost Concepts

Where there are multiple choices, the rational person will select one or more alternatives that maximize his or her satisfaction, or what an economist would call the person's utility; however, our utilities are specific, if not unique, to each of us. Although individual utilities are cumbersome to capture, aggregating the utilities of a population presents far greater problems. Thus, decisions that involve more than one person usually require a common measure. Most analyses are based on aggregating all of the costs and benefits to individuals regardless of whether their utilities are typical and to whom or from whom they accrue. That is why so many studies end up choosing dollars; however, not all agree on that. Whatever the metric chosen, one ends up with a ratio of benefits to costs, and the higher that ratio the better an alternative. In health care, however, we must also consider to whom these benefits and costs accrue.

Circular No. A-94 defines *cost-effectiveness* as "a systematic quantitative method for comparing costs of alternative means of achieving the same stream of benefits or a given objective." In other words, the economist would say no to the request to "get me the most for the least money," because it is a mathematical impossibility. The two feasible formulations are:

- Get me the most benefit for a given sum of money (i.e., maximize my benefit–cost ratio).
- Get me a given benefit package at the lowest cost (i.e., minimize my effectiveness–cost ratio).

Analysts often retreat to their previously prepared position of trying to produce a set of benefits defined by the politicians at the least possible cost and then labeling the results cost-effectiveness, even though it is really cost-minimization. That leaves the hardest part, the valuation of benefits, up to the political process. At higher levels of government where the trade-offs are between noncomparable benefits such as health care, highways, police protection, and recreational services, the only comparable means of comparison usually turns out to be money. The analyst has to be clear which is called for and be consistent in reporting the results. Pauly (1995) suggested that where money is used to measure benefits and (1) there is a fixed budget and (2) there is little variation in the preferences for outcomes, then cost-effectiveness analysis should be used, but where there is a variable budget and varying utilities of outcomes, cost-effectiveness is "much less suitable, in theory than cost–benefit analysis" (p. 111).

At this point, the analysis splits into two streams. One stream estimates the costs, whereas the other values the outcome. This chapter looks next at the cost side, which is the easier path to consider.

AGREEING ON THE RESOURCES REQUIRED

All too often the analysis team begins by talking about monetary costs. This is the wrong place to start in a cost analysis. When trying to compute the costs of a wedding reception, few people would start with a dollar figure per guest; instead, most would consider estimates of the number of guests, the menu for food and drink, the portions offered, the number of helpings per person, and the staffing needed. After these are defined, it is a simple matter to determine the costs by multiplying these resources by their market prices and totaling them up. That gives us an estimate of the total variable cost of the reception. Then there are the fixed costs of the reception, such as the chef and hiring the hall. However, the kitchen staff only has a certain capacity, and if the guest list exceeds a certain number, the staff would have to be augmented; therefore, many fixed costs apply only over a specific volume range. These are sometimes called step-variable costs or semi-fixed costs.

After we have the cost of our ideal menu and level of hospitality, it is time to figure out whether it falls within the acceptable budget range. Chances are it does not, and we would have to agree to spend more on the wedding than we had planned, cut some costs out of the reception, or cut down on some other aspect of the reception.

DETERMINING RELEVANT COSTS

Relevant costs are those affected by the decision being considered. There are two methods of estimating costs: aggregate costs and marginal costs. One arrives at aggregated costs by taking the total costs of a division, department, or other organizational unit and then dividing it by the number of service units or products produced. This figure is usually relatively easy to produce from existing departmental cost data, but using this method is not recommended. It does not take into account how processes, and hence costs, change with volume, nor does it include relevant costs that occur outside of the given organizational unit. Relevant costing ignores those costs that are not affected by a decision, including those that are real but fixed. For example, the comparison of two treatments for pneumonia would not include the costs of diagnostic tests unless different test protocols were associated with the new treatment regimen.

Relevant costs for the two treatments are likely to include the following:

- Changes in costs of medicines, consumable supplies, and tests caused by the introduction of the alternative method
- Changed labor costs, including physicians, nurses, and pharmacists, and ancillary services
- Costs altered by the changes in length of stay or location of treatment
- Changes in costs incurred by the patient and the patient's family, including access costs and lost income, if any
- Changes in overhead costs associated with the new alternative including amortization of new specialized equipment and altered space requirements

Hospital costs represent an especially difficult problem because so many costs are lumped into the overhead cost categories and then allocated to the various operating departments.

A process-based cost study is usually a must in the hospital setting. The usual hospital cost reports are so loaded with fixed costs that it is necessary to map out the process, directly identify the resource inputs required, and then price them.

Marginal/Incremental Cost Concepts

Where demand is changing, the appropriate cost is not the average cost of the service, but the cost of adding the next additional service unit (the marginal or incremental unit) or subtracting it. Even though pricing, and hence revenue, may be related to the average cost of a unit of service, the cost of changing output is not. If I am the dean of a medical school and am asked to add 10 more students, I may find that my costs of the preclinical lectures are nil, because there are extra seats in the lecture hall. However, during the clinical years I may find that I have to divert clinical faculty from clinic hours to rounding with students at considerable opportunity cost of revenue. I will also have to add desks in the anatomy lab and secure more cadavers. These incremental costs may be very different from what one gets by dividing total existing costs by the current number of students.

Handling Inherent Process Uncertainty

Earlier chapters dealt with the technological and political uncertainties of producing a desired outcome. The analysis team must decide how to deal with those uncertainties in its economic and financial analysis. Sometimes the uncertainty is handled with multiple analyses up front, a sort of branching in the analysis; however, the usual way of handling uncertainties is through sensitivity analysis in which the inputs of uncertain parameters are allowed to take on a realistic range of values to define the range over which the analysis is sensitive to that parameter.

For example, in the Washington State study of evidence-based treatment of substance abuse and mental illness disorders, the Washington State Institute for Public Policy conducted a sensitivity analysis with many different parameters using a Monte Carlo simulation technique. Researchers assigned a probability distribution to each range of values and ran the simulation model 10,000 times with the values of each variable sampled randomly from its distribution. This process indicated that there was only a 1% probability that the investment would provide a negative return to the taxpayers. This was very important to the credibility of the analysis, because so many of the measures and variables were so difficult to define and to measure (Aos et al., 2006).

Much of the value of a simulation would be to identify the interaction of various factors as a policy is implemented. For example, we have seen a number of governors prepared to ensure access to health care for virtually all their state's population; however, very little has been said about what will happen to health care demand and supply and the resulting prices. Given the rapid rise in prices following the starts of Medicare and Medicaid in 1965, this has to be a matter for concern given the access-expanding provisions of the Affordable Care Act (ACA).

Figure 11-3 illustrates one model that might be used to simulate the effects of increased access. As demand increases, so do the direct costs of services and the capital costs of providing the necessary delivery infrastructure, especially supplying sufficient primary care providers (PCPs), nurses, and community-based services; however, these changes will not

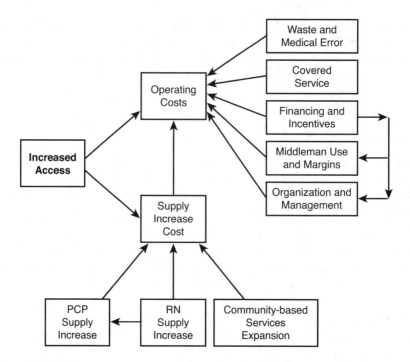

Figure 11-3 What happens to costs, if we resolve the general access problem.

take place in a vacuum. Policy variables can be manipulated to affect those costs, including the new covered service definitions, the management and organization of the new efforts, the amount of waste and medical error experienced, the financing and incentives of the program, and whether middlemen are used and what their margins will be. This again would seem to call for a simulation model to assess the overall impact of the planned interventions. The model is not revenue or budget constrained, but that component also could be added. This model might start as a spreadsheet model, but be converted to a Monte Carlo simulation if one wanted to see how sensitive the model would be to specific uncertain variables.

What additional variables and/or feedback loops would you like to add? If there are many loops, a feedback type of model might be used. Certainly, the organization and management of services and the financing and incentive available would affect the capacity changes that might be needed. For example, a Markov model of colon cancer disease states would have some Stage 3 patients fed back into the healthy but at-risk pool after surgery, whereas others would not respond to treatment and would stay at Stage 3 or progress to Stage 4.

VALUING THE OUTCOMES PRODUCED

A hard part of health care policy analysis is valuing the benefits. We have already addressed the willingness-to-pay argument versus the use of utility metrics such as QALYs saved or deaths avoided. Most utility comparisons are based on psychometric instruments that can be used to compare and rank order alternative outcomes. QALY is one example of a utility measure. It usually involves multiplying an incremental survival period by a subjective quality-of-life measure, indexed to a 0 to 1 scale, on which 0 is complete health and 1 is death. The attributes recognized in the comparisons include physical function limitations, social function limitations, emotional well-being, pain levels, and limitations on cognitive ability. Many intermediate states have been identified, from wearing glasses to acute pain to physical incapacitation. Any one individual may have a quirky utility curve, such as "I would rather be dead than a vegetable," but the scale is based on the aggregate values of a representative population and not the individual. That is why people are urged to think about their own utilities and express them in a living will. There are many other scales for specific diseases and disease states, because the QALY may not be sensitive enough over the range experienced by that specialized population or may not include a key variable. If one does try to develop a condition-specific measure, it could be useful to check out how well it maps on one of the generic psychometric quality-of-life measures and compare both against available objective measures of illness progression (Brazier et al., 2012). For example, in the case of rheumatoid arthritis, the most frequently used generic subjective utility measures seem to diverge from objective disease state measures as severity increases (Salaffi et al., 2011).

The estimated monetary value of a QALY varies considerably among analyses. A figure of $50,000 per QALY is often cited in the United States. However, Braithwaite and colleagues (2008) noted that that amount had been used for a number of years and had not been adjusted for inflation. They took a willingness-to-pay approach based on U.S. investments in health insurance versus changes in the mortality rates between the nonelderly adult insured and uninsured between 1950 and 2003 and determined a range of $109,000 and $297,000 per QALY. They ultimately argued that the true value was closer to the World Health Organization (WHO) estimate of $109,000. NICE (2013b) in the U.K. noted that a range of £20,000 to £30,000 pounds was still its cutoff for drug evaluations.

It is difficult to reconcile cost-utilities with the ranges of cost per life saved used by U.S. regulatory agencies. In 2004, the Office of Management and Budget suggested a possible range of $1 million to $10 million, but more recently has suggested an upper limit of $5 million (Applebaum, 2011). Lives-saved reconciliation is difficult to achieve due to lack of a quality adjustment. For example, many Americans might prefer dying in a car accident to a long bout with terminal cancer.

Determining the Present Value of Costs and Outcomes

If we asked you for $10 and paid it back tomorrow, you probably would be okay with that. If we requested $10 and said that we will return it to you in 5 years, you probably would decline the honor. The value of money has a time dimension with two components: (1) whether it will have as much utility in the future or whether inflation will reduce its purchasing power and (2) the lost opportunity to create utility with it in the interim. Analysts adjust for the latter by applying a discount rate. The discount rate may represent interest income forgone or what one would have to pay to borrow the money at interest to operate until the payoff takes place. Economists argue not over whether the time value of money should be recognized, but over the appropriate rates to use; however, there are legitimate concerns about how inflation adjusting and discounting tends to devalue programs such as preventive care that pay off a ways into the future.

Discounting

The time value of money concept also applies to discounting, except that the values of future benefits and costs are reduced to a net present value (NPV). Each stream of both costs and benefits needs to be brought back to a current value using the formula:

$$NPV\,(V_t, N, r) = V_0 + \frac{V_1}{(1+r)} + \frac{V_2}{(1+r)^2} + \frac{V_3}{(1+r)^3} + \ldots + \frac{V_N}{(1+r)^N}$$

where V_t = the value of the cost or benefit in time period t, N = the number of periods in the series, and r = the discount rate to be used.

Analysts can calculate these values directly using a spreadsheet model or function or they can use the discount factors from a NPV table similar to the one in **Table 11-1**. For example, if the annual benefit received from a program is $10,000 and the discount rate chosen is 6%, then the NPV of benefits received over 5 years would be worth $42,124 (NPV = $10,000 × 4.2124).

Table 11-1 Present Value of a Dollar Received in Year N at Discount Rate r

N r =	0.03	0.04	0.05	0.06	0.07	0.08	0.09	0.1
1	0.97087	0.96154	0.95238	0.9434	0.93458	0.92593	0.91743	0.90909
2	0.9426	0.92456	0.90703	0.89	0.87344	0.85734	0.84168	0.82645
3	0.91514	0.889	0.86384	0.83962	0.8163	0.79383	0.77218	0.75131
4	0.88849	0.8548	0.8227	0.79209	0.7629	0.73503	0.70843	0.68301
5	0.86261	0.82193	0.78353	0.74726	0.71299	0.68058	0.64993	0.62092
6	0.83748	0.79031	0.74622	0.70496	0.66634	0.63017	0.59627	0.56447
7	0.81309	0.75992	0.71068	0.66506	0.62275	0.58349	0.54703	0.51316
8	0.78941	0.73069	0.67684	0.62741	0.58201	0.54027	0.50187	0.46651
9	0.76642	0.70259	0.64461	0.5919	0.54393	0.50025	0.46043	0.4241
10	0.74409	0.67556	0.61391	0.55839	0.50835	0.46319	0.42241	0.38554
11	0.72242	0.64958	0.58468	0.52679	0.47509	0.42888	0.38753	0.35049
12	0.70138	0.6246	0.55684	0.49697	0.44401	0.39711	0.35553	0.31863
13	0.68095	0.60057	0.53032	0.46884	0.41496	0.3677	0.32618	0.28966
14	0.66112	0.57748	0.50507	0.4423	0.38782	0.34046	0.29925	0.26333
15	0.64186	0.55526	0.48102	0.41727	0.36245	0.31524	0.27454	0.23939

Cumulative Present Value of a Dollar Received Annually for N Years Discounted at Rate r

N	0.03	0.04	0.05	0.06	0.07	0.08	0.09	0.1
1	0.97087	0.96154	0.95238	0.9434	0.93458	0.92593	0.91743	0.90909
2	1.91347	1.88609	1.85941	1.83339	1.80802	1.78326	1.75911	1.73554
3	2.82861	2.77509	2.72325	2.67301	2.62432	2.5771	2.53129	2.48685
4	3.7171	3.6299	3.54595	3.46511	3.38721	3.31213	3.23972	3.16987
5	4.57971	4.45182	4.32948	4.21236	4.1002	3.99271	3.88965	3.79079
6	5.41719	5.24214	5.07569	4.91732	4.76654	4.62288	4.48592	4.35526
7	6.23028	6.00205	5.78637	5.58238	5.38929	5.20637	5.03295	4.86842
8	7.01969	6.73274	6.46321	6.20979	5.9713	5.74664	5.53482	5.33493
9	7.78611	7.43533	7.10782	6.80169	6.51523	6.24689	5.99525	5.75902
10	8.5302	8.1109	7.72173	7.36009	7.02358	6.71008	6.41766	6.14457
11	9.25262	8.76048	8.30641	7.88687	7.49867	7.13896	6.80519	6.49506
12	9.954	9.38507	8.86325	8.38384	7.94269	7.53608	7.16073	6.81369
13	10.635	9.98565	9.39357	8.85268	8.35765	7.90378	7.4869	7.10336
14	11.2961	10.5631	9.89864	9.29498	8.74547	8.24424	7.78615	7.36669
15	11.9379	11.1184	10.3797	9.71225	9.10791	8.55948	8.06069	7.60608

An Example

If a proposed program were to cost $100,000 but yield a stream of benefits annually starting at the end of 5 years for 5 more years, we would have the following calculations to make to arrive at a NPV using a 4% discount rate:
  Investment at the beginning of Year 1 of $100,000.

	Benefits		
Year 6	$40,000	NPV = $(40,000)/([1+.04]^6)$	= $31,612.58
Year 7	$40,000	NPV = $(40,000)/([1+.04]^7)$	= $30,396.71
Year 8	$40,000	NPV = $(40,000)/([1+.04]^8)$	= $29,227.61
Year 9	$40,000	NPV = $(40,000)/([1+.04]^9)$	= $28,103.47
Year 10	$40,000	NPV = $(40,000)/([1+.04]^{10})$	= $27,022.57
Total Benefit			**$146,362.94**

The same result can also be calculated assuming a 10-year stream of benefits from which the initial 5 years of the stream has been subtracted. Using a NPV table, we would then calculate the following:

NPV = 10-year stream – 5-year stream
    = $40,000 × (8.1109 – 4.4518)
    = $146,364

Computing Ratios

Ratios are easy to compute. In the previous example, the NPV of the investment is $100,000 and the total benefits are $146,364; thus, the benefit–cost ratio is (146,364/100,000), or 1.46. This would be a comparison figure to rank order with other social or corporate investments. Each investment would then be subjected to other comparative evaluations or perhaps a minimum target IRR. IRR is the discount rate at which the benefits and the costs equal each other (i.e., the rate that brings the NPV to 0). In the previous example, the IRR is 9.155% (computed by finding the r value in the preceding example that makes the present values of investments and benefits equal). This rate can then be compared with the cost of capital and/or financing the investment. It must also be evaluated in terms of the uncertainty of the values used, the distributional impact on various actors and bystanders, the impact on other programs (especially in terms of budgets available), and financial viability.

Inflation Adjusting

A constant inflation rate produces a cumulative geometric increase in costs. Over time, analyses can be very sensitive to the inflation effect, especially in health care, where overall inflation rates are high. However, the inflation rate in health care costs reported in the popular literature is the result of a number of factors, including the following:

- Input prices for labor and purchased goods
- Increasing technological opportunities, including pharmaceuticals
- Aging of the population

The costs of a given program, however, are not necessarily subject to all of these factors, and thus one has to be careful in the selection of an appropriate rate. Because the population is defined and the technology is assumed to be fixed for comparative purposes, the appropriate inflation rate for an analysis is often the first item chosen for sensitivity analysis because it affects the input prices for labor and purchased goods. A reasonable lower bound on this rate is the consumer price index (CPI), but because health care is a labor-intensive professional service that does not usually exhibit the same productivity improvements as much of the rest of the economy, the appropriate rate is somewhat higher than the CPI. Available indices applicable to components of an analysis include producer price indices for specific segments and medical care CPI price deflators. Newhouse (2001) estimated that historically inflation in health care costs has been about 2% above the overall CPI. He also noted that the available indices may be biased on the high side, in part, because of the lack of reliable data on real transaction prices. For example, the producer price index for pharmaceutical preparation manufacturing was as follows:

1995	253.9	2001	314.5
1996	259.1	2002	326.7
1997	290.1	2003	343.3
1998	298.5	2004	360.1
1999	306.6	2005	378.7

To determine a rate of change from raw data, use this formula:

1. Decide on the number of years in the interval (try 5 and 10).
2. Divide the ending index by the initial one:

   5 years $378.7/306.6 = 1.235$
   10 years $378.7/253.9 = 1.492$

3. Set the number of years equal to N, and take the Nth root of the appropriate value above.

   5 years $(1.235)^{(1/5)} = 1.0431$, meaning a 4.3% inflation rate
   10 years $(1.492)^{(1/10)} = 1.0408$, meaning a 4.1% inflation rate

If you were looking at the prices charged by pharmaceutical manufacturers, the forecast of prices would grow at whatever rate you thought appropriate. If you chose 4.2% over a 5-year period, then the price of drugs now at $200 would be calculated in the fifth year to be $200 multiplied by 1.042^5, or $245.68. This is based on a mixture of products, some of which might be going up rapidly, whereas others become generic and go down markedly.

DEALING WITH IMPORTANT UNCERTAINTIES

There are three approaches one might use to deal with important uncertainties in the financial analysis:

- Adding a risk premium to the discount rates used for uncertain parts of the calculations. This means that different streams of costs and benefits will be adjusted at different rates because they will have different uncertainties associated with them.
- Developing a subjective probability distribution for those values and applying that distribution to the modeling process. If there is a 60% chance that a program will cost $100,000, a 30% chance that it will cost $110,000, and a 10% chance that it will cost $90,000, the expected value would be:

$$([100,000 \times 0.6] + [110,000 \times 0.3] + [90,000 \times 0.1]) = \$102,000$$

This value could be substituted for the $100,000 value to adjust for uncertainty in costs.
- Investing in further research to reduce the uncertainty. For example, one could refine the cost estimate until one was relatively certain that $100,000 was the proper mean estimate of the cost and then use that.

Evaluating Public Health Interventions

Because medical care and public health are both government functions in the U.K., the government has wrestled with whether the two delivery systems should use a common set of evaluation measures. Edwards, Charles, and Lloyd-Williams (2013) have reviewed the guidance issued on this by the U.K. government and by international agencies. These documents seem to agree that QALYs are appropriate for medical care evaluations, but may not be so for public health investments. The latter often involve changing the behaviors of individuals and populations, and these changes typically take place over considerable periods of time and affect many other aspects of personal and public life. These documents suggest that programmatic effects that are not medical be included. Some would value all costs and benefits in local currency leading to a cost–benefit analysis. Others would use multidimensional scaling to include QALYs with other effects, such as personal competency, into a single metric. Money as a common metric allows a public investment approach that can use the IRR as the prioritizing metric.

IDENTIFYING FINANCING METHODS

Where is the money for the investment coming from, even if it is offset later by benefits? Those benefits may or may not generate adequate cash flow into the organization. For example, money spent on smoking cessation programs by a state government would ultimately reduce the costs of its Medicaid program, but much of the benefit accrues to the federal government, to insurers, and to individual citizens; thus, there must be a budgetary source of funding specifically for the advertising campaign. For this reason, one is unlikely to spend most of the available budget on one program with a highly favorable ratio because it would crowd out other meritorious programs and threaten the organizational and political coalitions that make a budget viable. To match the acceptable share of available funds better, any very large program investment is likely to seek multiple sources of funding or spread out the investment over multiple budget cycles.

CONSIDERING DISTRIBUTIONAL EFFECTS

Financial decisions affect both actors and nonactors. There are issues of externalities and free riders and moral hazard associated with some alternatives. There also are impacts on provider income, payer cash flows, and patient cash flows. In a financial sense, every proposal can be considered a zero-sum game in which there are winners and losers under our current set of incentives. Professionals are usually paid more for doing more. Vulnerable patients often end up paying more than those strong enough to monitor their own care and bargain on price. The health policy analyst must "follow the money" without becoming too cynical and attributing all motivation to greed. Health care is a mixture of necessities and consumption goods. Consider that during both the Great Recession of 2007 and the Great Depression of the 1930s, birth rates dropped to new lows as many families put off having more children.

There are four general methods of rectifying maldistribution if the market fails to correct the problem over time. According to Wheelan (2011), they are:

- Regulation or deregulation
- Incentives and disincentives, including taxes and subsidies
- Direct government services delivery
- Contracting with the private sector to deliver service

The ACA incorporated all four methods. Everyone must have health insurance or be taxed. Subsidies are provided to those who cannot pay the full premium. The government provides insurance exchanges to facilitate the market and also pays providers through Medicaid.

COMPARING WITH COMPETING ALTERNATIVES

The ratios that we have been studying (benefit/cost and cost-effectiveness) have little meaning in and of themselves. They are useful only in comparison with either a minimum standard value or in terms of rank ordering a set of alternatives. Sometimes a set of subcategories are used, such as the following:

- Absolutely necessary because of the regulation or risk to the patients
- High priority in terms of meeting overall organizational goals
- Medium priority
- Low priority

Where there are subcategories, the ratios may be used to rank order alternative investments within each category. Setting priorities may be one way to recognize some of the political pressures that might otherwise overwhelm simple league-table rankings (similar to those used to display team standings in sports).

FINANCIAL FEASIBILITY

An organization's financial system must be up to evaluating an alternative's costs and forecasting the financial implications of various funding alternatives. Cleverley and Cameron (2003) suggested three major target areas of financial strategic planning for health organizations:

- Revenue estimation
- Capital budgeting (more of a concern for organizations that pay income tax)
- Financing of operations and capital investments

They expanded on these by suggesting that the underlying financial systems must

- Provide data on revenue, costs, and capital requirements according to program or product lines.
- Adjust these estimates for inflation and increasing technology requirements.
- Supply ROI or IRR estimates for decision making.
- Estimate working capital and cash reserve requirements under expected operating conditions.
- Establish the desired capital structure given the organization's debt capacity.
- Provide procedures for the allocation of capital among competing internal programs and facilities.

The first three steps are the same in both the public and private sectors. The last two are especially important to organizations and companies operating in the private sector. Even governmental programs that are separately funded, such as Medicare, have to estimate flows and reserves. The actuaries at the Centers for Medicare & Medicaid Services (CMS) are the ones who keep telling us when the Medicare trust funds will run out.

It is important to recognize that different parts of the organization may disagree on the value of an activity, such as reducing the length of stay, depending on whether they are looking at full costs or marginal costs, whether they consider the organization to be at capacity or below it, and how the reimbursement system operates (Ward, Spagens, & Smithson, 2006). In response to this concern, Voluntary Hospitals of America (VHA) has developed a template for evaluating the cost, revenue, and cash-flow impacts of various proposals. **Figure 11-4** analyzes a proposal to improve hospital laboratory turnaround times, thus reducing the overall average length of stay by 0.1 days. It then proceeds to evaluate three types of costs: the cost of the project, the cash-flow impacts of the cost reduction, and the cash-flow impacts of the new patients that can be accommodated in the freed-up beds (called backfill).

Capital Allocation Processes

Capital investments is one area where facilities and services available to the poor and the uninsured are likely to be shortchanged over time as large multisite health care organizations seek to maintain reasonable payer mixes and returns on their investments (Hurley, Pham, & Claxton, 2005; Robinson & Dratler, 2006). The use of analytical techniques to estimate

Costs of Process Improvement			
Salaries	$	(100,000)	
Fringe Benefits	$	(100,000)	
Supplies & Services	$	(20,000)	
Other	$	-	
Costs of Process Improvement	**$**		**(220,000)**
Cash Flow Impact of the Improvement			
Changes in Net Revenue Associated with			
Case based reimbursement	$	-	
Per Diem reimbursement	$	(96,000)	
Percentage of Charges reimbursement	$	-	
Medical Device Revenue	$	-	
(Revenue = device cost and markup)			
Drug Revenue	$	(10,000)	$	(106,000)
(Revenue = drug cost and markup)			
Changes in Operating Cost Associated with			
Supply costs driven by changes in patient days	$	15,000	
Medical device changes	$	-	
Medication substitution	$	25,000	$	40,000
The Cash Flow Impact of the Improvement	**$**		**(66,000)**
Backfill Cash Flow Estimate			
Incremental Net Revenue Associated with Backfill			
Case based reimbursement	$	243,902	
Per Diem reimbursement	$	96,000	
Percentage of Charges reimbursement	$	48,780	$	388,683
Medical Device Revenue	$	-	
(Revenue = device cost and markup)			
Drug Revenue	$	10,000	$	398,683
(Revenue = drug cost and markup)			
Incremental Operating Costs Associated with Backfill			
Incremental supplies	$	(15,000)	
Medications	$	(25,000)	
Medical Devices	$	-	$	(40,000)
The Cash Flow Impact of Potential Case Backfill	**$**		**348,683**
Backfill Cash Flow Estimate			
Cost of Process Improvement	$	(220,000)	
Cash Flow Impact of the Improvement	$	(66,000)	
Net Cash Flow Improvement Exclusive of Potential Case Backfill	$		(286,000)
Cash Flow Impact of Potential Case Backfill	$		348,683
Total Cash Flow Impact from Process Improvement Initiative	**$**		**62,683**

Figure 11-4 VHA cash flow analysis template.

Source: Reproduced from: "Faster Labs: Process Improvement Initiative Cash Flow" spreadsheet from the Financial tab of "Building the Business Case for Clinical Quality". © 2006 VHA. All rights reserved.

rates of return over time is unlikely to lead to expansion of services for those who can pay little or nothing.

CONCLUSION

Decision makers need to know what a program will cost; what revenue, if any, it will generate; and how and by whom the balance will be financed. They also have to present a convincing case that the current and future benefits to patients, payers, and the public justify the investment. Cash-flow management also is important, even if it is not usually considered part of health policy analysis. Comparative tools, such as cost–benefit analysis and cost-effectiveness analysis, are basic tools of policy analysis, but they present a number of ethical and value-based concerns. They are critical to the budget and adoption approval processes and to gaining top-level support for proposals. Smaller organizations also have to worry about the sources of working capital necessary to undertake and sustain both current and higher levels of activity. For them, "cash flow is king." Although some may see financial viability analysis as "the dark side" of policy analysis, competency in this area is a must.

Case 11	Increasing the Federal Cigarette Excise Tax

When the Congressional Budget Office (CBO) (2012) published *Raising the Excise Tax on Cigarettes: Effects on Health and the Federal Budget*, its stated motivation was "to demonstrate the complex links between policies that aim to improve health and effects on the federal budget" (p. iii). According to this June 2012 report, "A policy that discourages smoking by raising the excise tax on cigarettes provides a good case study because a substantial body of research exists about the effect of changes in cigarette prices on smoking rates, as well as about the impact of smoking on health, health care spending, longevity, and (to a lesser extent) earnings" (p. 2).

Policy and budget analysts evaluated the impact of a hypothetical $0.50 increase (adjusted for inflation) in the federal excise tax on cigarettes and small cigars. At the time of the report, the federal tax was $1.01 per pack. It had been increased in 2009 from $0.39 by the ACA. State excise taxes ranged from $0.17 in Missouri to $4.35 per pack in

Case 11 *(continued)*

New York State, with an average $1.48 for all states. Additional city taxes increased the combined state and local taxes per pack to $5.85 in New York City and $5.66 in Chicago.

The CBO report noted:

> A policy initiative aimed at improving the health of the population would affect the federal budget through the following links:
>
> - The effects of the policy on people's behaviors.
> - The impact of changes in behavior on people's health, and
> - The implications for improvement in health for people's health care spending, life expectancy, and earnings. Specifically, better health would tend to reduce health care spending per capita . . . Better health might also lead to lower mortality rates and greater longevity, thus increasing size of the population and changing its age distribution. Better health could also affect total earnings, because healthier people might make different decisions about working and might be more productive at work.
>
> To produce comprehensive estimates of how such a policy initiative would affect the federal budget, CBO must assess the magnitude of each of these complex links. That process requires a great deal of analysis by CBO and a significant amount of research by outside analysts on which CBO can draw. (pp. iv–v)

The study projected the budget impacts of the status quo and the additional 50-cent excise tax on outlays and on revenues through 2085. The net result of the analysis was a $41 billion deficit reduction over 10 years (the usual CBO window for analysis), with smaller deficit reductions through 2085. After about 2025, federal outlays would increase slightly. Greater longevity and the costs of supporting the additional aged population would more than offset savings from health improvement, although there would still be deficit reductions for another 15 years or so because of increased tax revenue.

ESTIMATION TASKS

The flows of costs, payments, and revenues required estimates of the following:

- Response of smokers to the policy change
- Effects of smoking (including secondhand smoke) on health
- Effects of smoking on labor earnings, productivity, workforce participation, and disability
- Impacts of health care on Medicare, Medicaid, employment-based health insurance, subsidies through health insurance exchanges, and federal employee, military, and veteran benefits (i.e., retirements, pensions, and health care)
- Excise tax revenues
- Other federal revenues
- Inflation rates
- Longevity effects on Old Age and Survivors Insurance, Disability Insurance, Supplemental Security Income

ESTIMATING THE EFFECTS AND FLOWS

One of the most difficult estimates was the underlying future rate of smoking without the intervention. Smoking rates in the United States have declined relatively steadily since 1992—at first by 2% of the population per year, and then by 1% in the most recent years. The report referred to the slower rate of decline as "hardening of the target." The report assumed, based on the available literature, that without the increased excise tax the percentage of smokers would remain relatively constant at about 15% of the adult population.

The CBO had available a number of studies of the price elasticity of cigarettes for adults and youth, some of it from the tobacco settlement negotiations. One problem was that no price-related interventions had gone on in a vacuum. Other antismoking activities had also been taking place. The report was issued somewhat ahead of the current trend of employers and insurers penalizing smokers by charging higher health care premiums. The report argued that its findings are likely to hold up through a $1 excise tax increase, but suggested that savings from even greater tax increases might be offset, in part, by increased smuggling or international Internet sales.

The CBO report also discussed three analytical models appearing in the literature: longitudinal or life-cycle, cross-sectional, and policy simulation. The report seemed to dismiss the longitudinal models as unstable and presenting present value issues. It stated that longitudinal studies seemed to give conflicting results about lifetime health spending.

Case 11   (*continued*)

The study used a regression model to analyze the health care cost impacts and the longevity effect of reductions in smoking. The report noted that two different approaches often are used: disease-specific analysis and regression analysis. It cited a number of sources of strong disease-specific (bottom-up) evidence, but the CBO decided to rely on regression. The researchers did not want to assume that all differences in health care costs, income, and longevity between smokers and nonsmokers are due to the smoking habit. Education level, gender, alcohol use, and health risk tolerance were given as examples of cohort differences unlikely to be affected by smoking status. The disease-specific approach might also miss health effects of smoking not yet documented.

CBO'S ANALYSIS

The new work presented in the CBO report was based on cross-sectional analysis using regression followed by a set of policy simulations. The cross-sectional analysis for the effect of smoking on health care spending involved regressions conducted on data from the Medical Panel Expenditure Survey for five different age groupings. Smokers had higher costs than nonsmokers except in the 75+ age group. The CBO used a two-part model. A logistic regression model determined first the probability of having any expenditure in a given year and a second general linearized model estimated the amount of expenditures with nonzero values. The regressions controlled for sex, marital status, race or ethnicity, education level, geographic location, alcohol consumption, categories of body mass index, health insurance coverage, and attitudes toward risk taking.

The conclusion from the CBO regressions was that health care expenditures were higher for smokers and former smokers than for nonsmokers except for the 75+ age group. This analysis gave information on the differences between the groups. Those differences were sufficiently great that the CBO decided to construct a health care cost comparison between a smoker and someone who was not a smoker but had the same characteristics otherwise. The percentage of health care cost attributable to smoking ranged from 4% to 8%, with the greatest differences in the 45–65 and 65–75 age groups. The average was 7%.

This was consistent with most older studies, but higher than the 5% reported by a newer study.

To estimate the relationship between smoking and longevity, the CBO again used logistic regression with 1.0 being a death in the next year. The data came from the 1997–2004 National Health Interview Survey and death certification records from the National Death Index through 2006. Indicators (dummy variables) were added for the survey year to capture changes over time. Again the final comparison was between smokers and nonsmokers who share the same other characteristics. The conclusion was that smoking reduced longevity by 5–6 years.

LAG EFFECT IN SMOKING CESSATION RECOVERY

The increase in cigarette tax would affect only smokers; those who quit would gradually achieve improved health. The CBO constructed a longitudinal percentage recovery time series using disease-specific data supplied through the CDC on diseases responsible for 86% of deaths attributable to smoking. It was referred to as the "health response lag."

ESTIMATING EARNINGS IMPACT

The literature shows that smokers have more unemployment, lower wages, and perform less well at work, although these effects are not all due to smoking. Using data on both smoking and earning power from the Current Population Survey and its Tobacco Use Supplement, the CBO again used regression analysis and controlled for age, region, sex, race or ethnicity, education level, and marital status. The analysis indicated that apparent differences in earnings between smokers and nonsmokers with similar measured characteristics were greater than could be attributed directly to the smoking decision. Similar patterns were observed from regression analysis of the interaction between smoking and retirement based on the Health and Retirement Study. Again there seemed to be substantial unmeasured relationship as the pattern emerged that former smokers were doing better than nonsmokers who, in turn, were doing better than smokers, all with the same characteristics.

Even though the regressions indicated that smokers on average earned 11.7% less than nonsmokers and former smokers averaged 1.3%

Case 11 *(continued)*

more than nonsmokers, the CBO decided to use the following estimates of income differentials based on an evaluation of the evidence and consideration of the unmeasured factors:

- Ages 18–34: Smokers earn 4% less.
- Ages 25–44: Smokers earn 6% less.
- Ages 45–54: Smokers earn 5% less.
- Ages 55–64: Smokers earn 7% less.
- Ages 65–74: Smokers earn 5% less.

EXPOSURE TO SECONDHAND SMOKE

The CBO report considered several ways of accounting for the health effects of secondhand smoke. There was a self-reported rate of 15% for individuals subject to secondhand smoke, and the prevalence of nicotine in blood samples of nonsmoking adults was nearly 40%. The CBO chose to calculate the number of smoke-free households with and without the tax increase, even though that ignored smoking at work and other public places. Data from the National Health and Nutrition Examination Survey, the Medical Expenditure Panel, and the Current Population Survey were combined to determine that the benefits to health care spending and longevity from not being subject to secondhand smoke would be about 5% of the benefits accruing to those who stopped smoking.

MODELING THE FINANCIAL FLOWS OVER TIME

To model financial flows over time, first the study staff had to estimate the impact of the intervention on the size and age distribution of the national population and the relevant population segments over time, including smokers, quitters, quitters who resumed smoking, nonsmokers, and nonsmokers who started smoking, year by year. Then they could apply their estimates of the revenues, earnings, and expenditures for each subgroup year by year for each federal funding stream. They used this estimate for each year to calculate the amounts taken in and expended for each subgroup for each program. These programs were cited earlier, however, special adjustments were necessary. For example, the study took into account the revenue effects of the taxes on increased taxable incomes due to reduced health insurance premiums, changed disability program enrollments, changed cost-sharing and premium subsidies under insurance exchange provisions of the ACA, and the fact that disability programs had a higher population of mentally ill persons who were much less likely to quit smoking. The staff did not try to estimate the effect of reduced consumption due to price elasticity without stopping smoking. They cited the fact that people could and sometimes did offset their consumption of reduced numbers of cigarettes by buying stronger blends or adjusting the amount inhaled.

CBO CONCLUSIONS

Figures 11-5 and **11-6** show the overall findings of the study. The health improvement effects outweigh the costs of greater longevity for about

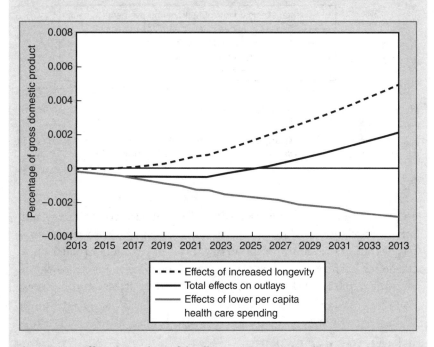

Figure 11-5 Effects on outlays of the illustrative increase in the cigarette tax.

Source: Reproduced from: Congressional Budget Office Report *Raising the Excise Tax on Cigarettes: Effects on Health and the Federal Budget* (Publication 44319), p. 18.

Case 11 (*continued*)

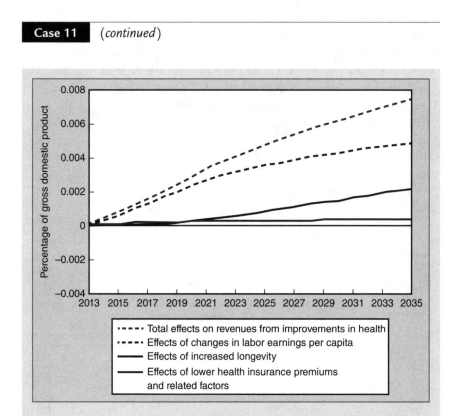

Figure 11-6 Health-related effects on revenues of the illustrative increase in the cigarette tax.

Source: Reproduced from: Congressional Budget Office Report *Raising the Excise Tax on Cigarettes: Effects on Health and the Federal Budget* (Publication 44319), p. 19.

10 years, and then the increased costs of Social Security, Medicare, and other programs would mount as the survivors aged. However, the cigarette excise tax revenues would offset this and yield a net reduction in the deficit each year for the next 75 years. The deficit reductions would amount to 0.02–0.03% of GDP, with the greatest effects in the earliest years.

A MAJOR DISCLAIMER

The report recognized that the budgetary analysis did not include all the factors involved in a decision to raise the federal cigarette excise tax:

If lawmakers were to consider raising the excise tax on cigarettes, or adopting other policies that would promote a healthier population, their proposals would depend on a variety of considerations besides the effects on the federal budget. Those other considerations would most likely include the impact of a proposed policy on people's health, views about the appropriate role of the government in influencing behavior, the burdens that the proposed policy might impose on people in different circumstances, and the effects of the policy on the budgets of state and local governments. Those other considerations lie beyond the scope of this analysis, which addresses only the impact of an increase in the cigarette tax on the federal budget (with related analysis of the effects on health and longevity). (p. 5)

Discussion Questions

1. How important are the budgetary effects likely to be in the decision to impose a further increase in the federal cigarette excise tax? What factors ought to have a major role in the debate? What would you add to the CBO's major disclaimer about its analysis? How important should its analysis be in any real decision-making process?

2. Make sure that you understand the differences between longitudinal analysis, cross-sectional analysis (including logit), and the simulation analysis approaches. Does it appear that the CBO used all three?

3. It does not appear that the CBO used a Monte Carlo simulation in the final modeling. Why do you think that it did not do so?

4. The states were making large increases in their cigarette taxes during this period. What would you speculate would be the interaction between the two (state and federal), and how would that affect your analysis? Do you think some of that effect was captured by the inclusion of "region" in the regressions?

Chapter 12

The Policy Analysis Process: Analysis of Values

An analysis that considers technological capabilities, economic outcomes, and political support will usually point toward a single health policy recommendation. Yet any final recommendation must take into account values, especially where there are competing trade-offs. You might ask this: Does not the political process, which a recommendation often goes through before it can be adopted and implemented, take care of those value concerns? Do not decision makers reflect their personal values and those of their constituencies in the positions they take during a policy debate and in their votes? Yes, the political process will reflect the current wider conflicts in American society over social mores, the nature of human life, the role of government, the economic marketplace, and collective versus individual rights. In this chapter, however, we consider some value issues relating specifically to health care and the health care professions. These values may or may not be considered in the political process and should be assessed as part of any robust analysis.

Value issues discussed briefly in this chapter include:

- Equitable access
- Efficiency and value
- Patient privacy and confidentiality
- Informed consent
- Personal responsibility

- Quality, variability, and malpractice reform
- Professional ethics
- Consumer sovereignty
- Social welfare
- Rationing
- Process equity

This chapter ends with the broader question of how a wide range of social institutions might be influenced by the growth of the medical sector of the economy.

EQUITABLE ACCESS

Priester (1992) suggested that the United States should reorder its values to give the greatest emphasis to fair equity, which he defined as giving each individual access to an "adequate level of care." Skipping over issues of residency and eligibility, he argued, "Assuring access to health care, regardless of cause or source of need, is society's responsibility"; however, he added that "this does not require access to all potentially beneficial care" (p. 92). He maintained that this is the only approach that would not exceed the available resources or deprive some segments of society of their opportunity for a reasonably full life. He saw this as a floor, not a ceiling; someone with more personal resources could choose to consume more health services. He saw the U.S. system as overemphasizing provider autonomy, individualism, and assumed abundance. He felt that we have too often let economic considerations outweigh ethical ones.

A similar argument could be made for removing health disparities; among the major causes of which is differential access to care. The Affordable Care Act (ACA) has made a step in the direction of fair access by moving toward universal coverage and by calling for a defined essential benefit package.

EFFICIENCY AND VALUE

If resource scarcity leads society to overlook some populations or to restrict necessary services to them, then efficiency is important. "Waste not, want not" is not always a fundamental value in a system in which one person's waste is another person's enhanced income. Porter and Teisberg (2006) argued against a "zero-sum" mentality that attempts to maximize each individual provider's share of the existing pie and favored reducing waste to enhance the value received by individual consumers. One could also promote the collective view that the services available to consumers collectively form a "zero-sum" game in which all will get more if the collective waste is minimized. One way or another, there is considerable merit in viewing waste negatively, rather than as enhanced income.

Because it is so hard to get individuals to pull together on efficiency and cost minimization, some policy experts have tended to emphasize "value." We now have value-based compensation experiments that allow sharing of the savings with providers and provide compensation for higher-quality outcomes. The sense here is that there is value created when you get greater quality for the same cost or the same quality for lower cost, or both positive outcomes concurrently.

In a survey that asked health industry leaders to rank 11 areas of innovation for their potential impact in terms of quality and cost over the next 5 years, the highest ranking went to process improvement. The other innovation areas likely to contribute to both improved quality and cost were data analytics, nonphysician delivery alternatives, disease management, and alternatives to fee-for-service. The respondents believed innovations in diagnostics, pharmaceuticals, and electronic medical records would help with costs but not quality, and they forecasted a low likelihood of help along either dimension from consumer incentives or from basic research (Chin et al., 2013). The good news is that process improvement is an area where any provider who wants to make a difference can contribute.

PATIENT PRIVACY AND CONFIDENTIALITY

Increasingly, electronic patient records, digitized information already collected for billing and claims, and specialized databases offer potential for finding out more about disease processes and care outcomes. At the same time, they offer possibilities for excluding individuals from care or for breeches of the confidentiality that one expects when encountering the health care system and is often guaranteed by laws such as the Health Insurance Portability and Accountability Act (HIPAA). News stories about stolen laptops with personal data crop up frequently. This is an area where trade-offs will continue to be difficult and frustrating, and it will continue to be important in policy analysis and decision making.

INFORMED CONSENT

Requirements for informed consent for patients and human subjects in research represent a constraint on provider autonomy. They add to the staff burden, but are a regulatory requirement. **Table 12-1** illustrates part

Table 12-1 Code of Federal Regulations Section 50, Subpart B, Informed Consent of Human Subjects

§50.20: General requirements for informed consent

Except as provided in 50.23 and 50.24, no investigator may involve a human being as a subject in research covered by these regulations unless the investigator has obtained the legally effective informed consent of the subject or the subject's legally authorized representative. An investigator shall seek such consent only under circumstances that provide the prospective subject or the representative sufficient opportunity to consider whether or not to participate and that minimize the possibility of coercion or undue influence. The information that is given to the subject or the representative shall be in language understandable to the subject or the representative. No informed consent, whether oral or written, may include any exculpatory language through which the subject or the representative is made to waive or appear to waive any of the subject's legal rights, or releases or appears to release the investigator, the sponsor, the institution, or its agents from liability for negligence.

Section 50.24 Basic elements of informed consent.

(a) In seeking informed consent, the following information shall be provided to each subject:

  (1) A statement that the study involves research, an explanation of the purposes of the research and the expected duration of the subject's participation, a description of the procedures to be followed, and identification of any procedures which are experimental.

  (2) A description of any reasonably foreseeable risks or discomforts to the subject.

  (3) A description of any benefits to the subject or to others which may reasonably be expected from the research.

  (4) A disclosure of appropriate alternative procedures or courses of treatment, if any, that might be advantageous to the subject.

  (5) A statement describing the extent, if any, to which confidentiality of records identifying the subject will be maintained and that notes the possibility that the Food and Drug Administration may inspect the records.

  (6) For research involving more than minimal risk, an explanation as to whether any compensation and an explanation as to whether any medical treatments are available if injury occurs and, if so, what they consist of, or where further information may be obtained.

  (7) An explanation of whom to contact for answers to pertinent questions about the research and research subjects' rights, and whom to contact in the event of a research-related injury to the subject.

  (8) A statement that participation is voluntary, that refusal to participate will involve no penalty or loss of benefits to which the subject is otherwise entitled, and that the subject may discontinue participation at any time without penalty or loss of benefits to which the subject is otherwise entitled.

(b) Additional elements of informed consent. When appropriate, one or more of the following elements of information shall also be provided to each subject:

  (1) A statement that the particular treatment or procedure may involve risks to the subject (or to the embryo or fetus, if the subject is or may become pregnant) which are currently unforeseeable.

  (2) Anticipated circumstances under which the subject's participation may be terminated by the investigator without regard to the subject's consent.

Table 12-1 Code of Federal Regulations Section 50, Subpart B, Informed Consent of Human Subjects (*continued*)

(3) Any additional costs to the subject that may result from participation in the research.

(4) The consequences of a subject's decision to withdraw from the research and procedures for orderly termination of participation by the subject.

(5) A statement that significant new findings developed during the course of the research which may relate to the subject's willingness to continue participation will be provided to the subject.

(6) The approximate number of subjects involved in the study.

(c) When seeking informed consent for applicable clinical trials, as defined in 42 U.S.C. 282(j)(1)(A), the following statement shall be provided to each clinical trial subject in informed consent documents and processes. This will notify the clinical trial subject that clinical trial information has been or will be submitted for inclusion in the clinical trial registry databank under paragraph (j) of section 402 of the Public Health Service Act. The statement is: "A description of this clinical trial will be available on http://www.ClinicalTrials.gov, as required by U.S. Law. This Web site will not include information that can identify you. At most, the Web site will include a summary of the results. You can search this Web site at any time."

(d) The informed consent requirements in these regulations are not intended to preempt any applicable Federal, State, or local laws which require additional information to be disclosed for informed consent to be legally effective.

(e) Nothing in these regulations is intended to limit the authority of a physician to provide emergency medical care to the extent the physician is permitted to do so under applicable Federal, State, or local law.

Source: Reproduced from: Code of Federal Regulations (2013, April 1). Protection of human subjects. Washington, D.C: Government Printing Office. Title 21, Volume 1, Part 50. Retrieved on December 17, 2013, at www.accessdata.fda.gov/scripts/cdrh/cfdocs/cfcfr/CFRSearch.cfm?CFRPart=50&showFR=1&subpartNode=21:1.0.1.1.20.2.

of the federal regulations governing informed consent by research subjects in federally funded research. You might ask yourself this: What values are represented here, and why were they made an added requirement of all research in the first place?

PERSONAL RESPONSIBILITY

A significant portion of the cost of health care can be attributed to lifestyle choices, such as smoking, lack of exercise, overeating or poor nutrition, not wearing seat belts or cycling helmets, and use of drugs and alcohol. Many policy proposals seek to change the behavioral risk factors or shift those costs to the individuals at risk. Smokers pay higher insurance premiums for long-term care, for example. Some analysts have suggested that those involved in risky behaviors, such as not wearing motorcycle helmets, post a bond to cover their incremental medical care costs in case of an accident. Most people would agree that individuals should take more responsibility for their behavior rather than have it borne as a collective risk, but there is less agreement on the effort society should expend to make healthy choices more attractive. There is considerable evidence, for example, that the development choices we make—our *built environment*—can encourage or discourage physical activity. A politician asked to support a bill to encourage "walkability" or "multimodal transportation hubs," however, may be inclined to attribute lack of exercise solely to, as one state legislator put it, "a lack of personal fortitude."

The question of personal responsibility comes up repeatedly in debates about health reform and the ACA in particular. Key elements of the reform can be seen as an attempt to balance a society's responsibility to ensure equitable access with an individual's responsibilities. The individual mandate legislates personal responsibility, using tax fines to ensure that young, healthy people can pay for their own care if they need it and do their share to support a larger system they will likely rely on as they age. When Governor Mitt Romney was considering the individual mandate as part of the Massachusetts reforms, he noted that the personal mandate was about personal responsibility, which is a fundamental Republican value (Starr, 2011). Yet, in a video released by *Mother Jones* during the campaign, Romney said that 47% of the population feel entitled to government handouts. "I'll never convince them that they should take personal responsibility and care for their lives," he said (*Mother Jones*, 2012). In his acceptance speech after winning another term, President Obama emphasized social responsibility:

> What makes America exceptional are the bonds that hold together the most diverse nation on earth. The belief that our destiny is shared; that this country only works when we accept certain obligations to one another and to future generations. The freedom which so many Americans have fought for and died for come with responsibilities as well as rights. And among those are love and charity and duty and patriotism. That's what makes America great.

QUALITY, VARIABILITY, AND MALPRACTICE REFORM

We hear a lot about malpractice reform and frivolous lawsuits and unreasonable awards for pain and suffering. We see local television advertisements by law firms seeking to represent clients "wronged" by providers and insurers. State and federal legislatures and courts debate whether to cap the size of awards or determine when they are excessive. Funding flows freely into campaign coffers from organizations on both sides of the debate; trial lawyers favor the Democratic Party, whereas insurers and organizations representing health providers and facilities favor the Republican Party. Putting political posturing aside, however, several values-related policy issues recur in the debates on this area, including the following:

- The value of a human life lost and of other negative consequences suffered unnecessarily
- The allocation of the responsibility for error between the individual provider and the overall care system
- The amount of variability in outcomes and events that is unavoidable and how much is unacceptable
- The appropriate way to compensate advocates for patient rights and to overcome inappropriate provider behavior
- How much to let the provider community police itself and how much and when to intervene in the public interest

PROFESSIONAL ETHICS

Access and rationing are aspects of distributive justice. Confidentiality, truthfulness, informed consent, respect for patient and professional autonomy, and the safety of the patient are all topics cited in discussions of professional ethics and in professional codes of ethics. Most professionals have had some indoctrination in biomedical ethics and are aware of key issues. Most professions have an ethical code or statement. Most such statements have become more general over time as patient autonomy has become more respected and monopolistic practices have come under government scrutiny. At the same time, professional societies may take strong positions without incorporating them into a code. For example, the American Nurses Association has long supported health care as a basic right delivered through a single-payer system.

What About Health Policy Experiments?

Daniels (2006) raised an interesting ethical question for health policy professionals: What if we required that health system transformations had to undergo an ethical review process similar to that required of medical research experiments? He noted that these social experiments can put significant populations at risk. He did not suggest what the mechanism for such reviews might be; however, he raised the issues of balancing the social value of the experimental policy changes with the risks to which those affected are exposed and how we might go about conducting such a review. He suggested three levels of analysis:

1. Select benchmarks for the ethical analysis in terms of their effect on:
   a. Equity
   b. Efficiency
   c. Accountability
2. Conduct an ethical evaluation of how well the design of the proposed reform meets its goals:
   a. How good is the evidence used to justify the intervention?
   b. Is the implementation planned adequate to test the results?
   c. Will the intervention measure the effect with sufficient sensitivity to evaluate the results?
   d. Are the key implementers involved in the planning and committed to an unbiased evaluation?
3. Determine whether there is sufficient oversight to protect the rights of those involved in the experiment. Informed consent might be impractical in many settings.

He mostly offered examples of international situations, but, overall, he noted, "Unfortunately, there is little experience in measuring how systems establish transparency, accountability, and fair process in decisions involving resource allocation" (p. 450).

CONSUMER SOVEREIGNTY

Those who want a highly competitive marketplace want the consumer to make decisions rather than the government. The examples in the box on the next page illustrate views of health policy analysts on both sides of this economic and political ideological divide. The typical health professional is in a bit of a straddle here. Most believe in patient autonomy but also recognize that consumer sovereignty often comes at the expense of professional power and influence, which some would call paternalism, but may positively affect patient compliance and clinical outcomes as well.

SOCIAL WELFARE

Interest groups at the table during policy formulation may or may not adequately represent the public's interests. There are a number of ways of evaluating outcomes in terms of social welfare. Some are economic; some

CONTRASTS IN ECONOMIC AND POLITICAL IDEOLOGY

Cannon and Tanner (2005) agreed in one respect with many who support a greater government role in health: that the health care sector of the economy is special. But they argued that because it is special, reliance on competition is even more critical:

> Unlike software, wireless communications, or banking, health care involves very emotional decisions, which often entail matters of human dignity, life, and death. However, we do not see the gravity of these matters as a reason to divert power away from individuals and toward government. Rather we see the special nature of health care as all the more reason to increase each consumer's sphere of autonomy. (pp. 146–147)

Richmond and Fein (2005) concluded otherwise. They would prefer to use public policy to create a more equitable society:

> Health and health care are vitally important in influencing life's chances and one's income and wealth should not determine the amount and quality of care one receives. We seek a system in which the financing and distribution of health services reflect our image of a just society, a society in which economic arrangements reflect a moral dimension. (p. 4)

are not. Economic models that would base policy decisions on benefit–cost or cost-effectiveness criteria raise issues of valuation, such as

- Willingness to pay
- Contribution to gross domestic product
- Social costs avoided, as in the case of support of a family when the breadwinner dies

At the same time there are other considerations, such as

- Lives saved
- Quality-adjusted life-years (QALYs)
- Longevity
- Pain and suffering avoided

In this arena, there are counterattacks to the economic arguments (Ackerman & Heinzerling, 2004):

> Cost–benefit analysis of health and environmental policies trivializes the very values that gave rise to these policies in the first place. Moreover, through opaque and intimidating concepts like willingness to pay, quality-adjusted life-years, and discounting, economic analysts have managed to hide the moral and political questions lying just under the surface of their precise and scientific-looking numbers. It is time to blow their cover. (p. 234)

Discounting is easy to do mathematically but difficult to interpret practically, politically, and ethically. The problem is in the trade-off between the present and the future, a difficult problem in all policy making. The standard economists' approach of bringing the costs and benefits back to a net present value explicitly biases the analysis against future events. Some advocates, therefore, argue for a discount rate of 0%.

Ackerman and Heinzerling also questioned the use of QALY metrics because they discriminate against the older population, who will naturally have fewer years ahead of them. The same can be said of any analysis dealing with contribution to gross domestic product, because the older population generates little output or will soon stop generating it and the output of children is so far into the future that any reasonable discount rate obliterates the benefits. This is why some suggest that economic analysis is useful for payers and for comparing treatment alternatives for specific illness, but that it really does not work well when comparing an array of different alternative public investments.

RATIONING

Bodenheimer and Grumbach (2005) suggested a two-part definition of rationing: (1) limiting care that is likely to be beneficial due to scarce resources, including money, and (2) a method of fairly distributing the resources that are available. To this we would add a third condition: (3) that the decision-making method is determined by society rather than a corporation or an individual. Bodenheimer and Grumbach noted that popular use of the term *rationing* tends to equate it with withholding of care and ignores the second necessary condition. That distinction separates arbitrary actions to decrease the cost of care from situations in which the system attempts to distribute its limited resources in a systematic and equitable way. There are a variety of notions of equity, and thus a rationing system may be designed to

- Reduce overall costs to a targeted level
- Maximize access
- Maximize the social welfare based on the contributions of the individuals within the population
- Maximize medical effectiveness:
  - Subject to a cost constraint
  - Subject to other resource limitations
- Combinations of the above

For example, the attempt of the British National Health Service (NHS) to limit the costs of care has led to at least one charge of rationing in which a woman with breast cancer was denied the drug Herceptin by a local health authority on the basis of cost. An account of this has been included in **Table 12-2**.

Reducing Overall Health Care Costs to a Target Level

An effective rationing system is not aimed at minimizing health care costs. They cannot be driven to zero; however, when there is a budgetary limitation or a fixed-revenue situation, a system must be in place to decide which services will not be provided to which individuals. In many cases, this is done by limiting the population served and limiting the services offered.

For example, one of the largest Medicaid expenses is paying for long-term care for older people, a service not covered by Medicare. States have quietly limited the amount they pay by limiting the number of new nursing home beds they license. They know that there is a strong linear relationship between the number of beds available and the amount of Medicare claims received.

Maximize the Social Welfare

When transplanted organs first became available, it was clear that there were not enough to go around. Institutions doing transplants set up committees of individuals concerned with medical effectiveness and medical ethics to determine who would get the next available organ. This process provides an example of how social welfare considerations can influence rationing and access decisions. The committees examined a mixture of personal, family, and medical data to determine literally who should live and who would, in all probability, die. Considerations included family status, work status, medical factors such as alcoholism and comorbidities, and psychiatric factors. Outside observers were also suspicious that ability to pay might be creeping into the decision making.

Table 12-2 Rationing and the Courts

Ann Marie Rogers, 54, sued the Swindon Primary Care Trust after it refused treatment for her early-stage HER2 breast cancer with the drug Herceptin (trastuzumab), even after her doctor prescribed it. The Roche drug is licensed for late-stage breast cancer, but some studies showed it to be effective for early-stage cancer as well. Ms. Hewitt, the British Health Secretary, had praised the efforts of other women to get the treatment, and the Health Department had ordered the local health services "not to withhold it solely on the grounds of cost," even while a government-appointed review panel was in the process of setting new guidelines for the use of the drug. Treatment with Herceptin costs $36,000–47,000 a year for each patient and was supplied under very different circumstances by the local health trusts. The Swindon trust had a policy of supplying Herceptin for early-stage breast cancer only in "exceptional circumstances." Ms. Rogers had pointed to her cancer being of the type responsive to the drug and the risk factors of the death of her mother and a cousin from cancer.

When the trust refused to fund her treatment, Ms. Rogers starting paying for the drug on her own, but had to stop when her own resources were used up. Thus, she sued the authority, citing the "postal code lottery," which determined who got treated and who did not. A lower court judge ruled in February 2006 that the Swindon health service's denial was lawful. In April, however, a three-judge appeals court overturned that verdict and said the local health service had acted unlawfully, noting that "once the Primary Care Health Trust decided, as it did, that it would fund Herceptin for some patients and that the cost was irrelevant, the only reasonable approach was to focus on the patient's clinical needs and fund patients within the eligible group who were properly prescribed by their physician." It observed that there had been "no rational basis for distinguishing between patients within the eligible group on the basis of exceptional clinical circumstances any more than on the basis for personal, let alone, social circumstances" (Lyall, 2006).

The National Institute for Clinical Excellence (NICE) issued a press release on April 12, 2006, in which NICE Chief Executive Andrew Dillon reaffirmed the importance of ensuring that new drugs are both safe to use, by having an effective system for licensing, and used in the right way through the work that NICE does. "Without these things, we risk exposing patients to risks and the health service to using its money unwisely," he said (NICE, 2006a).

After a public comment period that closed in June 2006, NICE issued guidance in August 2006. "Trastuzumab, given at 3-week intervals for 1 year or until disease recurrence (whichever is the shorter period), is recommended as a treatment option for women with early-stage HER2-positive breast cancer following surgery, chemotherapy (neoadjuvant or adjuvant), and radiotherapy (if applicable)" (NICE, 2006b, p.4).

In June 2012, NICE again addressed the breast cancer issue with Technical Appraisal 257, "Breast cancer (metastatic hormone receptor)—lapatinib and trastuzumab (with aromatiase inhibitor)." It stated that NICE did not recommend this as first-line treatment for post-menopausal women who have metastatic breast cancer that is hormone-receptor and HER2 positive. It explained its response as follows:

> NICE looks at how well treatments work, and also at how well they work in relation to how much they cost the NHS. NICE applies special considerations to treatments that can extend the lives of people who are nearing the end of their life. Lapatinib and trastuzumab (herceptin) do not provide enough benefit to patients to justify their high cost even when the special considerations were applied, so NICE did not recommend them. (NICE, 2012)

One problem with the social welfare criterion is that it goes well beyond issues that health professionals are comfortable with. Issues might include citizenship status, economic contribution, utility of one's work, and emotional impact on others. Reaching some agreement on the importance of each of these is unlikely given current value conflicts in our society. That does not mean that we cannot reach a social consensus, but rather that it would be very difficult to justify once we have reached it.

Maximize Utility and Medical Effectiveness

"The providing or withholding of care is ideally determined by the probability that the treatment will maximize benefits and minimize harm, i.e. by the criterion of medical effectiveness" (Bodenheimer & Grumbach, 2005, p. 137). This concept was operationalized in the Oregon Basic Health Services Act of 1989, which tried to guarantee health care for all and still control health care costs through an open, publicly accountable rationing process. At that time, one had to be at or below 58% of the federal poverty level to receive Medicaid benefits in Oregon, and this bill was intended to open that up to those below the 100% level. The state created a Health Services Commission to recommend the prioritization of health services. The 11-member body was to report its priorities to the governor and the Joint Legislative Committee on Health Care. An actuarial contractor would then estimate the cost of each of the prioritized services for the committee. After the Medicaid budget for services was set, the package of services offered to the Medicaid population would be developed using the priority lists. Essentially, the process would be to go down the list taking the next highest priority coverage until the estimated budget package was exhausted. Other services then would be outside this basic coverage. If the demand exceeded the funding provided, Oregon was prepared to reduce the benefit package rather than ration through eligibility thresholds or Medicaid reimbursement levels, as so many other states were doing (Calkthan, 1991).

The commission used three techniques to develop the prioritization of some 800 services. It held 11 open public hearings around the state. It also had Oregon Health Decisions, a respected advocacy group, conduct 47 community forums, including one in every county. Each forum featured a slide presentation, group discussions, and a questionnaire on the participants' opinions about the relative importance of specific health situations and categories. About 70% of the more than 1,000 individuals attending these forums were health care workers. The commission also supported a statewide random-digit dialing survey asking 1,000 individuals to rate 31 health care situations on a modified Quality of Well-Being (QWB) scale that had been validated elsewhere. That information was used to build a cost-utility scale called a "net benefit value" scale. That study produced a listing of 1,600 medical condition–treatment pairs. The orderings produced by the telephone survey were highly debatable. Fox and Leichter (1991) reported that "crooked teeth received a higher ranking than early treatment for Hodgkin's disease, and dealing with thumb sucking was ranked higher than hospitalization of a child for starvation" (p. 22). Because it was clear that the derived utilities were not workable in terms of overall values, commission members negotiated among themselves for an acceptable ordering. For example, the four consumer representatives on the panel argued for higher rankings for preventive services because that is what the public seemed to have been saying during this process. Rather than a continuous ranking, they came up with 709 pairs grouped according to three basic categories: essential, very important, and valuable to some individuals (Kaplan, 1995), and then under 17 subcategories of outcomes, using descriptors such as survival, degree of recovery, and degree of improvement on the QWB scale (Fox & Leichter, 1991).

Implementing this process required a federal Medicaid waiver, which the federal government denied on the grounds that the assessments of quality of life by healthy individuals tended to stereotype and discount the value of quality for the disabled, and the process, therefore, violated the Americans with Disabilities Act. Kaplan (1995) argued that this finding was in error and offered counterevidence.

Instead of debating these issues, Oregon chose to resubmit its application with the utility portion of the model excluded. Its revised waiver application considered probability of death and probability of moving up from a symptomatic to an asymptomatic state. By giving up the utility component of the model, Oregon ignored the fact that health states are valued (Kaplan, 1995). Priester (1992) argued that the plan had been flawed because it denied access to a reasonable level of care to some, but not to others. In 1993, the Clinton administration approved the revised Medicaid waiver.

Combinations of One or More

Table 12-3 contains a description of how the United Network for Organ Sharing (UNOS) allocates available organs (not including related donors). This contractor was set up after passage of the National Organ Transplantation Act of 1984. It emphasizes the likely medical outcome and then pays attention to one's length of time on the waiting list; however, the issue of

Table 12-3 How the Transplant System Works: Matching Donors and Recipients

Under the Organ Procurement and Transplantation Network (OPTN) contract with the U.S. Department of Health and Human Services' Health Services & Resources Administration, UNOS maintains a centralized computer network linking all organ procurement organizations and transplant centers. This computer network is accessible 24 hours a day, 7 days a week, with organ placement specialists in the UNOS Organ Center always available to answer questions.

A person who may benefit from a transplant is referred by his or her doctor to a transplant center, which evaluates the patient. The transplant center runs a number of tests and considers the patient's mental and physical health, as well as his or her social support system. If the center decides to accept this person as a transplant candidate, it will add his or her medical profile to the national patient waiting list for organ transplant. The candidate is not placed on a ranked list at that time. Rather, his or her information is kept in a constantly updated, computerized database. When a deceased organ donor is identified, a transplant coordinator from an organ procurement organization accesses the UNOS computer. Each patient in the database in matched against the donor characteristics. The computer then generates a ranked list of candidates for each available organ in ranked order according to OPTN organ allocation policies.

The match for each donor would be different and unique to the circumstances of the donor and the patients waiting. Factors affecting ranking may include tissue match, blood type, length of time on the waiting list, immune status, and the distance between the potential recipient and the donor. For heart, liver, lung, and intestines, the potential recipient's degree of medical emergency is also considered. The organ is offered to the transplant team for the first person on the list. Often, the top patient will not get the organ for one of several reasons. When a patient is selected, he or she must be available, healthy enough to undergo major surgery, and willing to be transplanted immediately. Also, a laboratory test to measure compatibility between the donor and recipient may be necessary. For example, patients with high antibody levels often prove incompatible to the donor organ and cannot receive the organ because the patient's immune system would reject it.

Source: Reproduced from: United Network for Organ Sharing. (n.d.). How the Transplant System Works: Matching Donors and Recipients. Richmond, VA: UNOS. Retrieved on December 27, 2013, from www.unos.org/donation/index.php?topic=fact_sheet_1.

whether the transplant takes place is also contingent on the availability of private insurance or Medicare or Medicaid funds to pay for it. By now you should be aware that trying to maximize one thing while trying to minimize or maximize another is often a mathematical impossibility. It is legitimate, however, to have a system in which one objective is traded off against another. The problem is that most attempts to do so never specify what the trade-off ratios are because trying to arrive at a consensus ratio is likely to generate conflict over the weightings that cannot be resolved without considerable loss of momentum and goodwill. Allocation rules, therefore, tend to remain fuzzy. You can see this even in the UNOS description. It is clear that the concept of a social welfare criterion is not really operative there.

PROCESS EQUITY

Not only must the outcome of the policy analysis and selection process—that is, the policy itself—be perceived as fair, but so should the process that produced it. For example, before settling on a policy, the policy analysts must ask themselves whether all interested parties participated. If not, have the underrepresented or disenfranchised had their issues addressed by the analysts? This was a relevant concern in the Oregon process, which, although highly rational, seemed dominated by health professionals and by more educated and civically involved individuals. It is not unusual for opponents of a policy to argue against the inclusiveness or integrity of the policy development process. Many governments have requirements for public hearings that are regionally representative in hopes that their process will be fairer to those concerned and to protect themselves against complaints about the process.

INFLUENCE ON SOCIETY: A BROADER QUESTION

With the medical care sector headed toward constituting 20% of the economy, we have to wonder about the long-term effects of this much emphasis on health in our society. Areas of concern might include:

- A focus on illness and the possible loss of a sense of well-being
- Commercial pressure to overemphasize medical problems
- The power of the medical–industrial–university complex

Is it healthy to be so conscious of our health? Is it healthy to be so stressed about our medical bills? Just about every sector of our society adds a health concern to its primary and previous missions. Churches add health ministry committees and/or health-trained staff members. Schools take on more responsibility in terms of children's medications and their special needs; some have even established school-based health clinics. Tax revenues previously devoted to education and infrastructure get diverted to health care. All of these individual decisions may be virtuous, but they also signal a changing societal focus from toughing it out to getting it fixed through health care, whether that works or not.

Because health care represents an opportunity for growth, we see more and more commercial pressure to expand its markets—and its "top of mind" awareness for the public. In a way, this is good because it creates more innovation. However, it can create demand for which there is not a significant need and siphon resources away from areas of true need. Two issues that illustrate this are the explosive growth in direct-to-consumer advertising,

PREHYPERTENSION

Many older doctors report that they were trained that the normal upper limit for systolic blood pressure was your age (at least up to 55 years) plus 100 millimeters of mercury over 90 (diastolic). Then, in 1977, the Joint National Committee on Prevention, Detection, Evaluation, and Treatment of High Blood Pressure issued its first report establishing the guideline of 120/80 mm Hg as optimal, 120–129/80–84 mm Hg as within the normal range, and 130–139/85–89 mm Hg as high normal. Then, in May 2003, it issued a new guideline stating that levels above 120/80 mm Hg constituted prehypertension and indicated increased risk for heart attack, stroke, or kidney disease. This new diagnostic entity was to be treated with the same methods as before—diet, exercise, and other lifestyle changes and, if these fail to do the trick, a diuretic. Critics argue that there is no randomized clinical trial evidence below 140 mm and suggest that the pharmaceutical industry, which might double its number of treatable patients, not only approved of the decision, but may have influenced it. They note that reducing salt intake will help some, but hinder others, and that treating blood pressure "by the numbers" is not good medicine, although it is tempting when a provider is pressed for time and faced with patients who expect a prescription. They point out that hypertension can have a number of causes and that it should be viewed as part of a "mosaic" of risk factors associated with cardiovascular care.

In November 2013, the American Heart Association and the American College of Cardiology issued a new set of joint guidelines for cholesterol treatment, calling for treatment for anyone with a 10-year risk factor for a cardiac event of 7.5% or more. The two organizations also issued a new risk calculator, a spreadsheet that considers age, race, cholesterol levels, blood pressure, and other factors. The risk calculator combined with the new threshold will result in a dramatic increase in the number of individuals that should be treated. The risk calculator came under immediate criticism because reviewers said the model overpredicted risk by 75% or more. The main complaint was that it relied on outdated demographic data.

Most of the public discussion focused on the use of statins to lower cholesterol, but treatment could also include prescribing drugs

(continues)

that lower blood pressure. Dr. H. Gilbert Welch, a Dartmouth medical professor, said the calculator treated the relationship between blood pressure and heart risk as if it was a straight line. "The model suggests that lowering systolic blood pressure from 130 to 100 is nearly as important as from 180 to 150," he told the *New York Times*. "I doubt there is a cardiologist that believes that" (Kolata, 2013).

A good classroom exercise would be to search out other newly emphasized conditions and track down their medical and commercial origins. You can start by turning on your television and noting all the ads for drugs that one must take regularly to suppress some distress such as acid reflux, erectile dysfunction, or insomnia.

especially on television, and the creation of new syndromes to justify new products, such as the hotly debated emergence of prehypertension.

In the United States, much debate centers on pharmaceutical industry advertising aimed directly at consumers, the cost of which ranges between $3 billion and $5 billion annually. Health care advertising, especially for prescription drugs, seems to have replaced all of the airtime and billboard space that had been taken up by cigarette and tobacco ads before they were banned. Are we that much better off from stopping one set of ads and substituting another? Other countries, including New Zealand, have barred this type of commercial activity.

Sterling offered a vision of a medically obsessed future in his novel *Holy Fire* (1996). In it, protagonist Mia Ziemann is 94 years old and still professionally active as a medical economist. In her world, wealth is all about how many medical procedures one can afford to extend one's longevity. The medical–industrial–research complex clearly dominates the entire economy, and young people are disenfranchised because employment opportunities rarely open through retirement or death. It is a disturbing vision, and yet one that is strangely familiar and highly plausible because Sterling draws on existing trends to shape his view of the late 21st century. Indeed, his major failing as a futurist may have been underestimating the rate of change.

CONCLUSION

Values are the fourth leg of the analyst's desk, working alongside technology, politics, and economics to support identifying a policy recommendation.

This chapter outlines a number of concerns that a policy analysis group must consider in addition to the other three as they factor in concern for the general welfare of our society and our democratic traditions. The issues of ethics and values are not just limited to professional decisions, but also play an important role in all analyses of policy alternatives.

| Case 12 | The Folic Acid Fortification Decision: Before and After |

BEFORE

At 5 p.m. on July 20, 1991, Dr. Godfrey P. Oakley, Jr., head of the Division of Birth Defects and Developmental Disabilities at the Centers for Disease Control and Prevention (CDC), took a phone call that, he says, "forever changed my life." On the phone was a member of the British Medical Research Council (MRC) Vitamin Study Group, calling to share study results that would be published the following month in *The Lancet* (SerVaas & Perry, 1999).

The MRC study focused on women who had previously had a pregnancy in which the fetus or child had a neural tube defect (NTD), a birth defect of the spinal cord or brain. In April 1991, the MRC halted its study after almost 8 years because the data indicated that daily folic acid supplementation before pregnancy and during early pregnancy resulted in a 71% reduction in the recurrence of NTDs (CDC, 1991). It was no longer ethical not to provide folic acid to all of the women.

Dr. Oakley told the Saturday Evening Post Society in 1999,

> Until that time, I thought that prevention of neural tube defects by taking folic acid supplementation was certainly no better than 50-50. If you really pressed me on what I would have thought the likelihood that a vitamin would have prevented neural tube defects, I would have said no more than 10% or 20%. But this was the first randomized, controlled trial designed and executed in a way that it proved folic acid would prevent spina bifida—not all but most of it. You could bet the farm that folic acid prevents neural tube defects. (SerVaas & Perry, 1999, p. 3)

The study ignited a policy debate lasting several years. In the United States, the question of how to increase folic acid consumption in woman

Case 12   (*continued*)

of child-bearing years was contentious in itself, but the issue was complicated further by the controversy that surrounded implementation of the Nutrition Labeling and Education Act (NLEA) of 1990, which required the Food and Drug Administration (FDA) to regulate the health claims of food manufacturers.

Among the tools policy makers had to help them sift through their options were three economic analyses: cost–benefit analyses produced in 1993 and 1995 and a cost-effectiveness analysis completed in 1996. All three predicted positive net economic benefits from fortifying foods with folic acid.

BACKGROUND

NTDs are a class of birth defects that involve the brain and spinal cord. The most extreme form is anencephaly, in which all or part of the brain is missing. Another form is spina bifida, in which the spinal cord is not fully encased in the spine. In the early 1990s, there were about 4,000 NTD-associated pregnancies per year in the United States.

Folates are a form of B vitamin that occurs naturally in leafy vegetable, legumes, nuts, and other foods. Folic acid is its synthetic form. Folates help cells replicate quickly.

Reports that increased folic acid intake could help prevent birth defects date back to 1965 (Hibbard & Smithells, 1965). Vitamin manufacturers learned how to add it to their supplements in the 1970s. The Saturday Evening Post Society launched its campaign to promote folic acid supplementation in October 1982 in the wake of a report that women who took a vitamin supplement with 400 mcg of folic acid experienced fewer NTD-affected pregnancies. In the late 1980s, the CDC held a workshop to discuss emerging research linking folic acids to reductions in the numbers of NTDs, which renewed interest among supplement manufacturers.

Support for folic acid was limited, however. *Post* writers Cory SerVaas and Pat Perry (1999) reported that they were ridiculed for their efforts to promote folic acid. Scientific evidence was sparse, inconclusive, and based on observational epidemiological studies. Around the time of the CDC workshop, in fact, the National Research Council advised the FDA that it should lower the recommended daily allowance. A 1990 report by the Institute of Medicine's Food and Nutrition Board called taking vitamin supplements to prevent NTDs "unjustified." The National Academy of Sciences also discounted the link between NTDs and folic acid in its 1990 *Report on Nutrition and Pregnancy*.

In the midst of this debate, the NLEA skated through Congress and was signed by President George H. W. Bush. The act directed the FDA to establish standards for nutrition labels and define how certain terms such as "low fat" and "low cholesterol" could be used on food packaging. Congress also directed the FDA to investigate 10 specific health claims and develop language food manufacturers could use to convey any valid claims on their packaging. One of those claims was that folic acid reduced the risk of neural tube defects. The FDA was hard at work on its proposed rules when *The Lancet* published the MRC study (MRC Vitamin Study Research Group, 1991).

The study involved more than a thousand women in 33 centers across 17 countries. Researchers divided the subjects into four groups. Those in the first group received 400 mcg of folic acid. Those in the second group received the same amount of folic acid plus a multivitamin supplement. Those in the third group received neither the multivitamin supplement nor folic acid, and those in the final group received only the multivitamins. NTDs recurred 1% of the time when mothers received folic acid, with or without other vitamins, and 3.5% of the time when they received nothing or only the multivitamin supplement.

The MRC study did not settle the debate. It investigated women who had already had a NTD-associated pregnancy and therefore might be predisposed to having another; the results were not necessarily applicable to the general population. An FDA-contracted study released in November 1991 said it was not possible to positively conclude that folic acid prevented NTDs, but it criticized the Institute of Medicine and National Academy of Sciences reports. FDA draft rules issued later that month rejected claims that high-folate foods prevented NTDs, but it called its conclusion "tentative" and left open the possibility of further review.

The CDC, however, was less equivocal. At a 1991 conference on "Vitamins, Spina bifida, and Anencephaly," participants generally accepted the notion that women who were pregnant or might become pregnant required more folic acid. They began to wrestle with what FDA Commissioner David Kessler would call "one of the most difficult issues" of his tenure—exactly how to go about providing that folic acid.

Case 12   (*continued*)

ALTERNATIVES

There were only a few ways to ingest more folic acid at the time: consume more foods naturally high in folates, take vitamin supplements, take folic acid pills, or eat fortified foods. Each option brought its own challenges. Working against the natural nutritionists was the fact that natural folates have lower bioavailability than folic acid and break down during cooking. A typical U.S. woman ingests only 25 mcg of naturally occurring folates daily, and thus it is hard to envision women ingesting 400 mcg through dietary changes.

At the time, folic acid by itself was only available in a 100-microgram prescription formulation. The level of folic acid in most multivitamin supplements was so low that a woman trying to hit the 400-microgram target would have to ingest toxic levels of other vitamins. One option was to make folic acid more readily available in larger doses. Another was to reformulate multivitamins. Both options suffered from the same problem: Only periconceptional intake (ingestion before pregnancy and during the first few weeks after conception) is effective; yet roughly half of all pregnancies occur without early prenatal care. You would have to convince all women to take pills to supplement their folic acid intake throughout their childbearing years or risk missing more than half the pregnancies.

That left the possibility of fortification (adding a nutrient to food that does not otherwise contain it). This approach would reach everyone, including all women who are or might soon become pregnant. Food fortification and enrichment (increasing the levels of a nutrient already in a food) has a long history in the United States, beginning in 1924 with the decision to add iodine to salt to prevent goiter and other iodine-deficiency disorders. Vitamin D was added to milk in the 1930s (much later, vitamin A was added to low-fat dairy products). Flours and bread have been enriched with various nutrients—1938 through 1942 saw the addition of thiamine, niacin, riboflavin, and iron.

Four hundred micrograms of folic acid, however, struck many as a pharmacological dose. Best-selling longevity authors Durk Pearson and Sandy Shaw said fortification was equivalent to medicating competent adults without informed consent (Junod, 2006). Scientists worried about adverse reactions. One known issue was that folic acid at daily doses of a microgram or more could mask vitamin B_{12} deficiency, particularly among the older population, prompting some scientists to worry that fortification would simply shift risks from developing embryos to adults with pernicious anemia (Gaull et al., 1996).

SUPPORT BUILDS

Fortification gained adherents after the MRC study appeared and supporters' ranks swelled as people became aware of two studies, as yet unpublished, conducted on women with no history of NTD-affected births. One, conducted in Hungary by Andrew Czeizel and his colleagues, showed benefits in the general population from consuming 800 mcg per day. Another, the "Werler study," studied women in Boston, Philadelphia, and Toronto. Although Werler and her colleagues recommended 400 mcg daily, they found that even 250 mcg offered some protection. In May 1992, Dr. Walter C. Willet argued in an *American Journal of Public Health* editorial that "fortification should be the long term goal" (Junod, 2006).

NEW PUBLIC RECOMMENDATION

In September 1992, the U.S. Public Health Service announced that women of child-bearing age should get 400 mcg of folic acid every day, a decision touted by the CDC but soft-pedaled by the FDA and the National Institutes of Health (Palca, 1992). The announcement did nothing to satisfy the two policy questions in the FDA's lap: whether to allow food products to promote their folic acid levels on their labels and whether to require that certain foods be fortified with folic acid.

Amid safety concerns, the FDA's folic acid advisory committee recommended against a folic acid health claim after a November 1992 meeting. In early 1993, the FDA, working under tight deadlines, adopted an NLEA rule that reflected this position and disallowed a health claim; however, the committee expressed an interest in fortification, and it reconvened in April 1993 to look at a variety of unresolved issues, including fortification. By October, the FDA had reversed its position, publishing a draft rule that would allow health claims for foods containing folic acid. There were many aspects of the rule, but its core was a provision that would allow health claims for foods that contained 40 mcg or more of folic acid per serving. On December 31, 1993, the rule became final.

Case 12   *(continued)*

The October 1993 draft rule had contained provisions about fortification, but fortification was not mandated as part of the New Year's
Eve ruling. The FDA and its folic acid advisory committee continued to
struggle with a variety of implementation questions.

COST–BENEFIT ANALYSIS

Federal agencies are required to conduct regulatory impact analyses as
part of rulemaking and starting in 1993 were required to assess expected
costs and benefits of significant rules. FDA staff conducted a CBA and
estimated that fortification with 140 mcg of folic acid per 100 grams
of cereal grain products would prevent 116 NTD-affected births per
year. This analysis tallied direct savings, notably medical care avoided,
and estimated a savings of $5 million for each case averted, resulting
in economic benefits of $651–786 million annually. The annual cost of
fortification would be $27 million, and thus the annual net economic
benefit would be $624–750 million (FDA, 1993).

In 1995, University of California researchers published a second
CBA. They estimated that 304 NTD-associated births would be avoided
through fortification. Using a different method that looked at lost productivity, they put the value of a case avoided at $342,500. The eco-
nomic benefit came in at $121.5 million. From this, the researchers
deducted not only the cost of fortification, which they put at $11 mil-
lion, but the cost of adverse events—namely 500 cases of neurological
damage annually at a cost of $16.4 million. Their calculations resulted
in an estimated net benefit from fortification of $93.6 million (Romano,
Waltzman, & Scheffler, 1995).

These two studies were before the advisory committee as it debated
folic acid implementation, and they played a role in shaping the draft
folic acid fortification rule published on March 5, 1996. A third analysis, published by the CDC that same year, was not influential. The CDC
estimated 89 averted NTDs at a total benefit of $16.1 million annually.
That was largely offset by the $11 million cost of fortification and an
estimated $350,000 in health costs related to 89 cases of neurological
damage. That left a net benefit of $4.7 million.

The FDA ultimately adopted a rule requiring fortification of cereal
grain products with 140 mcg of folic acid for every 100 grams of grain.

The rule went into effect on January 1, 1998. Between October 1998 and December 1999, the prevalence of reported cases of spina bifida declined 31%. Anencephaly declined 16%. Various studies over the years have put the total reduction of cases of spina bifida and anencephaly at 20–30%, much more than were reflected in the three ex ante economic analyses. (Not all of the improvement can be attributed to fortification, because women of childbearing age can expect to get only about a quarter of their recommended intake of 400 mcg through fortified grains, and public education campaigns continue to promote consumption of folic acid through vitamin pills.) **Figure 12-1** shows the type of product labeling allowed with folate-fortified products.

Nutrition Facts

Serving Size 1 cup (228g)
Servings Per Container 2

Amount Per Serving	
Calories 250	Calories from Fat 110

	% Daily Value*
Total Fat 12g	18%
Saturated Fat 3g	15%
Cholesterol 30mg	10%
Sodium 470mg	20%
Total Carbohydrate 31g	10%
Dietary Fiber 0g	0%
Sugar 5g	
Protein 5g	

Vitamin A	4%
Vitamin C	2%
Calcium	20%
Iron	4%
Folate	30%

*Percent Daily Values are based on a 2,000 calorie diet. Your Daily Values may be higher or lower depending on your calorie needs:

	Calories:	2,000	2,500
Total Fat	Less than	65g	80g
Sat Fat	Less than	20g	25g
Cholesterol	Less than	30mg	300mg
Sodium	Less than	2,400mg	2,400mg
Total Carbohydrates		300g	375g
Dietary Fiber		25g	30g

Supplement Facts

Serving Size: 1 tablet

Amount Per Serving		% Daily Value
Vitamin A	5000IU	100
Vitamin C	60mg	100
Vitamin D	400 IU	100
Vitamin E	30 IU	100
Thiamin	1.5mg	100
Riboflavin	1.7mg	100
Niacin	20mg	100
Vitamin B6	2mg	100
Folic Acid	400mcg	100
Vitamin B12	6mcg	100
Biotin	30mcg	10
Pantothenic Acid	10mg	100
Calcium	162mg	16
Iron	18mg	100
Iodine	150mcg	100
Magnesium	100mg	25
Zinc	15mg	100
Selenium	20mcg	100
Copper	2mg	100
Manganese	3.5mg	175
Chromium	65mcg	54
Molybdenum	150mcg	200
Chloride	72mg	2
Potassium	80mg	2

Figure 12-1 Two labels ("nutrition facts" for foods and "supplement facts" for vitamin supplements) showing how regulations allow display of folate content.
Source: Courtesy of the Office on Women's Health at the U.S. Department of Health and Human Services

THE RESULTS COME IN

Studies in Chile and Canada also reported the effectiveness of folate fortification programs. Canada mandated 150 mcg per 100 grams in

| Case 12 | (*continued*) |

1998; Chile required 220 mcg per 100 grams in 2000. Three Canadian population-based studies showed reductions in the incidence of NTD-related births of 50%, 54%, and 43%, respectively. A single study in Chile included measures of increased folate blood levels from fortification and reported a 43% reduction in the NTD rate within 6 months. Differences among these studies included differences in fortification levels and differences in measurement and reporting regarding the inclusion or exclusion of stillbirths and terminated pregnancies.

The CDC published a before and after epidemiological study in 2004 that reported that surveillance-based population studies from 1995 and 1996 (prefortification) and 1999 and 2000 showed a reduction in the estimated number of NTD-affected pregnancies from 4,000 to 3,000. These results are summarized in **Table 12-4**. An editorial note in the *Morbidity and Mortality Weekly Report* (*MMWR*) noted that a 26% reduction was somewhat less than earlier studies had indicated and short of the national goal of a reduction of 50% (CDC, 2004).

In 2005, Grosse and colleagues published an ex post economic study of fortification in the United States. It estimated 520 averted cases of spina bifida and 92 cases of averted anencephaly annually, which led to economic benefits per case of $636,000 and $1,020,000, respectively. That translated into $425 million in economic benefits ($146 million in direct costs, mostly medical) against an annual cost of fortification of $3 million. The authors did not identify any documented adverse health effects from fortification.

This study used a 3% discount rate but noted that Office of Management and Budget guidelines called for comparisons using both 3% and 7% discount rates (at least one ex ante study had used a 5% rate). Of the $636,000 savings per spina bifida case avoided, the study reported, $279,000 was direct costs, mostly medical, with the rest apparently indirect costs for nonmedical caregiving. For the anencephaly cases, almost all of the $1,020,000 in costs were indirect. In addition to the required 3% and 7% discount rate comparisons, the authors performed sensitivity analyses with only 80% of the cases avoided attributed to folate fortification and with a doubling of the fortification costs. Then they developed a worst-case scenario that assumed only 80% of the observed benefits attributed to the intervention, a doubling of the cost of fortification, and a $25 million allowance for the potential effects of

Table 12-4 Estimated Average Annual Numbers of Spina Bifida and Anencephaly Cases Based on Prevalence per 10,000 Live Births from Surveillance Systems—United States 1995–1996 and 1999–2000

	Systems with Prenatal Ascertainment		Systems Without Prenatal Ascertainment		Fetal Deaths and Elective Terminations
Prefortification	Prevalence	No.	Prevalence	No.	No.
Spina bifida	6.4	2,490	5.1	1,980	
Anencephaly	4.2	1,640	2.5	970	
Total		**4,130**		**2,950**	**1,180**
Postfortification	Prevalence	No.	Prevalence	No.	No.
Spina bifida	4.1	1,640	3.4	1,340	
Anencephaly	3.5	1,380	2.1	840	
Total		**3,020**		**2,180**	**840**

For systems with prenatal ascertainment, estimated total pregnancies included live births, stillbirths, prenatally diagnosed cases, and elective terminations. For systems without prenatal ascertainment*, estimates included live births, stillbirths, and fetal deaths through 20 weeks. Fetal deaths and elective terminations were calculated as difference between systems with and without prenatal ascertainment. The numbers of NTD-affected pregnancies and births were determined as prevalence multiplied by the average total number of U.S. births during the respective periods, as derived from the U.S National Vital Statistics System.

*Programs with prenatal ascertainment use specific case-finding techniques to identify prenatally diagnosed and electively terminated cases.

Source: Modified from: Centers for Disease Control and Prevention. (2004). Spina bifida and anencephaly before and after folic acid mandate: United States, 1995–1996 and 1999–2000. *MMWR*, 53, 362–365. Accessed December 11, 2013, at www.cdc.gov/mmwr/preview /mmwrhtml/mm5317a3.htm.

neurological damage from untreated anemia. This worst-case scenario still yielded annual net direct benefits of $88 million after expenditures of $6 million on fortification and an overall benefit of $312 million. The authors observed that the benefits were exceptionally large and noted that "few public health interventions beyond immunization and injury prevention are cost saving."

Hertkampf (2004) estimated that in Chile the fortification process cost approximately $280,000 annually. For spina bifida, she estimated the cost of surgery and rehabilitation for each of the 110 cases avoided annually at $100,000. She noted that bread is more of a staple of the Chilean diet. Commenting on the low priority given to folate fortification in most developing countries, she noted that prevalence data are

Case 12   (*continued*)

lacking and that NTDs are not recognized as an important cause of morbidity and mortality.

A meta-analysis of eight population-based studies found that folic acid food fortification reduced the incidence of NTDs by 46% (Blencowe et al., 2010). The authors estimated that in low-income countries, fortification could reduce the number of neonatal deaths stemming from congenital abnormalities by 13%.

NEW CONCERNS ABOUT ADVERSE EFFECTS OF HIGH DOSAGES

The earlier concerns about the masking of B_{12} deficiencies in the elderly have not been supported with reported cases. New concerns, however, surfaced by 2007 about the impact of high doses of folates on colorectal cancer (CRC). Animal studies suggested that high doses led to two conflicting effects. Doses higher than those normally introduced by fortification protected against the onset of CRCs, but also seemed to stimulate the growth rates of existing neoplasms. These observations, reported by Mason et al. in 2007, were not followed up by randomized controlled trials, which led the British Scientific Advisory Council on Nutrition (SACN) to report in January 2008, "The evidence for an association between folic acid and increased or reduced cancer risk is equivocal."

A 2009 report on two Norwegian clinical trials with high doses of folic acid and vitamin B_{12} in patients with ischemic heart disease showed significant increases in overall cancer rates (Ebbing et al., 2009). However, folic acid was considered to have a preventive effect toward heart disease and stroke (Wang et al., 2007).

Vollset and colleagues (2013) conducted a meta-analysis that examined 13 randomized trials of people taking folic acid supplements. The studies were all conducted before 2011 and combined they enrolled almost 50,000 subjects. No significant effects were found with regard to folic acid supplementation on the incidence of cancer of the large intestine, prostate, lung, breast, or any significant site. The authors noted that folic acid dosages in the study were an order of magnitude greater than intake from fortified food.

A CDC-sponsored study (Crider, Bailey, & Berry, 2011) that reviewed concerns about adverse effects found no evidence that fortification masked or exacerbated neuropathies related to anemia. It found no increase in cancer; no definitive studies showing adverse health effects from exposure to unmetabolized folic acid; and no evidence that folic acid was leading to epigenetic changes in human DNA. The researchers concluded, however, that future hypotheses addressing concerns about epigenetic changes would have to be explored. Crider and colleagues noted that careful monitoring of existing and proposed programs was needed to allow the scientific community to determine the blood folate concentrations required for NTD prevention as well as to evaluate and respond appropriately to concerns that may arise.

FORTIFICATION IN OTHER COUNTIES

To date, more than 50 countries have adopted mandatory fortification, but many of the programs have yet to be implemented (Crider et al., 2011). A number of English-speaking countries are considering a mandate at the recommendation of food safety agencies, but for a variety of reasons only Australia has completed its implementation.

Australia and New Zealand

Mandatory fortification of bread began in Australia in September 2009. Voluntary fortification had been allowed for more than 10 years. Food Standards Australia New Zealand (FSANZ) recommended mandatory fortification of bread in 2007 following an extensive review begun in 2004. The recommendation triggered a public comment period followed by approval of the Australia and New Zealand Food Regulation Ministerial Council, which is made up of the food and health ministers of the two countries. A 12-month phase-in period was to follow. FSANZ (2009) anticipated that a mandate would avoid about 14–48 of the 300–350 NTD-affected pregnancies that occur annually in Australia. New Zealand, however, put the plan on hold after a media campaign against fortification by bakers increased public concern about the proposed fortification. In August 2012, the New Zealand government announced that fortification would remain voluntary, with the goal of half of all bread products to be fortified eventually.

Case 12 (*continued*)

Ireland's Plans Derailed

In 1990, Ireland had one of the highest rates of NTDs in Europe, with 10–15 NTDs per 10,000 live births. Voluntary fortification and nutritional education were only marginally successful, so in 2002 the Department of Health turned to the Food Safety Authority of Ireland (FSAI). In 2003, FSAI recommended fortification, and the health minister established a National Committee on Folic Acid Food, which consulted the parties involved and in July 2006 recommended mandatory fortification. An Implementation Group on Folic Acid Fortification was formed with the expectation of final implementation. In 2008, however, the implementation group reported that folic acid intake by woman of childbearing age had increased 30% as a result of voluntary fortification, and the incidence of NTDs had been reduced to 9.3 per 10,000 live births. Although Ireland's daily folic acid intake of 90 mcg is well below international targets and other countries are achieving a much lower rate of NTD-associated births (5–6 per 10,000 live births), the group concluded that mandatory fortification would be of limited public health benefit at that time, although the decision is subject to future reconsideration.

Meanwhile, Back in the U.K.

The U.K. Food Standards Agency (FSA) first discussed the issue of fortification in 2002 amid concerns about possible risks to the health of older people. Then the Scientific Advisory Committee on Nutrition (SACN), an independent expert panel, reviewed the evidence and tracked the emerging science. SACN issued a November 2005 draft report (the final report was released in December 2006) that recommended mandatory fortification of flour, and in April 2006, the FSA agreed to consider four options for improving folate levels in young women:

- Do nothing.
- Increase efforts to encourage young women to change their diets and take supplements.
- Further encourage voluntary fortification of foods.
- Implement mandatory fortification of "the most appropriate food vehicle."

The FSA consulted with consumers, stakeholders, and industry in early 2007. A SACN briefing paper issued in January 2008 recommended fortification of flour but also called for the establishment of baselines for folic acid intake and folate concentrations in the blood so future surveillance programs could identify trends. It also called for standardized testing protocols (SACN, 2008).

In 2009, SACN concluded that there was not sufficient data to support concerns about cancer, and it reconfirmed its recommendation in support of mandatory fortification. The four chief medical officers for the U.K. then recommended mandatory fortification to the four health ministers.

CONCLUSION

Mandatory fortification with folic acid is established practice in the United States and voluntary or mandatory fortification has been introduced in more than 50 countries worldwide as a strategy to help women of childbearing age increase their intake of folate. In countries where it has been implemented, it dramatically reduced NTD-associated births. So far, no European country has adopted *mandatory* folic acid fortification. Voluntary fortification is widely practiced in the European Union under regulation 1925/2006/EC, which allows the fortification of all foods except unprocessed foods and alcoholic beverages. Foods fortified with folic acid are widely available on the European market, except in Sweden, where fortification is not practiced, and in Denmark and Norway, which require approval. The range of product categories that are fortified on a voluntary basis includes dairy products, breakfast cereals, cereal bars, fruit juices, fat spreads, bread, and beverages. Maximum levels for the addition of folic acid to foods are not yet set in European regulations. The levels vary widely, with the highest levels added to spreads. Further use of fortification around the world, including in poorer nations, could dramatically reduce the global burden of NTDs.

Discussion Questions

1. Describe the authorizing environment for folic acid fortification in the United States.

2. Why would a decision based on strong British studies influence the U.S. decision to fortify cereal products but yield a delayed response in the U.K.?

3. Contrast and compare the variables and their values used in the before and after CBA studies. What conclusions would you draw from them about that approach in this case? In general?

Chapter 13

Implementation Strategy and Planning

Health care delivery, like politics, is mostly local. No matter how good the policy analysis process, the policy selected as a result of that process will fail unless it elicits the support of its local implementers. Health-related activities exhibit deeply contrasting tendencies: health care processes are slow to change in some areas, yet the pace of change is rapid in other areas. Some argue that the adoption of new technologies is driving up costs, whereas others argue that failure to adopt new technology is partly responsible for escalating costs. Christensen, Bohmer, and Kenagy (2000) used the health care industry as an example of the need for disruptive technology to come in and overcome inertia. Their model applies very well in some areas, such as health information technology, but not in others, such as noninvasive surgery.

Dopson and Fitzgerald (2005) edited a book about the "implementation gap" for evidence-based health care in Britain's National Health Service, where centralization of management and financing would seem to create a more fertile environment for change. In a chapter contributed by Dopson and his colleagues (Dopson et al., 2005), the authors pointed out that failure to achieve goals that had been carefully planned has a long history in public policy analysis. Implementation failures could be explained as political bargaining as usual at a micro level; however, empirical studies suggest that implementation is a separate stage of the change process (Torenvlied & Thomson, 2003).

The policy process must consider how to implement a policy decision and how to promote that implementation. The Australian government considers implementation so important that it established a Cabinet Implementation Unit in late 2003 within the Department of the Prime Minister and Cabinet.

The White House might want to consider a similar unit after the Obama administration's experience with the 2013–2014 rollout of the Web-based insurance exchanges. One can make a substantial list of the basic requirements of effective program implementation that were violated in that process.

LEVELS OF IMPLEMENTATION FAILURE

There can be many reasons for a policy to be adopted but not implemented. Sometimes plans are unrealistic. Sometimes there is a failure to execute critical elements of a plan, whereas other plans are foiled by much more subtle (all too human) resistance. Still others are simply overtaken by events—wars, budget crises, changes of government, competing technologies, or differing ideologies. Many social programs started at the federal level with great effort and then failed in the field over time. McLaughlin (1984), noting how often legislators develop and adopt social programs that miss their intended objectives, observed:

> It is sometimes tragicomic to read the laws of entitlement, such as the one guaranteeing equality of education for the handicapped and exceptional children, and then see how they work out in group homes, classrooms and clinics. Some have blamed public parsimony. Others would cite professional narrowness, individual insensitivity, and bureaucratic myopia. But much of the blame falls on the haste with which public policy is adopted, implemented, and then displaced by new policy. (p. 83)

The "deinstitutionalization" effort of the 1970s is a good example of failure to execute. After early antipsychotic drugs became available, the inpatient populations of psychiatric hospitals began to decline. Community mental health centers created to serve people released from mental institutions were up and running in many areas. Medicaid and Medicare provided some funding, but despite promises to transfer budgetary resources that had previously gone into psychiatric hospitals to these centers and other community organizations, the funding never arrived in sufficient amounts to provide both direct care and supportive services such as housing and employment training. An entire new population of homeless individuals appeared in our cities, and the terms *revolving door* and *bag lady* entered the public vocabulary. Hospitals and community centers did not provide coordinated care; they were often separate systems that competed for the same resources. Furthermore, many community mental health centers drifted away from the goal of supporting deinstitutionalization of the mentally ill and began serving a much broader spectrum of patients. As Torrey (1997) noted, "Once trained, however, the vast majority of these professionals decide to provide psychotherapy for people with mental health problems rather than treat people who were mentally ill" (p. 185). It is not easy to keep well-intentioned policies from going off the tracks. As the saying goes, "The devil is in the details."

IMPLEMENTATION PLANNING

Implementation planning arrives early and stays late. It is important to involve all stakeholders, including the implementers. An Australian Cabinet Implementation Unit process guide referred to two implementation processes: (1) implementation assessment, which contributes to the documentation that accompanies the submission of a proposal to the cabinet, and (2) implementation planning, which continues that process in much greater detail once the decision is final. **Figure 13-1** outlines the stages of the Australian cabinet's implementation planning process. Several topics discussed below—scope, funding, risk management, and schedule (which is discussed as part of the work breakdown)—may also be inputs, alongside program objectives, outcomes, and governance considerations connected to the strategic decision-making process.

Scope

Policy making is an art, and the "who, what, where, when, and how" may be changed either subtly or substantially. Implementers must be aware of what was actually approved. There is a saying that the camel was intended to be a horse, but it was designed by a committee. Note the result: the camel is highly adapted to its environment, but it is something quite different from a horse. Consequently, it needs a very different management approach to operate it and evaluate its ultimate performance.

In the latter stages of implementation, it is important to establish lines of authority and accountability for implementation and to consider how the effort interacts with other initiatives and programs already under way.

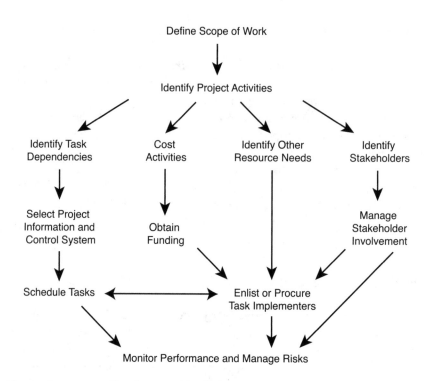

Figure 13-1 Stages of implementation planning.

It is also important to consider whether the new policy can be implemented effectively using existing organizational structures, management systems, and funding approaches or whether there is a need to establish a new structure designed to deliver the changed output.

Work Breakdown

This stage is a detailed analysis of the tasks generated by the implementation requirements of the policy. Political decision makers are likely to establish important dates (milestones) for implementation, dates that may or may not be achievable. Then the implementing organization must get to work:

- Identifying the tasks to be performed, such as submitting a detailed budget, hiring personnel, finding office space, issuing rules and regulations, establishing advisory committees, and specifying reporting requirements

- Identifying the units and individuals responsible for each task and gaining their commitment to complete the task within a specific time period
- Establishing reporting responsibilities for the status of each task
- Including coordination tasks as well as intradepartmental tasks
- Developing a master schedule and an estimated time of completion for the project along with mechanisms for monitoring progress

Depending on the complexity and urgency of the project, the project implementation staff may choose to use any one of a number of project management techniques and their associated software to show what the resulting project duration will be and whether the original target is likely to be met. If not, implementation planners may decide to undertake a number of efforts to "crash" the project in order to remain on schedule.[1] This process works best when the estimate of how long an activity will take comes from the individual or team that will be responsible for that activity. This encourages participants to make realistic estimates and then commit to meeting their own estimates. For example, the Obama administration shortened the testing period for the insurance exchanges and failed to have top-level oversight of the process to determine whether this mission-critical system was up to its assigned tasks.

Funding

Few proposals get considered without a cost figure attached; however, additional steps related to funding may need to be taken once that figure is approved. Congress authorizes many more initiatives than it funds. For example, in 1998, Congress passed and President Clinton signed the Ricky Ray Hemophilia Relief Act, which authorized a compassionate payment of $100,000 to each hemophiliac infected between 1982 and 1987 from contaminated blood products, or to their families if they had died. This was to compensate for lax government control of the blood supply. The authorization bill did not include the funding required, estimated to be $750 million. Only after considerable effort by advocacy groups was $75 million appropriated in fiscal year 2000, $100 million in fiscal year 2002, and $475 million in other years. By the time the program was terminated in 2005, $559 million had been dispersed.

---

[1]Many systems for project planning and scheduling are available, including the Critical Path Method (CPM) and the Program Evaluation and Review Technique (PERT). These methods enable staff to build a feasible schedule and to track performance, updating that schedule as the effort moves along. Microsoft Project is one such program that is usually readily available.

Risk Management

The Australian *Guide to Preparing Implementation Plans* states the following:

> By understanding the potential risks which may affect the implementation of a policy measure, agencies can reduce the likelihood or consequence of "unpleasant surprises" that may jeopardise the achievement of policy objectives." (Cabinet Implementation Unit, 2006, p. 23)

It suggests that likely risks include

- Unclear objectives and deliverables
- Unrealistic schedules
- Shortages of key resources—funds, people, equipment
- Lack of infrastructure and supports
- Lack of agency internal capacity

Whatever the risk, the planning process needs to assess the likelihood that it will occur, its severity and impact, how to mitigate it, and who is responsible for preventive measures. It also needs to address monitoring and how to initiate any needed actions. In situations of high uncertainty and high impact, such as national security intelligence, analysts are now required to report their estimates of their certainty regarding their findings.

One way for implementers to ensure that they will be able to respond to changing conditions is to keep the planning flexible. How does a plan stay flexible?

- By not getting too detailed too early
- By not planning to use the available resources up to their limit
- By checking in with all implementers from time to time to see if anything has changed
- By having the periodic reviews to allow other parts of the plan to adjust to the "as built" changes that naturally occur
- By making sure the staff knows from the start that there will probably be changes

This does not mean that the planning is not complete. However, it does mean that there are contingencies built in and that the people on the job are prepared to respond to unexpected situations as they arise.

Stakeholder Engagement

Implementation must include a review of the stakeholders, including the following:

- Who needs to be kept informed?
- Who needs to participate in what detailed planning activities?
- Who can be an opinion leader or champion of the program?
- Who needs further training and motivation?
- Who can be an enabler?
- Who can be a blocker and needs to be co-opted?

Then, as **Table 13-1** illustrates, implementation planners must identify the type of commitment needed from the implementation stakeholder, how to secure it, key messages that need to be delivered, and who is responsible for the relationship. Decisions about how to deliver the message and maintain the relationship follow. Should it be delivered personally, by email, through the media, through a representative, and so on? After those coordination and communication tasks are identified, they can be scheduled and assigned to someone.

It often is best to approach this work with stakeholders as meaningful consultation and collaboration. This can make initial implementation easier because stakeholders who feel that their ideas have been considered and their concerns addressed are less likely to try to subvert the process. Chances of success over time are greater if the people and organizations affected by the project recognize its value and are invested in its success. There will be times, though, when an implementing agency is given a mandate to implement a policy change on a specific timeline over the objections of important stakeholders, and this may force the implementation planners to develop a policy for "stakeholder management"—a term that is in disfavor but may be apt in such circumstances.

You may recall from discussions of evaluating political feasibility that most techniques involve collecting information from stakeholders. That

Table 13-1 Communications Strategy Tool

Key Stakeholder	Desired Commitment and Strategy for Securing Commitment	Key Messages That Need to Be Delivered	Responsible Officer

Source: Reproduced from: *Guide to Implementation Planning*. Licensed from the Commonwealth of Australia under Creative Commons Attribution 3.0 Australia License. © Commonwealth of Australia 2005.

is why the most popular framework for determining political feasibility is called "stakeholder analysis." Political feasibility inquiries can yield a lot of information that can be very important during the implementation process. If Delphi processes, key informant interviews, or other stakeholder outreach efforts were part of a feasibility evaluation prior to policy adoption, then implementers should review that material. Even if they feel they know the material, it could be helpful to turn to it with a fresh eye. A stakeholder concern that was not enough to prevent a policy's adoption, for example, could frustrate or even derail that same policy's implementation. Implementers might also consider employing such processes after the fact as part of their stakeholder engagement practices.

Resources, Including Sourcing and Procurement

Key resource needs should have been identified by this point in time because the funding requirements depend on the resources needed, especially personnel, equipment, and support systems. There may also be other less tangible resources that are mission critical, such as office space, computers and communication equipment, loaned personnel, and contractor personnel with special skills. For example, it is a frequent practice for contractors to assign their most competent personnel to preparing and marketing the proposal, but then substitute underutilized, less experienced, less skilled, or less costly personnel when the work gets under way. Implementation managers must stay alert to get the quality people and services that they expected originally.

Quality Assurance

The policy proposal usually specifies the quality and quantity of outcomes anticipated, and it may refer to the process and outcome measures to be used; however, implementation planners may still have to develop, validate, and install measures and measurement systems to monitor progress and suggest improvements as the implementation proceeds. When planning quality assurance measures, analysts should keep in mind the kinds of data, information, and documentation needed to conduct an evaluation after the policy has been implemented.

When it comes to sequencing these implementation activities, there is no magic order. After the proposal stage, many activities may have to go forward on parallel tracks, with the implementation team making adjustments as problems and opportunities are encountered. New technology or results from ongoing studies may lead to program changes after the policy makers have completed their work. If so, the implementation team should inform the policy makers of the change so that there will be no big surprises when the effort is being reviewed (e.g., during a site visit). The list of implementation activities is often quite detailed, and it is up to the implementation team to decide how much planning time to invest in each activity. The systems necessary to plan and monitor some of these stages may be in place already. The budgeting and scheduling functions should be basic management activities everywhere.

SETTING UP TO SUCCEED

Ample evidence suggests that implementation is enhanced by involving implementers early. This builds their commitment to the plan. Health care is going through a transition from a professional model that emphasizes individual responsibility, autonomy, and accountability toward an organizational one, hopefully one where organizational learning and transformation are norms. To succeed at implementation in this contentious environment, a number of things need to happen, including:

1. **Shared responsibility is accepted.** Team leaders and members at all professional levels must come to share overall responsibility while still accepting individual responsibility for assigned tasks. The industrialization of health care often means that treatment processes are carried out by multiple actors whose actions must be coordinated.

2. **Leadership takes place at multiple levels.** The team involved in developing a policy must have facts about how the system works at the operational level as well as the strategic level. Many developing countries still suffer from the system developed by the British Colonial Office for managing the Empire. This consisted of mostly locals organized into two cadres: one, the civil service, developed policy, whereas the other, the health service, for example, implemented it. A small group of British officials controlled the flow of information from one to the other. The policy makers produced brilliant analyses that circulated in files held together with red ribbon (called *red tape* by the English), but these analyses often proved unworkable for implementers in the field. It was an efficient way to use a small expatriate staff, but it did not necessarily produce effective delivery systems. All too many policies and plans have become "shelf art," sitting there unused because implementers do not see them as practical or relevant.

THE ORIGIN OF A POLICY

The labor, delivery, recovery, and postpartum nursing team at a community hospital was reviewing its procedures and cost items in order to become more competitive in their city. One policy that puzzled team members was sending 100% of the placentas to the pathology laboratory after delivery. They kept asking around for the source of that rule and found that it stemmed from an incident many years earlier. At the time, the daughter of the chief of obstetrics was having a difficult delivery and encountered a problem that might have been handled more effectively if the placenta from her delivery had been saved and analyzed. The angry chief thoroughly chewed out the OB nursing staff for not saving it. To avoid such a confrontation in the future, the nursing supervisor instituted the rule that all placentas would go to pathology. Both the chief of obstetrics and the nursing supervisor had long since retired, but the rule lived on. The three obstetricians currently practicing at the hospital developed a set of criteria for sending placentas to the laboratory. This new rule decreased the number of pathology reviews of placentas by 95%, resulting in substantial cost savings to the patients and the hospital.

3. **People understand the core business and technical processes, values, and mission of the organization.** Participants must be knowledgeable and consistent in their decision making about policies and implementation. Policies and processes rarely bolt out of control. More typically, they silently drift away from the optimal as individuals and groups make incremental local adjustments in response to local events, stimuli, and experiences. The example in the box on pathology review of placentas illustrates how one process moved away from its appropriate levels.

4. **Expectations are managed.** Some participants will be optimistic and expect too much, whereas others will be pessimistic or cynical and expect too little. Wilson and McLaughlin (1984) suggested that one needs to work out a psychological contract with the planning participants, one that recognizes the scarcity of resources and directly addresses the WIIFM (what's in it for me?) question. **Table 13-2** outlines some of the factors such a psychological contract might consider. In essence, the contract would specify what each party gets from the exchange beyond monetary considerations.

Table 13-2 The Psychological Contract

The Employee Gets

Performance standards that represent realistic trade-offs between funds, personnel, schedules, and service levels

Personal courtesy and respect

A supportive environment

Meaningful and purposeful work

Reasonable conflict and tension levels, mediated by clear standards for priority setting and evaluation of work

Opportunities for personal development

Profession and organizational recognition for good work

Security, as long as funds are available

Process for psychological contract change processes that reflect changing resource conditions

Scarce resources

The Organization Gets

An honest day's work, at least

Loyalty to the organization

Initiative, especially in resource use

Job effectiveness and efficiency in meeting overall organizational goals

Flexibility and willingness to wear multiple hats under tight staffing

Acceptance of reasonable trade-offs among professional norms and organizational needs

Participation in psychological contract change processes that reflect changing resource conditions

Source: Reproduced from: Wilson, M., & C. P. McLaughlin. (1984). *Leadership and Management in Academic Medicine*, p. 310. Josey-Bass.

5. **Planning is continuous.** The health care environment is continuously changing. There are many more opportunities and challenges than most organizations can take on at any one time. Through functional and cross-functional teams, managers involve providers and others in setting priorities, developing and evaluating alternatives, and meeting the many new challenges.

6. **Orientations are prospective rather than retrospective.** Dopson and Fitzgerald (2005) and Senge and colleagues (1994) observed that behaviors and beliefs take time to change and require both abstract reasoning and experiential reinforcement. It is often easier to do things the way they have always been done. Looking to the past

for precedent is usually a rational step in assessing a situation, but there is little assurance that what an organization has been doing is effective or will be so in the future. "Transformational leadership continually brings forward the vision of the future organization and indicates how the organization can get from where it is in the present to where it wants to be in the future" (Upshaw, Steffen, & McLaughlin, 2013, pp. 293–294).

7. **Performance is assessed and rewarded.** Effective policy change requires that the organization be prepared to commit real resources and provide support mechanisms for recognizing creativity and innovation. Personnel evaluation processes and procedures must be in place to encourage implementers, as well as policy makers, to seek new ways to get things done and to prepare for the changing future.

THAT ALL-IMPORTANT START

Starting right is critical. If a team is involved, especially a multidisciplinary one (which would be the case for just about anything clinical), plan to offer leadership throughout the team formation cycle, which usually progresses through the following four stages:

1. Forming
2. Storming
3. Norming
4. Performing

Forming

The team needs to understand fully the factors behind the policy change and how it links to the institution's strategies. The team's initial efforts should be well supported and include tasks that are carefully chosen to build a shared experience of success. At this stage, the team must also consider whether it includes representation of all the important implementers.

Storming

Because health care settings are complex and have many built-in tensions, team members often start out blaming, finding fault, or expressing distrust of others. The team members have to be kept focused on their task until they begin to understand it and accept each other's viewpoints.

Norming

The group can then set up norms of operation, detailing, for example, how decisions are made and how work is allocated. Do we vote? Do we have to have a consensus? What do we have to clear with higher authority? Do some professional groups have veto power?

Performing

After the barriers at each of the preceding stages are dealt with, the team can get on with its assigned tasks effectively or, having addressed them and failed to get over them, seek further guidance or facilitation.

PROVIDING FOR PERIODIC REVIEWS

Major change projects often require that multiple teams go forward in parallel. Again, one or more of these may veer off on its own path, so it is important to stage periodic review sessions in which each team reports what it is doing, compares its progress against measures such as budget and schedule, and shares what implementation barriers it is experiencing. This process enables management to assess overall progress and make adjustments to the current plan where necessary. It also allows individual team leaders to see where they need to interface with other teams in order to meet their objectives and how to adjust their efforts to reflect what they learn at the review. The larger and more complex the project, the more important these periodic reviews become.

IMPLEMENTING POLICIES THAT AFFECT CLINICAL OPERATIONS

One of the more problematic areas for implementing policy involves getting professionals to change the way they carry out professional tasks. This has been a topic of concern to those who study quality of care, provide continuing professional education, or sell pharmaceuticals and other supplies to the health industry. The move toward greater use of evidence-based medicine is a case in point. For example, Dopson and Fitzgerald (2005) provided a meta-analysis of a number of studies of implementing evidence-based practices in the U.K. Health Service, in which the concluding summary by Ferlie (2005) emphasized the role of leadership, organizational support, and the differences between *knowledge* (i.e., information) and *practice*:

In the best case examples, there appeared to be a circular relationship between research evidence and experience—they reinforced each other and were woven together. At other times, there was a tension between craft knowledge and formal evidence. It should be remembered that clinical practice contains an element of judgment and tacit knowledge more reminiscent of craft skills than traditional conceptions of science. It may be unwise to force a stark choice between the two modes (experience or science), but there may be a need to balance both. (Ferlie, 2005, p. 188)

Paul Batalden at Dartmouth has suggested that professional training include a microsystem approach to continuous improvement in health care, operating alongside issues- and organization-centered efforts. Mohr and Batalden (2006) identified eight dimensions of an effective, improvement-oriented microsystem (a teaching clinic or hospital service):

1. Constancy of purpose
2. Investment in improvement
3. Alignment of role and training for efficiency and staff satisfaction
4. Interdependence of the care team to meet patient needs
5. Integration of information and technology into work flows
6. Ongoing measurement of outcomes
7. Support from the larger organization
8. Connection to the community to enhance care delivery and extend influence

THE POSTMORTEM

Assuming that the group doing the analysis and planning will do this kind of thing again, it is critical to review the group's own performance. This postproject analysis should be done by the planning group if the project is small or medium-sized, or by an independent evaluator if it is large or mission critical. Evaluation should study two aspects of the project: process and outcome. Process analysis should take place relatively quickly after the final report is delivered and should ask this question: "If we had to do this analysis again, what would we do differently?" Because this can be threatening interpersonally, a little humor would not hurt. The list of phases of a project in **Table 13-3** can be used to lighten things up a little and may also point out opportunities for improvement.

Clearly, one has to avoid using the postmortem merely to assign blame and to make sure that the accolades and rewards go to all those who really contributed to the process.

Table 13-3 A Little Humor Might Help: Six Phases of a Project

1. Enthusiasm
2. Frustration
3. Panic
4. Assigning blame
5. Punishing the innocent
6. Rewarding the noncontributors

Source: Reproduced from: W. A. Fischer, personal communication. Used with permission.

Outcomes assessment has to wait until the outcomes are evident. It can only be justified for major policy proposals that were actually implemented; otherwise, a second analysis might be needed to focus on what might have been done differently to get that proposal implemented. The failure to implement might be primarily due to outside factors. Either way, one should be able to go back through the analysis and see how well the group defined the situation, assessed the technology, outlined the economics, adjusted to the political system, planned the implementation, and presented the product to the decision makers. Such a review is a key to improved organizational learning about policy analysis.

CONCLUSION

There is no silver bullet to make implementation easy; however, the elements of successful implementation are well known. They involve top management consideration and support. They require an understanding of the social context in which change takes place. Would-be implementers must focus on the players, their roles, their barriers to action, and the roles of leadership and influencers in bringing about change. From an academic viewpoint, all of these should be worked out so that strategic policies are not derailed by the implementation details; however, decision makers are usually not comfortable with that level of detail as they deal broadly with a wide range of issues. They are very uncomfortable with surprises after the fact, but they also do not want to be bogged down reading the fine print. That is just a managerial reality. Perhaps the best answer is to turn to the experienced presenters on the team who know the behavior patterns of key decision makers and ask for their assessment of the appropriate level of detail to present at each stage.

| Case 13 | 340B Drug Pricing Program Oversight |

Section 602 of the Veterans Health Care Act of 1992 was titled "Limitations on Prices of Drugs Purchased by Certain Clinics and Hospitals." It amended the Public Health Services Act by adding a new section, Section 340B, to that act. Section 602 of the Veterans Health Care Act read in part:

> Part D of title III of the Public Health Service Act is amended by adding the following subpart: "SUBPART VII – DRUG PRICING AGREEMENTS" LIMITATION ON PRICES OF DRUGS PURHASED BY COVERED ENTITIES "Sec. 340B (a) Requirements for Agreement with Secretary – "(1) In general. The Secretary shall enter into an agreement with each manufacturer of covered drugs under which the amount required to be paid . . . to the manufacturer for covered drugs . . . does not exceed an amount equal to the average manufacturer price for the drug under title XIX of the Social Security Act in the preceding quarter, reduced by the rebate percentage described in paragraph (2). "Rebate percentage defined. – (A) In general. For a covered outpatient drug . . . the 'rebate percentage' is the amount equal to – "(i) the average total rebate required under Section 1927(c) of the Social Security Act . . . for a unit of the dosage form and strength involved during the preceding quarter divided by "(ii) the average manufacturer price for such a unit of the drug during such quarter. . . ."

Section 340B applied Medicaid drug discounts to drugs purchased for clinics that served many outpatients who were not eligible for Medicaid at qualified safety-net institutions. For the most part, eligible clinics were associated with hospitals receiving disproportionate share payments under Medicare, pediatric hospitals, and community health centers. Also included were specialized clinics and projects for HIV/AIDS, hemophilia, black lung, tuberculosis, and family planning, as well as those serving Native Americans and Native Hawaiians. Hospitals were required to be governmental or nonprofit with a contractual commitment to provide services supported by governments, have a disproportionate share percentage greater than 11.75, and not obtain the covered drugs through a group purchasing agreement. The drugs had to be used for patients of the covered entity and could not be resold.

A key provision of Section 340B read "(10) No prohibition on larger discount. Nothing in this subsection shall prohibit a manufacturer from charging a price for a drug that is lower than the maximum price that may be charged under paragraph (1)." The Patient Protection and Affordable Care Act (ACA or PPACA) increased the 340B discount to 13% on generic drugs and 23.1% on branded drugs. Specific discounts have been reported to range from 15–60% on prescription drugs. The law prohibits getting both a state Medicaid rebate and a 340B discount on a drug.

BACKGROUND

In the 1980s, Congress established a discount drug purchasing program for the Veterans Administration. In 1990, it extended this discount program to Medicaid purchases on behalf of low-income and uninsured enrollees under the Medicaid Drug Rebate Program. Soon it became clear that this law conflicted with another requirement that state Medicaid programs receive discounts matching the lowest prices offered in non-Medicaid markets. Congress moved to remedy this problem. Otherwise, the participating pharmaceutical and biotechnology companies would choose to stop offering discounts across the board.

The 340B program is administered by the Office of Pharmacy Affairs within Health Resources and Services Administration (HRSA) of the Department of Health and Human Service. This office is tasked with auditing compliance with program requirements, especially the eligibility of covered entities, and program integrity concerning diversions and duplicate discounts and manufacturer pricing. However, this office has a very limited staff, and the number of institutions taking advantage of the program has been growing rapidly. HRSA also supports a number of other programs, such as the Ryan White HIV/AIDS program and community and rural health centers that are covered entities for 340B drug discounts.

The HRSA website describes the intent of 340B in a listing of Frequently Asked Questions to be "to permit covered entities to stretch scarce Federal resources as far as possible, reaching more eligible patients and providing more comprehensive services" [HR Rep. No. 102-384 384(II) at 12 (1992)].

Although there are limitations on billings to Medicaid patients, there are no constraints on billings to non-Medicaid patients.

Case 13 (*continued*)

The ACA freed up hospitals to choose among discount sources such as 340B and their group purchasing organizations. The ACA also made a number of provisions to strengthen program integrity.

Section 1703 of the ACA called for a Government Accounting Office (GAO) study of the program:

> . . . that examines whether those individuals served by the covered entities under the program under section 340B of the Public Health Service Act (42 U.S.C. 256b) (referred to in this section as the "340B program") are receiving optimal health care services.

> (b) RECOMMENDATIONS. – The report under subsection (a) shall include recommendations on the following:

> (1) Whether the 340B program should be expanded since it is anticipated that the 47,000,000 individuals who are uninsured as of the date of enactment of this Act will have health care coverage once this Act is implemented.

> (2) Whether mandatory sales of certain products by the 340B program could hinder patients access to those therapies through any provider.

> (3) Whether income from the 340B program is being used by the covered entities under the program to further the program objectives.

THE 2011 GAO STUDY

That study was issued by the GAO in September 2011. In the conclusions it noted:

> The 340B program allows certain providers within the U.S. health care safety net to stretch federal resources to reach more eligible patients and provide more comprehensive services, and we found that the covered entities we interviewed reported using it for these purposes. However, HRSA's current approach to oversight does not ensure 340B program integrity, and raises concerns that may be exacerbated by changes within the program. According to HRSA, the agency largely relies on participants' self-policing to ensure

compliance with program requirements, and has never conducted an audit of covered entities or drug manufacturers. As a result, HRSA may not know when participants are engaging in practices that are not in compliance. Furthermore, we found that HRSA has not always provided covered entities and drug manufacturers with guidance that includes the necessary specificity on how to comply with program requirements. There also is evidence to suggest that participants may be interpreting guidance in ways that are inconsistent with the agency's intent. Finally, participants have little incentive to comply with program requirements, because few have faced sanctions for noncompliance . . .

PPACA [i.e., ACA] outlined a number of provisions that, if implemented, will help improve many of the 340B program integrity issues we identified. For example, PPACA requires HRSA to recertify eligibility for all covered entity types on an annual basis . . . Additionally, PPACA requires HRSA to develop a formal dispute resolution process, including procedures for covered entities to obtain information from manufacturers, and maintain a centralized list of 340B prices—provisions that would help ensure covered entities and manufacturers are better able to identify and resolve suspected violations. PPACA also requires HRSA to institute monetary penalties for covered entities and manufacturers, which gives program participants more incentive to comply with program requirements. Finally, PPACA requires HRSA to conduct more direct oversight of manufacturers, including conducting selective audits to ensure that they are charging covered entities the correct 340B price.

However, we identified other program integrity issues that HRSA should also address. For example, the law does not require HRSA to audit covered entities or further specify the agency's definition of a 340B patient. While HRSA has developed new proposed guidance on this definition, it is uncertain when, or if, the guidance will be finalized.

Because the discounts on 340B drugs can be substantial, it is important for HRSA to ensure that covered entities only purchase them for eligible patients both by issuing more specific guidance and by conducting audits of covered entities to prevent diversion. Additionally, while PPACA included a provision prohibiting manufacturers from discriminating against covered entities in the sale

---

Case 13   (*continued*)

---

of 340B drugs, HRSA does not plan to make any changes to or further specify its related nondiscrimination guidance.

Absent additional oversight by the agency, including more specific guidance, access challenges covered entities have faced when manufacturers' have restricted distribution of IVIG at 340B prices may continue and similar challenges could arise for other drugs in the future. (GAO, 2011, pp. 33–34)

HOW IS THE PATIENT HELPED?

The ACA and the GAO report said little about getting the resulting savings to the patient's bill. As the law has been modified over the years, the direct link to the low-income, uninsured patient has weakened. The discounted drugs can even be used for commercially insured patients. The 2011 GAO report found that "some covered entities passed 340B savings on to patients by providing lower-cost drugs to uninsured patients. For example, many covered entities determined the amount that a patient is required to pay based on the lower cost of 340B-priced drugs" (p. 17). The report noted that some covered entities had indicated that without the discounts they would have to close their pharmacy or curtail other services.

> For a number of reasons, operating the 340B program in the hospital environment creates more opportunities for drug diversion compared to other covered entity types. First, hospitals operate 340B pharmacies in settings where both inpatient and outpatient drugs are dispensed and must ensure that inpatients do not get 340B drugs. Second, hospitals tend to have more complex contracting arrangements and organizational structures than other entity types—340B drugs can be dispensed in multiple locations, including emergency rooms, on-site clinics, and off-site clinics. In light of this and given HRSA's nonspecific guidance on the definition of a 340B patient, broad interpretations of the guidance may be more likely in the hospital setting and diversion harder to detect. Third, hospitals dispense a comparatively larger volume of drugs than other entity types—while representing 27 percent

of participating covered entities, according to HRSA, DSH hospitals alone represent about 75 percent of all 340B drug purchases. (GAO, 2011, p. 29)

OTHER IMPACTS OF THE ACA

The ACA added a number of classes of institutions, including affordable care organizations, freestanding cancer hospitals, clinical access hospitals, rural referral centers, and sole community hospitals. Many millions of uninsured individuals are to receive insurance. This would greatly increase the consumption of 340B drugs, even though one might argue that the original need for the 340B program was partially mitigated.

MANUFACTURER PUSHBACK

In early 2013, the Biotechnology Industry Organization (BIO) issued a white paper subtitled "A Review and Analysis of the 340B Program." It was cosponsored by the Community Oncology Alliance (COA), the National Community Pharmacists Association (NCPA), National Patient Advocate Foundation (NPAF), the Pharmaceutical Care Management Association (PCMA), and the Pharmaceutical Research and Manufacturers of America (PhRMA). The report's executive summary cited:

> Areas of most concern included the following:
>
> - Concerns that some uninsured, indigent patients may not be experiencing direct benefit from the program's existence.
> - Anecdotal evidence that clinical decision-making may be skewed by efforts to take advantage of the 340B discount.
> - Growing evidence of displacement of non-340B providers who serve a key role in providing patient access to important health care services. (BIO, 2013, p. 1)

The same executive summary cited the concerns expressed in the GAO report, as well as insufficient resources at HRSA to carry out its responsibilities under 340B and the ACA, the need for clearer guidance, and HRSA's use of "subregulatory" procedures to clarify definitions and establish interpretive guidelines.

The HRSA website contained the following observation:

Case 13   *(continued)*

PROGRAM GUIDELINES

> HRSA chose to publish guidelines in the *Federal Register* rather than regulations to administer the Section 340B program. Guidelines are the quickest and most flexible way to convey to all concerned parties how HRSA interprets the Section 340B requirements. Guidelines are also used to disseminate procedures that are acceptable under the statute. To ensure that the guidelines were as appropriate and responsive as possible to the legitimate concerns of the covered entities and manufacturers, comments were solicited on all of the guidelines before HRSA published them in a final notice.

The BIO white paper cited the changed guidance that allowed covered entities to use contract pharmacies as an example of HRSA expanding this program by administrative means. Subsequently, the number of 340B contract pharmacy arrangements climbed from about 3,000 in 2010 to more than 9,000 in 2012, with more than 12,000 projected for 2012. The white paper claimed these arrangements were forcing some community pharmacies out of business.

SENATOR GRASSLEY'S INQUIRIES

Senator Charles E. (Chuck) Grassley (R-Iowa) has often been critical of nonprofit hospitals, and his concern about their implementation of the 340B program is just one example. His office often follows up on public disclosures that provide an investigative opening and an opportunity to prod HRSA about its oversight of the program.

The UAB Inquiry

For example, as ranking member of the Senate Judiciary Committee, he sent a letter on May 19, 2012, to Dr. Carol Garrison, president of the University of Alabama (UAB) Hospital, stating that:

> The original intent of the program was to extend the Medicaid drug discount to the most vulnerable patients at PHS Clinics,

those who are mostly, "medically uninsured, on marginal incomes, and have no other source to turn to for preventive and primary care services." . . .

On February 16, 2011, Donna Evans, R.Ph., Senior Pharmacist, with University of Alabama (UAB) Hospital gave a presentation at the 340B Annual Conference in San Diego, California. In this presentation, Ms. Evans stated that the purpose of the Purchasing Committee is, among other things, to "maximize savings opportunities." Ms. Evan's presentation goes on to state that UAB Hospital tracks the top drug expenses for "possible change in admission[s] process." As an example of this change in admission process, Ms. Evans lists the drugs Melphalan and Busulfan and stated that the hospital "change[d] treatment protocol/location." Furthermore, Ms. Evans' presentation discussed the "discharge [of an IVIG patient] from [the] hospital to [a] Townhouse," for the purpose of maximizing savings opportunities associated with the 340B drug discount provided in an outpatient setting.

Ms. Evans' presentation is deeply disconcerting (Grassley, 2012, pp.1-2).

Senator Grassley asked the hospital to document the frequency and economics of such changes in admission status and 340B discounts in general, what the hospital did with the savings, and whether HRSA had ever audited it.

The North Carolina Major Hospitals Inquiry

In 2012, McClatchy newspapers in Charlotte and Raleigh, North Carolina, ran articles about major hospitals buying up oncology practices and substantially raising chemotherapy drug prices in these outpatient settings (Alexander & Garloch, 2012). In September 2012, Senator Grassley sent letters to three major hospitals cited in the articles, asking how much they earned by participating in the 340B Program, the breakdown of the 340B payer mix, and how they had reinvested those 340B dollars into serving the most vulnerable patients. Senator Grassley summarized their replies in a March 27, 2013, letter to Dr. Mary K. Wakefield, HRSA administrator:

Case 13 (*continued*)

First, all three North Carolina hospitals provided a summary of revenue generated by participating in the 340B program from 2008. Below is a revenue summary . . .

Carolinas Medical Center	UNC	Duke
2008: $12,970,012	2009: $33,087,329	2009: $88,953,570
2009: $16,697,500	2010: $38,451,076	2010: $109,700,400
2010: $16,910,620	2011: $52,580,763	2011: $131,759,091
2011: $21,065,620	2012: $65,391,050	2012: $135,539,459

These are not small amounts.

. . .

These numbers paint a very stark picture of how hospitals are reaping sizeable 340B discounts on drugs and then turning around and upselling them to fully insured patients covered by Medicare, Medicaid, or private health insurance in order to maximize their spread. (Grassley, 2013, pp. 1–2)

All three hospitals were able to provide their 340B payer mix for the period 2008–2010. The data for 2010 taken from Senator Grassley's letter is presented in the table below:

Hospital	Medicare	Medicaid	Self-pay	Commercial
UNC	23.1%	9.7%	12.0%	22.6%
Carolinas Medical Center	25.6%	18.3%	11.3%	41.9%
Duke	19%	8%	4%	68%

The *Raleigh News & Observer* of April 3, 2013, reported on Senator Grassley's inquiry and stated that "Last year, Duke University Hospital purchased $65.8 million in drugs through the program and received $135.5 million in revenue. Duke says it saved $48.3 million buying the drugs through the 340B program. That means the hospital made a profit of $69.7 million, instead of $21.4 million if it had not participated in the program"(Alexander, Neff, & Garloch, 2013, p. A1).

Sen. Grassley's letter then goes on to ask a series of questions seemingly aimed at getting HRSA to collect this type of data routinely.

Discussion Questions

1. What seems to be the true intent of the 340B drug discount program? How would you go about clarifying the legislative intent?

2. What conclusions do you draw from the data provided to Senator Grassley?

3. What data would you like to make the covered entities provide to HRSA on a routine basis?

4. Discuss the merits of using the "subregulatory" process versus the normal rule-making procedures.

5. As the ACA is implemented, what will be the impact of the 340B program on pharmaceutical and biotechnology firms?

6. What are the merits of using disproportionate share as a screen for whether acute care hospitals are covered entities? What about the average manufacturer's selling price as a denominator in calculating the discount? What alternatives would you recommend?

7. What are the merits of Senator Grassley's investigative methods, given that he holds formal hearings on health policy issues as well?

8. What events or policy shifts would support the contraction or expansion of the 340B program?

Part

III

THE PROFESSIONAL AS A PARTICIPANT

The Policy Analysis Process and Health Professionals

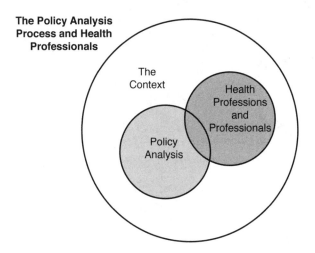

We expect that most users of this book will be current or future health professionals. They need to understand the role of the professions and professionals in the health policy process. Although not disinterested parties, they can bring to the table their commitment, their technical expertise, and their concern for the patient. However, they also bring their economic interests, as do all of the other actors, and their economic interests will be known to the other parties. Likewise, health professionals must understand the positions of the others at the table and be prepared to evaluate how they are affected by various policy alternatives.

Chapter 14 looks at what alternatives and approaches are likely to work, given current U.S. political processes. Chapter 15 addresses the leadership roles open to professionals and the skills that they need to develop to perform them appropriately. Chapter 16, the concluding chapter, sums up some of the issues raised in earlier chapters and sends you on your way, hopefully as an effective future participant in the policy process.

Chapter 14

Double-Checking for Contextual Change

Even when a specific policy had been thoroughly analyzed, it still has to be checked against a scenario about what is likely to happen to the system as a whole. Alternative visions, which we call *scenarios*, need to be considered. For example, a concern about moves that take us closer to universal coverage—whether that means the Affordable Care Act (ACA) as it is more fully implemented or future efforts (such as, potentially, a single-payer system)—is that we could be worse off unless there are concurrent system changes that reduce waste, expand primary care services, and address the impact on prices of treatment access for additional millions of low- and middle-income people. Various provisions of the ACA attempt to address each of these areas, but critics often say it does not do enough to control costs.

A comparison of two offsetting effects of an alternative decision is a trade-off analysis. That is one step in comparing outcomes, but it is still a very narrow picture in terms of the transparency of unintended consequences and secondary and tertiary effects. Trade-offs should be considered throughout the analysis. After the trade-offs have been evaluated and the alternatives narrowed down, the relevant scenarios will become apparent.

In the field of health policy, consensus is hard to come by, and even harder to sustain. There are certain conclusions, however, that seem to be inescapable:

- Without major interventions, health care will be near or at 20% of GDP over the next decade. No government is likely to risk too radical a change in that large a portion of the economy, especially while contending with other issues, such as international competition, immigration, terrorism, and government deficits.
- The moves of employers away from responsibility for paying health insurance premiums for workers, workers' families, and pensioners will continue despite the mandates in the ACA. The availability of an alternative path to coverage for employees of small businesses—namely the exchanges—is likely to accelerate this trend. Some larger employers may also chose to pay the penalty rather than provide "shared responsibility" coverage for all full-time employees.
- Insurance companies will come up with less expensive products for individuals (with lesser coverage) to adapt to the changing market. The risk has always been that these basic packages and new exclusions create another class of underinsured individuals and possibly drive up the premiums for the chronically ill and others who require more comprehensive coverage. This process will be shaped by the "minimum value" and "minimal essential coverage" provisions of the ACA.
- The unique aspects of health care in terms of uncertainty, agency conflict, and market failure will constrain the degree to which free-market solutions will take hold.
- Consolidation will increase the possibilities for better coordination of care but risk further increase in the market power of providers.
- Communicable disease events in other countries will affect the United States much more rapidly because of global transfers of people, foodstuffs, money, and information.
- The flow of physicians into the United States for training and their subsequent experiences practicing here will set up the potential for a competent workforce elsewhere, as we now see returnees performing hip and heart valve replacements in a number of countries at a third of the cost, with international middlemen brokering such services.
- Similarly, but more darkly, the illicit market in transplantable organs is growing rapidly, again through middlemen. There is also the international trade in prescription drugs, which is primarily attributed to Canada but is really wider and has great growth potential. Unfortunately, it opens up an entryway for counterfeit drugs as well.
- The perceived future insolvency of the Medicare "insurance" system will put pressure on the federal government, but that reckoning will likely be postponed because it will be beyond the reelection time horizons of most politicians. States will continue to deal with the burden of the working poor under the ACA and Medicaid. Even

states not participating in Medicaid expansion are expected to see increased enrollment and a rise in associated costs as a result of the ACA, and those participating in the expansion will pay 10% of related costs after 2016. That and the problems of local disasters, especially if a pandemic occurs, will lead to pressures on the federal government to provide more leadership. If the states are generally successful, the federal government will not seek a comprehensive solution. If the states fail, and that, in turn, threatens their fiscal integrity, Congress will be more likely to act.

- The states will continue to be a laboratory for implementing health policies, either through waivers or policies that are not directly related to Medicaid. The ACA allows each state to set up its own coverage system within the framework of federal law. In the wake of the ACA's passage, for example, Vermont began to develop its own system for universal coverage.

The greatest uncertainties, therefore, are not on the financing side, but on the cost-control side. Many cost-oriented measures that seem to work over time have been described previously. They could involve the following:

1. Removing provider incentives and opportunities for overutilization
2. Reducing contribution margins and incomes of providers and suppliers to levels comparable for other professional services through administered pricing or competition
3. Reducing the costs of malpractice coverage and the need for defensive medicine
4. Allowing more international competition to drive down prices
5. Constraining treatment choices to those that are most effective and efficient
6. Encouraging labor substitution for those process steps that can be made routine
7. Empowering primary care providers to control utilization and self-referral
8. Increasing the supply of providers to levels available in other countries
9. Allowing some longer waiting periods for elective procedures to slow consumption
10. Increasing use of information technology to avoid waste and medical error, but also trying to avoid the implementation of these systems in ways that are anticompetitive at both the provider and equipment supplier levels

If the states find they must demand more stringent measures from Washington, or if there is another economic meltdown, then we are likely to see further implementation of measures with more impact. Such measures could include the following:

- Full transparency in health care pricing, including bundled prices for all stages of a specific medical condition
- Legislation to amend the Employee Retirement Income Security Act (ERISA) to allow states to regulate self-insured plans
- Regionalization of care for complex or rare medical conditions, which would require greater patient travel but produce much less waste and better outcomes
- Stronger control of the referral process by primary care providers
- Other aspects of value-based competition (Porter & Teisberg, 2006) in the marketplace, including the following:
  - Integrated IT systems reporting bundled prices and quality performance for many more procedures and diagnoses.
  - Attention to the total process of care, making it better coordinated and more effective.
  - Shifting research budget priorities from developing and evaluating new treatments to evaluating methods already in use and innovating more in process improvement rather than in new product development (Chin et al., 2013).
  - Limitations on allowable price discrimination, perhaps along the lines of the Robinson-Patman antitrust law, but applied to individuals.
  - Phasing out of laws governing corporate practice of medicine, as well as other restrictive regulations, in order to open up competition on price and results. This needs to be accompanied by licensure procedures that are more closely linked to performance.

Are we saying that the future of our health care depends more on the willingness of others to underwrite our debt—factors that if they change significantly could precipitate an economic breakdown—than on our own democratic processes? That is possible. Noted health economist Victor Fuchs (2002) has suggested that major health system change, such as national health insurance, will come only after the "kind of change that often accompanies a war, a depression or large scale civil unrest" (p. 1824).

TRADE-OFFS

It is popular to talk about a country, if not a world, divided over values, but that is not the entire story. This book illustrates that there are many trade-offs—trade-offs everywhere one turns. **Table 14-1** lists a number of these,

Table 14-1 Illustrative List of Trade-offs, Impacts, and Some of the Proposed Solutions

Trade-off	Versus	Current Impact	Proposed Solutions
First-dollar coverage	Catastrophic insurance	Many see payouts, motivating participation, but not enough money for both	Major medical option Means testing (spend-downs and Medicaid) Risk pools for high-risk patients
Selective underwriting	Community rating	Adverse selection Lifetime limits Prevention disincentives	Minimum coverage for all, with add-ons allowed
New drug safety and efficacy	Rapid deployment of effective technology	Current focus on drugs for continued use A lack of new drugs to fight acute illnesses	Sponsored development Reduced approval cycles Stronger postmarketing surveillance
Direct-to-consumer advertising	Health education campaigns	Higher drug costs Overutilization Misallocated research funds Disease mongering	Constraints on proportion of costs in advertising Redefining health Health education (counter detailing)
Liability for vaccines' effects	Vaccine development and production capacity	Inability to respond to surges in demand Failure to develop new vaccines and production methods	Limited liability Support for nonprofit producers Subsidies for standby capacity
Linked electronic medical records	Consumer privacy	Medical errors Duplicate tests Slow responses to acute problems	Designing in privacy safeguards Firewalls
Need to train new health professionals	Desire to increase faculty incomes and cross-subsidize research	Overstressed learners Decreased quality of care	Better funding of supervision Reduced charges for learner-produced services
Investment driven by utilization growth	Certificate of need	Efforts to increase demand Duplication of services Reduced competition	Wider disease-specific catchment areas Capital rationing Global budgeting

showing the two sides, the impacts of the current status quo, and some possibilities for responding to them. The fact that these trade-offs have been issues for as long as they have shows that they are currently at an equilibrium position (or an impasse). Some would argue that having a less than rational system with unresolved conflicts and continuing inefficiencies is not all bad because it provides high-income employment. It does that, but one might also question how productive much of that employment is.

We expect that managing trade-offs, rather than implementing radical changes, will be grist for health policy analysts' mill for some years to come. Each time a new program or regulation is proposed to deal with one aspect of health care access, cost, and quality, the policy analyst must present to the interested parties the trade-offs that have to be made, their magnitude, and their consequences, intended and otherwise. The policy analyst will have to look at the desired impact, the unintended consequences, the distributional effects, the ethical issues, the technological impact, the financial feasibility, the political feasibility, and the best way to implement the proposal, and from that come up with a justified recommendation to the parties involved, the politicians, and the public. Such analyses do not necessarily lead to earthshaking decisions because there is no one answer. However, they are necessary if we are to make things better rather than worse. If they succeed, it will be a product of leadership as much as anything else; however, those who would lead, especially from a professional position, must participate both in effective analysis and in rational leadership.

WORKING OUT YOUR OWN SCENARIOS

Someone could push the policy envelope by considering extreme scenarios against the status quo and seeing what kind of health care system might result; however, getting single-event estimates is only one step in the process. An event may be acceptable on its own, but its interaction with other events may result in an overall outcome that is totally unacceptable. For example, encouraging kidney transplants for end-stage renal disease patients is one thing, but if the supply is totally inadequate and promotes a sizable international traffic in involuntarily harvested human kidneys, would that be acceptable? We have set up an illustrative example with multiple scenarios to compare. We have provided five scenarios, three of which are extreme:

A. Extrapolating current trends
B. Extreme reliance on free market
C. Extreme industrialization

Table 14-2 Building Some Scenarios for Cost Reduction

Change Scenario	A	B	C	D	E
1. Remove provider incentives to overutilize.	N	N	N	Y	
2. Major changes in staffing requirements.	N	Y	Y	Y	
3. Major reductions in provider and staff incomes and contribution margins.	?	Y	N	Y	
4. Reduced costs of malpractice coverage.	Y	?	Y	Y	
5. International competition reducing prices.	Y	Y	?	?	
6. Constraining treatment choices to those most effective and efficient.	N	N	Y	Y	
7. Encouraging labor substitution where process can be industrialized.	N	Y	Y	Y	
8. Empowering primary care providers to control utilization and self-referrals.	N	N	Y	Y	
9. Increasing supply of providers to levels in other countries.	N	Y	N	?	
10. Increased waiting periods and other devices to increase competition.	N	N	Y	Y	
11. Increasing use of IT to reduce waste and medical error without constraining competition.	Y	Y	N	?	
12. Global budgeting of hospitals and other institutions to ration capital, perhaps on a regional basis.	N	N	Y	Y	
13. Stripping away less essential services or covering outside health insurance system.	?	?	Y	Y	
14. Return of more voluntarism in the health sector.	N	Y	N	N	

Y = likely, N = not likely, and ? = not predicted

Scenario A is the extrapolation of the current trends in the current system.

Scenario B is the case of an extremely strong move toward a free-market health care system.

Scenario C is the case of an extremely strong move in the direction of industrialization and corporate governance of health care.

Scenario D is the case of a major economic crisis that leads the country to a major overhaul of government programs, including health care, and major changes in the tax code, such as a shift from the income tax to a value-added or some other form of consumption tax.

Scenario E provides all citizens a voucher for basic health coverage, replacing current insurance and Medicaid and ultimately Medicare. It would be financed with a value-added tax and add administrative systems to oversee coverage, technology assessment, and quality measurement and to replace the current tort system for malpractice with administrative law.

    D. National economic crisis resulting in major tax code reform

    E. The Emanuel-Fuchs proposal

In **Table 14-2**, we have provided, by way of illustration, event predictions for 15 changes that fit the first four of these scenarios. A rational person can certainly come up with others, and thus we have included **Table 14-3**, which encourages you to build your own predictions, redefining the scenarios and then assessing the impact of a set of events that you are free to augment.

Scenario A: The Status Quo Extrapolated

As you look down column A of Table 14-2, you see that not much new is happening to reduce costs. We might expect to see some responses as volume increases due to access improvements under the ACA, reductions in malpractice insurance costs, and international competition to reduce the prices of some procedures. There are also possibilities that as consumers and insurers find it harder and harder to pay their bills provider incomes will fall further, along with institutional contribution margins. Health information technology (IT) will move into place, but it may still be subject to the complaint that despite increased deployment of health IT the motivation to share information in still lacking. Thus, one might see some internal waste and medical error reduced, but very high investment costs with relatively little immediate impact on operating costs. Some major changes might occur on the funding side, however; thus, you might want to repeat the exercise with an added set of rows representing programmatic changes on the funding side.

Scenario B: Extreme Reliance on the Free Market

Here we would be likely to see little or no action to reduce costs, except to increase the competitive pressures from foreign competition and to increase the supply of providers. The primary argument for consumer-centered health care—that consumers will make choices to lower their own costs of care—is not addressed in this listing. Again, you might want to repeat the exercise with some events related to consumer-driven health care as an additional set of rows; however, with the lower resulting profit margins and professional incomes, more providers are likely to improve efficiency to compete on cost, resulting in staffing changes, better use of information technology for scheduling and coordination, and more use of volunteers.

Table 14-3 Your Exercise on Building Cost-Reduction Scenarios

Change Scenario	A	B	C	D
Remove provider incentives to overutilize.	N			
Major reductions in provider and staff incomes.	?			
Reduced costs of malpractice coverage.	Y			
Constraining treatment choices to those most effective and efficient.	?			
Encouraging labor substitution where process can be industrialized.				
Empowering primary care providers to control utilization and self-referrals.				
Rationing capital available to institutions.				
Increased waiting periods and other devices to increase competition.				
Increasing use of IT to reduce waste and medical error without constraining competition.				
Global budgeting of hospitals and other institutions, perhaps on a regional basis.				
No-fault health insurance, perhaps with tiered premiums				

Y = likely, N = not likely, and ? = not predicted

Scenario A is the extrapolation of the current trends in the current system.

Scenario B is _____.

Scenario C is _____.

Scenario D is _____.

Scenario C: Extreme Industrialization

Under the corporate, industrializing scenario, the resulting oligopolistic firms will likely try to resist and/or seek protection from a number of cost-reduction pressures, such as foreign competition and increasing the supply of providers. At the same time, they will likely make a number of internal policy choices that limit provider options, restrict capital investment, constrain institutional budgets, and break jobs down into repetitive tasks doable by lower-level, lower-paid personnel. They will also be likely to resist and lobby against measures to limit overutilization, as long as those limits affect their revenues.

Scenario D: National Economic Crisis Resulting in Major Tax Code Reform

In this scenario, the nation is in severe economic difficulties, and radical change is in the air. There is near universal coverage. At the same time, there is a much higher level of regulation affecting choices of treatments, capital availability, and staffing coupled with a defined minimum acceptable coverage. Resources will be very tight; thus, waiting lines will lengthen, and there will be pressures to put hospitals on fixed budgets, reduce services that are not absolutely necessary, and concentrate specialized treatment capacities to increase throughput and effectiveness.

Scenario E: The Emanuel-Fuchs Proposal

In a one-page article in *Fortune,* Emanuel and Fuchs (2006) offered a suggestion on "How to cure U.S. health care." They offered a comprehensive five-part program, the centerpiece of which would be a health care voucher for every citizen currently younger than age 65. It would cover currently accepted levels of care with existing or new health plans. Each individual would then have a choice of 5 to 10 plans that would have to accept all comers.

The vouchers would be paid for by an earmarked 10% value-added tax that would be offset by replacing current employment-based insurance premiums, Medicaid expenditures, and individual and corporate tax deductions for health care premiums. Medicare recipients would be grandfathered (so to speak) under the current system, but those in the new program would stay with it past age 65, and Medicare would gradually be phased out.

To administer it, there would be a new system of federal and regional boards, much like the Federal Reserve System, to provide accountability, specify and modify the benefit package, and oversee technology assessment and quality evaluations. Malpractice cases would be assigned to a separate administrative system that would adjudicate and pay claims and oversee linkages to quality measurement and the licensure process. We have left column E of Table 14-2 blank for you and your colleagues to assess and fill in.

Interpreting the Cost-Reduction Scenarios

As you can see, virtually every scenario in Table 14-2 has elements to which U.S. patients would strongly object, and each is likely to generate strong opposition from one or more interest groups. That is why the most radical departures from current trends of more intramarket competition and more industrialization are likely to occur only if there is a continuing economic crisis or a more serious meltdown of the economic system, forcing a return to bipartisanship and evoking new, strong domestic leadership with the will to take the government in a very different direction; however, it is apparent that each of the first three scenarios is weak in terms of its likely effects on health care costs, and, ultimately, draconian measures may be taken. In other words, nothing in these scenarios is likely to work until the society either runs out of money or reaches some consensus as to when enough health care is enough. Economists differ on whether that will be 10, 20, or 25 years from now (Hall & Jones, 2007).

TRY YOUR OWN SCENARIOS

We purposely offered scenarios that omitted some key policy possibilities (such as consumer-oriented health care) in hopes that you and your associates would undertake your own evaluative process and (1) flesh out your own list of changes to be tried, (2) match them against your own list of scenarios, (3) debate the effects of each change on the outcome of each scenario, and (4) come up with your own concepts of what would or would not work in the United States under various conditions. There are no pat answers. Most alternatives have been tried elsewhere in the world with mixed results. What would you want the United States to try next, perhaps on a small scale, to see how it works here?

CONCLUSION

This chapter emphasized the importance of putting event forecasts into scenarios to highlight how events and measures will interact. The initial step is to outline and evaluate the trade-offs involved with each alternative. A number of examples of health care trade-offs are provided. Possible outcome scenarios can be developed from your own lists of trade-offs. Four illustrative outcome scenarios were considered dealing with the status quo ante, more industrialization, more governmental involvement, and more of a free market; however, even these were not examined exhaustively, and further examination would be warranted on your part.

Case 14	Partnership for a Healthy North Carolina

In early February 2013, the administration of newly elected Republican governor Pat McCrory began the process of Medicaid reform with a request for information (RFI). Based on those responses, the newly appointed leaders of the state Department of Health and Human Services, Aldona Wos, MD (secretary), and Carol Steckel, MPH (Medicaid director), held a number of information-gathering meetings around the state. On April 3, 2013, the governor and the heads of both legislative houses held a press conference to announce that they would seek legislative approval of a Medicaid waiver request to Washington to substantially change the state's Medicaid system.

The governor and the secretary had referred to this effort as a "Partnership for a Healthy North Carolina." This was also the title of a report published by the John Locke Foundations and the Foundation for Government Accountability (Ingram & Restropo, 2013). Art Pope, a significant contributor to the John Locke Foundation and other libertarian causes and Republican candidates, was the governor's newly appointed associate budget director.

That report viewed as positive recent reforms in Florida, Louisiana, and Kansas. It suggested that North Carolina could save $1 billion annually, or 8% of its Medicaid costs, using the design cited in the report, as follows:

KEY ASPECTS OF THE PARTNERSHIP FOR A HEALTHY NORTH CAROLINA

- The state awards contracts to three or four comprehensive care entities (CCE).
- CCEs operate statewide, ensuring fair and equal access for patients in both rural and urban areas.
- All CCEs use the same financial vendor to reimburse medical providers, increasing speed and efficiency of repayments.
- Patients can choose from among the several plans available and pick the one that best meets their individual health concerns.
- Plans compete for patients based on the value and quality of the service they can provide.

- Patients unhappy with their plans can drop them and choose new ones that will better serve them.
- These plans would be paid on a risk-adjusted, capitated basis. (Ingram & Restropo, 2013)

Many of North Carolina's Medicaid patients had already been enrolled in a medical home program that was fee-for-service with a per-member-per-month (PMPM) management fee. This nonprofit system of local networks, organized and operated by community physicians, named Community Care of North Carolina, has been credited with saving the state close to a billion dollars over a 4-year period. It has also been recognized as a national leader in improving Medicaid quality and cost and has been expanding to serve other populations as well.

THE GOVERNOR'S POINT OF VIEW

The governor had frequently stated that Medicaid was "broken" and that he envisioned a system "to provide care for the whole person by uniting physical and behavior health, increase administrative ease and efficiency for providers, create a predictable and a sustainable Medicaid program for taxpayers" (Office of the Governor, 2013). House Speaker Tom Tillis (R-Mecklenburg) was quoted as saying, "We cannot continue to have frequent unplanned Medicaid shortfalls that wreak havoc on the budgeting process. Medicaid must stop being a budgetary time bomb."

Senate President Pro Tempore Phil Berger (R-Rockingham) was quoted as saying, "Medicaid's out-of-control costs are undermining our ability to fund core constitutional obligations like education, transportation and our judicial system. The budget we introduce next week must include over $1 billion in additional funding for out-of-control Medicaid costs."

The governor's administration could also point to an audit of the Medicaid program conducted by State Auditor Beth Wood (D). It had been commissioned by his predecessor, Governor Bev Perdue (D), but the report was not issued until January 17, 2013. The audit discovered that there had been major overruns in the Medicaid entitlement program and that administrative costs paid directly were high compared to other states. North Carolina's population was growing and had been hard hit by the Great Recession, thus enrollment had increased rapidly. The Kaiser Family Foundation credited North Carolina with

Case 14   (*continued*)

the smallest per capita costs in the Southeast and the nation's slowest growth in program costs (Hoban, 2013a). Assertions about the relative level of administrative cost varied greatly. Some states contracted out administrative functions that others produced directly with budgeted resources. Some state health and human services departments loaded allowable collateral costs into the Medicaid budget to maximize the inflow of federal dollars. For example, North Carolina was charging half of the cost of the Medicaid-eligibility specialists in county social services departments back to Medicaid.

The disastrous 2013 rollout of a new computerized Medicaid payment system was also cited as a symbol of the need for change. In the interest of full disclosure, we must note that one author of this text served as chair of the North Carolina Medicaid Medical Care committee some 30 years ago, and the department had severe problems using its data for systematic analysis then, as now. It could not compete effectively in the IT labor market and had trouble even administering its IT contracts to get necessary management information out of what was essentially a transactional system.

There were also widely acknowledged problems with the state's mental health system, which depended largely on Medicaid. For example, mental health provider agencies, called local management entities (LMEs), had for the past 2 years been bearing the risk of providing mental health care services using a set amount of money each month. However, given the financial problems that many of these LMEs suffered, as evidenced by the failure of the Asheville-based Western Highlands Network, Steckel decided that this was not the most effective way of managing financial resources that had been set aside for mental health (Hoban, 2013b).

Critics of the governor were quick to suggest that he was using the "Medicaid is broken" issue as a cover for his refusal to develop a state insurance exchange under the ACA.

MANAGED MEDICAID IN NORTH CAROLINA

The last state health maintenance organization (HMO) contract for Medicaid recipients, serving only Mecklenburg County, including

Charlotte, ended in 2006. A number of other HMO contracts, mostly serving urban areas, had been in operation between 1986 and 2002.

Community Care North Carolina (CCNC) and its earlier version, called ACCESS, has been credited with increasing the number of physicians accepting Medicaid patients. According to the Kaiser Family Foundation (2009), "CCNC was adopted as an alternative to capitated managed care that was embraced by physicians and was able to successfully operate in both urban and rural areas."

Since 1991, a 1915(b) waiver from the Centers for Medicare & Medicaid Services (CMS) has been in effect for primary care case management programs. The state launched a successful pilot program that was then expanded statewide. The participating providers were paid a PMPM management fee for coordinating care and compensated fee-for-service for treatment. This system evolved and expanded and was spun off from state government into CCNC. This system of 14 primary care provider (PCP) networks serves as the medical home for more than half of the state's Medicaid enrollees. The networks are nonprofit and managed locally but fall under the umbrella of the nonprofit, statewide CCNC organization, which develops procedures and standards and provides information services, education, and evaluation. The system also had a Section 646 waiver to serve dual eligibles and high-risk uninsureds.

As of 2013, the state Department of Health and Human Services requirements for a Medicaid PCP to participate included the following:

> A candidate for participation must meet the criteria below:
>
> - Perform primary care that includes certain preventative services;
> - The ability to create and maintain a patient/doctor relationship for the purpose of providing continuity of care;
> - Establish hours of operation for treating patients at least 30 hours per week;
> - Provide access to medical advice/services 24/7;
> - Maintain hospital admitting privileges or have a formal agreement with another doctor based on ages of the members accepted;
> - Refer or authorize services to other providers when the service cannot be provided by the PCP;
> - Use reports provided by the DMA managed care section as guides in maintaining the level of care that meets the goals of CCNC and patient needs. Reports are available via the web and paper copies that are mailed. (NC DHHS, 2013, p. 9)

Case 14   (*continued*)

The responsibility of managing care rested with the network. Physician leaders had been developing evidence-based tools for the networks, including implementing best practices and disease management for

- Asthma
- Congestive heart failure
- Diabetes
- Hypertension
- Ischemic vascular/cardiovascular disease

Physicians also sought to develop case management procedures for high-risk/high-cost patients.

Process performance measures were in place for all of these, and almost 30,000 chart reviews supporting quality improvement were conducted among the 1.3 million (out of 1.8 million) Medicaid enrollees and 1,350 PCP practices in a recent year. CCNC had had a streamlined electronic medical record system available since 2009. Reviews were conducted randomly within diagnosis, and several registries were supported.

The PCPs had a limited gate-keeping role:

> . . . the PCP is contractually obligated to refer patients and authorize treatment for patients when unable to provide the necessary service. It is the domain of the PCP to refer/authorize treatment and define the scope . . . which includes the number of visits being authorized and the extent of the diagnostic evaluation. The PCP should be informed if a secondary referral . . . should be made. A provider who has received a referral should consult the PCP before referring to a secondary provider for situations not related to the diagnosis of the first referral. The PCP may authorize care retroactively; however, it is at the discretion of the PCP. (NC DHHS, 2013, p. 9–10)

The document then proceeds with a page-long list of "Exempt from Authorization by the PCP"; the list includes emergency departments, hospital-owned urgent care centers, hospices, hospital-based lab and diagnostic procedures, and health departments.

WHERE DOES NORTH CAROLINA GO NEXT?

The governor's announcement created considerable concern, especially in the medical community. For example, one letter from a physician in the *Raleigh News & Observer* read:

> I appreciate the governor's desire to control Medicaid spending. I know of few physicians who would argue against reining in medical costs or making improvements. But the governor's proposal runs counter to what North Carolina has been doing with its award-winning approach to Medicaid.
>
> The national Kaiser Family Foundation even recently reported that North Carolina had the lowest rate of growth in Medicare spending in the nation.
>
> So why change direction now? And why use private managed care companies that have been shown to be more costly and less effective in many cases? (George, 2013)

The *Triangle Business Journal* commented:

> ... health care providers say Medicaid reimbursements barely cover costs as it is, so it's difficult to see where a potential CCE could find real savings. . . . The state has a history of making health care demands that private companies find unachievable. Last year, the state put out requests to outsource inmate health care, but abandoned the idea when Corizon Inc., one of the largest providers of such services, said that the state's requests "contain several provisions that are either completely unattainable or add significant and unnecessary cost that will likely mitigate any savings that can be achieved." (deBruyn, 2013)

Later in the year, Secretary Wos was involved in other controversies, and in October, Medicaid Director Steckel resigned to go into the private sector. On November 6, 2013, the governor invited 30 state health care leaders to the governor's mansion to discuss Medicaid reform. The governor reported that there was a new advisory group working on a proposal. It would hold public hearings and recommend a waiver request to the legislature on March 17, 2014. One participant reported that the governor felt that no one state had all the answers and that

Case 14   (*continued*)

North Carolina had resources that could be leveraged, including CCNC and the LMEs currently delivering mental health services. The number of entities would probably be reduced. The medical care managers would probably number five to seven, and physical and mental health would be integrated. The legislature would likely act in May 2014 and waivers submitted to Washington soon after so that requests for proposals could go out in time to put the system in place in late 2015 or early 2016 (Dihoff, 2013).

Discussion Questions

1. What are the apparent strengths and weaknesses of the current Medicaid care management system in North Carolina?

2. How does one separate out the effects of IT failures, budget overruns, and exogenous changes in enrollment?

3. What would be the governor's likely proposal to the legislature? Why?

4. What should CCNC do to prepare for the changes that seem to be in the wind?

5. How does one best integrate physical and mental health services?

Chapter 15

Health Professional Leadership

Normal is getting narrower and narrower.
> —Personal observation by an experienced nurse practitioner

Health professionals can be important participants in health policy processes. They bring their experiences, their knowledge of both science and art, their ability to distinguish between the two, and their commitment to the patient. Typically, they also bring a commitment to lifelong learning. The power of the professions, especially physicians, has been waning of late, but that has a lot to do with the height of their dominance in the past. In an open, market-driven, information-rich society, the old monopoly power described by Starr (1982) is not sustainable. Health professionals now need to undertake new leadership roles or else their status will be further undermined by those actively seeking a greater share of the pie. Those new roles will have to focus more on collaboration and coordination of care.

DISINTERESTEDNESS

Much of the diminished respect for health professionals stems from the public's perception of reduced disinterestedness. Current fashion in economics seems to deny the concept of disinterestedness—the concept of lack of bias and freedom from special interests, the ability to set aside one's own interests and to seek the best possible outcome for others. The opposite is the oft-repeated phrase, "All they care about is money." Money is harder to come by in most parts of the health care system because of utilization controls and deep discounts to health care plans, and thus the increased concern is understandable; however, that is not reassuring to the public. Much of the literature on the rising costs of care blames the current fee-for-service system for making it in the providers' interest to promote overutilization. Schlesinger (2002) argued that this loss of faith seemed to intensify with the advent of Medicare and Medicaid, and that that has led to a loss of political power as well. One parameter of successful professional leadership will be the ability to engender faith that the professional and the profession have the interests of other constituencies in mind.

INFORMATIONAL CREDIBILITY

Disintermediation in general and direct-to-consumer advertising in particular have affected the informational monopoly of the health professions. This is not a one-way street. The claims and counterclaims of the various interested parties can be hard to sort out. One leadership role for the health professional is to guide the general public through that welter of information. This is not just a physician's task. It involves all health professionals. An article in *BusinessWeek* asked, "How Good Is Your Online Nurse?" and compared the online patient portals of the three largest health insurers: WellPoint, United Health Group, and Aetna (Weintraub, 2006). The trends reported in the article included greater integration with patient records, more add-on purchased counseling, and more personalized responses. It concluded, "A bit like Big Brother? Sure. But as health care gets more complex, it's comforting to have a virtual coach" (p. 89). Despite the word "nurse" in the title, the article compared the companies' automated systems that tailored the information. One insurer did offer written and telephone nutritional consultations for a fee, but the professional component was largely invisible in the process. Maintaining the power of the professions in the future will require efforts to maintain acceptance as a unique and relevant information domain. There is relatively little art in computerized communications, and the public might well want more in the way of art, if it is offered. Procedural control alone is a slender reed upon which to stake the future of a profession. Conceding the informational domain to others is risky. The countertrend is the rise of boutique medical services, which offer more access and attention for an annual fee.

TO INFLUENCE GLOBALLY, START LOCALLY

The health professional's power to participate effectively in the political process is earned through leadership in one's profession, in one's institution, and in one's community. Although some leaders and spokespersons appear to have burst onto the national scene directly—Dr. Donald Berwick in government and health quality improvement, for example; Dr. Atul Gawande with his *New Yorker* articles and his books; and Dr. Paul Farmer in international health—most rise slowly through the ranks of their profession as team players. The routes to leadership positions are varied. Health professionals are in leadership roles in medical centers, community hospitals, government agencies, and insurance companies. Each presumably came by his or her position by training, intelligence, hard work, and usually trustworthiness. They were able to convince others to work beside them and for them because they could be trusted to take the interests of others into account.

Leadership career paths often overlooked in the health policy arena include those in corporations and in entrepreneurial ventures. A number of very influential health professionals have stopped delivering care directly and have moved into the management of health institutions, insurance companies, occupational health, medical device and supply companies, pharmaceutical companies, and government agencies. They represent those institutions, and many seem able to do so without negating the trust of health care decision makers. Their leadership roles may have been thrust upon them, or they may have sought them. In either case, they took a prepared mind and a sense of what they wanted to accomplish in an arena of health care policy.

The press seems to emphasize the importance of careers in publicly held companies, as considerable wealth can be created by developing a company and taking it public. After the company goes public, however, it is beholden primarily, if not solely, to one set of stakeholders, the stockholders; therefore, there is still a major role in health care for the nonprofit organization that does not have stockholders and can balance a number of competing interests. A deeper knowledge of nonprofit organizations and their behaviors is necessary for determining their role in setting and implementing health policy. This is especially true of entrepreneurial nonprofit organizations that can participate in the marketplace as fully as a stock corporation. Leaders must understand the similarities and differences in how these types of organizations function. The term *governance* is often applied to the roles of management, staff, and boards of both for-profit and nonprofit organizations. The professional leader must be able to function effectively and help govern effectively in one or the other or both.

PROCESS INNOVATION

There seems to be a consensus developing that there is great potential in the area of process innovation. This goes well beyond improving current processes and moves into major changes that meet the criteria outlined by the Institute of Medicine's (IOM) Learning Health System initiative and its Innovation Collaborative (IOM, 2012a, 2012b). Those criteria included:

- A participatory, team-based transparent culture
- Patient-anchored and patient-tested processes
- Fully active and engaged patients and the public
- Informed, facilitated, shared, and coordinated decisions
- Care that starts with best practice every time
- Transparent and constantly assessed outcomes
- Incentives aligned for value
- Knowledge that is an ongoing, seamless product of services and research
- Health information that is a reliable, secure, and reusable resource for the patient and the common good
- Leadership that is multifocal, networked, and dynamic

There is plenty there to work on locally and nationally.

RISK TAKING

Moving out of a traditional professional role requires dealing with new classes of risks and accepting success as well as failure. There are many successful health professional entrepreneurs and leaders and also some unsuccessful ones. Recent events have shown us situations where successful professional leadership has been followed by failure. An example is the rise of large physician practice management organizations that grew very rapidly in the 1990s but failed as their leaders strayed from their areas of expertise and listened, not to their customers, but to those who were concerned only with increasing stock prices. Chin et al. (2013) point out that the innovators have to accept failure as a natural learning experience and keep trying until things work. That is very different from practicing defensive medicine.

HEALTH POLICY ANALYSIS: A RELEVANT SCHOOL FOR LEADERSHIP

Participating in policy discussions and analyses can also help prepare one for leadership. By reviewing and critiquing the alterative scenarios provided by scholars—such as the consumer-oriented free-market approach of Her-zlinger (1997) versus the community-based planning approach of Short-ell and colleagues (1996) versus new approaches being undertaken by the various states—one can learn a great deal. These debates offer a number of intellectual leadership roles for trained policy analysts with professional backgrounds and skills.

Evaluating the alternatives calls for an understanding of the types of risks that health care organizations and health care managers may choose to handle or not handle in the design of their system. These risks have been described as follows (McLaughlin, 1997; McLaughlin & Kaluzny, 1997):

- Underwriting
- Marketing
- Clinical operations
- Financial
- Regulatory
- Integrative

The would-be professional leader has to think through the following questions:

- Which of these risks am I now comfortable handling?
- Which other ones do I need and want to learn to handle?
- How can I use my work or educational experiences to learn to handle those that I want to or will need to handle?

This exercise can help the potential professional leader outline what he or she needs to learn about managerial skills and activities. One must learn to analyze the various organization forms used for health care delivery in terms of how to allocate these risks and facilitate their handling.

GOVERNANCE

Not only do health care professional leaders make decisions, they also provide what Karl Weick (1995) called "sensemaking" for those being led. They must be able to understand and articulate the role of the governance process in their operation. Health care professionals guard and maintain the technological core of their organizations. They demand a role in their governance processes and governance mechanisms, which are the keys to effective technical and organizational change. Their leaders must understand how these processes operate and how their professions and the other actors can best work together in the policy-making process. Through understanding the risks to be encountered, analyzing the nature of local markets and delivery organizations, and meeting the governance needs of organizations delivering care, health profession leaders can become equipped to analyze local health care systems and how they are best led.

PLANNING ALTERNATIVES

Professional leaders must analyze policy issues for specific communities and specific segments of health care. These have to be analyzed against specific criteria of quality, access, and cost. One can also master less familiar risks, such as pricing. Leaders must consider quality measurement and improvement and disease-management approaches. Imbedded in such studies are opportunities to develop insights about the ability or inability of organizations to handle high levels of inherent variability in definitions, patients, events, costs, and so on. This needs to be a continuing theme in analysis, one relating back to the issues of art versus science and Deming's (1986) notions about special cause variation and common cause variation. Health care professions have historically treated all situations, whether art or science, as if they were science. Consequently, they have assumed that any negative consequences were the result of special cause variation, holding the individual practitioner responsible for adverse events. What future managers have to learn from the Deming approach is that health care is a field that will have high variability, even without special cause variation, and that administrative systems have to be tailored to that reality. Success in health care is as much dependent on a team's functioning in an effective system as it is on any individual professional. Deming, a pioneer in continuous quality improvement, noted (1986) that most quality problems were not due to worker errors, but to problems in the design of the production system that failed to handle inherent variability effectively. Professional leaders must come to understand that assessing and adapting to this inherent variability is a key element of the manager's role in health care delivery.

COMMUNITIES

If professionals are to manage populations rather than just individuals, they must develop a sense of how that can be done in a community setting. They must experience and participate in change processes undertaken by groups involving payers, providers, public health agencies, and patient organizations in their own community. They need to understand the limits of community-based cooperation and planning in a market-driven health care system. Leaders must develop sufficient respect among their colleagues to be trusted with data needed for community health improvement when it might otherwise be seen as proprietary information for competitive use.

ENHANCING THE PROFESSIONAL'S ROLE

Professional performance in health policy roles can be enhanced in a number of ways, including the following:

- Preparation
- Skills development
- Training others
- Educating the public
- Networking
- Practicing leadership

Preparing to Learn and to Lead

Professionals need opportunities to adapt to policy analysis roles above and beyond those normally associated with clinical care. Potential leaders have to walk in the shoes of those who are leading, consider the multiple sides of the issues, use hard facts and fit them into conceptual and mathematical models that allow one to reduce and refine the array of available alternatives, and then select those that are likely to succeed in the field. Health policy analysis invites the potential leader to step back from narrow professional roles, think in terms of what is best for the patient and for society, and see the changes in health care more in the sweep of time. Intellectual integrity also is needed as a bulwark against being swept along with the fads.

One very important role for the health care professional is as a team member. Policy analysis teams require a wide range of skills, including management, economics, operations, and medicine. As the owners of the technological core of medicine, health care professionals can always claim a place at the table; however, they must also be prepared to contribute to the overall progress of process analysis and improvement efforts.

Developing Skills

The policy analyst must also understand the financial implications of what is being discussed; think in terms of markets and competition; adjust to social, economic, and political change as they play out in U.S. society; analyze and optimize processes; and motivate individuals and teams. All of these move in the direction of exhibiting the competence, demonstrating the mastery, and gaining the respect of one's peers and colleagues expected of a potential contributor to a senior management team. Another skill of senior leadership is that of sensemaking; that is, being able to interpret publicly what is going on in a way that supports positive outcomes. One practice arena would be in explaining the changes in the health care landscape, such as the implementation of the remaining provisions of the Affordable Care Act (ACA), to one's peers, patients, and the public.

Learning and Training Others

One function of professional leadership is training the next generation of professionals. For example, if health policy is going to focus on motivating the system to reduce waste, as suggested by Porter and Teisberg (2006), then the present and the next generation are going to have to think in terms of value-based patient care and focus on managing the entire medical condition from start to finish. Paul Batalden and others at Dartmouth have already started to incorporate this into their training of physicians there and elsewhere. They refer to it as employing microsystems strategies as compared with organization-centered or issue-centered strategies for process improvement (Mohr & Batalden, 2006). They suggest that there are eight dimensions of effective microsystems (Mohr, Batalden, & Barach, 2006, p. 408):

1. Constancy of purpose
2. Investment in improvement
3. Alignment of role and training for efficiency and staff satisfaction
4. Interdependence of the care team to meet patient needs
5. Integration of information and technology into workflows
6. Ongoing measurement of outcomes
7. Supportiveness of the larger organization
8. Connection to the community to enhance care delivery and extend influence

These eight dimensions align very well with the concepts of the value-based competition model offered by Porter and Teisberg (2006). Adopting that approach in both clinical process improvement and in clinical training is one way to walk the talk, to learn the full implications of such an approach, and to develop the skills and insights applicable at higher levels of policy analysis. If one does not normally use something, one of the best ways to come to understand it fully is to try to teach it to others.

Building Networks

An intriguing part of health policy analysis is that it takes place in a virtual network of participants, professions, and organizations. One learns how influence is exerted nationally, locally, and in one's work group by knowing when to speak up and when to hold back, when to be the advocate and when to be the analyst, and how to support and move forward the multidisciplinary team—the key element of health care leadership for many years to come. By doing so, one develops skill at working with other disciplines and the contacts that become important assets as one attempts to exert leadership at higher and higher levels in the policy analysis process.

Practicing Leadership

Potential professional leaders have many opportunities to experiment with leadership roles in their interactions with program peers inside and outside their usual work setting. They can try out new concepts and compare experiences with their colleagues. Buttressed by the knowledge and skills gained, they can gradually assume leadership based on competency and commitment to personal and institutional change. One need not wait for a senior management opening to put that new knowledge to use.

CONCLUSION

Professionals play a very important role in policy analysis; however, they need to acquire those skills necessary to achieve positions of leadership in health policy making. Professionals, especially physicians, must learn to take a disinterested view in many of their interactions with others, offsetting the growing public perception that they are much too concerned with the monetary aspects of care. If they fail to do so, their professional and political influence will continue to wane as their informational and procedural monopolies weaken.

To start, professionals must begin to influence health policy locally. They have to gain experience and leadership skills at that level before moving up to higher levels. As they move up, they will learn about the governance processes of both for-profit and nonprofit organizations and the suitability of each for specific purposes. They will gain knowledge about managing nonclinical types of risks in the health care setting and about how to become a member of a team that can deal with the entire medical condition rather than their subspecialty's aspect of it.

Learning by doing is available in all settings, especially in training newer health professionals, improving local care processes, and health policy leadership at the community level. There is plenty of room for professional leaders in the health policy process, if they are willing to invest time and effort into learning to manage and lead in it.

| **Case 15** | **Australian Surgery Indicator Makes the Front Page** |

The front page of the *Sydney Morning Herald* of February 28, 2011, carried an exclusive headlined, "Thousands Hit as Hospitals Cancel Surgery" (Wallace, 2011). It cited public records from NSW Health, the ministry responsible for monitoring New South Wales' state health system. The records indicated that same-day surgery cancellations were "occurring regularly at three times the accepted standard." Many patients showed up at public hospitals operated by area health services expecting to go into the operating room, only to be sent home after fasting and having blood samples sent to the lab. In many instances, surgeries were canceled because the hospitals did not have beds waiting for the patients after their surgeries.

The article noted that the ministry's "Surgery Dashboard," a monthly snapshot of key performance indicators, sets a target of less than 2% for surgery cancellations. This is a stretch or "aspirational" goal, and some NSW hospitals were not meeting the previous standard of less than 5%.

The Surgical Service Taskforce developed the dashboard, and NSW Health incorporated it into its Pre-Procedure Preparation Toolkit, a guideline issued by the ministry's Health Service Performance Improvement Branch. **Table 15-1** lists the key performance indicators for both state and local levels.

The guideline indicators and targets were reviewed in November 2012, and the canceled surgeries target remained unchanged.

The reporter interviewed the chair of the local Australian Medical Association hospital practice committee, who was also a medical school faculty member. He suggested that the problem was worse than indicated, because patients who wanted surgery but were never booked were not counted. He observed that the benchmark percentage was "ambitious but clearly double or triple that figure is unacceptable." He called a ministry plan to add 400 public hospital beds per year insufficient.

The deputy director-general of NSW Health told the reporter that 40–45% of the cancellations were for "patient reasons," such as the patient not showing up or being ill on the day of surgery. He also noted that there were multiple reasons why hospitals could not accommodate surgery patients—when trauma patients unexpectedly tied up ICU beds, for example, or when necessary supplies and equipment were not available. He noted that when the benchmark had been less than 5% nearly all the hospitals had met it, so it was raised to an "aspirational" level of less than 2% in 2007.

Data extracted from the monthly reports by the newspaper indicated that some hospitals were usually failing to meet the less than 5% target and few had come close to the less than 2% level on a consistent basis. The same-day cancellation rate for six of the nine local hospitals was around 4%. This suggests that almost 9,000 same-day surgeries are canceled in New South Wales each year. The deputy observed that a cancellation rate of 4–5% was typical of other Australian states and that 91% of elective surgeries were "completed on time."

Table 15-1 Key Surgical Performance Indicators

State Level	
Booked patient cancellations on the day of surgery for any reason	< 2.0%
Patients canceled due to medical conditions (included above)	< 1.0%
Suggested for Local Level	
Patients through the preprocedure preparation process	100%
Percentage of patients processed by:	Target locally determined
Telephone interview	
General preadmission clinic	
Multidisciplinary preadmission clinic	
Average time spent by patient in preadmission clinic	
General (anesthetist and nurse)	2 hours
Multidisciplinary	4 hours
Other	
Patients who "do not attend" on the day of surgery	< 0.5%

Source: Data from: NSW Department of Health, Guideline: Pre-Procedure Preparation Toolkit, Document GL-2007_018, 02-Nov-2007, p. 18. Accessed December 9, 2013, at www.health.nsw.gov.au/policies/gl/2007/pdf/GL2007_018.pdf

Discussion Questions

1. Do the conclusions you draw from the case justify the headline? Why or why not?

2. Evaluate the indicators shown in Table 15-1. These are not the only indicators. Others included the waiting times for elective surgery by urgency category.

3. What do you estimate is the avoidable rate of canceled surgeries, and how would you develop an indicator for that?

4. How would you factor in the biases of both the doctors and NSW Health?

5. How might you manage the phenomenon that raising the benchmarks to "aspirational" levels means reporting more failures to the public?

6. Investigate the overlapping of private and public hospital systems in Australia. How does this complicate the issues of performance evaluation and improvement? In New South Wales, the Department of Health regulates private facilities and also manages the public ones. What are the strengths and weaknesses of such an arrangement?

Chapter 16

Conclusion: All Those Levers and No Fulcrum

The pragmatic method is primarily a method of settling metaphysical disputes that otherwise might be interminable. ... What difference would it practically make to any one if this notion rather than that notion were true? If no practical difference whatever can be traced, then the alternatives mean practically the same thing, and all dispute is idle. Whenever a dispute is serious, we (need to) be able to show some practical difference that must follow from one side or the other's being right.

Source: Reproduced from: *What is Pragmatism* (1904), from series of eight lectures dedicated to the memory of John Stuart Mill, *A New Name for Some Old Ways of Thinking*, in December 1904, from William James, Writings 1902–1920, The Library of America; Lecture II

WHERE TO STAND

A variety of levers can be used to try to move health care delivery in one direction or the other. All levers, however, require a strong fulcrum, a solid base against which the lever can operate when sufficient force is applied. In the United States, there is a clear absence of a reliable fulcrum. The passage of the Affordable Care Act (ACA) provides a fulcrum, albeit a sometimes shaky one, but its future is uncertain and there has been little stomach for movement since then.

Federal government bureaucrats know that the efforts of lobbyists, senior White House staffers, or chairs of congressional committees can undermine in a few days what has taken months of study and consensus building to achieve. At worst, one's program, or even one's agency, can disappear from the budget overnight. State offices are subject to the same risks, although governors sometimes stand more firmly because a state must meet its financial obligations, rather than print money or borrow more heavily.

Other potential fulcrums are likewise unreliable. Insurers continue to take their cut and pass on any added costs. Providers continue to maximize revenue. Employers continue to opt out of defined benefit programs. More and more of the costs of providing coverage and care accrue to state and federal governments through Medicare, Medicaid, and other programs. A 2013 survey of more than 200 key health care industry executives showed deep pessimism about our ability to improve both quality and inflation-adjusted costs, thus improving value. Only 1% were strongly positive, and 22% were strongly negative. To a parallel question about the current quality of U.S. health care, 16% were strongly positive, and 22% were strongly negative (Chin et al., 2013).

Fitting into Our Culture of Individualism

There are practical reasons for the on-the-one-hand and on-the-other-hand approach Harry Truman objected to when he called for a "one-handed" economist. Each of us brings a value system to any policy analysis, and those values inevitably get mixed up with the objective information that a scholarly approach offers decision makers. We are therefore understandably reluctant to declare one approach, one solution, or one system to be absolutely and unequivocally superior.

It is clear, however, that there are some things that fit well into the culture of the United States, and others that do not. One of our current cultural problems is that loud sets of voices are calling for one extreme or another with almost religious zeal. Reagan (1999) pointed to the horns of one health care dilemma. On the one hand, some would prefer that the federal government be the single purveyor of health care, but in a country that has long valued individualism and a free-market economic system it seems that there has to be some acceptance somewhere of some market forces in the process. On the other hand, it is clear that health care has been and will continue to be a highly imperfect marketplace. No matter how much information U.S. consumers receive, it is unlikely to be sufficient for them to make good decisions about all aspects of personal health care. Furthermore, it is clear that many segments of U.S. society cannot generate sufficient income to participate in that marketplace, whereas others may lack the skills or attributes necessary to participate fully and effectively in an unfettered health care market. Advocates of a single-payer system, who have been fond of saying that the United States is the only developed country without a national health system, are unlikely to see the United States fall in line with other nations anytime soon. Yet the current dependence on employers as the basic source of funding for care for workers and their families, while working and especially during retirement, is collapsing in the face of increasing international competition.

Limits of the Free-Market Approach

Those who argue that insurance, because it insulates health care consumers from any economic consequences, has been responsible for waste and overutilization have a strong point. Their efforts to shift more costs to the consumer will pay off some in terms of reduced utilization. There are three issues with that approach, however, in addition to the risk that for lower income individuals it will likely lead to underutilization with negative long-term consequences. The first is that much of its impact of cost-shifting may already have been achieved with the increases in deductibles and copays already in force, and the marginal effect may be much smaller than anticipated. The second is that information on quality and price is so opaque that the market cannot function very effectively until major changes take place to put realistic and relevant information into the hands of the consuming public. Those changes seem to be underway with respect to hospital prices and quality outcomes for specific institutions. Interpreting the data is still difficult in many cases.

The third constraint on the free-market approach is that some purchasers are quite capable of researching a medical condition and some are not. Educated individuals may be able to make an informed market decision because they:

- Have the technical information and the background to interpret it
- Have the market information on price and quality of providers of care for this medical condition
- Have the mental acuity to interpret it and make an appropriate decision
- Feel confident enough in their knowledge to act on it
- Have access to a primary care provider to test out their conclusions.

Six months later, however, they may have a set of symptoms that leaves them completely baffled and having to rely on the recommendations of their primary care provider or a local specialist, or are in pain and sedated at that moment. Yes, one may be capable of independent rational consumer decision-making behavior in the first instance, but not in the latter. In the second situation, one has to rely on one's agents, one's physicians, and, to a lesser extent, one's insurer.

If you have lived with gout for years, for example, you may be about as knowledgeable about the condition as most providers, but what if you have intestinal polyps and your personal physician sends you to a specialist who says, "I have this new technology that is less invasive than what is usually done and insurance will pay for it and you are a perfect candidate for it"?

Are you going to demur and go out and do a survey of methods and the market? Probably not. More likely, you say yes and then possibly look it up when you get home. But, if you cannot find out much about what it will cost and how effective it is and they tell you it is safe, then you are likely to keep your appointment and let your insurer cover it—especially if you have other things to worry about, like a paper due for your health policy class. The impact on health care costs of the market approach will be felt, but it will also be limited.

THE PHYSICIAN'S DILEMMA

What would likely changes do to the status of U.S. physicians? Many of the changes would clearly contribute to the industrialization of the health care sector and further weaken physician bargaining power. For example, if most medical centers were required to quote a single price up front for treating a medical condition and that single price bundles the professional, technical, and inpatient and aftercare components of that treatment, the physicians would have to bargain for their share, and they would likely be in a relatively weak position. In fact, it seems likely that more specialists will be on salary in community settings, just as they currently are in many academic medical centers. Some physicians might counter this development by setting up their own specialty hospitals, but one might anticipate further constraints on referrals if that response became very widespread.

More information on process, price, and quality; more bundling of pricing; more evidence-based protocols; requirements for reduced waste; and more intense case management would all, in part, constrain physician autonomy. At some point, health system policy makers will have to reconsider the patient–physician relationship and its attendant agency issues and try to reach an appropriate balance between industrialization and professionalism. One answer is for physicians to provide more assertive leadership when it comes to defining and maintaining the physician's role, especially the role of the primary provider, without trying to get back to the monopolistic mind-set that once tainted state and local American Medical Association efforts.

THE ERISA PROBLEM

Trying to make rational sense out of the health care system is difficult enough, but effectively having three complete sets of regulatory requirements, one under state insurance laws, one under the ACA, and one under the Employee Retirement Income Security Act of 1974 (ERISA), does not make sense, especially because the current responsibility for health and welfare in the United States rests principally with the states. At the time ERISA was passed, it was necessary as an enabler of nationwide collective bargaining by large employers and large industrial unions, but in an era when we have so many "model uniform codes" for so many types of commercial and personal business transactions, it would not seem to be an insurmountable obstacle to adopt a model uniform code for employer-based health insurance. The likely fly in the ointment is the health insurance industry itself, because the dual system for employer-provided health insurance blunts the ability of the states to mandate coverage requirements; however, the benefits of a uniform system are so great that legislatures, unions, and major corporations might be persuaded to fall in behind it and move it ahead. The requirement for a defined essential health benefit within the ACA-based exchanges is an initial step in that direction of establishing coverage mandates.

SO, WHAT IS LIKELY TO OCCUR?

The ACA will continue to be disruptive given continuing attempts to repeal it or roll it back and the high-stakes and often vicious political battles around its implementation. Conservatives have been focused on "repeal and replace," whereas liberals have been reluctant to start tinkering with it for fear of opening it up to major, undesired changes. Few analysts and policy makers, however, deny that some revisions will be necessary even if it is successful overall. Significant failure could force a reversion to earlier policies; major course adjustments; or further, far more extensive reforms. A small number of heath care advocates have openly stated that they see the ACA as a stepping stone to a single-payer system. That assessment assumes that the ACA will be a failed strategy, and that its failure will lead to greater government intervention rather than retrenchment.

Further major change is unlikely until the U.S. economy is threatened by other events and health care is seen as a part of the total package of changes that includes revisions in our tax code and is part of a compromise designed to deal with bigger overall problems. Short of that, we are likely to see incremental changes with an increase in the proportion of the gross domestic product devoted to health care. Regardless of the party in power, health care will compete for attention with other agenda items, such as national security, immigration reform, and inflationary pressures, due to overall lack of savings and the rising cost of interest necessary to attract foreign capital. Along the way, we will probably experience some positive effects from prevention programs, witness increased implementation of pay-for-performance, and see some offsetting federal efforts to strip out of Medicare and Medicaid some services that are not essential to health and safety in the short run. The pressure on both low-income working families and older people to pay a higher percentage of their income for health care will continue, despite the offsets from individual subsidies under the ACA.

WHY NOT AN UNRAVELING?

In January 2006, in advance of President Bush's State of the Union speech, *The Economist* published a scathing review of the U.S. health care system, including a forecast of a great unraveling. If true, such a disaster is still a number of years away for the following reasons:

- Measures undertaken will have some effect. In particular, the individual and employer mandates of the ACA will add to the revenue stream available.
- Efficiency improvement in other sectors, such as energy production, will enable consumers to allocate a larger proportion of the gross domestic product to their health care with somewhat less pain.
- Inflation in other sectors, such as food and shelter, could divert interest and support.
- Increasing employment in the health sector is seen by many as economically healthy given the absence of growth in other sectors.
- The increased use of modern information technology may ultimately reduce administrative costs in some segments of the industry.
- Increased patient participation in making choices about such things as purchasing policies from the exchanges and shopping among high-deductible plans has been making patients increasingly conscious of costs and interested in containing them.
- Additional actions may be taken to constrain the exploding costs of post-discharged care and biological drugs including those now used to treat wet macular degeneration, hepatitis, hemophilia, and many forms of cancer and autoimmune disease.

Measures Already Undertaken Will Have Some Effect

Although measures such as consumer-driven health care and the growth of integrated health systems are unlikely to solve the problems of the health sector, they will, like other measures before them, have some effect in slowing the rate of growth. Efforts to improve quality of care and introduce evidence-based medicine will have some impact, and so will efforts to get comparative price and quality information to consumers and payers. Reductions in provider incomes, although personally painful, are unlikely to reduce the care available and may increase productivity. Continued, accelerated deployment of health information technology may do the same. Given enough time, these many small improvements will have some cumulative effect, especially if institutions increase their focus on internal efficiency.

Inflation Could Offset Impact of Health Care Growth

Despite the longstanding opposition of the Federal Reserve, politicians may find it advantageous to allow a higher level of inflation in the overall economy, bringing growth to the rest of the economy and to tax revenues. Recently, more and more economists, including Federal Reserve insiders, have come to believe the national inflation rate in the late 1990s and early 2000s has been too low (Applebaum, 2013). If there are constraints on health care expenditures at the same time, the inflation rate in the overall economy might approach or surpass that of the health care sector and reduce the burden of added costs. International lenders may require more repayment of loans and force more favorable exchange rates, raising the costs of foreign goods, so that health care does not seem quite so exorbitant in comparison.

Employment in the Health Sector

As the proportion of national income devoted to health care increases, we see more and more employment in that sector. Like most other service sectors, health care employs a large number of individuals of moderate and low income. Continuing industrialization will mean that some higher-income workers will be displaced by lower-income workers as some tasks become rationalized and can be handled routinely. One risk to the country of having health care get so big is that a large proportion of the population will have their aspirations tied to the growth of that sector. Major cutbacks in expenditures, whether caused by improved quality and productivity or taken arbitrarily, will trigger a pushback by the affected employees. The growth of the health care sector is not a negative event from an employment point of view, especially as manufacturing and information-related service jobs continue to move out of the country.

Some economists argue that health care expansion is a key to maintaining employment and that a substantial proportion of the population will be willing to spend a greater proportion of their income on health care because they attach a high subjective utility to their own longevity and care (Cutler, Rosen, & Vijan, 2006; Hall & Jones, 2007). The problem with such growth is that it continues to force the transfer of wealth away from the young, the healthy, and the poor and toward the older population, the sick, and the professionals. At some point, those footing the bill will begin to object strongly to these transfers, and we will see much more stringent measures to control expenditures and reduce those transfer rates (Kolata, 2006). This is especially likely to create a political backlash if the income gap between low-wage service workers and higher-income knowledge workers and managers continues to expand.

From the perspective of cost control, one would hope that the rapid introduction of health information technology would lead to a reduction in employment of support staff in clinics and hospitals. Increased insurance coverage could also reduce the need for as many financial counselors and debt collectors.

Consumer Awareness and Participation in Purchasing Decisions

With some 20% of enrollees choosing high-deductable plans and with even more individuals having to buy their own insurance as employers pull back their contributions, we are seeing a more price-sensitive insurance market. Much of the slower inflation over the last year or two has been attributed to such consumer participation. The trends supporting this phenomenon are likely to continue and are supported by a number of transparency efforts visualized in the ACA.

Efforts to Constrain Growth in Areas Such as Aftercare and Costs of Biologicals

It is evident to most observers that there is an upper limit on the proportion of the national income that can be devoted to health care. It was that recognition that led many groups, such as hospitals, drug companies, and insurers, not to oppose the ACA the way they had opposed the Clinton health plan (Starr, 2011). If health care's share of the economy does not top out, high-growth sectors are likely to receive a heavy dose of regulation. In the aftercare market there is likely to be a further crackdown on fraud and abuse followed by price controls or special excise taxes like the one on durable medical equipment. Biological drugs are also likely to be subject to constraints on gross margins and limitations on use. An example of the latter would be restricting the newer, very expensive hepatitis C drugs to those patients for whom they are the only way to avoid death prior to availability of a liver transplant, those for whom comorbidities make transplantation impractical, or those who cannot tolerate the older treatments. Although, allowing people to sicken dramatically before treating them with readily available drugs (in many areas of this country, such as the San Francisco Bay Area, one must be nearly dead before qualifying for a liver) would be a scenario similar to the April 16, 2014, recommendation of NHS England's Clinical Priorities Advisory Group (NHS England, 2014), which would cover only about 500 patients if implemented.

A number of mergers and restructurings of pharmaceutical and biotech companies in early 2014 were attributed by various analysts to market recognition of the handwriting on the wall about drug margins. Constraints on health care expenditures are apparently much better accepted in corporate circles than in political ones.

CONCLUSION

The United States is unlikely to undertake major health care reforms at the federal level beyond those in the ACA in the near future. The states, however, will continue to lead the reform effort. A number of tweaking changes will move forward, but major reforms will not take place when the states are in financial trouble. Only dramatic problems financing the national debt are likely to lead to radical changes beyond the ACA. Employers may support the notions of value-based care, especially transparency in pricing, and an end to price discrimination. We are likely, however, to see limited excise taxes on specific health care goods and services and gainsharing incentive schemes added to programs like Medicare Advantage.

The position of specialists is likely to weaken as primary care providers are asked to reduce waste and improve efficiency, and capital-intensive, rare, and complex procedures will be concentrated at selected sites, often outside traditional market areas. Available measures and expected revenue adjustments are likely to delay the anticipated "unraveling" of the health care system. As the health sector grows, people may become increasingly concerned about upsetting the economy with radical measures. The issue that will have to be faced is not the size of the sector, but the distributional effects of its growth, the equity concerns of transfers of income from the young on behalf of the old and from the poor and middle class toward the wealthy. These will also generate pressures to reduce waste and overall cost in the health sector as employers, patients, and taxpayers resist further premiums or taxation.

References

Abelson, R. (2006a, March 8). Pay method said to sway drug choices of oncologists. *New York Times*. Retrieved March 9, 2006, from www.nytimes.com/2006/03 /08/health/08docs

Abelson, R. (2006b, June 28). Charities tied to doctors get drug industry gifts. *New York Times*. Retrieved June 28, 2006, from www.nytimes.com/2006/06 /28/business/28foundation.html?pagewanted=all&_r=0

Abelson, R. (2006c, August 18). Heart procedure is off the charts in an Ohio city. *New York Times*. Retrieved August 18, 2006, from www.nytimes.com/2006/08 /18/business/18stent

Ackerman, F., & Heinzerling, L. (2004). *Priceless: On knowing the price of everything and the value of nothing.* New York: The New Press.

Alexander, A., & Garloch, K. (2012, October 23). Hospitals probed on use of drug discounts. *Charlotte Observer*. Retrieved September 29, 2013, from www .charlotteobserver.com/2012/09/29/3566421/hospitals-probed-on-use of drug .html

Alexander, A., Neff, J., & Garloch, K. (2013, April 3). NC hospitals read profits from discount drugs. *Raleigh News & Observer*, pp. 1A, 6A.

Altman, S. H., Shactman, D., & Eilat, E. (2006). Could U.S. hospitals go the way of U.S. airlines? *Health Affairs, 25*(1), 11–21.

AMA vs. U.S., 1943.

American Academy of Pediatrics. (2007). *What is a medical home?* Retrieved February 1, 2007, from www.medicalhomeinfo.org/health/general

American Case Management Association. (2009). *Case management in hospital/ health care systems.* Retrieved July 11, 2013, from www.acmaweb.org/section .asp?sID=48mn=mn1&sn=sn1&wrg=mh

ANA (American Nurses Association). 2005. *Nurses' bill of rights.* Retrieved June 5, 2014, from www.nursingworld.org/NursesBillofRights

Anderson, G. F., Reinhardt, U. E., Hussey, P. S., & Petrosyan, V. (2003). It's the prices stupid: Why the United States is so different from other countries. *Health Affairs, 22*(3), 89–105.

Aos, S., Mayfield, J., Miller, M., & Yen, W. (2006). *Evidence-based treatment of alcohol, drug, and mental health disorders: Potential benefits, costs, and fiscal impacts for Washington state.* Olympia, WA: Washington State Institute for Public Policy.

Appelbaum, B. (2011, February 16). As U.S. agencies put more value on a life, businesses fret. *New York Times*. Retrieved November 12, 2013, from www.nytimes .com/2011/02/17/business/economy/17regulation.html

Applebaum, B. (2013, October 26). In Fed and out, many now think inflation helps. *New York Times*. Retrieved October 26, 2013, from www.nytimes.com/2013/10/27/business/economy/in-fed-and-out-many-now-think-inflation-helps.html?_r=0

Armstrong, D. (2006, December 13). Drug firm's cash sways debate over test for pregnant women. *The Wall Street Journal*, pp. A1, A12.

Arrow, K. J. (1963). Uncertainty and the welfare economics of medical care. *American Economic Review, 53,* 941–973.

Association of American Medical Colleges. (2005). Calls for modest increase in medical school enrollment. Press release. Retrieved from www.aamc.org./newsroom/pressrel/2005/05022

Association of Territorial and State Health Officers. (2012). *Primary care and public heath integration—primary care and public health strategic map.* Retrieved July 9, 2013, from www.astho.org/pcph-strategic-map.pdf

AusAID, UNAIDS, & National AIDS Council, Papua New Guinea. (2004, September). *HIV/AIDS Stakeholder Mapping in Papua New Guinea.* Retrieved August 5, 2013, from www.ausaid.gov.au/publications/Pages/8286_5720_261_8961_8145.aspx

Baker, F., Sheldon, A. C., & McLaughlin, C. P. (1970). *Systems analysis and medical care.* Cambridge, MA: MIT Press.

Barry, P., & Basher, B. (2007). Health our system. *AARP Bulletin, 48*(3), 12–14.

Basch, P. (2006, September 10). Pay-for-performance: Too much of a good thing—or too worried about the wrong things? *Health Affairs eLetters.* Retrieved January 6, 2007, from http//content.healthaffairs.org/cgi/eletters/25/5/w412

Becker, H. (Ed.). (1955). *Prepayment and the community.* New York: McGraw-Hill.

Belluck, P. (2007, January 10). Massachusetts could serve as a guide in California's health insurance bid. *New York Times.* Retrieved January 11, 2007, from www.nytimes.com/2007/01/10/us/10mass

Berry, L. L., & Saltman, K. D. (2007). *Management lessons from the Mayo Clinic.* New York: McGraw-Hill.

Berwick, D. M. (2009). What 'patient-centered' should mean: Confessions of an extremist. *Health Affairs, 28*(4), w555–w565.

Biotechnology Industry Organization. (2013). *The 340B Drug Discount Program: A review and analysis of the 340B Program.* Retrieved September 15, 2013, from www.bio.org/sites/default/files/340B%20White%20Paper%20FINAL.pdf

Blackley, B. G. (2006, June 27). Testimony before the U.S. Senate Special Committee on Aging, Washington, DC, "The Globalization of Health Care: Can Medical Tourism Reduce Health Care Costs?" Retrieved from www.aging.senate.gov/hearings/the-globalization-of-health-care-can-medical-tourism-reduce-health-care-costs

Blencowe, H., Cousens, S., Modell, B., & Lawn, J. (2010). Folic acid to reduce neonatal mortality from neural tube disorders. *International Journal of Epidemiology, 39*(Suppl 1), i110–i121.

Blendon, R. J., Brodie, M., & Benson, J. (1995). What happened to America's support for the Clinton Health Plan? *Health Affairs, 14*(2), 7–23.

Blendon, R. J., Schoen, C., DesRoches, C. M., Young, J. T., DesRoches, C. M., Osborn, R., et al. (2002). Inequities in health care: A five country survey. *Health Affairs, 21*(3), 182–191.

Boden, R., & Epstein, D. (2006). Managing the research imagination? Globalisation and research in higher education. *Globalisation, Societies and Education, 4*(2), 223–236.

Bodenheimer, T. S., & Grumbach, K. (2005). *Understanding health policy: A clinical approach* (4th ed.). New York: McGraw-Hill, Lange Medical Books.

Bohmer, R. M. J. (2009). *Designing care: Aligning the nature and management of health care*. Boston: Harvard Business Press.

Bohmer, R. M. J., & Lawrence, D. M. (2008). Care platforms: A basic building block for care delivery. *Health Affairs, 27*(5), 1336–1340.

Borger, C., Smith, S., Truffer, C., Keehan, S., Sisko, A., Poisal, J., et al. (2006). Health spending projections through 2015: Changes on the horizon. *Health Affairs, 25*(2), w61–w73.

Bradshaw, P. L., & Bradshaw, G. (2004). *Health policy for health care professionals*. London: Sage.

Braithwaite, R. S., Meltzer, D. O., King, J. T., Leslie, D., & Roberts, M. S. (2008). What does the value of modern medicine say about the $50,000 per quality-adjusted life-year decision rule? *Medical Care, 46*(4), 349–356.

Brazier, J. E., Rowen, D., Mavranezouli, I., Tsuchiya, A., Young, T., Yang, Y., et al. (2012). Developing and testing methods for deriving preference-based measures of health from condition-specific measures (and other patient-based measures of outcome). *Value in Health, 16*(32), 1–114. DOI: 10:3310/hta16320. Retrieved November 10, 2013, from www.hta.ac.uk

Brill, S. (2013, February 20). Bitter pill: Why medical bills are killing us. *Time .com*. Retrieved March 3, 2013, from http://healthland.time.com/2013/02/20 /bitter-pill-why-medical-bills-are-killing-us/?

Brown, L. D. (2006, April 11). Impermanent politics: The Hillsborough County health care plan and community innovation for the uninsured. *Health Affairs, 25*(3), w162–w172.

Brugha, R., & Varvasovszky, Z. (2000). Stakeholder analysis: A review. *Health Policy and Planning, 15*(3), 239–246.

Bunker, J. P., Barnes, B. A., & Mosteller, F. (1979). *The costs, risks and benefits of surgery*. Princeton, NJ: Princeton University Press.

Cabinet Implementation Unit. (2006). *Guide to preparing implementation plans*. Canberra, Australia: Department of the Prime Minister and Cabinet.

Calkthan, D. (1991). Commentary: Ethics and priority setting in Oregon. *Health Affairs, 10*(2), 78–87.

Callaghan, P. (2006, February 16). One Democrat stands in the way of Washington state tobacco bill. *Tacoma News Tribune*. Retrieved October 14, 2006, from www .shns.com/shns/g_index2.cfm?action=detail&pk=CALLAGHAN-02-16-06

Cannon, M. F., & Tanner, M. D. (2005). *Healthy competition: What's holding back health care and how to free it*. Washington, DC: The Cato Institute.

Centers for Disease Control and Prevention. (1991). Effectiveness in disease and injury prevention use of folic acid for prevention of spina bifida and other neural tube defects: 1983–1991. *MMWR Weekly, 40*(30), 513–516.

Centers for Disease Control and Prevention. (2000). Folate status in women of childbearing age: United States 1999. *MMWR Weekly, 49*(42), 962–965.

Centers for Disease Control and Prevention. (2004). Spina bifida and anencephaly before and after folic acid mandate: United States, 1995–1996 and 1999–2000. *MMWR Weekly, 53*(17), 362–365.

Centers for Disease Control and Prevention. (2006). National, state, and urban area vaccination coverage among children aged 19–35 months: United States 2005. *MMWR Weekly, 55*(36), 988–993.

Centers for Disease Control and Prevention. (2010). *Healthy People 2020 Objectives.* Retrieved from www.healthypeople.gov/2020/topicsobjectives2020/objectives list.aspx

Centers for Medicare and Medicaid Services, Office of the Actuary. (2012). *National health expenditure projections, 2011–2021.* Retrieved from www.cms.gov /Research-Statistics-Data-and-Systems/Statistics-Trends-and-Reports /NationalHealthExpendData/Downloads/ProjPDF.pdf

Centers for Medicare and Medicaid Services. (2013). *Key features of the affordable care act by year.* Retrieved May 5, 2013, from www.healthcare.gov/law/full /timeline.html

Chin, W. W., Hamermesh, R. G., Huckman, R. S., McNeil, B. J., & Newhouse, J. P. (2013). *Forum on healthcare innovation: 5 imperatives.* Retrieved July 29, 2013, from www.hbs.edu/healthcare/pdf/Forum-on-Healthcare-Innovation-5-Imperatives.pdf

Christensen, C., Bohmer, R. M. J., & Kenagy, J. (2000). Will disruptive innovations cure health care? *Harvard Business Review, 78*(5), 102–111.

Cleverley, W. O., & Cameron, A. E. (2003). *Essentials of health care finance* (5th ed.). Gaitherstown, MD: Aspen Publishers.

Clinton, H. R. (2003). *Living history.* New York: Scribner.

Code of Federal Regulations. (2013, April 1). *Protection of human subjects.* Washington, DC: Government Printing Office. Title 21, Volume 1, Part 50, Subpart B.

Congressional Budget Office. (2012). *Raising the excise tax on cigarettes: Effects on health and the federal budget.* Washington, DC: Author.

Conrad, P. (2007). *The medicalization of society: On the transformation of human conditions into treatable disorders.* Baltimore, MD: The Johns Hopkins University Press.

Cooper, M., & Chan, S. (2006, November 28). Panel said to call for closing 9 New York hospitals. *New York Times.* Retrieved November 28, 2006, from www .nytimes.com/2006/11/28/nyregion/28hospitals

Courneya, P. T., Palattao, K. J., & Gallagher, J. M. (2013). HealthPartners online clinic for simple conditions delivers savings of $88 per episode and high patient approval. *Health Affairs, 32*(2), 385–391.

Coye, M. J., & Kell, J. (2006). How hospitals confront new technology. *Health Affairs, 25*(1), 163–173.

Crider, K. S., Bailey, L. B., & Berry, R. J. (2011). Folic acid food fortification—its history, effect, concerns, and future directions. *Nutrients, 3*(3), 370–384.

Cutler, D. M., Rosen, A. B., & Vijan, S. (2006). The value of medical spending in the United States 1960–2000. *New England Journal of Medicine, 355*(9), 920–927.

Daniels, N. (2006). Toward ethical review of health system transformations. *American Journal of Public Health, 96*(3), 447–451.

Davis, F. D. (1989). Perceived usefulness, perceived ease of use, and user acceptance of information technology. *MIS Quarterly, 13*(3), 319–340.

Davis, K. (2004). Consumer-directed health care: Will it improve health system performance? *Health Services Research, 39*(4, Pt. II), 1219–1233.

deBruyn, J. (2013). *McCrory's Medicaid plan sprouts more questions than answers.* Retrieved from www.bizjournals.com/triangle/blog/2013/04/mccrorys-medicaid-plan-sprouts-more.html

Deming, W. E. (1986). *Out of the crisis.* Cambridge, MA: MIT Center for Advanced Engineering Study.

Dihoff, D. (2013, November 6). Medicaid reform discussion with Governor McCrory. *Heard in the Halls,* Edition 53. Raleigh, NC: National Alliance for Mental Illness North Carolina.

Donabedian, A. (1980). The definition of quality and approaches to its assessment. *Explorations in quality assessments and monitoring* (Vol. 1, pp. 95–99). Ann Arbor, MI: Health Administration Press.

Dopson, S., & Fitzgerald, L. (Eds.) (2005). *Knowledge to action? Evidence-based health care in context.* Oxford, UK: Oxford University Press.

Dopson, S., Lacock, L., Gabbay, J., Ferlie, E., & Fitzgerald, L. (2005). Evidence-based health care and the implementation gap. In Dopson, S., & Fitzgerald, L. (Eds.), *Knowledge to action? Evidence-based health care in context.* Oxford, UK: Oxford University Press, pp. 28–47, pp. 182–197.

Doran, T., Fullwood, C., Gravelle, H., Reeves, D., Kontopantelis, E., Hiroeh, U., et al. (2006). Pay-for-performance programs in family practices in the United Kingdom. *New England Journal of Medicine, 355*(4), 375–384.

Dror, Y. (1969). *The prediction of political feasibility.* Santa Monica, CA: The Rand Corporation.

Dror, Y. (1988). Uncertainty: Coping with it and with political feasibility. In Miser, H. J., & Quade, E. S. (Eds.), *Handbook of systems analysis: Craft issues and procedural choices.* New York: Elsevier Science Publishing.

Drucker, P. F. (1974). *Management: Tasks, responsibilities, practices.* New York: Harper & Row.

The Economist. (2006, January 26). Editorial: Desperate measures. Retrieved June 10, 2006, from www.economist.com/world/PrinterFriendly.cfm?story_id=4326968

Ebbing, M., Bønaa, K. H., Nygård, O., Arnesen, E., Ueland, P. M., Nordrehaug, J. E., et al. (2009). Cancer incidence and mortality after treatment with folic acid and vitamin B12. *JAMA, 302*(19), 2119–2126.

Edwards, E. T., Charles, J. M., & Lloyd-Williams, H. (2013). Public health economics: A systematic review of guidance for the economic evaluation of public health interventions and discussion of key methodological issues. *BMC Public Health, 13,* 1001. Retrieved November 16, 2013, from www.biocentral.com/1471-2458/13/1001

Einthoven, A. C., & Tollen, L. A. (2005). Competition in health care: It takes systems to pursue quality and efficiency. *Health Affairs, 24*(Suppl. 3), W5-420–W5-433.

Elwyn, G., Rix, A., Holt, T., & Jones, D. (2012). Why do clinicians not refer patients to online decision support tools? Interviews with front line clinics in the NHS. *BMJ Open* 2:e001350. Retrieved March 26, 2013, from http://bmjopen/bmj.com

Emanuel, E., & Fuchs, V. (2006, November 13). How to cure U.S. health care. *Fortune,* p. 78.

Epstein, A. M. (2006). Paying for performance in the United States and abroad. *New England Journal of Medicine, 355*(4), 406–408.

Epstein, A. M. (2007). Pay for performance at the tipping point. *New England Journal of Medicine, 356*(5), 515–517.

Farias, M., Jenkins, K., Lock, J., Rathod, R., et al. (2013). Standardized clinical assessment and management plans (SCAMPs) provide a better alternative to clinical practice guidelines. *Health Affairs, 32*(5), 911–918.

Feldstein, M. (2005). *Rethinking social insurance.* Retrieved November 18, 2006, from www.nber.org/feldstein/aeajan8.pdf

Ferdows, K. (2006). Transfer of changing production know-how. *Production and Operations Management, 15,* 1–9.

Ferlie, E. (2005). Conclusion: From evidence to actionable knowledge. In Dopson, S., & Fitzgerald, L. (Eds.), *Knowledge to action? Evidence-based health care in context* (pp. 182–197). Oxford, UK: Oxford University Press.

Fisher, E. S., Wennberg, D. E., Stuckel, T. A., & Gottlieb, D. J. (2004, October 7). Variations in the longitudinal efficiency of academic medical centers. *Health Affairs,* Suppl Variation, Var 19–32. Retrieved April 20, 2007, from www.healthaffairs.org/RWJ/variations_Fisher.pdf

Fleurence, R. L., Naci, H., & Jansen, J. P. (2010). The critical role of observational evidence in comparative effectiveness research. *Health Affairs, 29*(10), 1826–1832.

Food and Drug Administration. (1993). Food standards: Amendment of the standards of identity for enriched grain products to require addition of folic acid. *Federal Register, 58,* 53305–53312.

Food Standards Australia New Zealand. (2009). *Mandatory folic acid fortification—summary of emerging evidence on health outcomes.* Retrieved November 5, 2013, from www.foodsafety.govt.nz/elibrary/industry/proposed-amendment-nz-folic-acid-standard/fsanz-summary-of-emerging-evidence-on-health-outcomes.pdf

Fox, D. M., & Leichter, H. M. (1991). Rationing care in Oregon: The new accountability. *Health Affairs, 10*(2), 7–27.

Fox, P. D. (2001). An overview of managed care. In Kongstvedt, P. R. (Ed.), *The managed health care handbook* (pp. 3–16). Gaithersburg, MD: Aspen.

Freidson, E. (2001). *Professional power: The third logic.* Cambridge, UK: Polity Press.

Freudenheim, M. (2006, January 26). Prognosis is mixed for health savings. *New York Times.* Retrieved January 26, 2006, from www.nytimes.com/2006/01/26 /business/26accounts

Friedman, T. L. (2005). *The world is flat: A brief history of the twenty-first century.* New York: Farrar, Straus, and Giroux.

Frist, B. (2002). Public health and national security: The critical role of increased federal support. *Health Affairs, 21*(6), 117–130.

Fuchs, V. R. (2002). What's ahead for health insurance in the U.S. *New England Journal of Medicine, 346*(23), 1822–1824.

Fuchs, V. R. (2013). The gross domestic product and health care spending. *New England Journal of Medicine, 369*(2), 107–109.

Fuhrmans, V. (2007a, January 19). California gets health response. *The Wall Street Journal,* p. A10.

Fuhrmans, V. (2007b, January 10). A novel plan helps hospital wean itself off pricey test. *The Wall Street Journal,* pp. A1, A11.

Gardner, E. S., Jr., & McLaughlin, C. P. (1980). Forecasting: A cost control tool for health care managers. *Health Care Management Review, 5*(3), 31–38.

Garrison, L. P., Jr. (2009). Editorial: On the benefits of modeling using QALYs for societal resource allocation: The model is the message. *Value in Health,* 12(Suppl. 1), 536–537.

Gaull, G. E., Testa, C.A., Thomas, P. R., & Weinrich, D. A. (1996). Fortification of the food supply with folic acid to prevent neural tube defects is not yet warranted (fortifying policy with science—the case of folate). *The Journal of Nutrition, 126*(3), 773S–780S.

Gaynor, M. (2006). What do we know about competition and quality in health care markets? NBER Working Paper 12301. Retrieved November 12, 2006, from www.nber.org/papers/w12301

George, A. (2013). *McCrory's plan would ruin an enviable health care program.* Retrieved April 26, 2013, from www.newsobserver.com/2013/04/2847759/mccrorys-plan-would-ruin-an-enviable.html

Gilabert, P., & Lawford-Smith, H. (2012). Political feasibility: A conceptual expansion. *Political Studies, 60,* 809–825.

Gilfillan, S. C. (1952). The prediction of technical change. *Review of Economics and Statistics, 34*(4), 368–385.

Gilliam, F. D. (2005, December 6). Framing health care reform for public understanding and support. Presentation delivered at Health Legislative Conference, Seattle, WA. Retrieved January 30, 2007, from http://depts.washington .edu/rchpol/docs/legcon05/Gilliam.ppt#1

Gilson, L., Erasmus. E., Borghi, J., Macha, J., Kamuzora, P., & Mtei, G. (2012). Using stakeholder analysis to support moves towards universal coverage: Lessons from the SHIELD project. *Health Policy and Planning, 27*(Suppl 1), i64–i76.

Goddard, B. (1998, March 25). Public policy advocacy campaigns. Speech delivered at Duke University, Durham, NC. Retrieved January 30, 2007, from www .pubpol.duke.edu/centers/dewitt/papers/archive/15/15_2.doc

Goldman, D., Shekelle, P. G., Bhattacharya, J., Hurd, M. D., Joyce, G. F., Lakdawalla, D. M., et al. (2004). *Health status and medical treatment of the future elderly: Final report*. Santa Monica, CA: The RAND Corporation, TR-169-CMS.

Goldman, D. P., Shang, B., Bhattacharya, J., Garber, A. M., Hurd, M., Joyce, G. F., et al. (2005). Consequences of health trends and medical innovation for the elderly of the future. *Health Affairs, 24*(Suppl. 2), W5-R5–W5-R17.

Goldsteen, R. L., Goldsteen, K., Swan, J. H., & Clemeña, W. (2001). Harry and Louise and health care reform: Romancing public opinion. *Journal of Health Politics, Policy and Law, 26*(6), 1325–1352.

Government Accounting Office. (2011). *Drug pricing: Manufacturer discounts in 340B program offer benefits, but federal oversight needs improvement*. GAO-11-836. Retrieved April 15, 2013, from www.gao.gov/new.items/d11836.pdf

Grassley, C. (2012). Letter to Carol Garrison from Sen. Grassley on behalf of U.S. Senate Committee on the Judiciary of May 10, 2012. Retrieved May 31, 2014, from http://www.grassley.senate.gov/sites/default/files/about/upload/2012_05_08-CEG-to-UAB-Hospital-340B.pdf

Grassley, C. (2013). Letter to Mary K Wakefield from Sen. Grassley on behalf of U.S. Senate Committee on the Judiciary of March 27, 2013. Retrieved December 21, 2013, from www.grassley.senate.gov/about/upload/2013-03-27-CEG-to-HRSA-340B-Oversight-3.pdf

Grol, E. (2006). *Quality development in health care in the Netherlands*. The Commonwealth Funds. Retrieved June 5, 2006, from www.cmwf.org/publications/publications_show.htm

Grosse, S. D., Waitzman, N. J., Romano, P. S., & Mulinare, J. (2005). Reevaluating the benefits of folic acid fortification in the United States: Economic analysis, regulation and public health. *American Journal of Public Health, 95*(11), 1917–1922.

Hacker, J. S. (1997). *The road to nowhere: The genesis of President Clinton's program for health security*. Princeton, NJ: Princeton University Press.

Hadler, N. M. (2004). *The last well person: How to stay well despite the health-care system*. Montreal: McGill-Queens University Press.

Hadler, N. M. (2011). *Rethinking aging: Growing old and living well in an overtreated society*. Chapel Hill, NC: The University of North Carolina Press.

Hadler, N. M. (2013). *The citizen patient: Reforming health care for the benefit of the patient, not the system*. Chapel Hill, NC: The University of North Carolina Press.

Haislmaier, E. F. (2006). The significance of Massachusetts Health Reform. Web Memo #1035. Washington, DC: The Heritage Foundation. Retrieved January 3, 2007, from www.heritage.org/Research/HealhtCare/wm1035.cfm

Hall, R. E., & Jones, C. I. (2007). The value of life and the rise in health spending. *Quarterly Journal of Economics, 122*, 39–72.

Hansmann, H. (1996). *The ownership of enterprise*. Cambridge, MA: The Belknap Press of Harvard University Press.

HealthCare.gov. (2013). Timeline for implementation of the Affordable Care Act. Retrieved May 5, 2013, from www.healthcare.gov/law/full/timeline.html#2014

Heath, I. (2005). Promotion of disease and corrosion of medicine. *Canadian Family Physician*. Retrieved June 10, 2006, from www.cfpc.ca/cfp/2005/Oct /vol51-oct-editorials-2

Henderson, J. W. (2002). *Health economics and policy* (2nd ed.). Cincinnati, OH: Southwestern/Thomson Learning.

Hertkampf, E. (2004). *Folic acid fortification: Current knowledge and future priorities (discussion paper)*. Santiago, Chile: Institute of Nutrition and Food Technology, University of Santiago.

Herzlinger, R. E. (1997). *Market driven health care*. Reading, MA: Addison-Wesley.

Hibbard, E. D., & Smithells, R. W. (1965). Folic acid metabolism and human embryopathy. *Lancet, 1*, 1254–1256.

Hibbard, J. H., Green, J., & Overton, V. (2013). Patients with lower activation associated with higher costs: Delivery systems should know their patient "scores." *Health Affairs, 32*(2), 216–221.

Hing, E. & Bhuiya, F. (2012). Wait time for treatment in hospital emergency departments: 2009. *NCHS Data Brief*, 102. Hyattsville, MD: National Center for Health Statistics.

Hoban, R. (2013a, April 15). How 'broken' is NC Medicaid? *North Carolina Health News*. Retrieved September 7, 2013, from www.northcarolinahealthnews. org/2013/04/15/how-broken-is-nc-medicaid/

Hoban, R. (2013b, April 16). NC Medicaid has strengths, weaknesses, but "broken"? *North Carolina Health News*. Retrieved November 9, 2013, from www.north carolinahealthnews.org/2013/04/16/nc-medicaid-has-strengths-weaknesses/

Holstein, W. J. (2006, December 31). For better care, work across lines. *New York Times*. Retrieved from www.nytimes.com/2006/12/31/jobs/31advi.html

Homer, J. B., & Hirsch, G. B. (2006). System dynamics modeling for public health: Background and opportunities. *American Journal of Public Health, 96*(3), 452–458.

Houghton, A. (1995, September 28). In memoriam: The Office of Technology Assessment, 1972–1995. *House of Representatives—Congressional Record, Extension of Remarks* (pp. E1868–1870). Retrieved from www.princeton.edu/˜ota/ns20 /hough_f.html

Hsiao, W. C., Kappel, S., & Gruber, B. (2011, February 17). Health system reform design: Achieving affordable universal health care in Vermont. Burlington: Vermont State Legislature. Retrieved July 29, 2013, from www.leg.state.vt.us /jfo/healthcare/FINAL%20REPORT%20Hsiao%20Final%20Report%20-%20 17%20February%202011_3.pdf

Hurley, R. E., Pham, H. H., & Claxton, G. (2005). A widening rift in access and quality: Growing evidence of economic disparities. *Health Affairs, 24*(Suppl. 3), W5-566–W5-576.

Ingram, J., & Restropo, K. (2013). *The Partnership for a Healthy North Carolina*. Charlotte, NC: John Locke Foundation. Retrieved November 1, 2013, from www .JohnLocke.org/acrobat/policyReports/PartnershipRevised.pdf

Institute of Medicine. (2000a). *Bridging disciplines in the brain, behavioral and clinical sciences*. Washington, DC: National Academies Press.

Institute of Medicine. (2000b). *To err is human: Building a safer health system*. Washington, DC: National Academies Press.

Institute of Medicine. (2001). *Crossing the quality chasm: A new health system for the 21st century*. Washington, DC: National Academies Press.

Institute of Medicine. (2012a). Best care at low cost: The path to continuously learning health care in America. Retrieved August 3, 2013, from www.iom.edu /Reports/2012/Best-Health-Care-at-Lower-Cost-the-Path-to-Continuously-Learning-Health-Care-in-America.aspx

Institute of Medicine. (2012b). *The Learning Health System and its Innovation Collaborative—update report*. Retrieved August 3, 2013, from www.iom.edu/Activities /Quality/~/media/files/Activity%20Files/Quality/VSRT/Core%20socuments /ForEDistrib.pdf

Jacobson, M., O'Malley, A. J., Earle, C. C., Gaccione, P., & Newhouse, J. P. (2006). Does reimbursement influence chemotherapy treatment for cancer patients? *Health Affairs, 25*(2), 437–443.

Jones, A. P., Homer, J. B., Murphy, D. L., Essien, J. D. K., Milstein, B., & Seville, D. A. (2006). Understanding diabetes population dynamics through simulation modeling and experimentation. *American Journal of Public Health, 96*(3), 488–493.

Jonsson, P. (2006, September 29). Union blocks foreign healthcare plan. *Christian Science Monitor*, p. 2. Retrieved October 11, 2006, from www.csmonitor /com/2006/0929/p02201-usec

Junod, S. W. (2006). *Folic acid fortification: Fact and folly*. U.S. Food and Drug Administration. Retrieved January 7, 2006, from www.fda.gov/oc/history/making history/folicacid.html

Kaiser Family Foundation. (2009). *Policy brief: Community Care of North Carolina: Putting health reform ideas into practice in Medicaid*. May. Retrieved from www.kaiser familyfoundation.files.wordpress.com/2013/01/7899.pdf

Kaiser Family Foundation. (2011). *Summary of the Affordable Care Act*. Retrieved July 8, 2013, from http://kaiserfamilyfoundation.files.wordpress. com/2011/04/8061-021.pdf

Kaiser Family Foundation. (2012). *Disparities in health and health care: Five key questions and answers*. Retrieved May 27, 2013, from http://kaiserfamilyfoundation .files.wordpress.com/2013/01/8396.pdf

Kaiser Family Foundation. (2013). Kaiser Health Tracking Poll: April 2013. Retrieved October 10, 2013, from http://kff.org/health-reform/poll-finding /kaiser-health-tracking-poll-april-2013/

Kaplan, R. M. (1995). Utility assessment for estimating quality-adjusted life years. In Sloan, F. A. (Ed.), *Valuing health care: Cost, benefits and effectiveness of pharmaceuticals and other medical technologies* (pp. 31–60). Cambridge, UK: Cambridge University Press.

Kibbe, D. C., & McLaughlin, C. P. (2004). Getting from A to C: Lifecycle lessons for e-health deployment. *International Journal of Electronic Healthcare, 1*(2), 127–138.

Kindig, D. A. (2006). A pay-for-population health performance system. *Journal of the American Medical Association, 296*(21), 2611–2613.

King, J., & Moulton, B. (2013). Group Health's participation in a shared decision-making demonstration yielded lessons, such as role of culture change. *Health Affairs, 32*(2), 294–301.

Kingdon, J. W. (1984). *Agendas, alternatives, and public policies.* New York: HarperCollins Publishers.

Kleinke, J. D. (2005). Dot-gov: Market failure and the creation of a national health information system. *Health Affairs, 24*(5), 1246–1262.

Kolata, G. (2006, August 22). Making health care the engine that drives the economy. *New York Times.* Retrieved August 22, 2006, from www.nytimes.com/2006/08/22/health/policy/22pros

Kolata, G. (2013, November 17). Risk calculator for cholesterol appears flawed. *New York Times.* Retrieved November 24, 2013, from www.nytimes.com/2013/11/18/health/risk-calculator-for-cholesterol-appears-flawed.html

Lamson, E., & Colman, V. (2005). *Nutrition and physical activity: A policy resource guide.* Washington State Department of Health. Retrieved January 31, 2007, from www.doh.wa.gov/cfh/steps/publications/nutrition_activity_policy_guide_final.pdf

Lauer, M. S., & D'Agostino, R. B., Sr. (2013). The randomized registry trial—the next disruptive technology in clinical research? *New England Journal of Medicine, 369*(17), 1578–1581.

Leape, L. L., & Berwick, D. M. (2005). Five years after to err is human: What have we learned? *Journal of the American Medical Association, 293*(19), 2384–2390.

Leavitt, M. O. (2006a). Letter from Secretary Mike Leavitt to CEOs. Retrieved January 30, 2007, from www.hhs.gov/transparency/employers/ceo

Leavitt, M. O. (2006b). *Better care, lower cost: Prescription for value-driven health care.* Washington, DC: Department of Health and Human Services. Retrieved January 30, 2007, from www.hhs.gov/transparency

Levitt, S. D., & Dubner, S. J. (2005). *Freakonomics.* New York: HarperCollins Publishers.

Lewin, K. (1951). *Field theory in social science.* New York: Harper and Row.

Lin, G. A., Halley M., Rendle, K. A., Tietbohl, C., May, S. G., Trujillo, L., et al. (2013). An effort to spread decision aids in five California primary care practices yield low distribution, highlighting hurdles. *Health Affairs, 32*(2), 311–319.

Lindenauer, P. K., Remus, D., Roman, S., Rothberg, M. B., Benjamin, E. M., Ma, A., et al. (2007). Public reporting and pay for performance in hospital quality improvement. *New England Journal of Medicine, 356*(5), 486–496.

Lyall, S. (2006, April 13). Court backs Briton's right to a costly drug. *New York Times.* Retrieved from www.nytimes.com/2006/04/13/world/europe/13britain.html

MRC Vitamin Study Research Group. (1991). Prevention of neural tube defects: Results of the Medical Research Council Vitamin Study. *Lancet, 338,* 131–137.

MacRae, D. (1976). *The social functions of social science.* New Haven, CT: Yale University Press.

Mandel, M. (2006, September 27). What's really propping up the economy. *BusinessWeek,* pp. 55–62.

Martin, D. F., Maguire, M. G., & Fine, S. L. (2010). Identifying and eliminating the roadblocks to comparative-effectiveness research. *New England Journal of Medicine, 363*(2), 105–107.

Martin, D. F., Maguire, M. G., Fine, S. L., Ying, G. S., et al. (2012). Ranibizumab and bevacizumab for treatment of neovascular age-related macular degeneration: Two-year results. *Ophthalmology, 119*(7), 1388–1398.

Masalin, L. (1994). The Orton Hospital. Unpublished case study, University of Helsinki and Kenan-Flagler Business School, University of North Carolina at Chapel Hill.

Mason, J. B., Dickstein, A., Jacques, P. F., Haggarty, P., Selhub, J., Dallal, G., et al. (2007). A temporal association between folic acid and fortification and an increase in colorectal cancer rates may be illuminating important biological principles: A hypothesis. *Cancer Epidemiology, Biomarkers & Prevention, 16*(7), 1325–1329.

Mattoo, A., & Rathindran, R. (2006). How health insurance inhibits trade in health care. *Health Affairs, 25*(2), 358–368.

Mayer, T. R., & Mayer, G. G. (1985). HMOs: Origins and development. *New England Journal of Medicine, 312*(9), 590–594.

McGinnis, J. M., & Foege, W. H. (1993). Actual causes of death in the United States. *Journal of the American Medical Association, 270*(18), 2207–2212.

McLaughlin, C. P. (1984). *The management of nonprofit organizations.* New York: John Wiley & Sons.

McLaughlin, C. P. (1997). Management in practice: A case of risks and rewards. In Miller, K. A., & Miller, E. K. (Eds.), *Making sense of managed care. Vol. III: Operational issues and practical answers* (pp. 99–113). Tampa, FL: American College of Physician Executives.

McLaughlin, C. P. (1998). Evaluating the quality control system for managed care in the United States. *Quality Management in Health Care, 7*(1), 38–46.

McLaughlin, C. P. (2014). *One-sentence health care reforms,* in press.

McLaughlin, C. P., & Kaluzny, A. D. (1997). Total quality management issues in managed care. *Journal of Health Care Finance, 24*(1), 10–16.

McLaughlin, C. P., & Kaluzny, A. D. (2006). *Continuous quality improvement in health care: Theory, implementation and application* (3rd ed.). Sudbury, MA: Jones & Bartlett.

McLaughlin, C. P., & Sheldon, A. (1974). *The future and medical care.* Cambridge, MA: Ballinger.

McNamara, R. M. (2006). *Emergency medicine and the physician practice management industry: History, overview and current problems.* Retrieved June 6, 2006, from www.aaem.org/corporatepractice/history.shtml

Medical Board of California. (2006). *Corporate practice of medicine.* Retrieved June 5, 2006, from www.medbd.ca.gov/Corporate_Practice.htm

Mendelson, D. N., Abramoff, R. G., & Rubin, R. J. (1995, September). State involvement in medical technology assessment. *Health Affairs, 14*(2), 83–98.

Mohr, J. J., & Batalden, P. (2006). Integrating approaches to health professional development with improving patient care. In McLaughlin, C. P. & Kaluzny, A.

D. (Eds.), *Continuous quality improvement in health care: Theory, implementation and application* (3rd ed.) (pp. 281–317). Sudbury, MA: Jones & Bartlett.

Mohr, J. J., Batalden, P. B., & Barach, P. (2006). Inquiring into the quality and safety of care in the academic clinical care microsystem. In McLaughlin, C. P. & Kaluzny, A. D. (Eds.), *Continuous quality improvement in health care: Theory, implementation and application* (3rd ed.) (pp. 407–423). Sudbury, MA: Jones & Bartlett.

Morgan, M. G. (1995, August 2). Death by Congressional ignorance: How the Congressional Office of Technology Assessment—small and excellent—was killed in the frenzy of government downsizing. *Pittsburgh Post Gazette.* Retrieved March 5, 2006, from www.wws.princeton.edu/ota/ns20/ota95_n.html

Mother Jones. (2012, September 19). Full Transcript of the Mitt Romney Secret Video. Retrieved November 27, 2013, from www.motherjones.com/politics /2012/09/full-transcript-mitt-romney-secret-video

Naim, M. (2005). *Illicit: How smugglers, traffickers, and copycats are hijacking the global economy.* Norwell, MA: Anchor.

National Association of State Budget Officers. (2012, December 20). Summary: NASBO state expenditure report. NASBO: Washington, DC. Retrieved July 29, 2013, from www.nasbo.org/sites/default/files/Summary%20-%20State%20 Expenditure%20Report_0.pdf

Newhouse, J. (2001). Medical care price indices: Problems and opportunities. NBER Working Paper 8168. Retrieved July 6, 2006, from www.nber.org/papers/8168

NHS England. (2014, April 16). NHS England agrees funding for life-saving hepatitis C drug. *NHS News.* Retrieved April 21, 2014, from www.england.nhs .uk/2014/04/16/hepatitis-c/

NICE. (2006a). NICE issues statement following ruling of appeal court in Herceptin case. London, England: Author. Retrieved May 14, 2006, from www .nice.org/page.aspc?0=306959

NICE (2006b). *Trastuzumab for adjuvant treatment of early-stage HER-2 positive breast cancer.* London, England: Author. Retrieved November 27, 2013, from www .nice.org.uk/nicemedia/live/11586/33458/33458.pdf

NICE. (2012). *Breast cancer (metastatic hormone-receptor)—lapatinib and trastuzumab (with aromatase inhibitor) (TA257).* London, England: Author. Retrieved August 1, 2013, from http://guidance.nice.org.uk/TA257

NICE. (2013a). *How we work.* London, England: Author. Retrieved March 1, 2013, from www.nice.org.uk/aboutnice/howwework/how_we_work.jsp

NICE. (2013b). *Experts dismiss claims NHS drug decisions are "flawed."* London, England: Author. Retrieved December 17, 2013, from www.nice.org/newsroom /news/ExpertsDismissClaimsNHSDrugDecisionsFlawed.jsp

Nord, E., Daniels, N., & Kamlet, M. (2009). QALYs: Some challenges. *Value in Health, 12*(Supl.1), 510–515.

North Carolina Department of Health and Human Services. (2013). *Overview and history of managed care in NC.* Retrieved April 25, 2013, from www.ncdhhs.gov /dma/ca/overviewhistory.htm

Oberlander, J. (2003, August 27). The politics of health reform: Why do bad things happen to good plans? *Health Affairs,* Suppl Web Exclusive, W3-391–W3-404.

Office of the Governor. (2013). Governor Pat McCrory Announces Joint Effort to Reform Medicaid. Press Release. Retrieved November 6, 2013, from www .governor.nc.gov/newsroom/press-releases/20130517/governor-pat-mccrory-announces-joint-effort-reform-medicaid.html

Office of Management and Budget. (1972). *Circular No. A-94 guidelines and discount rates for benefit-cost analysis of federal programs.* Washington, DC: Author.

Office of Minority Health. (2001). *National standards for culturally and linguistically appropriate services in health care: final report.* Washington, DC: U.S. Department of Health and Human Services. Retrieved December 28, 2006, from www .omhrc.gov/assets/pdf/checked/finalreport.pdf

Office of Minority Health. (2013a). *National standards for culturally and linguistically appropriate services (CLAS) in health and health care.* Washington, DC: U.S. Department of Health and Human Services. Retrieved November 5, 2013, from https://www.thinkculturalhealth.hhs.gov/pdfs/enhancednational classstandards.pdf

Office of Minority Health. (2013b). *National standards for culturally and linguistically appropriate services in health and health care: A blueprint for advancing and sustaining CLAS policy and practice.* Washington, DC: U.S. Department of Health and Human Services.

Office of Technology Assessment. (1980). *The implications of cost-effectiveness analysis of medical technology Paper 1: Methodological Issue and Literature Review.* Washington, DC: Author, Congress of the United States.

Oliver, T. R. (2006). The politics of public health policy. *Annual Review of Public Health, 27,* 195–233.

Oliver, T. R., & Singer, R. F. (2006). Health services research as a source of legislative analysis and input: The role of the California Health Benefits Review Board. *Health Services Research,* 41(Pt. II), 1124–1158.

Organisation for Economic Co-operation and Development. (2013). OECD health statistics 2013—frequently requested data. Retrieved March 13, 2013, from www.oecd.org/els/health-systems/oecdhealthdata2013-frequentlyrequested data.htm

Palca, J. (1992). Folic acid: Agencies split on nutrition advice. *Science, 257*(5078), 1857.

Papanicolas, I., Cylus, J., & Smith, P. C. (2013). An analysis of survey data from eleven countries finds that 'satisfaction' with health systems performance means many things. *Health Affairs,* 32(4), 734–741.

Park, C. H. (2000). Prevalence of employer self-insured health benefits: National and state benefits. *Medical Care Research and Review,* 57(3), 340–360.

Park, L. (2013, March–April). A cardiac conundrum. *Harvard Magazine.* Retrieved November 5, 2013, from http://harvardmagazine.com/2013/03 /a-cardiac-conundrum

Parks, J. (2006, September 13). First employers send your jobs overseas. Guess what? You're next. *AFL-CIO Now.* Retrieved October 11, 2006, from http://

blog.aflcio.org/2006/09/13/first-employers-sent-your-job-overseas-guess-what-you-are-next

Pauly, M. V. (1995). Measuring health care benefits in money terms. In Sloan, F. A. (Ed.), *Valuing health care: Cost, benefits and effectiveness of pharmaceuticals and other medical technologies* (pp. 99–124). Cambridge, UK: Cambridge University Press.

Pear, R. (2006, April 11). Employers push White House to disclose Medicare data. *New York Times.* Retrieved from www.nytimes.com/2006/04/11/washington/11medicare.html?pagewanted=all

Pearson, S. D., & Bach, P. B. (2010). How Medicare could use comparative effectiveness research in deciding on new coverage and reimbursement. *Health Affairs, 29*(10), 1796–1804.

Pell, M. B. (2011, April 20). Huge hospital markups burden patients. *The Atlanta Constitution.* Retrieved May 8, 2013, from http://ajc.com/news/business/huge-hospital-markups-burden-patients/nQsmJ/

Peterson, M. A. (1995). How health policy information is used in Congress. In Mann, T. E., & Orenstein, N. J. (Eds.), *Intensive care: How Congress shapes health policy* (pp. 79–125). Washington, DC: AEI/Brookings.

Phelps, C. E. (1997). *Health economics.* New York: Addison-Wesley Longman.

Portela, M. C. (1995). *A Markov model for the estimation of costs in the treatment of AIDS patients.* Unpublished PhD dissertation, Department of Health Policy and Administration, School of Public Health, University of North Carolina at Chapel Hill.

Porter, M. E., & Teisberg, E.O. (2006). *Redefining health care: Creating value-based competition on results.* Boston: Harvard Business School Press.

Priester, R. (1992). A values framework for health system reform. *Health Affairs, 11*(1), 84–107.

Rao, R. (2006, June 27). Testimony before the U.S. Senate Special Committee on Aging, Washington, DC, "The Globalization of Health Care: Can Medical Tourism Reduce Health Care Costs?" Retrieved from www.aging.senate.gov/hearings/the-globalization-of-health-care-can-medical-tourism-reduce-health-care-costs

Rastegar, D. A. (2004). Health care becomes an industry. *Annals of Family Medicine, 2*(1), 79–83.

Reagan, M. D. (1999). *The accidental system: Health care policy in America.* Boulder, CO: Westview Press.

Reinhardt, U. E. (2006). The pricing of U.S. hospital services: Chaos behind a veil of secrecy. *Health Affairs, 25*(1), 57–69.

Rice, T. (1998). *The economics of health reconsidered.* Chicago: Health Administration Press.

Richmond, J. B., & Fein, R. (2005). *The health care mess: How we got into it and what it will take to get out.* Cambridge, MA: Harvard University Press.

Robert Wood Johnson Foundation. (2000). *Advances, 1,* 1.

Robinson, J. C., & Dratler, S. (2006). Corporate structure and capital strategy at Catholic Healthcare West. *Health Affairs, 25,* 134–147.

Robinson, J. C., & MacPherson, K. (2012). Payers test reference pricing and centers of excellence to steer patients to low-price and high-quality providers. *Health Affairs, 31*(9), 2028–2035.

Rogers, E. M. (1983). *Diffusion of innovations*. Glencoe, NY: The Free Press.

Romano, P. S., Waltzman, N. J., & Scheffler, R. M. (1995). Folic acid fortification of grain: An economic analysis. *The American Journal of Public Health, 85*(5), 667–676.

Rosenthal, M., & Milstein, A. (2004). Awakening consumer stewardship of health benefits: Prevalence and differentiation of new health plan models. *Health Services Research, 39*(4, Pt. II), 1055–1170.

Rosenthal, M. B., Zaslavsky, A., & Newhouse, J. P. (2005). The geographic distribution of physicians revisited. *Health Services Research, 40*(6, Pt. 1), 1931–1952.

Rubio, D. M., Schoenbaum, E. E., Lee, L. S., Schteingart, D. E., Marantz, P. R., Anderson, K. E., et al. (2010). Defining translational research: Implications for training. *Academic Medicine, 85*(3), 470–475.

Rychlik, R. (2002). *Strategies in pharmacoeconomics and outcomes research*. Binghamton, NY: Pharmaceutical Products Press/Haworth Press.

Sackett, D. L., Rosenberg, W. M., Gray, J. A., Haynes, R. B., & Richardson, W. S. (1996). Evidence-based medicine: What it is and what it isn't. *British Medical Journal, 312*, 71–72.

Sahney, V. K. (1993). Evolution of hospital industrial engineering: From scientific management to total quality management. *Journal for the Society of Health Systems, 4*(1), 3–17.

Salaffi, F., Carotti, M., Ciapetti, A., Gasparini, S., & Grassi, W. (2011). A comparison of utility measurement using EQ-5D and SF-6D preference-based generic instruments in patients with rheumatoid arthritis. *Clinical and Experimental Rheumatology, 29*(4), 661–771.

Saul, S. (2006, May 4). Doctors object to gathering of drug data. *New York Times*. Retrieved May 8, 2006, from www.nytimes.com/2006/05/04/business/04prescribe.html?pagewanted=all

Schick, A. (1995). How a bill did not become a law. In Mann, T. E., & Orenstein, N. J. (Eds.), *Intensive care: How Congress shapes health policy* (pp. 227–272). Washington, DC: AEI/Brookings.

Schlesinger, M. (2002). A loss of faith: The source of reduced political legitimacy for the American medical profession. *The Milbank Quarterly, 80*(2), 185–235.

Schoen, C., Osborn, R., Huynh, P. T., Doty, M., Davis, K., Zapert, K., et al. (2004, October 28). Primary care and health system performance: Adults' experiences in five countries. *Health Affairs*, Suppl Web Exclusive, W4-487–W4-503.

SCI. (2006). *The state of the states*. Seattle, WA: AcademyHealth.

Scientific Advisory Committee on Nutrition. (2008). Paper for information: Briefing for review of SACN recommendations for mandatory fortification. SACN/08/00. Retrieved from www.sacn.gov.uk/pdfs/sacn_08_00.pdf

Senge, P. M., Ross, R., Smith, B., Roberts, C., Kleiner, A. (1994). *The fifth discipline fieldbook: Strategies and tools for building a learning organization*. New York: Doubleday/Currency.

SerVaas, S., & Perry, P. (1999). A flaming failure. *Saturday Evening Post, 27*(5), 62-ff.

Shekelle, P. G., Ortiz, E., Newberry, S. J., Rich, M. W., Rhodes, S. L., Brook, R. H., et al. (2005). Identifying potential health care innovations for the future elderly. *Health Affairs, 24*(Suppl. 2), W5-R67–W5-R76.

Shortell, S. M., Gillies, R. R., Anderson, D. A., Erickson, K. M., & Mitchell, J. B. (1996). *Remaking health care in America: Building organized delivery systems*. San Francisco: Jossey-Bass.

Skocpol, T. (1996). *Boomerang: Health care reform and the turn against government*. New York: W.W. Norton & Company.

Sloan, F. A. (2003). Arrow's concept of the health care consumer: A forty-year retrospective. In Hammer, P. J., Haas-Wilson, D., Peterson, M. A., & Sage, W. M. (Eds.), *Uncertain times: Kenneth Arrow and the changing economics of health care* (pp. 49–59). Durham, NC: Duke University Press.

Smith, M., Saunders, R., Stuckhardt, L., McGinnis, J. M. (Eds.). (2012). *Best care at lower cost: The path to continuously learning health care system*. Washington, DC: National Academies Press.

Solomon, D., & Wessel, D. (2007, January 19). Health-insurance gap surges as political issue. *The Wall Street Journal*, pp. A1, A12.

Sommers, R., Goold, S. D., McGlynn, E. A., Pearson, S. D., & Danis, M. (2013). Focus groups highlight that many patients object to clinicians' focusing on costs. *Health Affairs, 32*(2), 338–345.

Sowell, T. (2002). *A conflict of visions: Ideological origins of political struggles*. New York: Basic Books.

Stanton, M. W. (2004). Hospital nurse staffing and quality of care. *Research in Action, 14*, 1–9. Retrieved from www.ahrq.gov

Starr, P. (1982). *The social transformation of American medicine*. New York: Basic Books.

Starr, P. (2011). *Remedy and reaction*. New Haven, CT: Yale University Press.

State Health Access Data Assistance Center. (2006). *The state of kids coverage, August 2006*. Minneapolis, MN: Author.

State Health Facts. (2013). Health status. Retrieved May 30, 2013, from http://kff .org/state-category/health-status/

State of Victoria. (2013). *Effective engagement: Stakeholder analysis (stakeholder matrix)*. Victoria, Australia: Author. Retrieved July 29, 2013, from www.dse.vic.gov.au /effective-engagement/toolkit/tool-stakeholder-analysis-stakeholder-matrix

Sterling, B. (1996). *Holy fire*. New York: Spectra.

Sterman, J. D. (2006). Learning from experience in a complex world. *American Journal of Public Health, 96*(3), 505–514.

Strauss, W., & Howe, N. (1991). *Generations: The history of America's future, 1584 to 2069*. New York: William Morrow.

Substance Abuse and Mental Health Services Administration. (2011). *Shared decision-making in mental health care: Practice, research and future directions*. Washington, DC: Author. Retrieved March 26, 2013, from http://store.samhsa.gov /shin/content/SMOAG-4271/SMOAG-4371.pdf

Texas Health and Human Services Commission. (2007). HHSC stakeholder public forum: Medicaid Reform—Preparing for the 80th Legislative Session, January

8, 2007. Retrieved January 30, 2007, from www.hhsc.state.tx.us/medicaid/reform

Tolley, K. (2009). *What are health utilities?* Retrieved November 12, 2013, from www.whatisseries.co.uk/whatis/pdfs/what-are-health-util.pdf

Tomkins, C. P., Altman, S. H., & Eilat, E. (2006). The precarious pricing system for hospital services. *Health Affairs, 25*(1), 45–56.

Torenvlied, R., & Thomson, R. (2003). Is implementation distinct from political bargaining? A micro-level test. *Rationality and Society, 15,* 64–84.

Tornatzky, L. G., & Klein, R. J. (1982). Innovation characteristics and innovation adoption-implementation: A meta-analysis of findings. *IEEE Transactions on Engineering Management, EM-29,* 28–45.

Torrey, E. F. (1997). *Out of the shadows: Confronting America's mental illness crisis.* New York: John Wiley & Sons.

Turoff, M. (1970). The design of a policy Delphi. *Technological Forecasting and Social Change, 2*(2), 149–171.

United Network for Organ Sharing. (n.d.). *How the transplant system works: Matching donors and recipients.* Richmond, VA: Author. Retrieved December 27, 2013, from www.unos.org/donation/index.php?topic=fact_sheet_1

University of Birmingham. (2003). *A training manual for health impact assessment.* Birmingham, UK: Health Impact Assessment Unit.

Upshaw, V. M., Steffen, D. P., & McLaughlin, C. P. (2013). CQI, transformation and the "learning organization." In Sollecito, W. M., & Johnson, J. K. (Eds.), *McLaughlin & Kaluzny's Continuous quality improvement in health care* (4th ed.) (pp. 277–310). Burlington, MA: Jones & Bartlett Learning.

Veroff, D., Marr, A., & Wennberg, D. E. (2013). Enhanced support for shared decision making reduced costs of care for patients with preference-sensitive conditions. *Health Affairs, 32*(2), 285–292.

Victor, B., & Boynton, A. C. (1998). *Invented here.* Boston: Harvard Business School Press.

Vollset, S. E., Clarke, R., Lewington, S., Ebbing, M. Halsey, J., Lonn, E., et al. (2013). Effects of folic acid supplementation on overall and site-specific cancer incidence during the randomised trials: Meta-analyses of data on 50 000 individuals. *The Lancet, 381*(9871), 1029–1036.

Wallace, N. (2011, February 28). Thousands hit as hospitals cancel surgery. *Sydney Morning Herald.* p. 1, Retrieved December 11, 2013, from http://newsstore.smh.com.au/apps/viewDocument.ac?page=1&sy=s...ine&rc=10&rm=200&sp=nrm&clsPage=1&docID=SMH110228LS6946ERKRJ

Wang, X., Qin, X., Demirtas, H., Li, J., Mao, G., Huo, Y., et al. (2007). Efficacy of folic acid supplementation in stroke prevention: A meta-analysis. *Lancet, 369,* 1876–1882

Ward, W. J., Jr., Spragens, L., & Smithson, K. (2006). Building the business case for quality. *Healthcare Financial Management, 60*(12), 92–98.

Washington State Board of Health. (2003). *Nationwide survey of state boards of health.* Olympia, Washington: Author. Retrieved April 23, 2007, from www.sboh.wa.gov/Pubs/documents/StateBoardsReport_Final.pdf

Weaver, C., & Mathews. A. W. (2013, May 28). Rx for health law: Self-insure. *The Wall Street Journal*, pp. B1, B2.

Weick, K. E. (1976). Educational organizations as loosely coupled systems. *Administrative Science Quarterly, 21,* 1–19.

Weick, K. E. (1995). *Sensemaking in organizations*. Thousand Oaks, CA: Sage.

Weinstein, S. M., & Stason, W. B. (1977). Foundations of cost-effectiveness analysis for health and medical practices. *New England Journal of Medicine, 296*(13), 716–721.

Weintraub, A. (2006, February 20). How good is your online nurse? *Business Week,* pp. 68–69.

Weissert, C. S., & Weissert, W. G. (2002). *Governing health: The politics of health policy.* Baltimore, MD: The Johns Hopkins University Press.

Welch, H. G., Schwartz, L., & Woloshin, S. (2007, January 2). What's making us sick is an epidemic of diagnoses. *New York Times*. Retrieved January 2, 2007, from www.nytimes.com/2007/01/02/health/02essa.html

Wennberg, J. E., Fisher, E. S., & Skinner, J. S. (2002, February 13). Geography and the debate over Medicare reform. *Health Affairs,* Suppl Web Exclusive, W96–W114.

Wessel, D., Wysocki, B., Jr., & Martinez, B. (2006, December 19). As health middlemen thrive, employers try to tame them. *The Wall Street Journal,* pp. A1, A4.

Wheelan, C. (2011). *Introduction to public policy*. New York: W.W. Norton Co.

Whoriskey, P., & Keating, D. (2013, December 7). An effective eye drug is available for $50. But many doctors choose a $2,000 alternative. *The Washington Post.* Retrieved December 8, 2013, from www.washingtonpost.com/business/economy/an-effective-eye-drug-is-available-for-50-but-many-doctors-choose-a-2000-alternative/2013/12/07/1a96628e-55e7-11e3-8304-caf30787c0a9_story.html?hpid=z1

Wilensky, G. R. (2012). The shortfalls of "Obamacare." *New England Journal of Medicine, 367*(16), 1479–1481.

Wilson, M. P., & McLaughlin, C. P. (1984). *Leadership and management in academic medicine*. San Francisco: JosseyBass.

Woolhandler, S., Campbell, T., & Himmelstein, D. U. (2003). Costs of health care administration in the United States and Canada. *New England Journal of Medicine, 349*(8), 768–775.

World Health Organization. (1999). *Health impact assessments: Main concepts and suggested approach (the Gothenburg Consensus Paper)*. Brussels: European Centre for Health Policy, WHO Regional Office for Europe.

World Health Organization. (2005). Constitution of the World Health Organization. Retrieved March 13, 2014, from http://apps.who.int/gb/bd/PDF/bd47/EN/constitution-en.pdf

Yergian, J. M., Dardess, P., Shannon, M., & Carman, K. L. (2013). Engaged patients will need comparative physician-level quality data and information about their out-of-pocket costs. *Health Affairs, 32*(2), 328–335.

Index

Note: Page numbers followed by *f*, or *t* indicate materials in figures or tables respectively.